ORDERED LIBERTY

Ordered Liberty

A CONSTITUTIONAL HISTORY OF NEW YORK

by

PETER J. GALIE

Fordham University Press
New York

Copyright © 1996 by Fordham University Press
All rights reserved
LC 95-31878
ISBN 0-8232-1651-9

Library of Congress Cataloging-in-Publication Data

Galie, Peter J.
   Ordered liberty : a constitutional history of New York.
     p. cm.
   Includes bibliographical references and index.
   ISBN 0-8232-1651-9
   1. New York (State)—Constitutional history. I. Title.
KFN5681.G35 1995
342.747'029—dc20
[347.470229]   95-31878
                                                                             CIP

ISBN 0-8232-1652-7 (paperback)
Second printing 2001

To Frannie

CONTENTS

Preface	ix
Introduction: New York State and the American Constitutional Experience	1
1. Colonial Roots	9
2. The First Constitution, 1777: Constitutional Sobriety in a Revolutionary War	36
3. Establishing the New Government: 1777–1800	56
4. The First Constitutional Convention: 1801	64
5. Property and Participation: The Constitutional Convention of 1821	71
6. Commerce, Canals, and the Common Man: The Constitutional Convention of 1846	95
7. The First Failure: The Constitutional Convention of 1867	117
8. New Modes of Constitutional Revision: The Birth of the Constitutional Commission, 1868–1894	137
9. On the Threshold of the Twentieth Century: The Constitution of 1894	159
10. The Progressive Movement and the Constitutional Convention of 1915	188
11. Re-establishing the Government: Constitutional Development, 1915–1938	204
12. Constitution-Making During the Depression: The Constitutional Convention of 1938	230
13. Constitutional Change Between Conventions: 1938–1967	262
14. Modernizing the Constitution: The Constitutional Convention of 1967	307
15. Contemporary Constitutional Developments: 1968–1995	332
16. Toward the Year 2000: Reflections on New York's Constitutional Tradition	358
New York Constitutional History: A Guide to Sources and Commentary	377
Table of Cases	395
Index	398

PREFACE

Writing constitutional history is an enterprise that is currently not in vogue in academic circles. The "new" social history has shifted the focus and redirected the energies of a generation of historians. However productive this shift has been, it has nonetheless created an unfortunate consequence: the neglect of state constitutional history, an area traditionally ignored by scholars. Nowhere is this more prominently illustrated than in New York State. There is no constitutional history of New York currently in print. The most comprehensive constitutional history of the state was a five-volume work published in 1906 under the title *A Constitutional History of New York From the Beginning of the Colonial Period to the Year 1905*[1] by Charles Z. Lincoln. Lincoln was a legal advisor to Governors Morton, Black, and Roosevelt and a delegate to the constitutional convention of 1894. His work, one of the best produced by lawyers in the nineteenth and early twentieth centuries, is a documentary history, containing copies of all the constitutions and amendments adopted between 1777 and 1905. His commentary, though primarily legal in approach, is reliable and, by the standards of the day, free from partisan bias. That work, however, is out of print as well as out of date. The only one-volume constitutional history of New York is J. Hampden Dougherty's *A Constitutional History of New York*, published in a second edition in 1915.[2] Like Lincoln's, it is dated and out of print.

This is not to say that there has been no research since these early twentieth-century works. Indeed, monographs, articles, reports, and dissertations on various aspects of New York's constitutional tradition have appeared. While other scholars have done justice to particular constitutional conventions and developments, the 225 years of the state's constitutional tradition has not been addressed as a whole. The present work hopes to offer the reader a single-volume account of New York State constitutional history that augments and extends the work of Lincoln and Dougherty with the more specialized scholarship of recent years. It makes no claims to novel understandings of the tradition and relies heavily on the work of others, though of course I have made my own study of the primary sources.

Needless to say, any attempt to encompass two centuries of constitutional history in a single volume necessarily means selectivity and a focus on the dominant values and events which have shaped that history. I have provided a fairly comprehensive bibliographic essay for those who wish to explore individual topics or conventions in more depth.

This volume is intended to provide a readable chronicle of New York State's constitutional history for those who wish to understand our state's constitutional tradition, including college instructors who teach New York history or government, elementary and secondary school teachers who are required by the Board of Regents to teach New York history and government, and lawyers and judges who may wish to put the current Constitution in the historical context out of which it emerged.

The author would like to single out four individuals from among the many who have assisted in the writing of this history: Francine Gray, secretary to the Political Science Department at Canisius College, who gave unstintingly of her time and advice and whose copyediting improved every aspect of the book; Christopher Bopst, my student research assistant, whose research skill, determination, and suggestions were indispensable to its successful completion; the anonymous reviewer whose comments proved invaluable; Gerald Benjamin, who gave me encouragement, intellectual support, and friendship; and Amy Romessor, my student research assistant, who helped compile the index.

Notes

1. (Buffalo: William S. Hein & Co., 1994 [orig. publ. 1906]).
2. (New York: Neale Publishing Co., 1915).

Introduction: New York State and the American Constitutional Experience

FOR TOO LONG Americans have tended to identify their constitutional tradition with the U.S. Constitution and its development. This identification has fostered neglect of state constitutions and their constitutional traditions, and created a misunderstanding as to the character of the national constitutional experience.[1] That experience is a complex interaction of state and national constitutional development, an interplay that gave rise to and sustains the federal system.

A proper understanding of our constitutional tradition should begin at least as early as the eleven years between 1776 and 1787, a period in which the original states adopted constitutions. These state constitutions were the culmination of a long colonial tradition and it was an age during which the states, first separately and then as a nation, more or less invented written constitutions. The U.S Constitution is derived from these constitutions by way of imitation or via a negative reaction to what was perceived as their missteps. This interaction did not cease with the adoption of the national charter. Newly admitted states sought guidance from the national document and from their sister states.[2]

The national Constitution is dependent on state constitutions in a more immediate and direct fashion. Without them, as Donald Lutz has pointed out, the national Constitution is, in a number of ways, an "incomplete document." The states are referred to fifty times in forty-two separate sections of the U.S. Constitution. Striking evidence of this dependence is evident when one realizes that the U.S. Constitution does not contain a definition of citizenship!ial[3]

Despite the growth of the national government and the expansion of national constitutional power, state constitutions continue to be an indispensable part of the American Constitution and our constitutional tradition. Reference to this constitutional tradition must include not only the national Constitution and the Declaration of Independence, but also the state constitutions. The group traditionally understood as our Founding Fathers is in need of enlargement both in numbers and time; an understanding of their intent must include their expectation that we read the state constitutions as well as the national document when interpreting our constitutional tradition.

The national document is dependent on the state documents in other areas as well. The existence of a concise national document was made possible, in part at least, by the fact that the state constitutions existed and addressed a number of complex matters such as education, police powers, and local government—subjects which could be taken for granted at the national level by virtue of the existence of the state charters. Moreover, by leaving some of the most controversial topics, such as slavery and the establishment of religion, for the states to grapple with, state constitutional systems helped diffuse conflict by giving the national government a constitutional "honeymoon." Finally, states have been continuous laboratories of constitutional experimentation, holding over 233 constitutional conventions, adopting nearly 150 constitutions, and passing over 5,000 amendments.[4] They have proved a source of constitutional reform as well as policy guidance. Issues such as the right to die, no-fault insurance, and surrogate parenting are currently being debated in the political and constitutional arenas of state governments.

State constitutions, however, are significant not only because they complete the national document and are the pillars of the federal system, but also because of their importance in their own right. As the fundamental law of the states, they establish the ground rules for how public business is conducted and public policy is made. Within the limits set by the national document, all these are determined by the state constitutions. The national Constitution does not dictate that New York keep the Adirondacks and Catskills "forever wild," as does the New York Constitution (Art. XIV, Sec. 31), nor does it require the state to allow the people to decide every twenty years whether to hold a convention for the purpose of revisiting the state constitution. These are state constitutionally mandated practices.

State constitutions and the policies made pursuant to them are most likely to affect the daily lives of citizens. Taxes, the administration of justice, licenses, transportation, education, resource production, and economic development are issues in which the states are the primary actors.

State constitutions also protect our liberties. An examination of the New York Constitution, and of court decisions interpreting that document, reveals that, in significant ways, citizens of New York enjoy greater protection of civil liberties and individual rights than the U.S. Supreme Court has granted under the national Bill of Rights. For example, right to counsel protection in New York is one of the strongest in the nation and exceeds the protections mandated by the Sixth Amendment.[5] The New York Constitution mandates the protection of the environment and care by the state for the needy and dependent segments of the population.

STATE AND NATIONAL CONSTITUTIONS: SIMILARITIES AND DIFFERENCES

State constitutions are strikingly similar to one another and to the national document with regard to basic principles and structures. All but one—that of Nebraska—contain bicameral legislatures; all embrace explicitly or implicitly the doctrine of the separation of powers, ratification by popular vote (except Delaware), a four-year gubernatorial term (except Rhode Island and Vermont), and, with a few exceptions, a willingness to amend and/or revise their constitutions. All contain a statement of rights and adopt republican forms of government; all have accepted the power of judicial review; all have extensive provisions dealing with matters of public finance and the raising and spending of money; all provide for local government; and all but that of Vermont have preambles. John Kincaid suggests that the similarities can be explained by the general consensus about political fundamentals, the sharing and borrowing of constitutional ideas among the states, and constitutional reform movements, such as Jacksonian Democracy, that have swept periodically through many states.[6]

How do state constitutions differ from the national Constitution? One way, at least in theory, is that the national government is one of delegated powers, meaning that whatever powers cannot be found or fairly implied from provisions in the U.S. Constitution cannot be exercised. State constitutions, conversely, are constitutions for governments possessed of plenary powers, meaning that unless there is found some limitation on the powers of the government in the constitution, the state is at liberty to undertake the activity. In practice, the disillusionment with and distrust of state governments, particularly state legislatures, in the nineteenth century led to the insertion of numerous restrictions on legislative power. In turn, these restrictions led to the necessity of adding grants of power to the legislatures in the constitution, authorizing them to undertake action in certain areas. These authorizations were soon transformed into restrictions on legislative power, on the theory that what was not granted was withheld. In practice, and under the influence of a political culture suspicious of political power to begin with, what appeared to be affirmative grants of power were frequently metamorphosed into restrictions on power. State governments have operated like governments of delegated rather than plenary powers, whereas the national government, particularly as understood by the Marshall Court and the post-World War II Supreme Court, has often appeared to be a government of plenary powers.

State constitutions also differ from the federal document in that they must deal with various complex matters that were, initially and for most of the country's history, outside the scope of the national government. The distribution of power between the state and local government has been a central issue of state constitutional law throughout our history, and, until very recently, that issue was decided exclusively on state constitutional or policy grounds. The vast areas of regulatory policy encompassed by the phrase "police power," including the power of the state to regulate for the health, welfare, and safety of the community, require the state and thereby state constitutions to address questions unlikely to arise in federal law. Another area of central concern for states and state constitutions has been education. Nearly every state constitution has provisions concerning education, and some, like that of New York, provide not only for free common schools but also for a Board of Regents with responsibility for all educational activity.

The position of the states in the federal system made it almost certain that state constitutions would develop their own characters. Frequently, the character and extent of rights protected by state constitutions differ from those protected at the national level. A number of states have Equal Rights Amendments.[7] State constitutions adopted in the twentieth century contain not only guarantees of freedom for the individual against enumerated types of government interference, but they also state claims that the individual should have upon the government. For example, the New York Constitution contains a number of "social rights," such as the rights of labor, the right to care if one is needy, and a mandate to provide low-cost housing.

State constitutions, as a rule, are more easily amendable than the national Constitution. In New York, passage of a proposed amendment by majority vote of the legislature in two sessions and ratification by majority vote at the polls is sufficient.[8] Nineteen states allow for some form of amendment by initiative.[9] Moreover, the New York Constitution contains a provision (Art. XIX, Sec. 2) requiring that the question of holding a constitutional convention to revise the constitution should be placed before the voters every twenty years. If a convention is held and revisions are made, they must be approved by a majority at the convention and ratified by a majority at the polls. It is not surprising that the New York Constitution of 1894 has been amended over 200 times since 1900 and been revised by one constitutional convention (1938). One result of the ease and willingness to amend state constitutions has been an increase in the size of the documents. Unlike the U.S. Constitution, which contains fewer than 8,000 words, the average length of state constitutions is 26,150 words. Only one state constitution, Vermont's, contains fewer words than the national document. The current New York Constitution contains over 50,000 words. The addition of numerous amendments often makes state constitutions resemble statutory or administrative codes. Much of the impetus for this "amendomania" originated with those distrustful of state government who wish to place as many restrictions as possible on state power. These restrictions, in turn, require further amendment when they become straightjackets on the necessary exercise of governmental power.

A second source of amendments is the activity of interest groups. If a group can place its values and goals in the constitution, it has not only achieved a significant symbolic victory, but an instrumental victory in that altering that policy will prove more difficult than changing an act of the legislature. Various groups concerned with New York canal policy were able to incorporate their policy goals in the constitution. Rural interests successfully inserted a reapportionment policy in the constitution which made it virtually impossible for New York City to receive an apportionment in the legislature commesurate to its population. As Governor Al Smith observed, the New York legislature was made "constitutionally Republican." Labor was successful in placing a Labor Bill of Rights into the constitution at the 1938 convention.

A third source for these amendments has been the need to erase the effects of unwanted court decisions. As a result, state constitutions, particularly those not recently revised and streamlined, provide an excellent picture of a state's past. Like layered geological formations, the various provisions accumulate. These accretions make the document unwieldy as well as difficult to decipher. Some measure of the neglect of our state constitutions is manifest in their unkempt and detailed length.

Another difference between the national and state constitutional traditions is the different roles of their respective judiciaries. The federal Constitution has been changed primarily by the decisions of the Supreme Court, which has acted as a continuous constitutional convention. The document itself has remained as brief as it has because the necessary changes are imbedded in the nearly five hundred volumes of Supreme Court Reports. State supreme courts have not played nearly as important a role in altering state constitutions. State constitutions have been shaped by the tradition of majoritarian democracy; direct popular consent has shaped state constitutional change to a degree not approached at the national level. New Yorkers have had nine constitutional conventions, five of them successful, and they have amended those constitutions hundreds of times.

The differing character of the two documents has led many to use the federal Constitution as the standard for judging the quality of a constitution, and by that standard state constitutions have been found wanting. This judgment ignores the fact that the American constitutional tradition consists of both state constitutions and the national Constitution, thus a tradition of dual constitutionalism.

Constitutions can be understood in two different ways. The first way, exemplified by the federal model, is to see a constitution as a document limited to the fundamentals, simple in design, establishing the framework for government, providing a bill of rights and a method for amendment, and not much more. This is the approach of the National Municipal League, which, since 1921, has published a Model State Constitution. It is also the approach of most good-government groups and academics. It would seem to demand that experts be primarily responsible for the drafting of the document, with the electorate confined to ratifying or rejecting their work. In that way, the document will remain uncluttered, streamlined, and able to provide a government strong enough to meet the responsibilities thrust upon it.

Another way to look at constitutions is to view them as we view language. Both function in the political and social marketplace, used and abused, willy-nilly, by many for a variety of purposes. Constitutional growth in a democratic, pluralist order is likely to resemble that of a Banyan Tree, complex and baroque in character. A constitution is political in the fundamental sense that it is shaped by the various forces present in the public arena, and as such it is likely to take on the irregular and inconsistent contours that such a political order produces. These two understandings of a constitution present the images of the engineer and the gardener, with their respective objects. The two images appear to be antithetical, but they are mutually dependent, the latter providing vitality and responsiveness and the former effectiveness and order. The argument over simplifying state constitutions is a classic example of the tension between the two metaphors. Constitutional brevity is only one value, and not necessarily the most important one. A state constitution will reflect and address the problems and concerns of its citizens. Such reflections are unlikely to resemble the work of a draftsman. States have sacrificed orderly, efficient, and clear documents at the altar of democratic participation. The national document, by and large insulated—by design—from the same direct participatory mechanism, remains a model of clarity and elegant parsimony. This has been achieved at the expense of democratic participation and has produced an enlarged—one could say hypertropic—role for the Supreme Court in adjusting the document to the felt needs of the time. It may be possible to create more orderly and simple state constitutions; some states, e.g., Alaska, have done so, and some, e.g., Vermont, have managed to keep their documents under 10,000 words. Such successes, however, may be atypical.

State constitutions also differ from one another. Such differences are a function of the peculiar traditions and history of each state. New York's constitution contains the residue of the major problems and public policy issues the state has faced over its 210 year history. To that history we now turn.

NOTES

1. For similar criticisms see John Kincaid, "State Constitutions in a Federal System," *Annals of the American Academy of Social and Political Science* 496 (March, 1988), pp. 12–15; and G. Allan Tarr, "Understanding State Constitutions," paper presented at the annual meeting of the American Political Science Association, August 30—September 2, 1990, p. 1.
2. This borrowing at times has amounted to "unabashed plagiarism" (G. Alan Tarr, "Understanding State Constitutions," p. 11).
3. "The United States Constitution as an Incomplete Text," *Intergovernmental Perspective* 13 (Spring, 1987), pp. 14ff.
4. Albert Sturm and Janice May, "State Constitutions and Constitutional Revision: 1984-1985," *The Book of the States, 1986–87* (Lexington, Ky.: Council of State Governments, 1986), p. 4; Janice May, "State Constitutions and Constitutional Revision, 1992-93," *The Book of States, 1994–95* (Lexington, Ky.: Council of State Governments, 1995), p. 4.
5. Vincent Bonventre, "State Constitutionalism in New York: A Non-Reactive Tradition," *Emerging Issues in State Constitutional Law* 2 (1989); Peter Galie, "State Constitutional Guarantees and the Protection of Defendant's Rights: The Case of New York, 1968-1978," *Buffalo Law Review*, 28 (1979).
6. John Kincaid, "State Constitutions in a Federal System," *Annals of the American Academy of Social and Political Science* 496 (March, 1988), p. 18.
7. Including Alaska, Colorado, Florida, Illinois, New Hampshire, Texas, Washington, Pennsylvania, Virginia, Wyoming, Louisiana, Montana, Utah, Hawaii, Maryland, Massachusetts, Connecticut, and California.
8. Some state constitutions are more easily amendable than others. Gerald Benjamin and Melissa Cusa have calculated the likelihood of a legislature offering constitutional amendments under the various procedures, concluding that states which allow constitutional amendment by extraordinary majorities of the legislature with single-session passage, or those with simple majorities and single-session passage, provide a greater liklihoood of legislative passage than schemes wich require dual passage by the legislature. "Amending the New York Constitution Through the Legislature," Temporary State Commission on

Constitutional Revision, *The New York Constitution: A Briefing Book*, ed. Gerald Benjamin (Albany: The Nelson A. Rockefeller Institute of Government, 1994), pp. 68–70.

9. Janice May, "State Constitutions and Constitutional Revisions, 1993–94," p. 23. The scope of these initiative procedures varies widely.

1
Colonial Roots

FOUR FACTORS in colonial New York played a decisive role in shaping the first constitution of New York State in particular and the constitutional tradition of New York in general. These were: the existence of a prominent and politically active elite, many of whom were provincial gentry whose economic base consisted of large estates; the early development of a heterogeneous society with accompanying factional politics; the existence of a tradition of charters functioning as instruments of government; and a strong commitment to liberty protected by and rooted in the common law, Magna Carta, and various acts of parliament.

New York has been called "the most aristocratic of all of Britain's North American colonies."[1] The state's colonial history was dominated by great landowners and merchant families. Intermarriage, and marriage with outsiders such as James Duane, John Jay, and William Smith Jr.—all of whom married Livingstons—helped to ensure their interconnectedness and to infuse the families with extraordinary talent. The most influential of these families, politically speaking, were the Livingstons, Van Cortlandts, Morrises, Philipses, and Van Rensselaers. Among the merchants the most prominent was James DeLancey. Their interconnectedness notwithstanding, New York's political elites were plagued with family and factional quarrels that frequently spilled over into the political arena.

The great baronial estates, roughly thirty in number, contained the largest tenant population in the North American colonies.[2] This extensive landlord-tenant system, though significant for the political and economic conflicts which occurred in seventeenth- and eighteenth-century New York, was not the exact equivalent of its English or Dutch ancestors: it was more fluid, fairer, and less oppressive than traditionally portrayed.[3] Almost from the beginning, those controlling this land system were on the defensive for a number of reasons. Migrating New Englanders in the first half of the eighteenth century carried with them a strong tradition of private ownership. Conflicting border claims with other colonies, which put land titles in jeopardy, was a second factor. A third factor was the increasingly unfriendly posture of the imperial authorities toward these holdings. Finally, the availability of vacant, inexpensive land enabled colonists to rise from tenant to owner.[4] New York manor leases, usually for life, turned over on average every ninth year.[5] Most tenants viewed tenancy as a temporary condition, "a way station on the road to independency."[6] Since the colony was unable to sustain a stable tenancy, the dependency which was necessary for tenancy as well as for a hierarchical society was undermined.

Factionalism among the landowners and the unstable land system did not prevent these families from providing talented individuals who would play pivotal roles both in colonial politics and in the creation of New York's first constitution. When the unstable, near anarchic conditions of the colony were exacerabated by the widening rift between colonist and crown, these "men of rank and ability" provided voices of moderation and conservatism. The interplay between those voices and claims from the "men of middling or low rank" created a fruitful tension from which emerged the Constitution of 1777.[7]

A second characteristic of New York colonial society was its heterogeneity. This heterogeneity was evident in all aspects of the social order: ethnic, religious, political, and economic. The state was not a single, geographically compact area as were other colonies of the English. Rather, it was a series of trading posts all distant from, and not easily accessible to, one another.

By the close of the seventeenth century the population of the colony consisted of five nations of Native-Americans, Dutch, English, African-Americans (both free and slave), Swedes, French-speaking Walloons, French Catholics, French Huguenots, Scots, and Germans. New York was the most polygenetic of all the British possessions in North America.[8] By the middle of the eighteenth century there were 73,348 inhabitants in the colony, 10,592 of whom were African-Americans.[9] Ethnic diversity spawned religious diversity—Dutch Reformed, Church of England, Presbyterians, Quakers, Anabaptists, Jews, Lutherans, French Protestants, Catholics, and Independents. Economic diversity was no less evident: agriculture on large estates and yeoman farmers, merchants and fur trappers, lawyers and "mechanics" (a general term referring to those who worked with their hands).

This religious, ethnic, economic, and geographic diversity created frictions which were expressed in a variety of ways, from lively factional politics to mobbing and riots. The variety of interests arising from this diversity created what has been called "A Factious People."[10] Factions—the groups formed around these interests—fostered a colonial, and later, a state politics dominated by party spirit. In eighteenth-century colonial New York "Faction was the instrument not simply of class, or interest or ideology, but of all this and something more—of politics, which contained and absorbed everything else."[11] Early on, the already sophisticated politics of faction, self-interest, and pluralism was crucial in moving the constitutional structure of New York away from the traditional Whig conception of politics (characterized by direct citizen participation in civic affairs, a small homogeneous community, simple government, a consensus regarding public good and virtue) toward the Federalist conception (characterized by a large, heterogeneous, commercial society, with checks and balances to control, in the service of the general good, the diverse and contentious pursuit of self-interest) which would triumph with the adoption of the national Constitution.

These tensions, however, had more vigorous manifestations. The mixture of religions, races, and real estate was an explosive combination. Popular uprisings and riots were a part of the provincial life.[12] Edward Countryman lists fifty-seven incidents of "riot" or examples of "popular upheavals" during the period 1764–1777. Such street actions—some politically charged, others less so—were an indication of the inability of colonial authorities to govern effectively and to cope with the dynamics and diversity of the colony. Racism was another manifestation of these tensions: African-Americans suspected of crimes or conspiracies frequently received vindictive treatment.[13]

During this period the provincial government was subject to a torrent of abuse—pamphlets, satiric broadsides, newspaper articles, and protest meetings.[14] One prominent example of this criticism occasioned the trial of John Peter Zenger in 1735 for seditious libel.[15] His acquittal by a jury in the face of legal guilt suggests the extent to which libertarian ideas had taken hold in the colony.[16]

The "radicalism" of the American revolution was not expressed so much in the institutions adopted or the economic system embraced, but in the changes in social relations, "the way people were connected one to another." The colonist moved from "monarchical, hierarchy-ridden subjects on the margin of civilization, [to] the most liberal, the most democratic, the most commercially minded, and the most modern people in the world."[17] In New York various forms of political activity created a new political culture, a participatory political culture in which new groups mobilized, legitimized, and developed a sense of their ability to act and think politically for themselves.[18] It was to this new political culture, among other things, that the writers of the 1777 Constitution had to respond.

The third factor, the existence of a tradition of charters and a strong commitment to self-government and freedom from arbitrary government, was of the greatest significance for New York's constitutional history. As Benjamin Wright noted over fifty years ago, "these charters were to serve, in one way or another, sometimes for a few years, sometimes for over a century, as instruments of government beyond the power of the companies, the proprietors, or the colonists to alter."[19]

Charters, first established by the Dutch in New Netherlands and subsequently by the English when they obtained the colony and renamed it the Province of New York, were at the heart of the founding of the colony. In 1614 a charter was granted to several Amsterdam merchants, awarding them exclusive right to trade in the new territories.[20] Another charter was granted in 1621 to the better-financed Dutch West Indies Company, creating a large corporation with comprehensive administrative and judicial powers. The government of this corporation was administered by a director and a council who exercised all executive, legislative, and judicial power, subject only to appellate review by the authorities in Holland. The company chartered by the States General of the Netherlands was managed at home by five chambers representing different parts of the Dutch union. This chamber in turn delegated its powers to the Board or Assembly of Nineteen sitting in Amsterdam.

Until 1641 the colony was governed exclusively by the director and his Council. In that year, in response to serious conflicts with the Indians which led to the killing of some settlers, Director William Kieft decided to take severe reprisal measures. He was, however, unwilling to assume all the responsibility for his decision. On August 23, 1641, he dispatched a notice informing all the "masters" and heads of families living in the vicinity that he wished them "to come to Fort Amsterdam . . . for the consideration of some important and necessary matters."[21] At that meeting twelve selectmen were elected to study the matter. These twelve are recognized as the first representative body chosen by the colony, and its formation as the first step in the direction of representative government taken in the colony.[22]

Once selected, this group turned its attention to matters other than those posed by dangerous Indians, including governmental reform. They petitioned: "so that taxes may not be imposed on the country in the absence of the twelve . . ." and that four persons elected from the commonalty (heads of households) should be represented on the colonial council.[23] A quarter century prior to English domination of the colony, the spirit of liberty and the demand for consent of the governed was manifested by this group of Dutch colonists. While admitting the legitimacy of their demands, Director Kieft would not recognize the legitimacy of their actions, claiming they exceeded the scope of their authority.[24] This demonstration of independence so alarmed Kieft that on February 8, 1642 he issued an order forbidding the delegates from calling any further meetings "as the same tends to a dangerous consequence, and to the great injury both of the country and of our authority."[25] Nevertheless the practice of summoning the people and/or their representatives for advice and support would continue.

Another crisis with the Indians found Kieft again seeking the advice and consent of the commonalty "in a manner to which he would not have resorted in time of peace."[26] In September 1643 the commonalty elected eight men from among their number "maturely to consider the propositions submitted by the Director and Council of New Netherland."[27] Frustrated by a persistently uncooperative director, the eight took the unprecedented step of communicating with the authorities in Holland, in this case the College of XIX. In their memorial they recount their frustrations with the director: "no sooner did they [the eight] open their mouths to propose anything tending in their judgment to the public good, than the Director met them with sundry biting and scoffing taunts. . . ." They recounted how, on one occasion when they refused to support any more taxes on the penurious colonists, the director said, "I have more power here than the Company, therefore I may do whatever I please." The memorial concluded with the following request:

> For it is impossible ever to settle this country until a different system [of government] be introduced here, and a new Governor sent out with more people who will settle in suitable places . . . in the form of villages or hamlets, and elect from among themselves a Bailiff or Schout and Schepens, who will be empowered to send their deputies and give their votes on public affairs with the Director and Council; so that the entire country may not be hereafter, at the whim of one man, again reduced to similar danger.[28]

Although some of the accusations against Kieft may have been exaggerated, he was indeed autocratic, and used his power to "further his schemes according to his own personal likes and dislikes."[29] The company finally yielded to the wishes of the eight. It recalled Kieft in December 1644, demanding justification for his administration.

Peter Stuyvesant, a consumate soldier, was chosen to succeed Kieft. He ruled the colony for seventeen years, the longest tenure in the history of colonial New York. Though conscientious, like his predecessor he was endowed with an autocratic and tyrannical disposition, and his "hostility to popular demands and rights, and his outbreaks of passion, led to continual trouble."[30]

In response to petitions and remonstrances to Holland he brazenly declared, "If any one during my administration, shall appeal, I will make him a foot shorter, and send the pieces to Holland, and let him appeal in that way."[31]

Realizing that raising necessary revenues would be unsuccessful without the cooperation of the colonists, Stuyvesant's council advised the director to allow some measure of representation. Stuyvesant ordered an election held in which the colonists in the towns would elect eighteen representatives from which the director would select nine. The nine chosen would assist the council and the director in promoting the commonwealth. Stuyvesant named these men "The Tribunes of the People." From the eighteen the director selected three merchants, three farmers, and three citizens. The share in the government for the commonalty which this step represented is less significant than the fact that its creation marked another stage in the progression toward a political system wherein all the major segments of the community would be consulted.[32]

Stuyvesant tolerated the nine as long as they agreed with him, but treated them with contempt when they brought matters to his attention that needed correction. Frustrated with his obduracy, they agreed to send a remonstrance to Holland. Stuyvesant objected, arguing that all correspondence must go through him. The nine refused to accept that position and petitioned the director for permission to consult the commonalty. Stuyvesant denied this right, but the nine perservered, even attempting, literally, to ascertain public opinion by going "door to door." This attempt met with harassment and arrests. Stuyvesant's recalcitrance and his escalating resort to repressive measures against all who opposed him brought censure from the States-General in Holland. The nine persisted, presenting a petition of the commonalty to the States-General on July 26, 1649. Among their requests were "suitable municipal government . . . resembling the laudable government of our Fatherland." In a supplement to that petition, "Additional Observations," the petitioners blamed the poor condition of the colonies on, among other things, "unsuitable government," which they defined as "bad and intolerable . . . wholly ruinous." Government should not be "intrusted to a set of hairbrained people, such as the Company flings thither, but to such as obtain in New England."[33] Some relief was forthcoming. The director was ordered to continue the nine in office, municipal government was eventually granted to New Amsterdam, and Stuveysant was to be recalled, replaced by "a suitable person."[34] However, conflict between the Chamber and the States General delayed the recall, Stuyvesant remained Director, and the disputes continued unabated.

The Dutch Company was constantly beset with problems of all sorts, two of which were fundamental: "the lack of legitimacy in public institutions and excessive pluralism in political society."[35] These two are vividly illustrated by the conflict that arose in the early 1650s between the Dutch director and English settlers on Long Island. On November 26, 1653, responding to troubles in the colonies, nineteen delegates from the City of New Amsterdam and from eighteen villages met at city hall. Ostensibly their purpose was to discuss measures of common defense, but other matters of common interest were included in the deliberations. The assemblage adjourned until December, enabling representatives from Dutch settlements to attend. This action alarmed the director, who wrote that such actions "border on revolt." Stuyvesant was particularly infuriated by the decision of the assembly to expel two members of his council from their proceedings. When the director objected to the meeting, the assembly, with much boldness, informed him that "he might prevent it if he could."[36] While referring to the "jealousies, troubles and quarrels" connected with such assemblies, Stuyvesant realized they would meet with or without his approval. To avoid the embarrassment of the latter, Stuyvesant gave his reluctant approval.[37] On December 11 a remonstrance and petition to the director was drawn up. Heading the list of eleven grievances was the "apprehension of the establishment of an Arbitrary Government among us." No clearer statement of limited constitutional government can be found than their elaboration on this apprehension:

> 'Tis contrary to the first intention and genuine principles of every well regulated government, that one or more men should arrogate to themselves the exclusive power to dispose, at will, of the life and property of any individual, and this, by virtue or under pretense of a law or order he, or they, might enact, without the consent, knowledge or election of the whole Body, or its agents or representatives.

They went on to "submit that 'tis one of our privileges, that our consent or that of our representatives is necessarily required in the enactment of such laws and orders."[38] Such sentiments have induced historians to label this convention "the most important that had yet been held in New Netherland."[39]

The director, stung by this rebuff to his authority and this ringing affirmation of the right to self-government, argued that his rule was consistent with his legal authority as delineated by the directives from Holland, that the three villages lacked authority to send delegates, and therefore the assembly had exceeded its authority.[40] In response to Stuyvesant's narrow, legalistic approach to their demands, the delegates appealed to "the laws of Nature" which "give to all men the right to gather for the welfare and protection of their freedom and property."[41] This appeal to the traditions and laws of the home country, followed, when necessary, by appeals to the laws of nature, is one which colonists in the middle of the eighteenth century would repeat in their debates with England—an amalgam from the common law rights of Englishmen and the natural rights of man.[42]

Stuyvesant, argument exhausted, ordered the delegates to disperse "on pain of an arbitrary correction," stating: "We derive our authority from God and the Company, not from a few ignorant subjects. . . ."[43]

The most interesting aspect of this confrontation is that much of the impetus came from the English settlers on Long Island. The remonstrance of December 11, 1653 was written by George Baxter, formerly the director's English secretary. Indeed, Stuyvesant acknowledged the English role when he wrote about the "Englishmen, who are the authors of and leaders in these innovations" and sarcastically targeted the Dutch colonists with the remark that "The cleverness of Burgomasters and Schepens may be inferred herefrom, when a stranger or Englishman must prescribe, what they should remonstrate and demand."[44]

The leaders of the convention were not intimidated; they wrote to Amsterdam to acquaint the authorities with current developments. Stuyvesant was in a bind: he wanted nothing to do with a representative assembly acting independently of his authority. However, he needed the cooperation and support of the colonists for revenue and defense of the colony. Another provincial assembly, suggested by the leaders of the towns, was convened on November 1, 1663. For once the director and delegates were in accord as the critical state of the colony overrode other differences. A final general assembly with even broader representation was held on April 10, 1664.

The delegates to these assemblies did not achieve much in the way of tangible results. They certainly did not establish representative government. Nevertheless, the Dutch colony was moving toward institutionalized executive and legislative bodies, the latter providing the representation necessary to legitimize governance in the eyes of the colonists. Each succeeding assembly became more important in the governance of the colony. This process came to an abrupt, if temporary, halt with the conquest of New Netherlands by the English and the granting of the colony to the Duke of York. A strikingly similar set of conflicts over autocratic governance would resume the process of institutionalization of a representative assembly as an integral part of the government. What is of significance is that principles fundamental to constitutionalism and constitutional government were being asserted and propagated. Such principles would take root and, though dormant after the colony passed into English hands, would re-emerge. By 1664, when the Dutch relinquished control of the colony, religious liberty had been achieved. That freedom, however, was not based on a philosophy of tolerance or on theological principles; rather, it was fostered from the need to populate the colony and encourage trade and commerce. Officers in Holland favored toleration because toleration cultivated trade and growth. The policy of allowing private individuals of any faith to practice religious observance while publicly plying their trades was a policy the English would inherit.

The English conquered New Netherlands in 1664. The Articles of Capitulation contained provisions that suggest how deeply entrenched charters of governance and the protection of personal rights were. Reading much like a frame of governance and set of protections, the Articles allowed all citizens of the colony to continue as free inhabitants, disposing of their lands, houses, and goods as they pleased (Sec. 3); provided liberty of conscience for the Dutch (Sec. 8); and allowed the towns of Manhattan to choose deputies who "shall have free voices in all public affairs, as much as any other Deputies." (Sec. 21)[45]

James, Duke of York, was granted a patent (a grant of property)—in this instance, the province of New Netherlands—from his brother, Charles II, King of England. This patent also gave James the right to give the law, subject to the sole restriction that such laws be agreeable to the laws and statutes of England. The king and his Privy Council reserved the right to hear appeals from inhabitants of the colony. There was no provision for an assembly and the duke was authorized to appoint and discharge governors and other officers of the province. The duke appointed Richard Nicolls first governor of the province of New York; a secretary and four councillors were also appointed. With this apparatus he hoped to govern the colony.

Governor Nicolls, probably reflecting the duke's views, intended to govern the colony with a strong executive hand without the interference of an assembly or any other elected body. From this perspective the Dutch were likely to be better subjects than the English, especially those New Englanders who had settled on Long Island and in West Chester, and who carried with them their tradition of local self-government. That Nicolls was aware of this sentiment is revealed in a letter he wrote to the Earl of Clarendon after his laws were promulgated. "Democracy hath taken so deepe a root in these parts that ye very name of a Justice of the Peace is an Abomination."[46] The colony was, after all, a propriety, not a self-governing colony, and above all the duke wished it to be a profitable enterprise. The governor and his Council were the supreme governing body of New York, and the duke intended to keep it that way.

Two days after the surrender of the Dutch, Nicolls, in apparent gratitude to the Long Island English who opposed the Dutch, proposed that "Deputies shall in Convenient time and place, be summoned to propose and give their advice in all Matters tending to [ye] peace and benefitt of Long Island."[47] Apparently in fulfillment of that pledge, Governor Nicolls wrote to the residents of Long Island in February 1665 that in light of the "grevious inconveniences, and discouragements occasioned partly from their subjection . . . [such that] few or no lawes could bee putt in due Execucon . . . [and] Civill Libertyes interrupted . . . ," he would convene a general meeting which was to consist of deputies chosen by the majority of the freemen.[48] In fact, Nicolls had already compiled a set of laws, known now as "The Duke's Laws," which he presented as a fait accompli to the convention. The meeting took place at Hempstead. Nicolls arrived with a frame of government and a legal code. He faced delegates who had no veto power or, for that matter, legislative authority. They were there only to ratify his work, which they did with some hypocritical obsequiousness, proclaiming their unanimous "cheerful submission to all such Lawes. . . ."[49] The laws were a melange of the Mosaic-based codes of Connecticut and Massachusetts and of English and Dutch law, and were an obvious attempt to deal with the bi-polar character of the colony. They made no provision for an elected assembly. Popular government was limited to the election of overseers of each town. A judicial organization for the new government was put in place. Provision was made for religious liberty for those "who profess Christianity." Criminal procedure protections included assigned counsel for the poor and bail in line with English practice; jury size was limited to no more than seven, except in "special causes upon life and death," and unanimous juries were required only in capital cases.[50] These last two provisions were inconsistent with English practice at the time.

The laws were consciously intended to restrict local autonomy and strengthen central government authority. Nicolls wrote as much to Lord Clarendon: "I have upon due Consideration of His Majesty's Interest layd the foundations of Kingly Government in these parts so farre as is possible, which truly is grievous to some Republicans. . . ."[51]

James had created an absolutist state—government by a fixed code without an assembly—but with the promise of religious toleration to all Christians. This policy was a politic response to the polyglot character of New York, whose inhabitants included Dutch Reformed; Lutherans from Holland, Germany and Sweden; French Calvinists; Presbyterians from the British Isles; Puritans; Separatists; Baptists; Quakers; and small numbers of Jews and Catholics. More telling was the absence "of anyone who claimed membership in the Church of England."[52] In light of these sentiments and the fact that most of the Dutch towns were excluded from the convention, it appears that the real purpose of the meeting was to have the English-speaking inhabitants understand immediately the character of the new regime.[53]

The Hempstead Convention was greeted with hostility and resentment by the townsmen. Expecting representative government, they got authoritarian government; hoping for local autonomy, they got centralized direction. The discontent created by the duke's decrees was dampened by Nicolls's rule, which, for the most part, was fair and prudent. Another factor in relieving the pressure for less authoritarian government was the fact that however centralized the new regime was politically and constitutionally, it was socially, economically, and juridically decentralized.[54] Nonetheless, discontent created by the absence of an assembly and the lack of local autonomy persisted. In 1669 a petition was presented to the highest court in New York, the Court of Assizes, signed by representatives of the principal towns, complaining that they had been promised all the privileges of the king's subjects; participation was among those privileges. The court, consisting of the governor, his council, and the justices of the peace, responded directly to this petition: the governor had made so such promise.[55] Governor Francis Lovelace was not pleased. He called the petition "scandalous and seditious" and ordered the documents burned, emphasizing his displeasure by having the burning done by the public hangman.[56]

Upon the recapture of New York from the Dutch in 1674, Edmund Andros was appointed governor. Aware of the demands for an assembly and realizing the difficulty of effectively governing a colony in its absence, Andros delicately raised the issue with the duke. The problem was particularly acute in the area of raising and collecting revenue. The primary source of revenue for the province was from customs, but collecting that revenue proved difficult, to say the least.[57] Initially, the Duke was unsympathetic. He believed assemblies dangerous and unnecessary in light of the existence of the council and the ability of colonists to petition the Court of Assizes. Nonetheless, in January of 1676, still claiming that assemblies would be both dangerous and unnecessary, he wrote to Andros, "if you continue of [the] same opinion, I shall be ready to consider of any proposalls you shall send to [that] purpose."[58]

By 1681 the colony's financial position was precarious. More funds were needed, but both the duke and his governor knew that demands for more taxes would intensify resentment and resistance. A grand jury had indicted an official of the Andros government, William Dyer, because the governor had inadvertently failed to renew his authority to collect duties on imports. The merchants refused to pay the duties, and when Dyer attempted to collect them, he was indicted on a charge of traitorous conduct "for [exercising] Regall Power and Authority over the King's Subjects . . . Contrary to the great charter of libertyes, [and] the Peticon of Right. . . ."[59] In addition, the grand jury presented to the Court of Assizes the absence of an assembly as a grievance against the government. The petition begged relief from:

> inexpressible burdens by having an arbitrary and absolute power used and exercised over them by which a yearly revenue is exacted from us against our wills . . . our liberty and freedom enthralled and the inhabitants wholly shut out and deprived of any share, vote, or interest in the government . . . contrary to the laws, rights, liberties and privileges of the subject. . . .

The petition asked for relief in the following form: "government . . . be settled and established, ruled and governed by a governor, council and assembly; which assembly be duly elected and chosen by the freeholders of Your Royal Highness' colony. . . ."[60] The duke relented. The collapse of the duke's absolutist regime immediately after Andros's departure suggests the degree to which colonists, particularly the New England population living on Long Island and what is now Westchester County and the Bronx, had committed themselves to assembly government and limitations on royal power. This commitment was strengthened by the fact that the adjacent colonies of Pennsylvania and New Jersey had assemblies with real power, and New York faced the prospect of losing settlers to these freer colonies. This intercolonial context explains why governing authority collapsed immediately after Andros left the colony in 1681.[61] A new governor, Thomas Dongan (1683-1688), was appointed and instructed to issue writs for a general election for "a General Assembly of all [the] Freeholders." As to the power of legislation the duke wrote: "if such laws shall be propounded as shall appear to me to be for the manifest good of the Country in generall and not [prejudicial] to me, I will assent unto and confirm [them]. . . ." The instructions allowed the governor an absolute veto over such laws, thus requiring assent from both the governor and the duke for passage of any legislation. In addition the governor was given the power to adjourn and dissolve the assembly and to call a new one at any time. Most intriguing, the instructions contain a provision which embodied the substance of Article 39 of the Magna Carta:

> I doe hereby require and comand you [that] noe mans life, member, freehold, or goods, be taken away or harmed in any of the places [under your] government but by established and knowne laws not repugnant to . . . the laws of the kingdome of England.[62]

These instructions are a watershed in New York's constitutional history. Though less radical than their counterparts in Pennsylvania and West New Jersey, the charter did end absolutism in New York until 1685. The acceptance of limited government such as these instructions provide is best seen as part of a series of developments in which the exercise of arbitrary power provoked resistance and calls for limited and regularized government. Many, though not all, of these conflicts were provoked, on the one hand, by the colonist's attempts to protect their economic interest, particularly with regard to the government's power to tax, and on the other hand by the need of the governors to raise revenue to ensure effective colonial government and profits for the duke. In this instance the duke's agreement to allow an assembly can be viewed as a quid pro quo, the return being a regular source of revenue by which the costs of colonial government could be met.

The problem lay deeper than a dispute over taxes. Administering a complex enterprise like the province of New York was simply too much for a private proprietor. The colony was becoming more like a subordinate commonwealth. As such, the problems were not simply those of administering and raising revenue as in a private corporation; they were, in fact, the problems of a community of freemen.[63] The governors were in the middle of two conflicting realities, the legal reality of a propriety enterprise (the perspective of the duke) and the political reality of an incipient commonwealth (the perspective of the colonists). There was no effective way in which these two understandings could be reconciled.

The development of constitutional and representative government can be seen as the result of a hard-won understanding on the part of rulers and ruled that a productive, successful colony needed the support of the colonists as well as competent governors. To achieve that support, institutions had to be developed which would legitimize the exercise of political power. Given the political and legal traditions of the Dutch and English, and the successful assertion of English power on the continent, it is not surprising that that legitimacy included the rule of law, representative institutions, and liberty.

On October 17, 1683, the first general assembly of the province of New York, composed of ten councillors and seventeen representatives, met in City Hall and was addressed by the governor. They sat for three weeks and passed fourteen acts, the first of which was by far the most significant. It was entitled "The Charter of Liberties and Privileges Granted by His Royal Highness to the Inhabitants of New York and its Dependents." Strictly speaking, it was not a charter but an act of the legislature, assented to by the governor.

The first substantive provision provided that supreme legislative authority under the king and duke "shall forever be and reside in a Governor, Council and the people met in General Assembly." The structure provided for is a clear example of a mixed regime where the powers of the government are balanced among democratic, aristocratic, and monarchic elements. It provided for meetings of the assembly at least once every three years, freehold status for voting in elections (freehold was left undefined), qualifications for membership, protection of representatives for what they said or did in connection with assembly business, and a provision guaranteeing that no taxes would be laid but by act and "consent of the governor, council and representatives of the people in general assembly met and assembled." Section 15 is practically a verbatim repeat of articles 39 and 40 of the Magna Carta: "No freeman shall be taken and imprisoned or be disseized on his freehold or liberty or free custom or be outlawed or exiled or in any other way destroyed nor shall be passed upon adjudged or condemned but by lawful judgement of his peers and law of his province." Section 17 provides for trial by jury of twelve men, peers and equals of the neighborhood, county, or shire where the crime occurred; grand jury indictment in felonies (capital cases); bail in non-capital cases; a clause prohibiting the quartering of soldiers; and a provision guaranteeing religious liberty to all Christians who do not behave "licentiously or disturb the peace." The charter continued the practice of allowing churches to be locally established upon approach of two-thirds of the voters (the duke's laws had required a simple majority), thus making all Christian denominations eligible for public recognition and financial support. This arrangement, though not contemplating the establishment of any particular church, did contemplate a system of multiple establishments more closely resembling the tradition that would develop in Canada than the separatist tradition that took root in the United States.[64] The charter had one other important effect: it "imposed an English constitutional system on a colony that was still mostly Dutch."[65]

All in all, the charter was a remarkable document and a milestone in the development of constitutional liberty in New York. It was New York's first experiment with representative government.

The duke approved the Charter. However, before he communicated that approval to the colony, King Charles died in February 1685. The colony passed from proprietary status to royal colony when the duke became King James II. The new king, believing the charter too republican in character and likely to interfere with kingly prerogatives, vetoed the charter on March 3, 1685. What most affronted the king was the phrase "The People met in a General Assembly." He noted that this phrase appeared in no other constitution in America.[66] Nonetheless, during this period three meetings of the Assembly took place. John Murrin calls the 1685 Assembly meeting "the only true general election in the colony's entire history before the Glorious Revolution—that is, the only occasion on which freeholders and freeman in all constituencies had an opportunity to vote directly for their representatives.[67] The Charter Assembly met for the last time in 1687; in that year it was dissolved by proclamation of the governor. The government reverted to a hierarchical pattern with the governor empowered to make all laws, statutes, and ordinances with the advice and consent of the council. During this period, however, Governor Dongan granted liberal charters to the cities of New York and Albany, allowing them a measure of self-government with certain immunities and privileges (trade monopolies).

Of great significance for the constitutional development of New York were the events that occurred in England and New York in the years 1688 to 1691. On December 11, 1688, James II fled from Whitehall and abandoned the throne. On February 13, 1689, the English crown was offered to and accepted by William and Mary. This momentous upheaval in England led to rebellion in the colonies. New York had been for some time a colony in discontent: opposition to authoritarian government and arbitrary taxation, religious conflict, fear of Indians, ethnic conflict between Dutch and English, and economic conflict between farmers and merchants. This unstable pluralism was exacerbated by the absence of an assembly to legitimize the government. Rumors that the French and Indians were planning an attack on Albany provided the proximate cause of the rebellion, and one Jacob Leisler, a wealthy merchant, ship captain, and former army officer, assumed leadership. He issued a call for an assembly despite the fact that the new governor-in-chief, Henry Sloughter, had been appointed in November 1689 and had been authorized to call a general assembly. Sloughter was instructed, "by and with the consent of our Council and Assembly or the major part of them," to enact for the colony "Laws, Statutes, and Ordinances."[68] This was, in effect, a revival of the policy initiated and later rejected by the Duke of York in 1683.

The new governor eventually quelled the rebellion, Leisler was hanged, and a new assembly met on April 9, 1691 under the authority of the new king. One of the first acts of this assembly was to pass a Charter of Liberties. In most respects it reaffirmed the provisions of the Charter of 1683, but with noteworthy differences. The assembly would meet annually instead of every three years. The definition of a freeholder was made explicit. Bail was permitted in certain felony cases, consistent with the law in England. With regard to religious liberty, a provision attempted to ban Roman Catholics from holding office; strictly interpreted, it would also have excluded Jews and Quakers. The charter omitted any mention of support for established churches, leaving that issue unresolved.

The charter was approved by the governor, but like its predecessor it was rejected by the government of William III in 1697, for reasons similar to those given by James II. It was in force only six years, but its rejection did not prevent the principles and practices embodied in the charter from being implemented. Absolutism suffered irreparable blows between 1664 and 1691; domesticating the royal prerogative would take much longer.[69] Henceforth some form of balanced or mixed government would exist in the colony.

By the beginning of the eighteenth century the constitutional structure of New York resembled the pattern that had developed in England after the Glorious Revolution. There would be a powerful governor appointed by the Crown who, with the advice and consent of the council, would administer the colony. There would be an assembly whose support for raising revenue and passing legislation was to become indispensable. The "charter" that was not a charter, the law that was not law for long, nonetheless provided a constitutional base for the colony.

One other significant change resulted from these events: the acceleration of the anglicization of the colony. Among the laws passed by the new assembly was one reorganizing the judiciary. The Supreme Court was given general jurisdiction and thus the opportunity to homogenize the law throughout the colony. This homogenization would take place according to the principles and precedents of the common law, as the statute required courts to decide "whatsoever as all or any of the said Judges of the severall Courts of Kings Bench, Common Pleas & the Exchequer in England Legally doe."[70] The beginnings of a legal profession also contributed to what Michael Kammen has called "a remarkable transformation in a relatively brief period of time" of Roman-Dutch civil law to English common law.[71]

Colonial lawyers played a major role in the developing notions of constitutionalism and the importance of the rule of law in the governing process. These men articulated the positions of the colonists and couched such arguments in legal terms. They thought in terms of the rule of law and the importance of law as a protection against arbitrary power. Colonial resistance to royal prerogative and hierarchical authority was given shape and direction by lawyers. Edmund Burke, English statesman and political thinker, marvelled at the extent to which the law was studied in New York: "The profession itself is numerous and powerful, and in most provinces it takes the lead."[72] Lieutenant-Governor Cadwallader Colden (1761–1775) wrote constantly to England regarding the "opposition and resentment of the whole profession of the Law," of their "insolence," and that "a dangerous combination may subsist between the Bench and the Bar"—dangerous, that is, to "His Majesty's prerogative."[73] Armed with Whig political ideas and a constitutional tradition stretching back to the Magna Carta, these lawyers displayed remarkable skill and energy in the disputes over prerogative power.[74] The cases of *Cosby v. Van Dam* (1733) and *Forsey v. Cunningham* (1764) are illustrative.

Cosby v. Van Dam involved a dispute over salary between Governor Cosby and former Acting Governor Rip Van Dam. Cosby sued Van Dam for recovery of salary payments. Cosby's dilemma was in finding a court to initiate the action. He thought his chances slim in a common law court where juries would be unsympathetic to a newly arrived Irish governor.[75] Chancery Court, the other logical choice, was unavailable because the governor sat on that court. Cosby's solution was to have the council authorize the Supreme Court to act as a court of exchequer. The case was heard before the three judges of the Supreme Court. The judges split on their decision, Chief Justice Lewis Morris arguing that the Supreme Court could not exercise equity jurisdiction. Though the legal results were inconclusive, the political repercussions were not.[76] Radical Whigs in the assembly had the arguments reprised before them by counsel representing Van Dam and the government. In the assembly the narrow legal question became a constitutional and political one concerning the status of the courts in the colony. Could the governor, acting on royal instructions, erect a court of exchequer—or any court, for that matter—or extend existing jurisdiction without an act of the assembly? Whig lawyers in the assembly argued that to do so was an act of arbitrary power. Cosby clearly viewed Justice Morris's opinion as a threat to royal prerogative. It was based on what he referred to as "Boston principles"[77] which, if allowed to spread, would undermine royal government in all the colonies. Cosby's solution was to remove Morris from his position. This removal did nothing to dampen debate, and a flood of literature was produced over this fundamental question regarding the extent of the royal prerogative in America.

Forsey v. Cunningham (1764) began as a criminal case in a common law court known as a Court of Oyer and Terminer (to hear and decide) which had jurisdiction over criminal matters. Cunningham was found guilty in the jury trial. In a subsequent civil suit he was required to pay Forsey 1,500 pounds in damages. Claiming the award excessive, he petitioned the Supreme Court for leave to appeal to the governor and council. Until this time it was generally assumed that such an appeal from a decision of a common law court could only be on a writ of error—that is where review is confined to errors of law, not of fact or on the merits of the case. Cunningham's own attorney refused to draft his petition, believing such an action to be a dangerous threat to jury trials. Indeed, none of the attorneys in the town would appear for Cunningham or advise the governor.[78] The lieutenant governor, Cadwallader Colden, found a notary public to assist in drafting the writ directing the chief justice of the Supreme Court to bring the proceedings to the governor and council. The Supreme Court refused to obey the order. The attorney general, John Tabor Kempe, agreed with the Court, calling the action unprecedented, and the council agreed with him.[79] Governor Colden ordered the judges to appear before him and demanded that they produce the record. Justice Daniel Horsmanden, the chief justice, stood firm, offering as a defense of his position that to admit such an appeal would disturb "the Ancient, and wholsome Laws of the Land," place jury trials in jeopardy, and arbitrarily introduce a novel procedure "repugnant to the Laws both of England and this Colony."[80] Colden's request for a decision on the matter by the Privy Council met with what appeared to be support for his position.[81] With this apparent backing of the Privy Council, Colden forced the council to accept the appeal.[82] Opponents of the government did what colonists had been doing and would continue to do right up to the break with England: they resorted to both the law and the streets. The Supreme Court again refused to send up the record. The assembly passed a series of strongly worded resolutions denouncing Colden's actions. A mob attempted to seize Fort George where Colden was staying, burned him in effigy, and invaded his coach house, making a bonfire of its contents.[83]

The matter was concluded when the Board of Trade, in consultation with Crown legal officers, held that only a writ of error could provide the basis for an appeal to the council. They recommended redrafting the law to specify that interpretation.[84]

During the eighteenth century the key constitutional disputes involved the question of who possessed sovereignty—the governor, the legislature, or both. Changes in patterns of interaction among the executive, council, and assembly anticipate the form the first constitution would give the three branches of government.

Initially the governor sat with the council, which was at various times composed of anywhere from five to twelve members. These members were appointed by the Crown, with the governor possessing the power to fill vacancies. The bifurcated character of the council was pointed up by a ruling of the attorney general and solicitor general in January 1735 in which the council was seen to have two capacities: "as one part of the Legislature, and as a Council to advise & assist the Governor in all political cases . . . and the Governors are restrain'd by their Instructions not to act without the advice and consent of the Majority of them, in many cases."[85] This double function would be reflected in the powers given the senate in the Constitution of 1777 and in the senate established by the national Constitution of 1787.

The Home Office in England ruled in 1735 that the governor could not sit and vote as a member of the council. With this ruling a significant step was taken in separating the institutions, if not the powers, of the colonial government. The council was on its way to becoming the direct precursor of the upper house or senate in the state's first constitution. The council began choosing its own presiding officer, who was called the speaker. In 1736 the common council adopted a resolution that used the phrase "both houses of the legislature," in effect treating the governor's council as a separate and independent branch of the legislature. The council took the name "legislative council," though in formal correspondence it was referred to as "His Majesty's Council."[86]

Early on, the assembly asserted its right to exclusive jurisdiction over money bills, as had the Commons in England. That right, though not supported by rulings of the English government, was continually asserted by the assembly throughout the first three quarters of the eighteenth century. By the late 1730s the assembly had complete financial control, and was both willing and able to defy governors' requests or threats as well as royal instructions. In 1749, when Governor George Clinton threateningly demanded that the assembly grant the government permanent revenue for five years that he might be independent of the people, the assembly remained firm: "Your conduct is arbitrary, illegal and in violation of our privileges, and we will not comply with your demands." In 1775 the assembly, disregarding royal instructions prohibiting further issuance of paper money unless authorized, ordered over $100,000 in bills of credit.[87]

The structure in place by the middle of the eighteenth century proved satisfactory enough to be adopted, with minor changes, in the first Constitution of New York. Along with political liberties connected with self government, protection in four other areas developed apace: religious liberty, freedom of speech and press, criminal procedure rights, and economic or property rights.

The settlement of North America was intimately connected with property rights. Land and its attendant wealth, along with religious liberty, were prime inducements to those emigrating to the new world. As Willi Paul Adams noted, the "acquisition and cultivation or exploitation of land was the very raison d'etre for the colonies."[88] The legal basis for the protection of private property was in English common law, and there was nearly unanimous agreement on the value of protecting property rights.[89] Appeals to the Magna Carta and similar charters were as often made in the name of protecting property rights as they were to protest arbitrary government. Indeed, for the colonist the protection of private property was synonymous with the protection of political liberty. One's political independence depended, to a large extent, on one's economic independence. If the government was going to take this property by taxation or by more direct means, then it should to do so only with the consent of the governed and by due process of law.

Ranking with private property in importance is the protection of religious liberty. Very early in the history of the colony a policy regarding religion and religious liberty was debated. "Proposed Articles for the Colonization and Trade of New Netherland" of 1638 designated the Dutch Reformed Church as the established church of the colony but allowed other religions to co-exist. This proposed policy of toleration, however, was rejected by the States-General. Two years later an official policy was announced: "No other Religion shall be publicly admitted in New Netherland except the Reformed . . ."[90] As in other areas of colonial life, a wide gap existed between official policy and actual practice. There is no indication that any serious attempt was made to apply this policy to its letter, with the exception of Director Peter Stuyvesant in the 1650s. The acceptance of Quaker refugees expelled from Massachusetts, and the fact that English settlers were permitted to organize their churches without interference, suggests a de facto policy of toleration.[91]

Peter Stuyvesant's attempt to restrict the religious liberty of Quakers, and subsequently of Lutherans and Jews, was greeted with formal protest by colonists and a rebuff from Holland. Freemen representing diverse religious viewpoints sent a remonstrance to Director Stuyvesant asserting the right to liberty of conscience. The document is an affecting and courageous statement in which a need to respect the conscience of others is derived from a deeply religious perspective.[92] It is a signal example of an argument for religious toleration that predates the attempts by enlightenment thinkers to rest toleration on secular grounds.

The authorities in Holland, while not rescinding their official policy, admonished the director to pursue a policy of toleration. "You may therefore shut your eyes, at least not force people's consciences, but allow every one to have his own belief, as long as he behaves quietly and legally. . . ."[93] This became the official policy of the colony in 1661 when oppressed Christians were offered "full liberty to erect a Colony. . . ."[94]

When the English gained control of the colony, the Articles of Capitulation specified that the Dutch "shall enjoy the liberty of their consciences in Divine Worship and church discipline."[95] With regard to the remainder of the colony, Charles II instructed Governor Nicolls to be very careful not to give indication that liberty of conscience would be threatened.[96] This policy was reaffirmed and codified in the Duke's Laws of 1665 which guaranteed religious liberty to those who professed Christianity, while concurrently providing for the establishment of multiple churches. This toleration was extended to all religions in 1674 when the Duke of York instructed Governor Andros to permit all persons of "what Religion soever" to live in the colony unmolested in any way, provided they "give no disturbance to [the] publique peace, nor doe molest or disquiet others in [the] free exercize of their religion."[97] This policy allowed the broadest protection for religious liberty New York had yet experienced. When the duke was crowned king he issued instructions to Governor Dongan to promote the Anglican Church, but Dongan did not interpret those instructions to mean a rescision of the earlier policy.[98]

The Glorious Revolution of 1688 ushered in a constitutional monarchy in England, but also marked the beginning of anti-Catholic policies. The new regime pursued an active policy of ensuring that the Anglican Church had a privileged position in the colony. The practice of Roman Catholicism was proscribed and Catholics were prohibited from holding office under the Charter of Liberties of 1691 by a provision requiring an oath of all officials denying the doctrine of transubstantiation (Sec. 29). In 1700 Catholic priests were ordered expelled from the province.[99]

The Dutch Church succeeded in getting established, but other churches were initially denied that opportunity. In 1770 the legislature allowed other churches to incorporate.[100] This policy would disappear with the adoption of the Constitution of 1777.

In colonial New York, speech deemed seditious was prosecuted. That policy continued to the end of the seventeenth century. The king in 1686 instructed Governor Dongan to "keep any press from printing or any book . . . or other matters whatsoever [from] being printed without [first obtaining] your especial leave and license."[101] Even as prior restraint in the form of licensing disappeared in the eighteenth century, subsequent prosecutions for seditious libel continued, at first on behalf of the Crown and later, after the Zenger case, on behalf of the assembly. The prosecution of Zenger for seditious libel ended in a jury's refusal to convict in the face of legal doctrine that mandated conviction. One important effect of the Zenger victory was to shift prosecutions from the Crown to the assembly; however, even prior to the Zenger case there were instances of punishment by the assembly of individuals for things they said.[102] Such instances prompted lively debates on the dangers of an unlimited assembly and what it could do and was doing. This fear accounts, in part, for the unwillingness of the drafters of the 1777 Constitution to embrace completely the doctrine of legislative supremacy and instead hedge assembly power with checks and balances.[103]

As with religious toleration, speech and press freedom were almost certainly more widely practiced than legal doctrine would suggest. There is substantial evidence to indicate that the press "operated as if the law of seditious libel did not exist."[104] Since juries could not make law, the Zenger case established no legal precedent. The decision, however, gave impetus to an already active and vigorous press, which had been printing material as libelous as anything Zenger had written. This was the tradition the colonists would take with them as they embarked on their journey toward independence.

In the area of criminal procedure protection, colonists received the same protections guaranteed by English common law and relevant statutes. These protections included the fundamental notion, found in the Magna Carta, that no person should be deprived of life, liberty, or property except by the law of the land or due process of law. It included the following specific protections: trial by jury of one's peers, twelve in number; bail in non-capital cases; presentment by grand jury; some protection against self-incrimination; right to an attorney in a criminal trial. This latter right was limited in England to misdemeanor cases or cases involving treason but was more liberally applied in the colonies.[106]

Not only were political institutions in place which could serve as the basis for the 1777 Constitution, but also fundamental notions of due process, freedom of speech and the press, property rights, and religious liberty were so entrenched that the first constitution would largely ratify and legitimize colonial practice.

Notes

1. Milton Klein, *The Politics of Diversity: Essays in the History of Colonial New York* (Port Washington, N.Y.: Kennikat Press, 1974), p. 35.
2. Sung Bok Kim, *Landlord and Tenant in Colonial New York Manorial Society: 1664–1775* (Chapel Hill: University of North Carolina Press, 1978), p. vii.
3. The traditional view is represented by Irving Mark, *Agrarian Conflicts in Colonial New York, 1711–1775* (New York: Columbia University Press, 1940); Carl L. Becker, *The History of Political Parties in the Province of New York, 1760–1776* (Madison: University of Wisconsin Press, 1968 [orig. pub. 1909]); Staughton Lynd, *Class Conflict, Slavery and the United States Constitution: Ten Essays* (Indianapolis: Bobbs-Merrill, 1967), pp. 63–77. Kim, *Landlord and Tenant*, challenges this view, arguing that more openness and fairness

existed in the system. Mary Lou Lustig's *Privilege and Prerogative: New York's Provinvial Elite, 1710-1776* (Canbury, N.J.: Associated University Presses, 1995) reasserts the traditional interpretation and rejects Kim's thesis, but does not address his argument or his data. Lustig argues that initially, New York's elite did not want change and that revolutionary "free white urban lower classes spurred the movement to independence." Later Lustig suggests that elite discontent with British imperial authority also gave impetus to the revolution: "Ultimately it was not only elite discontent . . . but the determination of the lower classes to effect change in society" that caused the revolution. This apparent shift and the ambiguous use of "Ultimately" suggests ambivalence and/or inconsistency in her argument. Finally, Lustig (pp. xvii, 180-181) argues that lower-class radicals remained in control until 1774, when elites "ursurped" the movement. Leaving aside the difficulties involved in such a reading, Lustig is surely right in suggesting that elites provided leadership and gave shape to the post-revolutionary constitutional order. That leadership was all the more imperative given the notorious lack of political stability in the province.

4. Patricia Bonomi, *A Factious People: Politics and Society in Colonial New York* (New York: Columbia University Press, 1971), p. 199.

5. Gordon Wood, *The Radicalism of the American Revolution* (New York: Vintage Books, ed. 1993), p. 114.

6. Bonomi, *A Factious People*, p. 200

7. Governor Francis Bernard of Massachusetts as quoted by Klein, *Politics of Diversity*, p. 45.

8. Milton Klein, "New York in the American Colonies: A New Look," in Jacob Judd and Irwin Polishook, eds., *Aspects of Early New York Society and Politics* (Tarrytown, N.Y.: Sleepy Hollow Restorations, 1974), p. 16.

9. Michael Kammen, *Colonial New York: A History* (New York: Charles Scribner's Sons, 1975), p. 180. By this time New York had a larger proportion of slaves (15%) than any other northern colony. Phyllis Field, *The Politics of Race in New York* (Ithaca, N.Y.: Cornell University Press, 1982), p. 31.

10. Bonomi, *A Factious People*.

11. Ibid., p. 286.

12. Edward Countryman, *A People in Revolution: The American Revolution and Political Society in New York, 1760-1790* (New York: Norton, paperback ed., 1989 [orig. pub. 1981]), pp. 36-45. See also Paul A. Gilje, *The Road to Mobocracy: Popular Disorder in New York City, 1763-1834* (Chapel Hill: University of North Carolina Press, 1987), pp. 5-68. Douglas Greenberg, *Crime and Law Enforcement in the Colony of New York, 1691-1776* (Ithaca, N.Y.: Cornell University Press, 1976, p. 146), notes an increase in riot prosecutions between 1750-1776; these increases were found in every rural section of the colony.

13. Klein, "New York . . . A New Look," pp. 21-22.

14. Countryman, *A People in Revolution*, pp. 89ff.

15. Criticism of the government, whether true or false, intended to create distrust and contempt which threatens its survival or well being.

16. See pp. 29-30 for further discussion of this case. Bonomi, *A Factious People*, pp. 112-120; Stanley, Katz, ed., *A Brief Narrative of the Case and Trial of John Peter Zenger, Printer of the New York Weekly Journal by James Alexander*, 2nd ed. (Cambridge: Belknap Press, 1972), pp. 34-35.

17. Wood, *The Radicalism of the American Revolution*, pp. 6-7.

18. Countryman, *A People in Revolution*, p. 295. Countryman claims this

radicalism was so extensive that "little more than the name of New York and the continuing fact of private property within it, remained the same" (p. 296).

19. "The Early History of Written Constitutions in America," in *Essays in History and Political Theory in Honor of Charles Howard McIlwain* (Cambridge: Harvard University Press, 1936), p. 346. More recently, Bernard Bailyn reaffirmed this judgment: "these documents formed a continuous tradition in colonial American life, and drifted naturally into the thought of the Revolutionary generation." *The Ideological Origins of the American Revolution*, enlarged ed. (Cambridge: Belknap Press, 1992) p. 197.

20. Edmund B. O'Callaghan and Berthold Fernow, eds., *Documents Relative to the Colonial History of the State of New York*, 15 vols. (Albany: Weed Parsons & Co., 1853–1887), I, pp. 11–12 (hereinafter cited as *N.Y. Col. Docs.*).

21. As quoted in James Sullivan, ed., *History of New York State, 1523–1927*, 5 vols. (New York: Lewis Historical Publishing Co., 1927), I, p. 180.

22. Charles Z. Lincoln, *A Constitutional History of New York*, 5 vols. (Rochester: Lawyers Co-operative Publishing Co., 1906), I, p. 415.

23. *N.Y. Col. Docs.*, I, p. 202.

24. John Brodhead, *History of the State of New York to 1691*, 2 vols. (New York: Harper & Bros., 1853–1871), I, pp. 327–328.

25. *N.Y. Col. Docs.*, I, p. 203.

26. Ibid.

27. Ibid., I, p. 192.

28. Ibid., I, pp. 212–213.

29. Ibid.

30. Ibid.

31. As quoted by Brodhead, *History of the State of New York to 1691*, I, p. 472.

32. The procedure apparently fell into disuse after the middle of the seventeenth century. Edmund O'Callaghan, *History of New Netherland*, 2 vols. (New York: D. Appleton & Co., 1846–1848), reprints the Charter establishing the procedure (II, pp. 36–39).

33. *N.Y. Col. Docs.*, I, pp. 260, 262, 266.

34. Ibid., I, pp. 390–391.

35. Michael Kammen, *Colonial New York*, p. 51.

36. As quoted by Lincoln, *A Constitutional History*, I, p. 419.

37. *N.Y. Col. Docs.*, XIV, p. 229.

38. Ibid., I, p. 551.

39. O'Callaghan, *History of New Netherland*, II, p. 242.

40. *N.Y. Col. Docs.*, XIV, p. 232.

41. Ibid., XIV, p. 237.

42. Clinton Rossiter, *The Political Thought of the American Revolution*, Pt. III of *Seedtime of the Republic* (New York: Harcourt, Brace & World, 1963) pp. 52–63; Forrest McDonald, *Novus Ordo Seclorum: The Intellectual Origins of the Constitution* (Lawrence: University of Kansas Press, 1985), pp. 57–66.

43. As quoted by O'Callaghan, *History of New Netherland*, II, p. 262.

44. *N.Y. Col. Docs.*, XIV, p. 233.

45. Ibid., II, pp. 250–252.

46. Nicolls to the Earl of Clarendon, April 7, 1666, *Collections of the New York Historical Society for the Year 1869* (New York: printed for the Society, 1870), II, p. 119.

47. *N.Y. Col. Docs.*, XIV, p. 556.
48. Ibid., XIV, p. 564.
49. Ibid., III, p. 91.
50. *The Colonial Laws of New York from the Year 1664 to the Revolution*, 5 vols. (Albany: J. B. Lyon, 1896), I, pp. 1ff.
51. *Collections of the New York Historical Society, 1869*, II, p. 119.
52. Paul Finkelman "The Soul of the State: Religious Liberty in New York and the Origin of the First Amendment," in Stephen L. Schechter and Richard B. Bernstein, *New York and the Union* (Albany: New York State Commission on the Bicentennial of the United States Constitution, 1990), p. 89.
53. Robert C. Ritchie, *The Duke's Province: A Study of New York Politics and Society 1664-1691* (Chapel Hill: University of North Carolina Press, 1977), p. 33.
54. Kammen, *Colonial New York*, p. 80.
55. *N.Y. Col. Docs.*, XIV, pp. 631-632.
56. Ibid., XIV, p. 646. Lincoln, *A Constitutional History*, I, p. 425.
57. Ritchie, *The Duke's Province*, p. 104.
58. *N.Y. Col. Docs.*, III, p. 235.
59. Ibid., III, p. 289. Robert Ritchie, "London Merchants, New York Markets and the Recall of Edmund Andros," *New York History*, 57 (1976).
60. *Collections of the New York Historical Society for the Year 1912* (1913), pp. 12, 15-17.
61. "The Menacing Shadow of Louis XIV and the Rage of Jacob Leisler: The Constitutional Ordeal of Seventeenth Century New York," in Schechter and Bernstein, *New York and the Union*, p. 41.
62. The instructions and law of the land provisions are found in "Instructions for Governor Dongan," *N.Y. Col. Docs.*, III, pp. 331-332.
63. Charles Andrews, *The Colonial Period of American History*, 3 vols. (New Haven: Yale University Press, 1934-1037), III, p. 101.
64. The charter is found in *The Colonial Laws of New York*, I, chap. I, p. 1683, 111ff. Leonard Levy, *The Establishment Clause: Religion and the First Amendment* (New York: Macmillan, 1986), p. 11.
65. John M. Murrin, "The New York Charter of Liberties, 1683 and 1691," in *Roots of the Republic: American Founding Documents Interpreted*, ed. Stephen Schechter (Madison, Wisc.: Madison House Publishers, 1990), p. 56.
66. *N.Y. Col. Docs.*, III, p. 357-358.
67. Murrin, "The Menacing Shadow," p. 42. Dongan also granted liberal charters to the cities of Albany and New York, allowing them a measure of self-government with certain privileges and immunities.
68. *N.Y. Col. Docs.*, III, p. 624.
69. McMurrin, "The New York Charter of Liberties," p. 64.
70. *Colonial Laws of New York*, I, ch. 4 (1691), pp. 226-231.
71. Kammen, *Colonial New York*, p. 129.
72. "Speech on Conciliation with America," March 22, 1775, in Robert A. Smith, ed., *Edmund Burke on Revolution* (New York: Harper Torchbooks, 1968), p. 60.
73. *N.Y. Col. Docs.*, VII, pp. 677, 679-680.
74. Milton Klein, "Prelude to Revolution in New York: Jury Trials and Judicial Tenure," in *Politics of Diversity*, pp. 154-177. Klein examines a number of clashes involving judges and jury trials.

75. Stanley Nider Katz, *Newcastle's New York: Anglo American Politics, 1732–1753* (Cambridge: Belknap Press, 1968), p. 64.

76. The events surrounding the case are recounted in Cadwallader Colden's "History of William Cosby's Administration . . . and of Lieutenant-Governor George Clinton's Administration, Through 1737" in *The Letters and Papers of Cadwallader Colden* (New York: Printed for N.Y. Historical Society, 1918–1937), 9 vols., IX, pp. 283–355; Governor Cosby and Lewis Morris' accounts of the case are found in *N.Y. Col Docs.*, V, pp. 942–955. Katz, *Newcastle's New York*, pp. 63-8-70 provides a dispassionate summary of the events.

77. *N.Y. Col. Docs.*, V, p. 948.

78. Ibid., VII, pp. 676–677.

79. *Calender of Council Minutes, 1668–1783* (Albany: New York State Library Bulletin No. 58, 1902), pp. 509–510.

80. *Cadwallader Colden Papers*, VI, pp. 380–381.

81. *N.Y. Col. Docs.*, VII, p. 803.

82. *Calendar of Council Minutes*, p. 514.

83. Helen Hill Miller, *The Case for Liberty* (Chapel Hill: University of North Carolina Press, 1965), p. 200. The night of the riot was also the night the Stamp Act was to take effect.

84. *N.Y. Col. Docs.*, VII, pp. 762–763. The most careful and detailed account of the case, with emphasis on the Privy Council's actions, is Joseph Henry Smith, *Appeals to the Privy Council from the American Plantations* (New York: Columbia University Press, 1950), pp. 390–416.

85. *N.Y. Col. Docs.*, VI, p. 41.

86. Lincoln, *A Constitutional History*, I, pp. 445–446.

87. Benson Lossing, *The Empire State, A Compendious History of the Commonwealth of New York* (Hartford, Conn.: American Publishing Co., 1888), pp. 158–159, 164.

88. *The First American Constitutions: Republican Ideology and The Making of the State Constitutions in the Revolutionary Era* (Chapel Hill: University of North Carolina Press, 1980), p. 191.

89. James W. Ely, Jr., *The Guardian of Every Other Right: A Constitutional History of Property Rights* (New York: Oxford University Press, 1992), p. 10; Forrest McDonald, *Novus Ordo Seclorum*, pp. 3–4.

90. *N.Y. Col. Docs.*, I, for initial proposal, pp. 110–111; for rejection, p. 115; for new policy, p. 123.

91. Nelson Mead, "Growth of Religious Liberty in New York City," *Proceedings of the New York Historical Association* (New York State Historical Association) XVII (1919), p. 142.

92. *N.Y. Col. Docs.*, XIV, pp. 402–403.

93. Ibid., XIV, p. 526.

94. Ibid., III, p. 37.

95. Ibid.

96. Ibid., III, p. 58.

97. Ibid., III, p. 218.

98. Ibid., III, pp. 372–373.

99. *Colonial Laws of New York*, I, p. 428 (August 9, 1700, Chap. 89, 7th Assembly).

100. *Ecclesiastical Records, State of New York*, Hugh Hastings, ed., 7 vols. (Albany: J. B. Lyon, 1901–1916), VI, p. 4179.

101. *N.Y. Col. Docs.*, III, p. 375.

102. Leonard Levy, "Did The Zenger Case Really Matter? Freedom of the Press in Colonial New York," *William & Mary Quarterly*, 3rd Series, Vol. 17 (Jan., 1960), pp. 35-50. Even so, Katz claims this was an advance "for it is one thing to be prosecuted and judged by one's elected representatives and quite another to be assailed by the surrogates of the Crown." *A Brief Narrative of the Case and Trial of John Peter Zenger Printer of the New York Weekly Journal by James Alexander*, ed. by Stanley Katz (Cambridge, Mass.: Belknap Press, 1972) p. 31.

103. Edward Countryman Jr. notes this war of words in his "Legislative Government in Revolutionary New York, 1777-1788" (Ph.D. Diss., Cornell University, 1971), pp. 64-67.

104. Leonard Levy, *Emergence of a Free Press* (New York: Oxford University Press, 1985), p. x. Nonetheless, Levy argues that the colonists were only as free as its legislature permitted: "In practice, all political comment was tolerated as long as criticism did not affront the people's representatives" (pp. 47-48). But cf. Countryman's conclusion: "Between 1765 and 1775 New York writers subjected their province's government, and especially its *assembly*, [my emphasis] to a barrage of criticism, abuse and ridicule." *A People in Revolution*, p. 89.

105. Juries in libel cases in the eighteenth century were authorized only to decide whether the defendant had published the statement in question. The court would then rule on its criminality. The jury in the Zenger case disregarded the law and the judge's instructions and returned a verdict of not guilty. This was an early example of jury nullification.

106. Melvin Urofsky, *A March of Liberty: A Constitutional History of the United States* (New York: Alfred A. Knopf, 1988), p. 32. Leonard Levy and Lawrence Leder, "Exotic Fruit: The Right Against Compulsory Self-Incrimination in Colonial New York," *William & Mary Quarterly*, 3rd Series, XX (Jan., 1963), pp. 3-32. For a thorough treatment of criminal procedure practice see Julius Goebel and J. T. Raymond Naughton, *Law Enforcement in Colonial New York: A Study in Criminal Procedure, 1664-1776* (New York: Commonwealth Fund, 1944). George Dargo, *Roots of the Republic: A New Perspective on Early American Constitutionalism* (New York: Praeger Publishers, 1974), Chap. 3, "The Legal Rights of Early Americans," pp. 53-76.

2

The First Constitution, 1777: Constitutional Sobriety in a Revolutionary War

> "Our Free and Happy Constitution"
>
> Governor George Clinton,
> Inaugural Address, 1777

ECHOING THE THOUGHTS of the great social contract thinker John Locke, a committee of the Third Provincial Congress of New York reported on May 27, 1776, that the "old form of Government is becoming, ipso facto dissolved," and recommended a new election be called, as "the right of framing, creating, or remodelling Civil Government is and ought to be in the People."[1] These elections provided the authorization for that body to frame a new constitution for New York.

On July 9, 1776, delegates selected at this special election convened at the Court House in White Plains as the Fourth Provincial Congress. Their purpose was, as they put it, "to institute and establish such a government as they shall deem best calculated to secure the rights, liberties and happiness of the good people of this colony. . . ."[2] The Congress renamed itself "The Convention of Representatives of the State of New York" on July 10, 1776, though it was simultaneously a wartime legislature and a constitutional convention. The Third Provincial Congress, troubled by the lack of any mandate to frame a new government, had called for a special election that would produce a body so authorized. It did not think it necessary, however, to form a special body explicitly for this purpose, nor did it require that the results be submitted to the people for ratification. The absence of popular ratification was the basis for objections raised by artisans and "mechanicks" of New York City who disputed the right of a Provincial Congress to declare and to adopt the fundamental law of the state.

This power, they argued, belonged exclusively "to the inhabitants at large." It was a right "which God has given them, in common with all men, to judge whether it be consistent with their interest to accept or reject a Constitution framed for that State of which they are members."[3] The concept of a constitutional convention was slow to develop, as was the idea of constitutional law as superior to legislative enactment. Even so, the Third Provincial Congress's decision to repair to the electorate for a mandate to frame a new government was a step in the direction of recognizing both distinctions.

The Convention selected a committee on August 1 to "report a plan for instituting and framing a form of Government [and] report . . . a Bill of Rights ascertaining and declaring the essential rights and privileges of the good people of this State as the foundation for such form of Government."[4] The committee was charged to report back on August 26. When that date elapsed without action, and when September gave way to October, the committee's continued inactivity drew increasing criticism. Committee member Henry Wisner informed General George Clinton: "the formation of government goes on very slow indeed; we have done little or nothing about it."[5] The work of this convention in drafting a constitution was not completed until April 20, 1777. The principal source of this delay was, in some ways, the most obvious: The new state's provisional government was literally a government on the run as the Revolutionary War was being fought in New York and the British had gained control of the southern part of the state, including its largest urban area, New York City. The constitution was created in an atmosphere charged with gunpowder. The convention was forced to move from New York City to White Plains, then to Fishkill, and finally to Kingston to keep ahead of the British. Benjamin Butler, in one of the earliest surveys of New York's constitutional history, reports that the delegates, while at Fishkill, were compelled to arm themselves against the possibility of attack by the British or their adherents.[6] Two delegates to the convention remarked that it would be well "first to endeavor to secure a State to govern, before we established a form to govern it by. . . ."[7] The war made it difficult for the committee to obtain a quorum as some of its members were serving in the army, and committee members Robert R. Livingston, John Jay, and Robert Yates were serving on a secret committee to obstruct the British war effort. Indeed, these delegates convinced the convention that their work on that committee was more important than the work of the convention.[8]

There is some reason to suspect the delay was not entirely induced by the problems of war. Delegates like Jay and Livingston were concerned that if action were too swift, the constitution thus produced would resemble too closely the radical document adopted by neighboring Pennsylvania in September 1776. Livingston wrote: "You know that nothing but well-timed delays, indefatigable industry, and a minute attention to every favorable circumstance could have prevented our being exactly in their [Pennsylvania's] situation."[9] Whatever the exact mix of reasons, nearly eight months lapsed before James Duane stood before the convention on March 12, 1777 and read the draft of the committee's work. For the next six weeks delegates debated, article by article, the proposed draft. The constitution was approved on Sunday, April 20, 1777, marking that day the birth of New York as a constitutional state. Two days following its adoption, it was read by the secretary of the convention, who stood on a barrel in front of the old courthouse in Kingston before a group of New Yorkers gathered to hear it.[10]

Until recently, John Jay has been given credit as the writer and prime force behind the 1777 Constitution. Research by Bernard Mason and others indicates that Jay's role in the drafting process was primarily that of refining the draft, giving it clarity and economy of language.[11] No doubt Jay, along with Livingston and Gouverneur Morris, made significant contributions in shaping floor debate on the document, but the constitution as adopted reflects the joint efforts of the drafting committee and the contributions of many of the delegates who attended floor debates.[12] In the end, thirty-three of the thirty-four delegates present at the final vote supported the new constitution.[13]

The Work of the Convention

Reconstruction of the work of the Committee on Government is difficult for a number of reasons. For one, the Provincial Congress was simultaneously a governing body, a war board, and a constitutional drafting convention. This multi-purposed character is reflected in the records of the congress, which shift back and forth among these functions. Moreover, there is no verbatim record of convention or committee debates. Records of votes are incomplete and only a few of the minutes of the committee's private meetings survive. Nevertheless, careful research has been done in tracing the progress of the various drafts of the document as it moved through the committee and was debated by the convention.[14]

Five drafts were produced by the Committee on Government, and at least three alternative constitutional structures circulated among the delegates. These ran the ideological gamut from democratic to conservative or traditional. The former provided for a dominant legislative branch consisting of a council and house of deputies, with the council electing an executive president without a veto power. All taxpayers would have the right to vote regardless of property holdings. The conservative alternative was little more than a modified version of the colonial structure prior to independence.[15] These proposals replicated at the state level the models for government presented by Thomas Paine in his *Common Sense* (1776)—simple, unicameral legislative government—and John Adams's response in his *Thoughts on Government* (1776)—balanced government and separation of powers. Robert Livingston was aware of Adams's work, and undoubtedly others at the convention had read it. One scholar, Edward Countryman, asserts that Adams's *Thoughts on Government* was "the starting point in drafting the constitution."[16] There was unanimity on the need for balance or mixture in the committee; the real debate involved the nature of this mixture, that is, arguments took place not between the followers of Paine and the followers of Adams, but between those who would follow Adams closely and those who would modify the Adams model in the direction of majoritarianism. A comparison of the successive drafts produced by the committee reveals a movement toward those favoring the Adams model, generally identified as traditionalist or conservative. Why this movement occurred is difficult to say with any degree of accuracy because of the difficulties connected with determining the ideological make-up of the delegates and their votes, since voting was done by county unit and dissents were not always registered.[17]

The prevailing view of twentieth century scholars has been that the drafting of the constitution was a "victory for the minority of stability and privilege."[18] The source of this viewpoint is Carl Becker's influential *The History of Political Parties in the Province of New York, 1760–1776.*[19] If this is the case, perplexing questions about how such a victory was achieved arise. The chair of the Committee on Government was Abraham Yates, a moderate majoritarian, and there were sufficient members of similar views to ensure that any document would have had to have their assent.[20] Moreover, a number of actions edging the document in a conservative direction were taken by the convention as a whole. The draft prepared by John Jay for the Committee required only taxpayer or freehold status as a prerequisite for voting, but the convention increased that to a 20-pound freehold or a forty-shilling renthold.[21] The committee draft would have eliminated viva voce voting in favor of secret ballot but the convention left that decision to the discretion of the legislature after the war. The picture of a conspiratorial elite is overdrawn and fails to explain fully what the convention did.

Studies of the convention delegates indicate that delegates divided roughly into three groups: radicals, characterized by those who wanted suffrage for all taxpaying males and legislative supremacy; conservatives, who desired higher property qualifications and more balance among the branches of the government; and moderates, who, as the name suggests, tended to take the middle position on these issues but leaned toward the conservatives.[22] Conservatives tended to be more cohesive and were comprised of men of higher stature and ability than the moderates or radicals. So why did moderates join with the conservatives rather than the radicals? Several factors appeared to be at work. Abraham Yates, chair of the committee, developed a severe fever and the gout, preventing him from attending most committee meetings in the early months of 1777. He did not attend the convention itself until five days prior to the approval of the constitution.[23] But there were other voices—men like John Morin Scott, Robert Yates, and Charles DeWitt. To be sure, they did raise their voices on a number of issues, but it appears that they acquiesced or actively supported the more conservative elements on key votes. Their immediate concern may have been in maintaining the unity of the revolutionary movement, and the prospect of failing to produce a document after eight months of labor also may have proved daunting.[24]

Of greater significance may have been the experience the delegates had had with the colonial assembly which, by the middle of the century, came to dominate provincial government. That experience suggested that an unchecked assembly could be as dangerous as an unchecked governor or monarch. Delegates of moderate view would be particularly susceptible to proposals aimed at balancing or limiting legislative power.[25]

The other great issue dividing conservatives from majoritarians was the issue of suffrage. The assembly requirement was not likely to disenfranchise any, save farm laborers, the urban poor, and seamen—groups identified in the minds of colonists as rootless. Republican/Whig ideology supported some property qualifications because those without such property, however minimal, were thought to have no will of their own, and thus unlikely to exercise the kind of independence necessary for civic virtue.[26] Moderate delegates at the convention would have found such arguments persuasive.[27]

THE INSTITUTIONS

The constitution begins with a preamble setting forth specific reasons for holding a convention, the erection of a new government, and the steps taken in New York for that purpose under the sanction of the Continental Congress. It includes the entire Declaration of Independence and the unanimous resolution of the convention of July 9, 1776 approving the Declaration and pledging the colony to its support. It concluded with the statement that "all power whatever therein hath reverted to the people thereof. . . ."

The constitution created a bicameral legislature consisting of an assembly and a senate, a governor, a Council of Revision, a Council of Appointment, and one court—the Court for the Trial of Impeachments and the Correction of Errors.

Legislative power was vested in two separate and distinct bodies. The assembly consisted of seventy members to be elected annually, and the senate, twenty-four members, of which one-fourth were to be elected every four years. The assembly members were apportioned among the fourteen counties according to the number of qualified voters. Setting the minimum size of the assembly at seventy made that body twice the size of its colonial predecessor. The apportionment requirement would insure that the assembly, unlike its predecessor, would reflect the population accurately. The constitution provided for a census every seven years which would be the basis for the reapportionment. New York's Constitution became the first state constitution to provide for both districts with equal numbers of inhabitants and periodic redistricting to accommodate population shifts. The assembly and senate were empowered to create new counties, allowing the assembly to expand to a maximum size of three hundred and the senate to one hundred.

Each house was given the powers and privileges of the Provincial Assembly of the colony, but surprisingly no grant of exclusive power to originate money bills was given to the assembly. This stipulation was made in almost every other state constitution with a bicameral legislature. Later, when the senate challenged the assembly's claim to originate such bills, the assembly had to resort to colonial precedents.[28]

The senate, though less closely related, is a successor to the colonial council as it had developed by the middle of the eighteenth century. For the election of senators the state was divided into four "great districts," the eastern with three senators, the southern with nine, and the middle and western each with six.

The supreme executive power of the state was vested in a governor who must be a freeholder, and chosen by votes of freeholders possessed of 100 pounds above debts. The term of office was three years. He was commander-in-chief of the army and admiral of the navy. As governor he possessed the power to convene the legislature in extraordinary session and to prorogue (discontinue or postpone) it, not to exceed sixty days in any given year. With the exception of treason and murder cases, he was given the power to pardon and grant reprieves. In such cases, however, he did possess the authority to suspend sentencing until the legislature acted. He was expected to deliver a message to the legislature on the situation of the state and to "take care that the laws be faithfully executed. . . ."[29]

The convention created as strong a governor as is found in any early state constitution. Delegates reacting to the weak and almost nonexistent executive in the Pennsylvania Constitution rejected proposals to create a "council of state" and all proposals to make the governor dependent on the assembly.[30] A lieutenant-governor was established who would succeed the governor in cases of death, resignation, or removal. The lieutenant-governor was made president of the senate with a casting vote, i.e., a vote in cases of ties, but held no vote otherwise.

Two powers generally associated with the executive power, the veto and appointment powers, were the basis for the creation of two unique institutions, the Council of Appointment and the Council of Revision. The power to appoint public officials was one of the most important topics considered at the convention. Its importance is suggested by the fact that this issue is mentioned in nine articles. Only the legislature was given more attention. The Council of Appointment was the result of a compromise between those who desired executive appointment and those who favored giving the legislature a predominate role. Dissatisfied with both of these alternatives, John Jay suggested a Council of Appointment consisting of the governor and one senator from each of the four districts, selected annually by the assembly. Ostensibly, the governor would have the exclusive power to nominate—but the constitution states "appoint" with the advice and consent of the council—all specified officers.[31] The use of the word "appoint" rather than "nominate" enabled members of the council to claim a concurrent right to nominate as well as to vote on nominees. It occasioned the first major dispute over the meaning of the constitution and necessitated a constitutional convention in 1801.

No doubt conservatives hoped the plan would help ensure that "ignorant or inattentive clerks" would not obtain office.[32] Further evidence of the fear that the appointment power would be used to expand power and ensconce individuals in office for life was a provision attempting to ensure rotation in office. Article XXVI prohibited the council from reappointing the same person sheriff or coroner for more than four consecutive years.[33] It is not surprising that the council was to have a tempestuous history and would be abolished at the convention of 1821.

The second institution connected with the executive office was the Council of Revision. Like the Council of Appointment it resulted from convention rather than committee action. John Jay convinced the convention that a collective body would be more suitable for the exercise of the veto power than a single individual. The council would be composed of a governor, the chancellor (the chief judge of the equity court system of the state) and the three judges (or any two) of the Supreme Court. It was empowered to revise or veto bills originating from the assembly. Such a bill would become law if the council failed to act within ten days of its receipt, or if vetoed, repassed by two-thirds of the legislature.[34]

The only court explicitly provided for by the constitution was the Court for the Trial of Impeachments and Correction of Errors. Taken for granted were the courts then in operation—the Supreme Court, Court of Chancery, Probate Court, and Courts of Admiralty. They were mentioned incidentally in provisions limiting the ages of the judges and the offices each might hold, and concerning the selection of clerks and appointment of attorneys, solicitors, and counsellors at law. The Court for the Trial of Impeachments was composed of the president of the senate, senators, the chancellor, and the three judges of the Supreme Court. It is likely that the practice of giving the upper house of the legislature appellate jurisdiction derived from the colonial practice of appealing to the council of the province.[35]

The procedure for impeachment is mentioned in no less than five articles. This attention reflects how saturated the colonists were with the "Whig apprehensions of misapplied ruling power."[36] This apprehension prompted the adoption of this ancient English procedure. Simultaneously it gave rise to a concern that the power should be used with the utmost scrupulous legal procedure and confined to use only in the clearest of cases. Thus while the assembly was given the power to impeach, two-thirds of that body would be necessary for a successful impeachment. The trial on the impeachment would be conducted before the Court for Trial of Impeachments. Judges were to be sworn to impartiality and specific provision was made to provide counsel in every impeachment proceeding. The desire to be able to remove corrupt officials competed with a concern that such a process could easily degenerate into political warfare, thus creating a constitutional ambivalence and the likelihood that despite all the attention paid to it the device would be little used.

The language of the article suggests that members of the assembly and the senate were not subject to impeachment. The grounds for impeachment were "mal or corrupt conduct" and such conduct was not restricted to criminal acts. The impeachment proceeding is similar to the one eventually adopted by the national Constitution.[37]

The Political Theory of the 1777 Constitution

To understand the 1777 Constitution, one must keep in mind three things: theory, compromise, and transition.

1. Theory: Whatever the specific disagreements expressed at the convention, the delegates formed a consensus on three theoretical concepts. First, they accepted republican government as the only form consistent with the traditions and genius of the people of New York. The 1777 Constitution opens with the declaration that no authority "shall in any pretence whatever be exercised over the people or members of this State but shall be derived from and granted by them" (Art. I).

The existence of a second chamber raises a number of questions regarding the delegates' understanding of republican government. What kind of institution was it intended to be? A new version of the colonial council? An elected version of the House of Lords? What function could a senate play in a strictly republican government? Was it part of an attempt to create a mixed regime in spite of the republican rhetoric of the opening articles? The tradition of a mixed regime in which monarchic, aristocratic, and democratic elements found their homes in a monarch, an upper house, and a popular assembly, respectively, usually coincided with a social order that was hierarchical. If such a hierarchical order did exist in colonial New York by virtue of the deference paid to one's "betters," it certainly did not exist in the New York of 1777.

Some saw it as a repository of Jefferson's "natural aristocracy," adding wisdom and experience to the governing process; others viewed it simply as a way to limit the powers of the assembly in the same way colonial Whigs sought to limit the royal prerogative; a third, more cynical group, saw it as an oligarchic bastion for the protection of private property. Deciphering the justifications for the senate may be an impossible task. Edward Countryman has concluded: "One can only assume that the makers of the Senate did not know what they wanted it to represent, persons, or property, or wisdom."[38]

Second, the delegates espoused the idea of constitutionalism, or rule of law, creating a government powerful enough to secure the polity's interests but not so powerful as to threaten other important values. Only a written constitution could achieve the rule of law—specifically, one providing for separation and division of governmental powers to ensure that no single branch became so dominant as to threaten the rule of law. The Council of Revision (Art. III), with the power to veto "laws inconsistent with the spirit of this constitution" and the provision continuing the common law in the state (Art. XXXV) are two examples of the rule of law and of constitutionalism expressed in the document.

Third, the commitment to individual liberty, the hallmark of classical liberalism, is present in the 1777 Constitution, specifically in its guarantees of liberty of conscience (Art. XXXVIII), the right to trial by jury (Art. XLI), and its restatement of Article XXXIX of the Magna Carta in Article XIII that "no member of this state, shall be disfranchised, or deprived of any rights and privileges secured to the subjects of this state, by this Constitution unless by law of the land or judgment of his peers."

2. Compromise: The commitment to republicanism, constitutionalism, and liberalism embodied in the 1777 Constitution did not forestall significant differences over the application of these concepts. The ideological divisions among those charged with drafting the document are a matter of some dispute, however. Generally speaking, a broad division appeared between those who wished to keep change to a minimum, variously called "traditionalists" or "conservatives," and those who wished for extensive change, variously call "majoritarians" or "Popular Whigs." Between these two there were the "moderates," so called only because they could not be classified in either of the first two divisions; they seemed to have had no coherent stable agenda at the convention.[39]

The central issues on which the debates focused were how far the consent of the people should be carried, and how power should be distributed among the various branches of government. The popular Whigs argued for minimal property qualifications and legislative supremacy; the traditionalists or conservatives argued for larger property qualifications and some sharing of power among the branches of government. The results were a series of compromises favoring the traditionalists.[40] Although controversy exists over the actual degree of enfranchisement in New York, nearly 60% of the adult males and 70% of the heads of families could vote for members of the assembly, but only approximately 29% of the adult males could vote for senators and the governor.[41] Another aspect of the suffrage question was the debate over voice voting versus secret ballot. The popular Whigs, fearing the influence of landlords on their tenants, pressed for the secret ballot. The convention compromised here as well, continuing voice voting during the war but authorizing the legislature to abolish it when the war ended (Art. VI).

The second major issue at the convention concerned distribution of power among the branches of the state government. Again, the convention resorted to compromise among the contending factions. The governor was to be elected directly by the voters for a term of three years, giving him an independence and stability not available to governors in other states at that time. He was made commander-in-chief of the military, given some pardoning power, the authority to convene and adjourn the assembly, and to make policy recommendations to the legislature. However, he was to share the veto power over legislation with the Council of Revision. The Council resulted from the convention's attempt to avoid the danger of a governor with too great a role in the legislative process and a veto-proof legislature. The Council, they hoped, would prevent executive despotism and place a check on the legislative branch.[42]

The fact that the Council was given power to veto bills "inconsistent with the spirit of the constitution or with the public good" meant that it could exercise both judicial review—voiding laws for legal reasons—and veto power—negating laws for political or policy reasons. This provision, in all likelihood, inhibited the development of judicial review in New York. The terms of the article suggested that approval by the Council removed both constitutional and political defects. Moreover, the membership of the Court for the Trial of Impeachments and Correction of Errors overlapped with that of the Council, both bodies having as members the chancellor and members of the Supreme Court. The Colonial Council and the King's Privy Council provided models for this institution.

The power to appoint to public office was a sensitive issue among colonists for two reasons. The first was a fear of the executive's use of the appointive power to aggrandize the power of that office. This fear, part of the Whig ideology that fueled the revolutionary movement, was prompted by the use of royal authority to appoint "improper men, from sinister designs . . . in places of trust or power."[43] Although not all-consuming in New York, such fear accounts for some of the uneasiness with placing the appointment power in the hands of the governor. Provincial assemblies viewed taxes and appointments as correlative powers since the salaries of royal officials were drawn from provincial taxes. A second, more pragmatic but related issue concerned the question of who was going to control and dispense the patronage connected with public office. The council was a compromise between those, like Gouverneur Morris, who wished the appointment power to reside with the governor, and those, like Robert Yates, who believed it should reside with the legislature.

The convention provided the judiciary additional independence by giving them tenure "during good behaviour" (Art. XXIV). It also stripped the governor of his equity and probate jurisdiction, which effectively insured the judiciary's separateness as well as its independence.[44] It is clear that the delegates' understanding of the separation of powers did not prevent them from adopting structures that combined the various powers for specific purposes. It may be that "hard political necessity" prevented them from consistently following doctrines like the separation of powers.[45] On the other hand, we can see the Council of Revision as precursor to the Federalist view that the great danger in republican government was the tendency for all powers to be swept into the legislative vortex. James Madison did not believe it to be a violation of the separation of powers when he advocated a Council of Revision to do for the House of Representatives what the Council of Revision in New York was to do for the legislative branch.[46] Seen in this light, the Council was an early attempt to combine the powers of government in order to keep the weaker branches (executive and judiciary) separate and independent.

3. Transition: Donald S. Lutz argues that the theory embodied in state constitutions during the revolutionary period was fundamentally different from that found in the United States Constitution of 1787. Despite the differences between the individual state constitutions, he claims they all shared a set of Whig assumptions regarding the nature of the polity.[47] The New York Constitution of 1777 stands out because it deviated from many of the assumptions and institutions which dominated early state constitution-making and because several of its provisions shaped comparable provisions of the federal Constitution, framed ten years later. It is thus, in many ways, a transitional document between Whig and Federalist political thought.

First, it provided for a stronger executive than all the other states, giving him the longest term (three years) with re-eligibility, direct popular election, and a share (with the judiciary) in the veto power. In the Council of Revision and the Court for the Trial of Impeachments and Correction of Errors, the judiciary was given more power than any comparable judiciary of its day. The Council of Revision unquestionably influenced debates at the federal convention. Gouverneur Morris, one of the architects of the 1777 Constitution, argued strenuously for a similar body as a Pennsylvania delegate to the federal convention in 1787.[48] In requiring property qualifications for those voting for governor and senators, and in choosing senators from only four great districts, the convention distanced the representative from the represented.[49] The term of office for senators was as long as any in the early constitutions, and the 1777 Constitution contained no requirements for petitions to or instructions of legislators. The senate was to be more a filter for, rather than a mirror of, popular sentiment. In this respect, New York moved away from Whig political theory and toward Federalist theory. Moreover, some of the sentiment for so structuring the state senate was similar to that which animated Madison and others at the federal convention: the need to restrain the "levelling spirit."[50]

Institutions such as the Council of Revision and the Council of Appointment indicate a focus on institutional checks by the various branches of the government on one another rather than a focus on "the relationship between government and the people."[51] It may be that the tendency to move toward a Federalist theory is attributable to the "greater degree of popular disorder" that existed in New York,[52] but the "popular disorder" was in fact part of a long history of regional, religious, and group conflict—a history which made New York seem, in the eyes of one observer, "mad with Politics."[53] As Milton Klein has put it, "In an age which looked on political factionalism as disruptive of public order, New Yorkers accepted it as . . . legitimate."[54] As previously noted, almost from the colony's inception group conflict was an integral part of New Yorkers' political culture. It is this pluralism that best explains the appearance of politics in the modern or Federalist sense, and helps explain the character of New York's Constitution as the bridge to the Federalist view embraced at the Philadelphia convention of 1787. Indeed, it is not an exaggeration to call the 1777 Constitution the first Federalist constitution.[55]

The Constitution of 1777: An Assessment

In forty-two sections and fewer than 7,000 words, the 1777 Constitution embodied the great ideas and institutions for which it is justly praised. Its preamble incorporated the Declaration of Independence. Along with the institutions and ideas it embraces, the document is noteworthy for what it does not contain. The constitution lacked a formal bill of rights and a method for amending; it failed to address the issue of slavery and made no mention of education.[56] Jay wrote to Gouverneur Morris lamenting the fact that there was not a "clause against the continuation of domestic slavery." Morris had introduced such a motion at the convention, but it was defeated.[57] Though the constitution did not outlaw slavery, it placed no restriction on suffrage based on race. African-Americans meeting the property qualifications could vote under the 1777 Constitution.

The delegates' reasons for not including a bill of rights are not entirely clear. The initial charge to the drafting committee was to declare the "essential rights and privileges of the good people of this State, as a foundation for such form of government."⁵⁸ Delegate Robert Yates offered one plausible explanation: "Our situation resembled a people in a state of nature . . . and as such, the constitution to be formed would operate as a bill of rights."⁵⁹ Yates's explanation foreshadowed that offered by Federalists such as James Wilson and Alexander Hamilton in 1787–1788 in response to demands by Anti-federalists, including Yates, for an explanation as to why the proposed United States Constitution lacked a declaration of rights. It is possible that the committee charged with drafting the document decided there was no need for a separate bill of rights. This view is reinforced upon recollection that the constitution contains provisions for trial by jury (Art. XLI), a right to counsel in felony cases (Art. XXXIV), a due process clause (Art. XIII), a prohibition of bills of attainder (Art. XLII), a clause protecting the right of conscientious objection for Quakers (Art. XL), an article protecting Indian land rights against fraudulent contracts and purchases (Art. XXXVII), and provisions providing religious freedom (Art. XXVIII).⁶⁰

The clauses bearing on the relationship of church and state and religious liberty merit further examination. Article XXV ended the system of multiple establishments in New York. It abrogated all parts of the common law and statutes "as may be construed to establish or maintain any particular denomination of Christians or their ministers. . . ." Article XXXVIII as finally adopted provides for "The free exercise and enjoyment of religious profession and worship, without discrimination or preference." That liberty was not absolute. Acts of "licentiousness" or "practices inconsistent with the peace and safety" of the state were prohibited. This provision reflects faithfully the tradition of religious liberty and toleration which had taken root in New York. In *People v. Phillips* (1813) a court in New York City was faced with the question as to whether a Catholic priest could be forced to testify in a court of law concerning matters learned in the confessional. Though the court settled the issue on common law grounds, it nevertheless proceeded "to more elevated ground," the constitutional question: "Religion is an affair between God and man, and not between man and man. The laws which regulate it must emanate from the Supreme Being, not from human institutions." After quoting in its entirety Article 38 of the Constitution, the court concluded that "it is essential for the free exercise of religion" that the secrecy of penance be protected, dismissing the prosecutor's claim that it was "inconsistent with the peace or safety of the state." The court's decision found a way not only to respect the claim of a superior religious obligation, but also to indicate that the polity—its justice and its laws—depends on something more than the will of the sovereign.⁶¹

But there was also a tradition of intolerance to Catholics, based on a fear of Catholics and the papacy arising from events in England in the late seventeenth century and reflected in the restrictions found in the Charter of Liberties of 1691 and subsequent legislation. John Jay, perhaps recalling the persecution suffered by his Huguenot ancestor Pierre Jay following the revocation of the Edict of Nantes, pressed ardently for provisions which would have restricted Catholicism in the state. One of his amendments would have had the effect of prohibiting Catholics from citizenship.[62] The convention rejected or softened most of Jay's amendments, but the document does contain some harsh, thinly veiled references to Catholicism, as in the opening of Article XXXVIII, which states that it is necessary to guard against "spiritual oppression and intolerance, wherewith the bigotry and ambition of weak and wicked priests and princes, have scourged mankind. . . ." In the naturalization Article (XLII) individuals applying for citizenship were required to "renounce allegiance to every foreign king, prince, potentate and state in all matters ecclesiastical as well as civil." The addition of "ecclesiastical" was clearly aimed at the papacy and could have been used to restrict Catholic immigration. That prospect never materialized, because the national Constitution, when adopted, made naturalization the exclusive province of Congress, and in 1790 Congress passed implementing legislation making Article XLII obsolete. Nonetheless, New York was the first state to abandon, by constitutional provision, the previously established churches. Of the first wave of state constitutions adopted between 1776 and 1784, New York came closest to establishing complete religious freedom.[63]

The constitution provided for a continuation of the common law, which was seen by the colonists as a bulwark of protections for their liberties. Whatever the reasons for not including a formal bill of rights, lack of concern for protection of liberties was not among them.

The 1777 Constitution failed to include an amending procedure. This was likely an oversight, but if it was not it suggests that the delegates believed that the legislature was the body to initiate constitutional change and determine how that change shall be effected. Evidence for this view is the enactment by the New York legislature in 1787 of a statutory bill of rights.[64] To the extent that this statute was considered a part of the state's fundamental law, it is inconsistent with the view that only the people, or the legislature pursuant to some specific mandate, is authorized to make fundamental law. As Bernard Mason has suggested, some decades passed after the adoption of their first constitution "before Yorkers comprehended fully the implications of a written constitution as a statement of popular sovereignty."[65]

It remains to note one final aspect of the 1777 Constitution: the document is remarkable for the continuity it maintains with earlier political practice. The assembly, with some changes, is the assembly of the colonial period; the senate replaces a council which had, by that time, become the upper house of legislature; and the governor is a slightly revised version of the colonial royal governor. The courts, with the exceptions of the chancellor (who assumed responsibility for equity and probate functions) and the new Court of Impeachment and Errors, remained as they had been in the colonial period. The common law, the laws of England, and colonial laws were continued in effect, with the exceptions noted in Article XXXV. To prevent interminable litigation, the constitution validated all inheritable land titles and leases granted by the King of England (Art. XXXVI).[66]

Among the reasons for the success of the 1777 Constitution was the fact that its creators did not tamper with those aspects of the governing process which had proven their effectiveness. That continuity, combined with the moderate character of the document, enabled it to achieve a legitimacy which in turn accounted for the relatively smooth transition from colony to constitutional republic.

Notes

1. Peter Force, ed., *American Archives, Consisting of a Collection of Authentick Records, State Papers, Debates and Letters and Other Notices of Public Affairs, the Whole Forming a Documentary History of the Origin and Progress of the North American Colonies . . . in Six Series*, 9 vols. (Washington, D.C.: M. St. Clair Clark, 1837–1853), 4th Series, VI, p. 1338, hereafter cited as *American Archives*.

2. Ibid., 5th Series, I, 1391. The preamble to the 1777 Constitution contains a similar statement.

3. "The respectful Address of the Mechanicks in Union for the City and County of New York, represented by their General Committee," *American Archives*, 4th Series, VI, p. 895.

4. Ibid., 5th Series, I, 1466. The members of the committee consisted of John Jay, John Sloss Hobart, William Smith, William Duer, Gouverneur Morris, Robert Livingston, John Broome, John Morin Scott, Abraham Yates, Jr., Henry Wisner, Sr., Samuel Townsend, Charles DeWitt, and Robert Yates. James Duane was added to the committee in September 1776. Of these, Hobart and Townsend never attended committee sessions. Generally considered conservatives or traditionalists were Jay, Morris, Livingston, Duer, and Duane. Those who could be classified as moderate majoritarians were Abraham Yates, Jr. (chair), Robert Yates, Henry Wisner, Charles DeWitt, and John Morin Scott. The difficulty and danger of classifying delegates is revealed most clearly in the case of John Morin Scott, who is classified by most commentators as a majoritarian but who voted to support an upper legislative house not based on any form of representation. See Bernard Mason, *The Road to Independence: The Revolutionary Movement in New New York, 1773–1777* (Lexington:

University of Kentucky Press, 1966), pp. 216–217; Edward Countryman, *A People in Revolution, The American Revolution and Political Society in New York, 1760–1790*, pp. 167–168.

5. Wisner to George Clinton, Oct. 4, 1776, *Public Papers of George Clinton First Governor of New York 1777–1785, 1801–1804*, Hugh Hastings, ed., 10 vols. (Albany: Wynkoop Hallenbeck Crawford Co., 1899–1914), I, p. 368.

6. "Outline of the Constitutional History of New York," *Collections of the New York Historical Society*, 2nd series (New York: Bartlett & Welford, 1848) II, p. 51.

7. Christopher Tappen and Gilbert Livingston to the Convention, August 24, 1776, *American Archives*, 5th Series, I, 1542.

8. *Journals of the Provincial Congress, Provincial Convention, Committee of Safety and Council of Safety of the State of New York, 1775–1777*, 2 vols. (Albany: Thurlow Weed Pub., State Printer, 1842), I, p. 568; see the comments of Bernard Mason, *The Road to Independence*, p. 218.

9. Livingston to William Dyer, June 12, 1777 as quoted by Mason, *The Road to Independence*, p. 231. But cf. Philip Schuyler's remark: "I am very apprehensive that much evil will arise if a Government is not soon established for this State. The longer it is delayed the more difficult it will be to bring the unprincipled and licentious to a proper sense of their duty and we have too many such amongst us" (*American Archives*, 5th Series, III, p. 1101). Countryman in his dissertation questions Mason's argument about the conservative conspiracy to delay. "Legislative Government in Revolutionary New York, 1777–1788" (Ph.D. Diss., Cornell University, 1971), pp. 80–85. Countryman appears to have changed his mind in his *A People in Revolution*, where he refers to the "trick" of the "delaying game" (p. 166). Stephan Bielinski, *Abraham Yates, Jr. and the New Political Order in Revolutionary New York* (Albany: New York State American Revolution Bicentennial Commission, 1975), pp. 27–29, reaffirms the older view of Lincoln's that the chaotic conditions were sufficient to explain the delays.

10. Alexander Flick, ed., *The American Revolution in New York* (Albany: prepared by the Division of Archives and History, University of the State of New York, 1926), p. 92.

11. Mason, *The Road to Independence*, pp. 225–229.

12. Alfred Young, *The Democratic-Republicans of New York: Their Origins, 1763–1797* (Chapel Hill: University of North Carolina Press, 1967), pp. 17–18; Edward Countryman, *A People In Revolution*, pp. 167–168.

13. Peter R. Livingston of Albany was the lone dissentor. Livingston was one of the upper manor Livingstons, who were among the few who rejected the constitution, believing it "savors too much" of the "levelling principle," as quoted by Young, *The Democratic Republicans of New York*, p. 21.

14. The first detailed examination of the work of the Committee and Convention was undertaken by Charles Lincoln, *A Constitutional History of New York*, I, 490–556. Lincoln discovered what he believed to be working drafts of the convention's deliberations. A careful re-examination of these, along with a newly discovered third fragment found in the papers of Abraham Yates by Bernard Mason, shows that these were in fact committee drafts. *The Road to Independence*, pp. 225–226. Proceeding on this assumption, Mason was able to establish a sequential order to these versions. Lincoln deserves credit not only for the discovery of the drafts and for his pioneering work, but for reprinting the drafts, as the originals were destroyed in the Capitol fire of 1911.

15. Mason, *The Road to Independence*, pp. 235–237; Countryman, "Legislative Government in Revolutionary New York," pp. 87–89.
16. Countryman, "Legislative Government in Revolutionary New York," p. 85.
17. Mason, *The Road to Independence*, pp. 243–245.
18. Frank Monaghan, *John Jay* (Indianapolis: Bobbs-Merrill, 1935), p. 97; quoted approvingly by Elisha Douglass, *Rebels and Democrats: The Struggle for Equal Rights and Majority Rule During the American Revolution* (Chicago: Quadrangle Books, 1965 [orig. pub. 1955]) p. 66; E. Wilder Spaulding, "The State Government Under the First Constitution," in Alexander Flick, ed., *History of the State of New York*, 10 vols. (New York: Columbia University Press, 1933–1937), IV, pp. 149–183.
19. Madison: University of Wisconsin Press, 1968 [orig. pub. 1909]. The class conflict view is also at the heart of Irving Mark's *Agrarian Conflicts in Colonial New York, 1711–1795* (New York: Columbia University Press, 1940).
20. Wilder Spaulding gratuitously suggests that "The patriot majority of the state was too much concerned with winning victories upon the battlefield to fight for popular rights upon the floor of the convention." *New York in the Critical Period 1783–1789* (New York: Columbia University Press, 1932), p. 95. Aside from the fact that he offers not a shred of evidence for the assertion, it is difficult to fathom exactly what it could mean or how it could be put into testable form.
21. Mason, *The Road to Independence*, pp. 240–241.
22. Ibid., pp. 246–248.
23. Stephan Bielinski, *Abraham Yates Jr.*, p. 33.
24. Ibid., pp. 33–34.
25. See below, pp. 83–84.
26. Gordon Wood, *The Creation of the American Republic 1776–1787* (New York: Norton Press, 1972 [orig. pub., 1969]), pp. 168–169.
27. Robert Yates, writing twelve years later under the pseudonym "Sydney," claimed that there was a consensus over granting the "middling" class suffrage since the dangers came from the two extremes, the rich and the poor. In Herbert Storing, ed., *The Complete Anti-Federalist*, 7 vols. (Chicago: University of Chicago Press, 1981), VI, p. 115. The essay appeared in *The New York Journal and Daily Patriotic Register* on June 14, 1788. It was part of the anti-Federalist campaign against ratification by New York of the Constitution of 1787. Yates's authorship has not been definitely established, but Storing believes the author to be Abraham Yates.
28. William Polf, *1777: The Political Revolution and New York's First Constitution* (Albany: New York State Bicentennial Commission, 1977), pp. 15–16.
29. This phrase appears in the national Constitution, Art. II, sec. 3.
30. Countryman, "Legislative Government," pp. 87–89.
31. Letter to Robert Livingston and Gouverneur Morris, April 29, 1977, ed., Henry P. Johnston, in *The Correspondence and Public Papers of John Jay*, 3 vols. (New York: G. P. Putnam's Sons, 1890–1893), I, p. 130. The letter indicates that Jay had intended for the governor to have the power to nominate and the council to confirm or reject.
32. Letter to Robert Livingston and Gouverneur Morris, April 29, 1777 in *The Correspondence and Public Papers of John Jay*, I, p. 130.
33. As J. M. Gitterman points out, this provision had the effect of rotating

a few persons through a series of officers. "The Council of Appointment in New York," *Political Science Quarterly*, VII (1892), p. 92.

34. Technically, to repass a bill over the veto, two-thirds of the members of the body in which the bill orginated and two-thirds of the members present in the other chamber.

35. DeAlva Alexander, *A Political History of the State of New York*, 3 vols. (New York: Henry Holt & Co., 1906), I, p. 12; Benjamin Butler, "Outline of the Constitutional History of New York," p. 53, suggests the House of Lords as its direct ancestor.

36. Wood, *Creation of the American Republic*, p. 141.

37. Art. I, Secs. 2, 3; Art. II, Sec. 4.

38. "Legislative Government in Revolutionary New York," p. 100. The fact that higher property qualifications and longer terms were required suggests that the senate was to perform other functions beyond mirroring the views of the citizens. But the fact that it was elective and that one could be a member of that body without possessing the 100-pound property qualification for voting in senate elections suggests confusion, if not inconsistency.

39. Mason, *The Road to Independence*, p. 231; Douglass, *Rebels and Democrats: The Struggle for Equal Political Rights and Majority Rule During the American Revolution*, p. 63; Young, *The Democratic Republicans of New York*, p. 17.

40. Young, *The Democratic Republicans of New York*, pp. 20–21; Douglass, *Rebels and Democrats*, p. 66; Mason, *The Road to Independence*, pp. 243–244; Countryman, *A People in Revolution*, p. 285.

41. Young, *The Democratic-Republicans of New York*, p. 84. Cf. Milton Klein, *The Politics of Diversity: Essays in the History of Colonial New York* (Port Washington, N.Y.: Kennikat Press, 1974), pp. 20–25 and n.43, for comments on Young's figures; and Chilton Williamson, *American Suffrage from Property to Democracy, 1760–1860* (Princeton: Princeton University Press, 1960), p. 111.

42. James Dougherty, *Constitutional History of the State of New York*, 2nd ed. (New York: Neale Publishing Co., 1915), pp. 51–52.

43. Wood, *The Creation of the American Republic*, p. 80.

44. This separateness is reinforced by Article XXV, which prevents the chancellor and judges of the Supreme Court, as well as the judges of county courts, from holding any other office except that of senator or delegate to the general Congress.

45. Bernard Mason, "New York State's First Constitution," in *Essays on the Genesis of the Empire State* (Albany: New York State Bicentennial Commission, 1979), p. 26.

46. Madison's advocacy, at the convention of 1787, of a Council of Revision consisting of the executive and the judiciary, is clearly indebted to the New York example: Max Farrand, ed., *The Records of the Federal Covention of 1787*, 4 vols. (New Haven: Yale University Press, 1911), II, p. 74. A good discussion is Charles F. Hobson, "The Negative on State Laws: James Madison, the Constitution, and the Crisis of Republican Government," *William and Mary Quarterly*, 3d ser., 36 (1979), pp. 215–235. For a sophisticated elaboration of this point in the federal context, see Garry Wills, *Explaining America: The Federalist*, (Garden City, N.Y.: Doubleday & Co., 1981), pp. 117–125.

47. Donald S. Lutz, *Popular Consent and Popular Control: Whig Political*

Theory in the Early State Constitutions (Baton Rouge: Louisiana State University Press, 1980), pp. 1–22.

48. Farrand, ed., *Records*, II, pp. 75–76.

49. Young, *The Democratic Republicans of New York*, p. 84.

50. Compare Madison's sentiments at the federal convention (Farrand, ed., *Records*, I, pp. 422–423) with those expressed by William Smith as quoted in Mason, *The Road to Independence*, pp. 235–236; and with John Jay's sentiments as quoted in George Pellew, *John Jay* (New York: Houghton Mifflin, 1897 [orig. pub. 1890]), pp. 76–104.

51. Lutz, *Popular Consent and Popular Control*, p. 235.

52. Ibid., p. 94.

53. Quoted in Milton Klein, "Shaping the American Tradition: The Microcosm of Colonial New York," *New York History* 59 (1978), p. 197.

54. Klein, "Shaping the American Tradition," p. 197.

55. Sol Wachtler and Stephen L. Schechter, "Liberty and Property: New York and the Origins of American Constitutionalism," *Law Studies* 14 (Spring, 1989), p. 4.

56. Jay desired a clause providing for the "support and encouragement of literature." Jay to Livingston and Morris, April 29, 1777, in *The Correspondence and Public Papers of John Jay*, I, p. 136.

57. *Journals of Prov. Cong.*, I, p. 887.

58. Jay to Livingston and Morris, April 29, 1777 in *The Correspondence and Public Papers of John Jay*, I, p. 136.

59. *Journals of Prov. Cong.*, I, p. 552.

60. "Sidney" [Robert Yates] in Herbert J. Storing, ed., *The Complete Anti-Federalist*, VI, p. 109.

61. Report of the trial is published as William Sampson (reporter), *The Catholic Question in America* (New York: Edward Gillespy, 1813), pp. 109–110. The case is analyzed by Michael McConnell, "The Origins and Historical Understanding of the Free Exercise of Religion," *Harvard Law Review* 103, pp. 1410–1412; and James R. Stoner, "Religious Liberty and Common Law: Free Exercise Exemptions and American Courts," *Polity* XXVI (Fall, 1993), pp. 20–24.

62. Bernard Mason suggests another reason: "a definition of rights would inhibit the government's flexibility in suppressing counter-revolutionary activities." Support for this is seen in the removal of the ex post facto clause in the drafting process and the modifications of the bill of attainder so as to permit attainder for crimes committed during the war. Mason, "New York State's First Constitution," p. 31.

63. *Journals of Prov. Cong.*, I, 852; Lincoln, I, pp. 544–545.

64. Paul Finkelman, "The Soul and the State . . . ," p. 79.

65. *Laws of the State of New York*, 1787, Chap. 1.

66. Mason, "New York's First Constitution," p. 32.

67. Nearly all the provisions connected with rights and due process were well established by common law, statute, or colonial practice. Even the clause protecting Native American land rights is based on a policy that goes back to the middle of the seventeenth century.

3

Establishing the New Government: 1777–1800

ON MAY 3, 1777, the convention appointed a Council of Safety to govern the state during the interim between the adoption of the constitution and its implementation. The convention also elected Robert Livingston as Chancellor, John Jay as Chief Justice, and Robert Yates and John Hobart Sloss as associate justices of the Supreme Court. Egbert Benson was appointed attorney general. Except Benson, all were members of the Committee on Government, which drafted the constitution.

If the high property requirement for voting in the gubernatorial election for governor was intended to ensure conservative control of that office, it failed from the beginning, as evidenced by the election of George Clinton over the conservative candidate, Philip Schuyler. At that same election members of the senate and assembly were elected. On September 10, 1777, the two houses of the first legislature met in the courthouse in Kingston to hear Governor Clinton's speech. The election, however, did not terminate the convention or the Council of Safety. When the legislature convened in October it assembled as a convention to provide for the safety of the state and thus appointed a new Council of Safety. It was one thing to write and adopt a constitution, literally under the gun, but it was quite another to carry on constitutional government during armed conflict. The tasks confronting New Yorkers were daunting: a viable government had to be erected; a war had to be fought and financed; Tories, of whom there were many, had to be suppressed; and chaotic socio-economic conditions had to be addressed.[1] The ruthless policies adopted in New York were likely related to the size of the loyalist population in the state and to the fact that British forces occupied New York City for so long.[2] These extra-constitutional bodies were given the same authority as the former convention and council: the power to govern. From April 3, 1775, the date of the last meeting of the colonial assembly, until January 15, 1778 when the legislature resumed session, all legislation enacted was by these conventions and councils. Their extra-constitutional—not to say unconstitutional—status raised a number of questions. When the legislature passed an act giving the Council of Safety power to embargo certain products, that act was vetoed by the Council of Revision. A recognition of the power of the Council to embargo would necessarily require "an acknowledgement of their right to make laws" and to recognize and give legal status to "a number of new laws, which have never been under the consideration of the Legislature, and perhaps repugnant to the Constitution. . . ."[3] The legislature mustered the two-thirds necessary to override, and, on June 9, 1778, claiming the "absolute necessity" of appointing such bodies, voted to validate all proceedings of the convention and council.[4]

In September 1780 the legislature passed a bill establishing a council to assist in the administration of the government while the legislature was in recess. The Council of Revision vetoed this bill on the grounds that the supreme legislative authority is vested in the assembly and senate by the people and cannot be delegated to an extra-constitutional body.[5] The legislature sustained the veto.

The legislature set about the business of implementing the constitution. In October 1778 the courts of the state, barely mentioned in the 1777 document, were reconfirmed and their procedures and jurisdiction specified. Rules governing the operation of the Council of Revision were provided, and the "great seal," representing the authority of the state, was adopted. Procedures governing the conduct of elections were detailed, and the state completed the transition from viva voce voting, a practice used prior to the adoption of the 1777 Constitution and continued during the war, to "paper-ticket" voting, or secret ballot.[6]

Wartime conditions placed a severe strain on constitutional regularity and the protection of individual rights. Measures aimed at the enemy and the prosecution of the war were, on occasion, punitive and excessive. One such act in March 1778 disenfranchised all those in the state who fell into anyone of thirteen specified categories, including those who, since June 9, 1775, acknowledged the sovereignty of the British king or parliament, held commissions under the British king or parliament, or held correspondence with the enemy prejudicial to the state. The Council of Revision vetoed this act, offering numerous objections. The Council argued that since the constitution already required an oath of allegiance or affirmation from all prospective voters (Art. VIII), such voters had a constitutional right to be admitted to such votes, and the legislature had no right to deprive them of that right. Moreover, punishment for those acts committed prior to the adoption of the constitution (April 20, 1777) constituted ex post facto legislation.[7] The legislature repassed the bill over the veto.[8]

The following year the legislature passed the "Confiscation Act."

This act contained a list of fifty-nine persons (including two former governors of the colony, William Tryon and John Murry, Earl of Dunmore) who were declared guilty of a felony and their estates forfeited.[9] Perhaps the worst feature was a provision allowing courts, on the oath of one credible witness, to indict a man as a Tory. If said person failed to appear after four weeks of advertising his newly determined status, his property would be confiscated. This act afforded less protection than the English Treason law which required two witnesses, trial at the site of the offense, and an overt action.

The Disenfranchisement and Confiscation Acts were followed by the "Trespass Act" of March 1783.[10] Its purpose was to enable citizens whose property had been invaded and occupied by British authorities during the military occupation to bring suit for damages against the occupants. Surprisingly, no report was issued from the Council of Revision on this bill. The forum for challenge would be the courts. The case of *Rutgers v. Waddington* commenced in the New York City Mayor's Court in February 1784 with Alexander Hamilton as counsel for the defendant. The plaintiff, Elizabeth Rutgers, sued Waddington, a British subject, for his use of her premises during the British occupation of the city. A treaty of peace with Britain, ratified by Congress in January 1783, contained a clause providing for mutual release of all claims by citizens and subjects of the two governments growing out of the war, which seemed to conflict with the claim made by Rutgers under the Trespass Act. In addition the claim seemed inconsistent with the law of nations, which allowed captors of a city the right to occupy and use abandoned real estate for authorized military purposes. Article XXXV of the 1777 Constitution adopted the common law, British statutes, and provincial acts as part of the law of the state with specific exceptions and with the general exceptions of all parts of the common law, statutes or provincial acts "repugnant to this constitution." Since the common law included the law of nations and the laws of war, Rutger's claim also appeared inconsistent with the state constitution. Although Article XXXV leaves it to the legislature to determine which parts of the common law would not be operative in the state, the language of the clause seems also to allow the possibility of legal suit involving the constitutionality of a British statute, or even parts of the common law. The Council was at that very moment rejecting statutes on the grounds that they were repugnant to the law of nations and the treaty with Great Britain.[11]

The case bristled with momentous issues: Were treaties made pursuant to the authority of the Articles of Confederation superior to state law? Did the authority of the law of nations supercede legislative authority? Could the judicial branch control the authority of the legislative branch? The opinion, delivered in August 1784 by Chief Judge James Duane, was a masterpiece of studied ambiguity. He avoided the question of whether the judiciary had the power to negate an act of the legislature, going out of his way to affirm the doctrine of legislative supremacy:

> When the main object of such a law is clearly expressed, and the intention manifest, the Judges are not at liberty, altho' it appears to them to be *unreasonable*, to reject it: for this were to set the judicial above the legislative, which would be subversive of all government.[12]

The operative phrases here are "object . . . clearly expressed" and "intentions manifest." Duane argued that when the legislature adopts a general statute which has an unreasonable effect—in this case conflict with the Treaty and the law of nations—the judges can fairly conclude that the legislators did not foresee these consequences. Since the legislature did not explicitly indicate its intent to contravene the law of nations or the Treaty of Peace, the Court would not give the law that interpretation. Duane concluded: "When the judicial make these distinctions, they do not controul the Legislature; they endeavour to give their *intention* it's [sic] proper effect."[13] The difficulty Duane faced—or, more precisely, did not face—was the fact that the act specifically and plainly stated that military orders or commands by the enemy could not be used as a defense to any action brought under the act. Duane seemed to be doing indirectly what he explicitly said was not within the power of the judiciary.[14]

This rather moderate decision provoked a storm of protests from the legislature and the press over the notion that any court could set aside an act of the state. The legislature not only condemned the decision, but even entertained a motion to have the Council of Appointment remove Duane from office.[15] Nonetheless, the notion that the judiciary might act as a limit on the legislative power by declaring statutes repugnant to the constitution was gaining strength in the state.[16]

Not all the legislation struck down by the Council was repassed by the legislature. A "Confiscation Act," passed in March 1779, would have deprived individuals of the right to trial by jury and seized the lands of the innocent as well as the guilty, but the act was voided as repugnant to "the immutable laws of justice" and "involved in such obscurity that this Council are at a loss to affix to it any precise meaning." After invoking the laws of natural justice and the constitution, the Council added two policy reasons for rejecting the act, viz., "it injures the national character of the State . . . [and] makes an ill return for the spirit and liberality with which our cause has been defended by many worthy patriots in the British dominions. . . ."[17]

The Council demonstrated solicitude for property rights and free enterprise when it vetoed an act aimed at "war profiteers." Those whose profits derived from commerce or trading would incur an additional tax over and above the assessment on their real and personal estates. This unequal taxation on an individual's capacity for legally acquiring property violated what in modern parlance would be called equal protection of the laws. Taxing individuals because they made a profit is to punish them for conduct which may be "offenses only against the moral law or the laws of God," such laws "being cognizable by Him alone." The Council added:

> It is an undoubted right of a freeman (whatever ill use he may make of it) that where no prices are fixed by law he is at liberty to ask what price he pleases for his land or goods, and he is amenable only to God and his conscience if he asks too much.[18]

When the legislature passed a bill with the laudable-sounding title "An act for the gradual abolition of slavery" the Council issued a veto. Contained in the bill was a provision which would have disenfranchised African-Americans. The Council called such a move a deprivation of "essential rights . . . shocking those principles of equal liberty which every page in that Constitution labors to enforce."[19]

Entails and primogeniture were abolished by law in July 1782, making property inheritance more democratic. Tenants who once held property in "fee-tail" (where there is a fixed line of succession) now held that property in "fee simple" (where inheritance is free of any condition, limitation, or restriction to particular heirs). The number and size of the great manors along the Hudson and Mohawk valleys which this law affected made this one of the most important results of the Revolution.[20] The abolition of manorial privilege did not affect the leases governing rented lands. As these were often oppressive, the failure to address this particular aspect of landlord-tenant relationships would result in agitation for legislative and constitutional reform throughout the first half of the nineteenth century.

Provision was made to compile such existing laws as were preserved by Article XXXV of the 1777 Constitution. The result was "An act concerning the rights of the citizens of this State," adopted on January 26, 1787. This act embraced the most important sections of the Magna Carta, the English Bill of Rights of 1689, the Habeus Corpus Act and other parts of the English Constitution. The Bill of Rights was a major component in the protection of rights in New York along with those rights mentioned in the 1777 Constitution. The act, along with such legislation as the Habeus Corpus Reform Act, demonstrated the commitment of the legislature to the protection of rights in the post-war period.²¹ It is likely that these rights were considered on a par with those found in the constitution, as the distinction between fundamental law made only with the consent of the people in their constituent capacity, and ordinary acts of the legislature, had not yet fully taken hold. Further evidence can be found in the decision of the legislature of New York to commit the state to the "Articles of Confederation and Perpetual Union" on February 6, 1778.²² By this act, New York ceased its existence as an independent state and joined the United States of America. This momentous decision was not submitted to the people for their approval!

Though unsuccessful in placing a clause abolishing slavery in the Constitution of 1777, efforts aimed at removing slavery from the state persisted. The slave trade was abolished in 1785, all children born after July 4, 1799 were declared free citizens by an act of that same year, and in 1817 all slaves born prior to 1799 were to be freed by 1827.²³

The Council of Revision, which has been described as "An Americanization of the King's Privy Council," played a significant role in New York politics during this period.²⁴ The council vetoed 169 of the 6,500 (2.57%) of the bills passed by the legislature. Fifty-one of these vetoes, almost one-third, were overridden, showing that the decision of the council was by no means final.²⁵ The real strength of the council was in its ability to act as a revisory body. Between 1779 and 1822, at least twenty-six bills were modified by the legislature to meet the objections of the council.

The role of the governor in the legislative process was diminished significantly by the presence of the council, the absence of sole veto power reducing his role to that of a symbolic consentor. While all of the opinions of the council were signed by the Chief Executive, and his presence was required at all deliberations, only two opinions were issued by the governor during the council's forty-five-year existence.²⁶ During this time the council provided the only protection individuals out of favor with the legislature would have, and, by and large, it exercised that power responsibly and prudently.

The power to decide the constitutionality of legislation may have provided the council de facto power to judge the wisdom of the legislation, but exercising the explicitly political power of passing on the wisdom of legislation created a direct confrontation with—not to say affront to—a central tenet of republican ideology, viz., that the public policy of the state was to be made by the people or its elected representatives. The exercise of the dual function was an inherently unstable one. Not surprisingly, the council would succumb in 1821 at the first convention in New York where the republican ideology prevailed. The two functions henceforth would be bifurcated, one going to the governor in the form of the veto and the other, eventually, to the judiciary in the form of judicial review.

With the disruptive and divisive war behind them, and the apparatus of government in place, New Yorkers were prepared to address the first constitutional crisis of the new order.

NOTES

1. Alexander Hamilton estimated that half the state was loyal to the king in the early stages of the war—a situation soon remedied by the vigorous, if not vengeful, policies adopted by the legislature. Henry Cabot Lodge, ed., *The Works of Alexander Hamilton*, 12 vols. (New York: G. P. Putnam's Sons, 1904), VIII, p. 69.

2. Allan Nevins, *The American States During and After the Revolution, 1775–1789* (New York: Macmillan, 1924), pp. 267–274.

3. Alfred Street, *The Council of Revision of the State of New York . . . and Its Vetoes* (Albany: William Gould, 1859) (hereafter cited as *Vetoes*), Veto of February 20, 1778, p. 206.

4. *Laws of the State of New York*, Chap. 37 (1778).

5. *Vetoes*, October 9, 1780, p. 234.

6. *Laws of the State of New York*, Chap. 12 (1778); Chap. 16 (1778); Chap. 15 (1787).

7. *Vetoes*, March 25, 1778, p. 211.

8. *Laws of the State of New York*, Chap. 16 (1778).

9. Ibid., Chap. 25 (1779).

10. Ibid., I, 6th Sess., Chap. 31 .

11. *Vetoes*, January 15, 1784, pp. 246–248.

12. Richard B. Morris, ed., *Select Cases of the Mayor's Court of New York City, 1674–1784* (Washington, D.C.: American Historical Association, 1935), p. 323.

13. Ibid., p. 324.

14. W. W. Crosskey, *Politics and the Constitution in the History of the United States*, 2 vols. (Chicago: University of Chicago Press, 1953), II, p. 964.

15. Julius Goebel, Jr. et al., eds., *The Law Practice of Alexandar Hamilton, Documents and Commentary*, 5 vols. (New York: Columbia University Press, 1964–1981), I, pp. 312–313. Hamilton's briefs in the case are found on pp. 336–392.

16. Gordon Wood, *The Creation of the American Republic*, p. 459.

17. *Vetoes*, March 14, 1779, pp. 220–221, 223.

18. Ibid., November 5, 1778, pp. 215–217.

19. Ibid., March 21, 1785, p. 268. E. Wilder Spaulding in his *New York in the Critical Period 1783–1789* refers to the veto of this bill as one of "numerous vetoes" of "progressive legislation" (p. 108). Frank Prescott and Joseph Zimmerman, in *The Politics of the Veto of Legislation in New York State*, 2 vols. (Washington, D.C.: University Press of America, 1980), I, p. 30, take Spaulding to task for this judgment. Calling the disenfranchisement of African-Americans a "progressive" measure can only mean that Spaulding read neither the provision of the bill nor the decision of the Council. Yet Spaulding does make reference to the disenfranchising provision of the bill on p. 41. Spaulding's

persistent efforts to paint the Council a reactionary shade to fit the procrustean thesis he held about the character of the 1777 Constitution led him, I believe, into this inconsistency. Spaulding and others of his school tended to judge the actions of the Council by whether the legislation it vetoed was "progressive" or not, and they paid little attention to the procedural or constitutional infirmities with which many of these bills were afflicted. In this respect Prescott and Zimmerman provide a useful corrective.

20. *Laws of the State of New York*, I, 6th Sess. (1782), Chap. 2; II, 9th Sess. (1786), Chap. 12; Chap. 36. Spaulding, *New York in the Critical Period 1783–1789*, p. 69.

21. *Laws of the State of New York*, II, 10th Sess. (1789), Chap. 1, Chap. 39.

22. Ibid., I, Chap. 1.

23. Ibid., II (1785), Chap. 68; Chap. 40; III, Chap. 28; Chap. 17; IV, Chap. 62.

24. Prescott and Zimmerman, *The Politics of the Veto*, p. 21.

25. *Vetoes*, p. 7. Prescott and Zimmerman compare the number of council vetoes overridden by the legislature with the number of vetoes overridden after the governor was granted exclusive veto power in 1821. Only sixteen gubernatorial vetoes were overridden during the period of 1823 to 1975. Prescott and Zimmerman, *The Politics of the Veto*, p. 55.

26. Ibid., p. 23.

4

The First Constitutional Convention: 1801

THE FIRST INSTITUTION created by the 1777 Constitution to cause difficulty was the Council of Appointment.[1] Article XXIII provided for a council composed of the governor and four senators selected annually by the assembly.

The originator of the council, John Jay, assumed that the governor would possess sole power to nominate candidates, who would then be accepted or rejected by the council; however, Article XXIII failed to say so explicitly.[2] The convention which adopted the constitution also seemed to believe that the power resided with the governor. In May 1777, a month following the adoption of the constitution, in an ordinance providing for new appointments and instituting the new government, the convention declared "the appointment of officers in this state is, by the Constitution thereof, vested in the governor, by and with the advice and consent of the Council of Appointment."[3]

The unity created by the Revolutionary War and the absence of party lines explains why so little conflict developed in the first fifteen years of the council's existence. During this period Governor George Clinton apparently exercised the sole power to nominate.[4] The rise of more or less clearly defined party lines between Federalists and Republicans, the latter sometimes referred to as Democratic Republicans, in the last decade of the eighteenth century ended that unity. The election of 1793 resulted in Federalist majorities in both houses of the legislature. Flushed with victory and with a desire to end Republican dominance on the council, the legislature enacted a provision which removed sitting members of the council even though the constitution specified their terms at one year. The first act of the newly constituted council was to appoint Egbert Benson to the Supreme Court. Governor Clinton had refused to nominate Benson. Philip Schuyler, a member of the council, proposed the nomination, which the council then voted to accept. This was the first time the council asserted a concurrent right to nominate candidates. Insisting that the right to nominate rested with the governor, Governor Clinton objected, but to no avail.[5] The result was a significant reduction of the governor's role on the council. Having successfully claimed a concurrent right to nominate along with the right to dismiss council members before their terms expired, and with a Federalist majority on the council, effective control of patronage passed to the majority party in the legislature.

In 1795 John Jay, a Federalist, was elected second governor of the state, with the Federalists retaining control of the council. With the dispute between Clinton and the council in mind, Jay, in his opening address to the legislature, requested a declaratory act on the question of the right to nominate.[6] The only response was a resolution passed by the assembly, calling such a declaration "inexpedient."[7] As both the council and the governor were of the same party there was no immediate need to settle the issue. In only one case did the council override the governor, appointing a secretary of state Jay did not want. All this changed in 1800 when the Federalists lost their majority in the legislature. Temporarily the governor's office and the council remained in the grip of the Federalists, reversing the situation of 1794. In 1801 Federalist council members were turned out of office. Governor Jay met the newly constituted council on February 11, 1801, and the battle was joined. The council refused to approve any of Jay's nominations, and Jay refused to put the question when a Republican member of the council, DeWitt Clinton, nominated a candidate. The council in turn refused to act on Jay's alternative nominee. Jay maintained that the council did not have a concurrent right to nominate, while the council steadfastly claimed that right. The result was deadlock. Jay, believing he would violate the oath of office if he yielded, refused to convene the council. On February 26 he sent a message to the legislature requesting a resolution.[8] The legislature refused to act, claiming it to be a constitutional question not within their authority to decide. Jay then turned to the chancellor and the judges of the Supreme Court. They also refused, claiming that the constitution did not allow them to issue advisory opinions.[9] With the appointment process at a standstill and all other avenues closed off, the legislature adopted what was probably the best possible course: it referred the question to the supreme power, a convention of the people.

Governor Jay had anticipated such a convention in a special message to the legislature in November 1800.[10] Therein he had pointed to a problem created by the 1777 Constitution concerning the size of the legislature. The 1777 Constitution called for a senate of twenty-four and an assembly of seventy members (Articles IV, X). Provision was made for increases in size until the senate reached a maximum of 100 and the assembly reached 300 (Article XVI). Rapid population increases affected the size of both houses more rapidly than anticipated, and the prospect of a large deliberating body prompted Jay's call for a convention to address this problem.

On April 6, 1801, the legislature passed "An Act recommending a Convention for the purposes therein mentioned."[11] Because the 1777 Constitution did not contain a procedure for amendment, such a step could only take the form of a recommendation to the people. No attempt was made to present the question of whether or not to hold the convention; rather, the act called for the selection of delegates to such a convention. The act recommending the convention directed the delegates to consider only two matters: the number of senators and assemblymen and "the true construction [sic] of the twenty-third article of the constitution . . . relative to the right of nomination to office; but with no other power or authority whatsoever." It is not at all clear what binding effect this limitation would have on a body called to exercise the constituent power, i.e., sovereignty. The enacting statute itself specified that "the determination of said convention respecting the several matters herein before mentioned shall be entered of record in one of the books of record in the [office of secretary of state] and such determination shall thereupon become and be considered as part of the constitution of this state." There is no further role for the legislature or the people required. The Council of Revision would not have jurisdiction since this was not an act of the legislature, and judicial review was not yet established for ordinary acts of the legislature, let alone the acts of a constitutional convention.

The Work of the Convention

The act calling for delegate selection permitted "all free white male citizens of this state, of the age twenty-one or upwards" to vote for and to be eligible to serve as delegates. This racial restriction was not present in the 1777 Constitution. Conspicuous is the absence of any property qualifications for delegates. No doubt this liberal voting provision reflected the tide of Jeffersonian Republicanism sweeping both the state and nation in the early 1800s.

In April 1801 George Clinton was elected governor and strong Republican majorities were returned to the legislature. When the delegates to the convention were selected in August the results were similar, with Republicans winning a large majority of the seats. The convention featured some of the most prominent figures in New York's history. Aaron Burr and DeWitt Clinton, rivals for control of the Democratic-Republicans, were present, as was Smith Thompson, subsequently an associate justice of the United States Supreme Court.

Daniel D. Tompkins, later vice president of the United States and governor of New York, made his first appearance as a public figure at this convention. The most vigorous proponent of the Federalist position was John V. Henry of Albany. Aaron Burr was elected president of the convention. This was somewhat surprising, given the bitter personal and political rivalry between Clinton and Burr. Two reasons have been offered for his selection. For one, as vice-president of the United States Burr was of higher standing than any other member of the convention. A second, more Machiavellian reason, was that as president and chairman he would have less influence than if he were a floor leader.[12] There is, however, good reason to believe that illness prevented Clinton from attending the convention, making Burr's selection less problematic.[13]

The convention began its deliberations in Albany on October 13, 1801, and as Burr acidly noted, "fifteen days would have been consumed in accomplishing the business of six hours."[14] The first order of business was that of legislative apportionment. Not viewed as a partisan issue, it was settled with dispatch. The amendments fixed the number of senators at thirty-two (Amendment III). By 1801 the senate had reached forty-three, therefore provision had to be made for reducing their number. The assembly number was set at one hundred, with provision for increases to a maximum of one hundred fifty (Amendment I). The convention required that the senators be apportioned among the counties and districts of the state "as nearly as may be, according to the number of electors [voters] which shall be found [therein]" (Amendment II). However, it added a proviso enabling the legislature to allow "one member of the assembly to each county heretofore erected within this state" (Amendment IV). This tradition of providing each county with at least one representative continued in New York State until the Supreme Court of the United States in *WMCA v. Lomenzo* (1964) declared the practice unconstitutional. The 150-seat limit on the assembly remains in the constitution to this day.

The convention took up the contentious issue of the Council of Appointment. Motions were defeated which would have given the senators and the governor exclusive right of nomination. The final resolution stated that the right to nominate officers other than those who were appointed resided concurrently in the governor as well as in each member of the Council of Appointment (Amendment IV). There was little doubt about the outcome, given the predominance of Democratic-Republicans, but the lopsided vote of eighty-six to fourteen reflected more than Republican dominance at the convention.[15] In the past both parties had supported concurrent nomination. The issue was not one of principle, but partisan political advantage.[16] A few, including Republican delegate Daniel D. Tompkins, opposed the council's position and voted against the resolution as a matter of principle.

Having resolved the two issues for which they were convened, the convention adjourned on October 26, 1801.

Assessment

Subsequent generations of New Yorkers have not judged kindly the work of the convention of 1801. All that remains of its work is the setting of the maximum size of the assembly at 150 seats. The senate size was subsequently altered and the Council of Appointment was abolished at the convention of 1821.

The decision to give concurrent nominating power to the council and the governor did resolve the immediate deadlock between governor and council, but it did so at great cost. By placing effective power in the hands of the legislature the way was opened for the creation of a powerful party machine for the control of political patronage. Though it is incorrect to claim that partisan political appointments began in 1801, it is fair to say that these decisions enabled the "spoils system" to reach its state of development in New York. The "clean sweep" of office-holders, a practice which did not precede the 1801 convention, became routine. By the time the 1821 convention met, it was estimated that nearly 15,000 offices were filled under the patronage system.[17] The blatant use of patronage by the council was the chief reason for its abolition in 1821.

In addition, the evidence is more strongly on the side of Jay's position with regard to the right to nominate. As Daniel D. Tompkins put it at the 1821 convention, "The Convention of 1801 was assembled to sanction a violent construction of the constitution."[18] The kindest words spoken about the system by a neutral observer were those of Howard McBain:

> ... while the system which he [DeWitt Clinton] instituted was more radical than anything which preceded it, yet it fell far short of a total dismissal of the federalists in office and was at least partially justified by the exclusive policy which had been pursued by the retiring federalists.[19]

In an age which views political institutions as less cause than reflection of economic and social forces, the claim of earlier political observers and historians regarding the responsibility of the Council of Appointment for the rise of the spoils system seem less compelling. Nonetheless, institutions do matter: how we channel and constrain new political forces makes a difference. The decision to provide a mechanism for centralizing patronage distribution made a difference as to how the parties and the polity operated in New York between 1801 and 1821, as did subsequent decisions in 1821 and 1846, which diffused that distribution.

NOTES

1. For an account of the conflict leading up to the convention, see J. M. Gitterman, "The Council of Appointment in New York," *Political Science Quarterly*, VII (May, 1892), pp. 91–103
2. *Journals of the Provincial Congress, Provincial Convention* . . . 2 vols., I, pp. 874–875. John Jay to Robert Livingston and Gouverneur Morris, April 29, 1777, in *The Correspondence and Public Papers of John Jay*, Johnson, ed., I, p. 128.
3. As quoted in Lincoln, *A Constitutional History of New York*. I, p. 598.
4. Ibid., I, pg. 598.
5. His objections are found in the *Albany Gazette*, October 23, 1794, as quoted by Howard McBain, *DeWitt Clinton and the Origins of the Spoils System in New York* (Ph.D. Diss., Columbia University, 1907), pp. 37–38.
6. Charles Z. Lincoln, ed., *Messages From the Governors . . . [1683–1906]*, 11 vols. (Albany: J. B. Lyon Co., 1909), II, pp. 360–361.
7. Ibid., I, p. 361.
8. Ibid., I, p. 472–476.
9. McBain, p. 91.
10. Lincoln, ed., *Messages From the Governors*, I, p. 468.
11. *Laws of New York*, V, 24th Sess. (1801) Chapt. 159.
12. Ray B. Smith, ed., *History of the State of New York, Political and Governmental*, 6 vols. (Syracuse, N.Y.: Syracuse University Press, 1922), Vol. I: 1776–1822 (Willis Fletcher Johnson), p. 210–211.
13. Howard McBain, *DeWitt Clinton and the Origin of the Spoils System*, pp. 122–123, claims that Clinton never attended the convention. He bases this conclusion on the fact that his name appears nowhere on the record and that he is unrecorded in any vote. McBain also notes that Clinton did not attend the fall meeting of the council, citing an illness that made it impossible for him to attend. In this respect Dorothie Bobbé, *DeWitt Clinton* (New York: Minton, Balch & Co., 1933) agrees with McBain. It appears that the source for the numerous commentators who have Clinton present and proposing amendments is Jabez Hammond in his *History of Political Parties*, I, pp. 165–166.
14. Matthew Davis, *Memoirs of Aaron Burr*, 2 vols. (New York: Harper & Bros., 1836–1837), II, p. 158.
15. New York State, *Journal of the Convention of the State of New York Begun and Held at the City of Albany, on the Thirteenth Day of October, 1801* (Albany: John Barber, printer to the Convention, 1801), pp. 26–27.
16. As a contemporary politician and historian, Jabez Hammond pointed out. *The History of Political Parties in the State of New York*, 4th ed., 3 vols. (Syracuse: Hall, Mills & Co., 1852), I, pp. 166–167.
17. Hugh M. Flick, "The Council of Appointment in New York State, The

First Attempt to Regulate Political Patronage, 1777–1822," *New York History*, XV (1934): p. 277

18. *Reports of the Proceedings and Debates of the Convention of 1821* . . . (Albany: E. & E. Hosford, 1821), p. 116. It should be noted that toward the end of his career DeWitt Clinton had cause to regret the system he had played such a large part in creating, calling it the source of "our divisions and distractions [and] incessant convulsions." As quoted in Gitterman, "Council of Appointments," p. 115.

19. McBain, *DeWitt Clinton and the Origins of the Spoils System*, p. 158.

5

Property and Participation: The Constitutional Convention of 1821

BY THE BEGINNING of the nineteenth century, the Democratic Republicans had achieved hegemony. Loosely linked by a commitment to the role of the citizen in government and to moderate humanitarian reforms, and with an antipathy to class privilege, party members otherwise clustered around individuals such as the Clintons, the Livingstons, and Aaron Burr. Factions were constantly forming and reforming as leaders gained and lost power. Party quarrels were generally unrelated to differences of principle.[1] DeWitt Clinton divided the party in 1812 by challenging James Madison's candidacy for the presidency, but with the support of the Federalists he managed to win the governor's office in 1817. Although there were valid and substantial reasons for calling a convention to revise the Constitution of 1777, the single most important factor was this conflict between the Clintonians, led by DeWitt Clinton, and the Anti-Clintonians. The latter were variously called Martling Men (adopted from the tavern in which they met), Tammanies (so-called because they belonged to the Tammany Society, a benevolent society formed in 1789 with strong political overtones), or Bucktails (taken from the badge they wore). Specifically, the moving force behind the 1821 convention was the desire of the Anti-Clintonians to destroy Governor Clinton. Clinton's alliance with the Federalists enabled him to enlist them to block policies deemed desirable by the Anti-Clintonians. In doing so he earned the enmity of the Republican leaders who feared a resurgence of Federalist power and resented Clinton's bid to become independent of Republican leadership. In 1819 Clinton broke openly with his party, causing those Federalists dissatisfied with his policies to join the Bucktails. By 1820 the tangled party lines had Federalists and Republicans supporting Clinton and Federalists and Republicans opposing him.

A means of achieving constitutional change in the state had not been established. The legislature had recognized this when it "recommended" a convention in 1801. Any change was dependent on the willingness of the legislature to act, and that meant when the party factions agreed.

There were a variety of ways by which demands for a convention could be expressed. Petitioning the legislature was a common technique for both policy and constitutional reform. Public meetings where calls for constitutional reform could be aired was another commonly used technique. The press provided a third avenue to express demands for change. There were, however, only a few scattered meetings around the state where cries for the abolition of the Council of Appointment and for the creation of additional elective offices were made, and the press played little or no role in creating or reflecting popular opinion on the convention question.[2] Only one newspaper, *The New York National Advocate*, the voice of Tammany Hall, whole-heartedly endorsed a convention.[3]

The lack of any vocal, organized popular demands for a convention, coupled with the legal limbo in which the amending process languished and the complicated maneuvers of the party factions on the convention question, created difficulties, delays, and, ironically, a convention with unlimited jurisdiction—a result neither party desired.

When the legislature passed a bill calling for a constitutional convention, the Council of Revision vetoed the measure on the grounds that it did not allow a vote on the issue. The council also cited the failure of the proposed ratifying process to give the people an opportunity to vote on the proposed amendments separately. The council's veto was particularly galling to the Bucktails, who, as the party of the people, had condemned the council as an obstruction to the people's will. Chancellor James Kent's opinion for the council claimed that no evidence existed to indicate a desire among the public for a convention. Whatever motivation lay behind the council's veto, Chancellor Kent's arguments addressed the unresolved issue of how and by whom constitutional change should take place. He began with a proposition based on Article I of the 1777 Constitution: the only authority exercised over the people is such that shall be derived from and granted by them. Since "The Constitution is the will of the people expressed in their original charter . . . it is perfectly consonant to the republican theory, and to the declared sense and practice of this country, that it cannot be altered or changed in any degree without the expression of the same original will."[4] Can a legislature, he continued,

> chosen only to make laws in pursuance of the provisions of the existing Constitution . . . call a Convention, in the first instance, to revise, alter and perhaps remodel the whole fabric of the government, and before

they have received a legitimate and full expression of the will of the people that such changes should be made.[5]

This was not the first expression of the view that only the people can adopt or approve the fundamental law of the state. The artisans and mechanics of New York City had expressed a similar claim with regard to the creation of the first constitution.[6]

Kent was faced with the precedent of the constitutional convention of 1801 which was "recommended" by the legislature and whose work was not submitted to the people for ratification. He attempted to distinguish the precedent, arguing that it was a limited convention called for two narrowly defined objectives, one of which was "merely to determine the true construction of one of its articles." Conceding that "it would have been more advisable that the previous sense of the people should have been taken," he did not wish to see a small misstep evolve into a precedent for denying the people any direct role in the process of constitutional change.[7]

These objections of the council were referred to a Select Committee of the Assembly, chaired by Michael Ulshoeffer. That committee issued a lengthy partisan reply to Kent's arguments. The report focused on past practices in New York State, those of other states, and the national Constitution. Excluding New Hampshire, none of these provided support for Kent's position.[8] In response to the objection that changes in the constitution should occur only following an expression of the people's will, Ulshoeffer replied: "the question however, to be decided is, in what manner the expression of this will is to be obtained?" The legislature possesses the "supreme legislative power within the state." As such, it is the representation of the people's will. The legislature in calling for the selection of delegates is, in fact, expressing the will of the people.

> No such law, it was taken for granted, would be passed, but in accordance with the public wish. The delegates represent the people, and act agreeably to their interests; and if such a case could occur as a Convention being called by theLegislature when none was desired by the people, it would be merely nugatory in its effects, as the delegates of the people would of course adjourn without any proceedings.[9]

Here in bold form was the doctrine of legislative supremacy—a doctrine which can trace its lineage to the radical Whigs of the eighteenth century.[10] The will of the legislature is the will of the people, and there can be no conflict because the legislature would not pass a law contrary to the wishes of the people.

The very existence of the Council of Revision was a rebuff to that doctrine and, not surprisingly, Ulshoeffer assailed the council as being inconsistent with "the principles of republican government."[11] The

1777 Constitution had settled the question by deciding in favor of some limit on the power of the legislature. This report revived that question with a vengeance. The council was soon to become a victim of an immaculate version of republican theory and a maculate partisan maneuver.

The council was especially vulnerable to attack by virtue of its constitutional charge to recommend revision or reject bills on political as well as legal grounds. It proved to be an unstable mixture. A system with the governor exercising a veto for political or policy reasons, and the judiciary exercising a veto for legal or constitutional grounds, would prove politically more palatable. The convention's decision to bifurcate the council's veto function put New York in line with federal practice. By the end of the nineteenth century all the states would adopt a similar separation.

Unable to garner sufficient votes to override the veto by the council, the legislature enacted a bill providing for the referendum. By a vote of 109,396 to 34,901, the electorate overwhelmingly approved the proposal to call a convention. Not until the 1846 convention would New York adopt a constitutional procedure for calling a convention.

Factional conflict may have been the proximate cause of the calling of the convention, but legitimate issues of constitutional reform demanded attention. When the first constitution was framed in 1777, the population of New York State was just over 190,000, with the majority of New Yorkers living in the Hudson Valley and along the Mohawk River east of Schenectady. By 1820 the state's population exceeded 1,300,000. Thirty-seven new counties had been created, thirty-two of them in the newly settled areas of the North and West. The new settlers, many from New England, were farmers, most of them debtors in need of capital, credit, and improvements in transportation. These settlers did not benefit from the constitutional structure established by the 1777 Constitution—particularly with regard to suffrage requirements, apportionment, and judicial service. The Western region voted for the convention with a larger ratio of aye to nay votes (nearly 10 to 1) than any other section.[12]

Two institutions in particular, the Council of Appointment and the Council of Revision, seemed to need re-evaluation and revision, if not outright abolition. The governor's power on the Council of Appointment was not clearly delineated by the provision; initially, governors claimed the power to make nominations, as well as the explicitly granted power to cast the deciding vote in cases of ties.[13] The powers of the Council of Appointment were defined by the constitutional convention of 1801. The right to nominate was declared a concurrent one, shared by the governor and the other members of the council. This solution had an unsuspected drawback: with the power of nomination not clearly anchored in any one person, no one could be held accountable for any given appointment. Control of the council became a substantial political prize, especially as it dispensed nearly 15,000 patronage jobs.[14]

By 1820 the council had established its power to nominate candidates and to appoint and remove officers at its pleasure. Legislative attempts to limit this discretion were rebuffed by the Supreme Court in *People v. Foot*.[15] The council had become a classic example of the spoils system in America, the constant target of escalating charges of corruption and bribe-taking. In his opening address to the legislature in January 1820, Governor DeWitt Clinton called the council "a principal of irritation in our constitution," responsible for New York's reputation as "more obnoxious to the excitement of party than any member of the federal union." He added that the "political tranquillity of the state demands a different arrangement of the appointing power."[16] A committee of the assembly made similar recommendations later that month.

The Council of Revision was assailed on a number of grounds. It violated the separation of powers, containing as it did members of the legislative, executive, and judicial branches. Additionally, the council's power to pass on the wisdom of legislation exposed the judges to the charge of partisanship. Finally, the duties attendant to council membership placed an extra burden on them.

The courts of the state were a patchwork affair stretching back to the colonial era. Moreover, the growth of the state in the western and central areas increased the burdens on these courts, rendering them ill-equipped to serve the newly populated areas effectively. By the 1820s the Supreme Court's docket was several years in arrears.[17]

The Work of the Convention

Although the constitution adopted non-establishment of religion, that principle was not viewed as inconsistent with a recognition by the delegates of a need for religious guidance. In the preamble to the 1821 document the delegates "acknowledge with gratitude the grace and beneficence of God in permitting us to make choice of our form of government. . . ."

Unlike the convention that framed and adopted the 1777 Constitution, delegates to the 1821 convention did not reflect a split between Federalists and Popular Whigs, nor were the convention's major conflicts decided by an informal alliance between Federalists and moderates. The traditional view of Dixon Ryan Fox—that the convention was the last desperate effort of the reactionary defenders of privilege and property to resist the forces of republicanism and reform—has not held up under subsequent scholarship.[18] Of the 126 delegates elected, all but eighteen were Bucktails or their allies. Numerical dominance was one thing; agreement was quite another. Examination of the votes cast at the convention indicates that delegates divided into four major groups: conservatives, including Federalists and Clintonian Republicans (thirty delegates); moderates, predominately Bucktails with some Clintonians and Federalists (thirty-eight delegates); radicals, nearly all Bucktails (thirty-nine delegates); and "outsiders," also nearly all Bucktails (eighteen delegates).[19] In the 1821 convention the major battles took place between Republican moderates, led by Martin Van Buren, and Radical Republicans, led by Erastus Root. By and large the victories went to the moderates.

Suffrage

A major focus of debate at the convention concerned suffrage. Delegates representing the large number of New England-born citizens (48 of the 126 delegates were born in New England) joined the mechanics of New York City in leading the fight to abolish freehold status as a qualification for the suffrage.[20] The majority of new landowners had mortgages on their property and thus were not considered freeholders, even though they paid taxes and served in the militia.

The convention adopted what in practice proved to be unlimited suffrage for white males. The vote was given to white, tax-paying males, those who served in the militia or as firemen and who had resided in the state for one year, and those who had resided in the state for three years who had worked on the highways.

On the other hand, the question of African-American suffrage, a matter which had not been an issue in 1777, became the focus of bitter controversy in 1821. Observers have noted a curious shift in party positions on this question. Republicans, who had led the campaign for expanded suffrage, fought to restrict African-American suffrage, while the Federalists and Clintonians, who resisted the effort to expand suffrage for white males, led the fight to treat both races equally. The existence of racial prejudice—a number of Bucktail delegates thought African-Americans "degraded" as a class[21]—was bolstered by political self-interest: the Bucktail Republicans believed the state's African-American voters had supported Clinton and the Federalists in earlier elections.[22] African-Americans who had been allowed to vote under the 1777 Constitution, providing they met the freehold requirement, were now required to possess a freehold free and clear of debt and worth $250 (Art. II, Sec. 1). This provision effectively disenfranchised all but a handful of African-American voters. In 1828, only 298 of the state's approximately 6,000 free adult African-American males could meet the requirement.[23]

The theory behind the suffrage amendment was that only those bearing some burden or making some contribution to the community should possess the franchise. It continued but broadened the principle behind the 1777 suffrage provision, that only those citizens demonstrating their independence and showing some tangible stake in the community should be permitted to vote. In 1777, as in 1821, rootless and impoverished men were not considered part of the community and thus had no claim to the suffrage. The convention's decision to adopt restrictive tests for African-American suffrage stemmed from the perception of many delegates that African-Americans were social outcasts lacking independence and contributing nothing to the community. The convention also permitted the legislature to disenfranchise those convicted of infamous crimes (Art. II, Sec. 2). The legislature had previously eliminated the pre-revolutionary practice of voice-voting, and the convention placed that policy in the constitution (Art. II, Sec. 4).

The constitution gave increased recognition to locality by guaranteeing one assemblyman to each county; the popular basis for representation was broadened from electors to "inhabitants, excluding aliens, paupers and persons of color not taxed" (Art. I, Secs. 6–7).

Through a variety of informal practices, the proportion of white males allowed to vote had already reached 78% by 1820. Thus, electoral reforms did not increase significantly the number of electors eligible to vote for assemblymen. The proportion of those who could vote in assembly elections increased modestly to 90%. The significant increase occurred in the category of New Yorkers eligible to vote for governor—from 33% to 84%.[24] Formal recognition of de facto white manhood suffrage was taken by an 1826 amendment abolishing all property qualifications. Subsequent suffrage battles in nineteenth-century New York would concern African-Americans and women, but no longer would the earlier republican tradition connecting land ownership with stability and virtue with independence play a significant role in constitutional debates. The 1820s marked the end of the classical republican tradition in New York and the beginning of a tradition foreshadowing the Jacksonian ideal of the common man.

COUNCIL OF APPOINTMENT

When the convention took up the question of modifying or replacing the Council of Appointment, it unanimously voted the council out of existence. The real dispute arose over what method of appointing officials should replace the council. The convention adopted a complicated procedure forged largely by partisan considerations and compromise. Justices of the peace would be nominated and selected at the county level. Sheriffs, county clerks, and coroners would be elected. Militia officers were to be elected by their men, with the exception of the highest-ranking officers, who were to be designated by the governor. The governor would nominate and, with the consent of the senate, appoint all judicial officers with the exception of justices of the peace (Art. IV, Sec. 7). The legislature would make all other appointments including the treasurer, attorney-general, comptroller, and surveyor-general (Art. IV, Sec. 6). Although the scheme dispersed the appointment power, the legislature emerged as the single most important source of patronage, with the governor the biggest loser.

COUNCIL OF REVISION

The Council of Revision, having little support, was also abolished by unanimous vote of the convention. In its place the convention followed the design of the United States Constitution, giving the governor sole control of the veto, with the possibility of a two-thirds vote of members present to override (Art. I, Sec. 12).[25] The arguments for the veto power ran counter to Radical Republican ideology. Proponents of the veto argued that the legislature was likely to enact too many laws, and that changing the laws too frequently was an evil to be avoided.[26] The legislature, they maintained, was by far the strongest of the three branches of the government and thus most likely to encroach on the executive or judicial branch. Although judicial review was available as a check on law-making, most delegates believed the period between the enactment of an undesirable law and its invalidation by the courts was too long.[27] Despite a rising tide of democratic expectations in New York and in the nation, the delegates maintained the countermajoritarian principle of checks and balances in their constitutional tradition. The forces supporting the veto power could cite evidence of legislative failures in other states, such as the Yazoo land fraud in Georgia, as well as failures within New York itself. In the face of a largely sorry record, it was difficult to convince delegates that the only check needed on the legislature was public virtue.[28]

The abolition of the Council of Revision undoubtedly accelerated the acceptance of judicial review by the judiciary. Judicial decisions challenging acts of the legislature were rare during the forty-five years the state operated under the 1777 Constitution. Charles Lincoln suggested that the scarcity of judicial activity was chiefly due to the scrutiny given legislation by the Council of Revision, which had the responsibility to pass on the constitutionality as well as the wisdom of legislation.[29] No doubt this was an important factor, but others were also at work. For one, the volume of legislation during this period was much less than it would be after 1822. Judicial review itself was neither fully developed nor fully accepted at the state level. The inchoate character of the doctrine thus also helps explain the paucity of cases.[30]

Rutgers v. Waddington (1784), usually cited as one of the handful of cases anticipating the establishment of judicial review by the Supreme Court of the United States, contained dicta and reasoning which, by implication, argued for a judicial role in judging the merit of legislation by more fundamental law.[31] Edward Corwin found eleven acts in which the legitimacy of statutes was challenged: three were sustained, five were voided, and three were curtailed in such a way as not to govern the case.[32] The one in which an act of the New York Legislature was struck down on the basis of a provision in the 1777 Constitution is *People v. Foot* (1821), involving the powers of the Council of Appointment.[33]

Other acts of the legislature were struck down by the courts during this period. Unlike *Foot*, these cases relied on the extra-constitutional doctrine of vested rights. That doctrine held property rights to be fundamental and any disturbance of these rights to be a violation of general principles limiting all constitutional governments. The first instance in which this doctrine was used to strike down an act of the legislature was *Dash v. Van Kleeck* (1811).[34] Judge Kent held that social legislation affecting vested rights was void. The doctrine of vested rights was to become a basic doctrine of American constitutional law in the nineteenth century and an important source for judicial review. That doctrine and the establishment of judicial review are considered the greatest achievement of the judiciary.[35] In New York, courts asserted the power to review acts of the legislature based on limitations not found in the constitution, suggesting that judicial review was derived from, or an instrument of, the doctrine of vested rights.[36] Further evidence can be found in *Gardner v. Newburgh* (1816).[37] The case concerned eminent domain, the power of the state considered an aspect of sovereignty, to take private property for public use. Chancellor Kent held that this power could be exercised only for public purposes and that the owner must receive full compensation. No mention of the public purpose or just compensation appeared in the 1777 Constitution. They would appear in the 1821 Constitution (Art. VII, Sec. 7) in language suggesting the influence of Amendment V of the national Constitution as well as the Gardner decision. Judicial review in New York thus took root in extra-constitutional soil, but was soon to find sufficient sustenance in the constitution itself—in particular, the due process clause.

ACTS OF THE LEGISLATURE STRUCK DOWN AS UNCONSTITUTIONAL*

1821—1847	14
1848—1867	66
1868—1894	132
Total	212

*Based on recalculation of data gather by Lincoln and Corwin. Lincoln, V, pp. 155–175; Corwin, "The Extension of Judicial Review," 306–311.

The increasing number of cases in which the judiciary struck down legislation indicates the growing role the judiciary was playing in the constitutional history of the state.

Two other important developments took place with regard to the doctrine of judicial review in New York between the adoption of the 1821 Constitution and the adoption of the Constitution of 1894. The courts shifted the character of their arguments from those relying on natural right and inherent limitations on legislative power based on a social compact theory, to those relying on due process, public purpose, and just-compensation provisions added to the constitution during this period. By the 1830s the notion of extra-constitutional restriction on legislative power had become suspect.[38]

The second development was the adoption of the doctrine of substantive due process by the judiciary of New York. The touchstone for this doctrine in New York is the 1856 case of *Wynehamer v. New York*.[39] The New York legislature had forbidden the sale of intoxicating beverages save for medicinal purposes. In addition, the statute penalized the sale of liquors on hand at the effective date of the statute. This latter provision was voided as a violation of the due process clause. An "act of destruction" was not within the power of the government "even by the forms which belong to due process of law."[40] That is, regardless of the procedure followed, certain substantive decisions of the legislature are not permissible. The legislature "cannot totally annihilate commerce in any species of property and so condemn the property itself to extinction."[41] Such actions were an unreasonable deprivation of a vested property right. In subsequent cases, such as *In Re Jacobs* (1885)[42], the Court of Appeals would expand the list of rights protected by the due process clause, as the following passage from the Jacobs case shows:

> Liberty, in its broad sense as understood in this country, means the right, not only of freedom from actual servitude, imprisonment or restraint, but the right of one to use his faculties in all lawful ways, to live and work where he will, to earn his livelihood in any lawful calling and to pursue any lawful trade or avocation. All laws, therefore, which impair or trammel these rights, which limit one in his choice of a trade or profession . . . are infringements on his fundamental rights of liberty, which are under constitutional protection.[43]

The New York judiciary led the way in developing and expanding the notion of substantive due process. This doctrine, especially in the economic area, has fallen from favor partly because of the mistaken belief that substantive due process was a contradiction in terms, created from whole cloth by conservative judges to protect property rights.[44]

Although the New York Court of Appeals began to play a more prominent role in shaping the state's constitutional tradition, it did not, and has not, exercised the kind of power the Supreme Court of the United States has played in shaping the national constitutional tradition. The existence of a majoritarian process for amending the constitution has meant that reversing unacceptable decisions would be much easier than at the national level, and New Yorkers have been quite willing to use that amendment process to reverse the consequences of court decisions. The state has had nine constitutional conventions, producing four constitutions; these conventions were not only at liberty to reshape the constitutional documents, but also to reverse decisions of the judiciary. The much-used majoritarian amending process and the willingness to convene constitutional conventions have combined to provide balance among the legislature, the people, and the courts in shaping the constitutional tradition of the state, a balance that is absent in the national level.

EXECUTIVE

When the convention approached the question of executive power, the delegates seemingly wished to balance each move to strengthen the governor's power with one to limit that power. The convention granted the governor the sole power to veto laws, but removed his power to adjourn the legislature. He was to receive a fixed compensation to protect his independence, but his term of office was shortened from three to two years (Art. III, Secs. 1, 4)—a reflection of the delegates' animosity toward Clinton. The governor retained the power to see that the laws are faithfully executed, but was no longer allowed to make an annual address to the legislature in person. Overall, the convention granted the governor more autonomy, but the shortened term and the reduced role in patronage made it less likely that the governor would be independent of his party.[45] That, after all, was exactly the complaint the Republicans had had with Governor Clinton—a problem they hoped the new constitution would eliminate.

Judiciary

One institution which both politicians and impartial observers agreed needed restructuring was the judiciary. The growth of the state's population and economy without corresponding growth in the judiciary made it impossible for the court system to keep pace with its caseload. Chancery (that is, equity) courts met exclusively in New York City and Albany, making these courts inaccessible to western New York, where most of the state's growth had occurred. In addition, the public perceived the judges as entirely too partisan and anti-reform.[46]

The critics of the courts had more on their agenda than simple reform. Nothing less than the destruction of the existing court system would satisfy the Radical Republicans. They maintained that the judiciary was subverting republican government with its obstructionism and penchant for complex legal reasoning.[47] Their proposals would have had the effect of creating a new judiciary more subservient to the legislative branch. Moderate Republicans, joined by Federalists, repelled this sweeping onslaught on the judicial branch, but the radicals achieved some success with the Supreme Court.

The Court of Impeachment and Correction of Errors and the Council of Appointment and Revision were the institutions that involved the greatest deviation from the doctrine of separation of powers. The Court of Impeachment and Correction of Errors was composed of senators, judges of the Supreme Court, the chancellor, and the lieutenant governor. It was a remnant of the colonial idea (in turn derived from the English Constitution) of the legislature as the final court of appeals. Federalists preferred a court composed entirely of jurists. Radical Republicans wished it to be composed of the senate alone, for only then would "common sense" triumph over "judicial refinement."[48] The convention was unable to generate a majority for either proposal, so the Court remained essentially unchanged (Art. V, Sec. 1). The chancellor's office was preserved, but equity jurisdiction would now be shared with the common law courts as the legislature saw fit (Art. V, Sec. 5). Such jurisdiction would be subject to the appellate review of the chancellor. The Supreme Court bore the brunt of the changes. It was reorganized, its membership reduced from five to three, and the incumbents' positions were to be terminated when the new constitution took effect. This was the most significant radical victory concerning the judiciary. A new district court system was created, bringing justice closer to the western part of the state. The chancellor, Supreme Court justices, and circuit court judges were prohibited from holding any other office of public trust (Art. V, Sec. 7). County judges and recorders would hold office for five years, subject to removal by the senate (Art. V, Sec. 6). In April 1823, the legislature implemented these provisions by creating eight district circuits and conferring concurrent jurisdiction in equity matters on common law courts.

Legislature

Reform of the legislature was not part of the partisan campaign for a convention, but the convention had to make some changes to adjust legislative districts and apportionment to accommodate the growth and shifts in the state's population. The reorganized senate represented eight districts instead of four; the redistricting was done in such manner as to ensure Bucktail victories in six of the eight districts.[49] The issue of origination of money bills was settled by Article I, Section 8: "Any bill may originate in either house. . . ."

The delegates resisted extending legislative power over the other branches of government. The convention insisted on a two-thirds instead of a simple majority vote for impeachment and a two-thirds assembly vote for removal of state officials from office (Art. I, Sec. 13). These changes, along with the failed attempts by the radicals to make the judiciary subservient to the legislature and to create a pliable governor, suggest the extent to which moderates dominated the convention. Even more conspicuous are the limitations the 1821 Constitution placed on the exercise of legislative power. The delegates set the salary of legislators at three dollars per day (Art. I, Sec. 9) They specified the method of paying the canal debt (Art. VII, Sec 10). They also mandated a two-thirds vote for any proposed law which would require disbursement of funds for private or local purposes, or for approving corporate charters. The latter was in response to the scandals accompanying the chartering of banks in the state (Art. VII, Sec. 9). This provision was the first step in the imposition of constitutional fiscal controls on the legislature. The convention prohibited the legislature from selling off the salt springs of the state and from adopting a lottery (Art. VII, Sec. 10). The convention incorporated into the constitution a provision authorizing payment of the state's canal debt, to ensure that these obligations would not be repudiated or altered by future legislatures.

The debates focused attention on the tension between the tradition of limited and balanced government, favored by the Federalists and moderate Republicans, and the tradition of democracy and majority rule with its attendant commitment to legislative supremacy, favored by the Radical Republicans. The distressing record of legislative mistakes and manipulations persuaded supporters of popular sovereignty to agree to restrictions on that branch. Some Republicans made a distinction between the will of the people and the will of the legislature.[50] As the public's perception of the gap between the popular and the legislative will grew, demands for further restrictions increased and found expression in a variety of constitutional provisions adopted throughout the rest of the nineteenth century.[51]

MILITIA

The convention delegates devoted five sections of a newly created Article IV to the militia. The subject initially appeared in the 1777 Constitution, but the militia had its foundation in New York's colonial history when armed citizens were a part of both the Dutch and English settlements. The articles in the 1777 Constitution contained a whereas clause whose solemn tones emphasized the importance of the subject:

> It is the utmost importance to the safety of the state that it should always be in a condition of defense; and it is the duty of every man who enjoys the protection of society, to be prepared and willing to defend it . . . (Art. XI).

The clause required the state militia to be prepared for service at any given time; Quakers, exempted from military service due to conscientious objections, were required to compensate financially in lieu of service, the sum determined by the legislature; the state must "forever" maintain a "proper magazine of warlike stores" proportionate to the population of the state.

The national Constitution gave Congress the power to provide for "the organizing, arming and discipling of the militia and for the governing of such part of them as may be employed in the service of the United States . . ." (Art. I, Sec. 8). The national government was empowered to "call forth" the militia only in specified emergencies. Reserved to the states was the "appointment of the officers, and the authority of training the militia according to the discipline prescribed by Congress. . . ." The state was not permitted to quarter troops in time of peace without congressional approval (Art. I, Sec. 10), but the Second Amendment assured that "a well regulated militia" was "necessary to the security of a free state." The state's laws were revised to accommodate the new relationship established between the state and federal constitutions.[52]

The 1821 Constitution removed the lofty whereas clause and added four sections, all concerning the mode of appointment, commissioning, and removal of officers. Top-echelon officers were appointed by the governor, second-level officers by officers under their command, and lower-ranking officers were elected by their men. The religious exemption was expanded to include "any religious denomination," despite testimony by some delegates that the exemption was being abused.[53] References to stores of armaments were removed.

BILL OF RIGHTS

Unlike its predecessor, the 1821 convention adopted a formal bill of rights (Art. VII). This article was derived largely from the English Bill of Rights, the Bill of Rights adopted by the New York legislature in 1787, and the United States Bill of Rights of 1791.[54] The sections dealing with habeus corpus, double jeopardy, self-incrimination, and just compensation for property taken for public purposes are virtually identical to their federal counterparts. A few delegates thought a bill of rights unnecessary. They believed that the national and state experiments in constitutional government had been so successful that a statement of the citizen's liberties seemed superfluous.[55]

The convention debates suggest that the 1821 bill of rights was designed as much with the judiciary in mind as with the legislature. The sections on free speech and libel were clearly aimed at limiting the role of the judiciary while increasing the role of juries.[56] The free speech clause is notable both for its content and its contrast with its federal counterpart:

> Every citizen may freely speak, write and publish his sentiments on all subjects, being responsible for the abuse of that right; and no law shall be passed to restrain or abridge the liberty of speech or of the press. In all criminal prosecutions or indictments for libels, the truth may be given in evidence to the jury; and if it shall appear to the jury that the matter charged as libelous is true, and was published with good motives and for justifiable ends, the party shall be acquitted; and the jury shall have the right to determine the law and the fact.

The justification for its inclusion was to prevent the legislature from restricting this freedom by statute. It differs from its federal counterpart in a number of ways: the freedom is stated in the affirmative; the initial sentence has no reference to a state action requirement; the provision is balanced by a responsibility for abuse clause; and there is a lengthy statement of the conditions governing prosecutions for libel. The debates at the convention were devoted almost exclusively to the libel provision.

In colonial practice truth was no defense against the charge of seditious libel. That began to change under the influence of libertarian forces unleashed in the early republic. In the case of *People v. Croswell* (1804)[57] the Supreme Court was divided on the question as to whether truth was a defense in criminal libel suits. In arguments reminiscent of those of Andrew Hamilton in the Zenger case, Alexander Hamilton asserted that freedom of the press included "the right to publish, with impunity, truth, with good motives, for justifiable ends, though reflecting on government magistracy or individuals."[58] Judge (later, Chancellor) Kent reiterated Hamilton's argument in his opinion; his restatement provided the basis for an 1805 statute allowing truth as a defense in criminal libel prosecutions. This section embodies that legislative decision.

The requirement of the truth told for good motives or justifiable ends as a defense in libel actions might strike post-Warren Court readers as quaint if not dangerous. But the conditions placed in this section were intended to ensure that the jury, and not the judge, would decide all crucial aspects of a libel suit.

The clause protecting religious liberty illustrated the tension between providing freedom for the individual and the concern for social stability and morality. It combined the absolute language of the First Amendment with language imposing responsibility for abuse of that right. The social and political instability that the delegates believed would follow from unlimited speech and religious freedom prompted the introduction of limiting clauses, which were obvious signals to the courts and legislature that some forms of religious behavior and speech were abuses of liberty and could be legitimately proscribed. This latter concern clashed with the goal of limiting judicial discretion in the area of individual liberty. The delegates also tempered their concern for protecting liberty with their desire that no one should receive special privileges. When granting conscientious objector status to Quakers, they also insisted on monetary payment in lieu of military service (Art. VII, Sec. 5).

Constitutionalizing Public Policy

The 1821 Constitution was the first in which the canal policy of the state appeared, and it also has the distinction as the first constitution to embody a public policy issue unrelated to the distribution of, or limit on, governmental power.[59]

By the second decade of the century the state had borrowed funds and had begun work on the great Erie Canal project, which. when completed in 1825, would provide a waterway spanning the length of the entire state. The convention in essence constitutionalized the canal policy adopted by the legislature. Revenues collected from the salt springs, from licenses sold to auctioneers, and from steamboat traffic on the canal were to be set aside specifically for reducing the canal debt. The legislature was prohibited from disposing of the salt springs or any part of the canals. The provisions were clearly aimed at insuring that funds devoted to payment of canal debt would not be diverted to other purposes and that general taxation would not be used to pay this debt. The process of constitutionalizing existing public policy originated at this convention, and with this provision. The process would eventually result in a constitution that often read like a statute book or the regulations of a department of the executive branch. The following, excerpted from the article on canal policy, illustrates the point:

> Rates of tolls, not less than those agreed by the canal commissioners and set forth in their report to the legislature on the twelfth of March, one thousand eight hundred and twenty-one, shall be imposed on, and collected, from all parts of the navigable communications between the great western and northern lakes and the Atlantic ocean, which are now, or hearafter, shall be, made and completed; and the said tolls, together with the duties on the manufacture of all salt, as established by the act of the fifteenth of April on one thousand eight hundred and seventeen, and the duties on goods sold at auction, excepting therefrom the sum of thirty-three thousand five hundred dollars, otherwise appropriated by the said act of the legislature. . . .

This provision continues for another fifteen lines in the same vein. The purpose of such inclusion was to insulate the policy from subsequent legislative change. A permanent and continuing fund, its proponents argued, should be just that. Placing it in the constitution would ensure that permanence. But there was spirited opposition. Opponents believed that ensconcing this specific policy in the document would hamper the canal commissioner and the legislature, making it difficult for them to alter policy as changing conditions might require. Policy issues should be left to the discretion of the legislature and not cast in constitutional stone.[60] In response, proponents of the clause contended that the legislature could not be trusted to spend the revenues collected solely for the purposes of reducing the canal debt. The debates on the canal issue revealed one of the earliest divisions between downstate delegates, whose constituents had loaned the money and demanded constitutional assurances of payment, and western delegates, who, though not opposed to such payment, thought the demand an insult.[61]

Provision for education also made its initial appearance in a New York constitution. Article VII, Section 10 required that all proceeds from the sale of state lands shall be committed to a perpetual fund devoted to "the support of the common schools of the state."

State lotteries were also the subject of attention. The use of lotteries was common in the colonial period. Private lotteries were forbidden as inimical to the public welfare and morals; however, the state authorized the use of lotteries to raise funds for all sorts of public purposes.[62] The delegates voted to ban public lotteries. Proponents of the prohibition contended that lotteries were legalized gambling, destructive of industry and frugality, loosened the moral fiber of the state, and would siphon revenue disproportionately from the poor. Opponents of the clause emphasized more pragmatic considerations. As long as bordering states permit lotteries, people will take advantage of them, and the net result of the ban would be to export revenue to neighboring states. Moreover, this issue belongs more appropriately with the legislature and not in the constitution of the state.[63] John Duer, Bucktail/Federalist from Orange County, responded: "This was exactly one of the subjects on which the discretion of an ordinary legislature was not to be trusted."[64] Such arguments as were expressed at the 1821 convention would reappear in constitutional and public debates to the present day.

The 1821 convention repaired a significant gap in the 1777 document by providing a method of amendent. Henceforth, amendments to the constitution would require the approval of a majority of elected members of the legislature, a two-thirds vote of the succeeding legislature, and final ratification by a majority at the polls (Art. VIII). Radical Republicans supported a simple majority in both legislative votes; others advocated a two-thirds vote in both the assembly and the senate. The procedure as finally adopted was an obvious compromise. Despite the controversy over the calling of the 1821 convention, and the requirement of the Council of Revision that the decision to hold a convention rests with the people, the delegates were silent on this question. No procedure for the calling of a convention would be built into the state constitution until 1846.

The convention submitted its work as a whole, notwithstanding the previous decision of the Council of Revision that the amendments be submitted separately. The electorate adopted the 1821 Constitution by a vote of 75,422 to 41,497.

The Political Theory of the 1821 Constitution

Both democratic and Federalist political theory, especially with regard to the separation of powers and checks and balances, shaped the 1821

Constitution. In turn, these doctrines were modified and sometimes blunted by party goals. Party considerations make it impossible to understand the 1821 Constitution solely in terms of political theory. Nonetheless, we can clearly see a theoretical structure underlying the modifications occasioned by more immediate and mundane party pressures.

The 1821 Constitution embodied a tension between democratic values, as represented for the most part by Radical Republicans, and the commitment to the balance and separation of powers found in the national Constitution, as represented by the moderate Republicans and the Federalists. The expansion of the suffrage and the categories of elective office are manifestations of the democratic impulse, as is the apportionment provision requiring equal population and periodic reapportionment in line with population changes. Also, the provision giving the legislature the dominant share of patronage and the power to remove state officials without cause illustrate the delegates' determination to make the people's will, as represented by the legislature, supreme.

As important as these democratizing elements are, more significant is the extent to which the 1821 Constitution was modeled on the United States Constitution in both its structure and its essential theory. The veto provision is directly patterned on the federal model. The clause imposing on the governor a duty to faithfully execute the laws is identical to the federal clause, as is the limitation on altering the governor's compensation. Although specific requirements are not identical, the age, citizenship, and residency requirements are patterned after those found in the United States Constitution.

A key theoretical feature of the work of the 1821 convention is its realigning of the constitutional structure with notions of separation of powers and checks and balances. The Councils of Appointment and Revision and the Court of Errors and Impeachment, all prominent features of the 1777 Constitution, were flagrant violations of the strict doctrine of separation of powers; moreover, the 1777 Constitution contained no restrictions on plural officeholding by non-judicial officials. The two councils were abolished, compensation protection for the executive was added, and other new provisions barred legislators from accepting positions in the executive or judicial branch and executive officials from serving in the legislature. Not all plural officeholding was proscribed, however. Under the 1821 Constitution, for example, county judges could seek election to the state legislature. The convention also attempted to provide checks and balances, most obviously in the governor's veto power.

Party considerations intruded in all areas, but in most the party's immediate organizational needs and governing ideology were not in conflict. Where pragmatic party needs and doctrinal concerns did diverge, the needs of the party usually prevailed. The delegates' refusal to eliminate all plural officeholding may have been prompted by the realization that party discipline could be enhanced by such plural officeholding.[65] The factions' reversal of positions on the question of African-American suffrage, as well as Martin Van Buren's refusal to support popular election of justices of the peace, were also examples of the party's organizational goals overriding ideological commitments. It is, nevertheless, noteworthy that significant reforms were introduced at the convention and elsewhere by opportunistic parties.

THE 1821 CONSTITUTION: AN ASSESSMENT

The convention was a political response to new political forces and economic developments, as well as a practical response to needed constitutional revision, both in turn shaped by the needs and goals of the party controlling the convention. The 1821 Constitution solidified the power of the Van Buren Republicans, subsequently known as the Democratic Party. The mild form of Jacksonian Democracy which provided the basis for the democratic reforms adopted by the convention was also the ideology that would undergird the Albany Regency. On the basis of this ideology the Regency equated its well-being with that of the people. Van Buren's new democracy became the model for party organization in the future.[66] He brought respectability to the idea that democratic majorities could be gathered and guided by a party, and that patronage could be something more than "dirty politics."[67] Henceforth, any party under the new constitution and political order wishing to attain power would have to address the citizenry on its own terms and with an ideology consistent with the people's aspirations.

What the convention accomplished cannot be described as either a conservative triumph or a democratic revolution. A constitution which increased the electorate by 160,000 voters, abolished the Councils of Appointment and Revision, adopted a bill of rights, reorganized the judiciary, made thousands of offices elective, and solidified the independence of each of the three branches can hardly be called conservative. It was, like its predecessor, a moderate document whose compromises displayed evidence of both Federalist political theory and republican ideas of popular government. The debate over property qualifications for voting has been called "one of the great suffrage debates in American history."[68] For the most part, the convention adjusted the document to accommodate the new political and demographic forces molding the state, and it mollified the various regions of the state, particularly with regard to canal policy and the judiciary. The 1821 Constitution, by allowing for the local election of justices of the peace, sheriffs, county clerks, and coroners, reduced legislative influence not only on the politics of local government but also on the administrative processes of those governments. The constitution gave increased recognition to locality by guaranteeing one assemblyman to each county. Such reforms, coupled with the decisions made at the 1846 convention, would lead to the reinvigoration of local governmental institutions.

On the other hand, the delegates' decision to ensconce key legislative policies such as those concerning canals and lotteries in the constitution indicated a distinct distrust of the legislature and made it difficult for future legislatures to deal flexibly with changing economic and financial conditions. Such provisions meant that change in those policies could be made only by further constitutional amendments. Escalating resort to the constitution for policy changes when conditions demanded inevitably created a more detailed and cumbersome document. The decision to treat the state constitution as a repository for the public policies of the state, first made in 1821, opened the way for future groups to use that constitution and its successors to insulate their policy goals from alteration by ordinary legislative process.

NOTES

1. Alvin Kass, *Politics in New York State, 1800–1830* (Syracuse: Syracuse University Press, 1965), pp. 18–22.
2. Helen Young, "A Study of the Constitutional Convention of New York State in 1821" (Ph.D. diss., Yale University, 1910), pp. 24–25.
3. John Antony Casais, "The New York State Constitutional Convention of 1821 and Its Aftermath" (Ph.D. diss., Columbia University, 1967), p. 11.
4. Albert Street, *The Council of Revision of the State of New York . . . and Its Vetoes*, p. 390 (hereafter cited as *Vetoes*)
5. Ibid., p. 391.
6. See above, p. 42.
7. *Vetoes*, p. 391
8. *Report of Select Committee of the Assembly, Assembly Journal*, 44th Sess. (1821), pp. 80–84, reprinted in *Vetoes*.
9. Ibid., pp. 466, reprinted in *Vetoes*.
10. Gordon Wood, *The Creation of the Republic*, pp. 162, 164, 273–282; Donald S. Lutz, *Popular Consent and Popular Control: Whig Political Theory in the Early State Constitutions*, pp. 6, 13.
11. *Report of Select Committee of the Assembly, Assembly Journal*, p. 456, reprinted in *Vetoes*.
12. Young, "A Study of the Constitutional Convention of New York State in 1821," pp. 2–4.

13. *Journals of the Provincial Congress, Provincial Convention*, I: 874–75; John Jay to Robert Livingston and Gouverneur Morris, April 29, 1777, in H. P. Johnston, ed, *The Correspondence and Public Papers of John Jay*, I: p. 128.

14. Dixon Ryan Fox, *The Decline of the Aristocracy in the Politics of New York* (New York: Columbia University Press, 1919), p. 231.

15. 19 Johns., 58 (1821)

16. Address to the Legislature, January 4, 1820, in Charles Z. Lincoln, ed., *Messages from the Governors*, II, *1777–1822*, pp. 1019–1020.

17. Subsequent analyses of the quality of the council's work have not supported the charges which led to its demise. Charles Z. Lincoln, in his magisterial *Constitutional History of New York* (I, p. 744), claims the council "rendered great service." This judgment is affirmed by the most recent scholarly study of the council, which concludes that the council "took its responsibilities seriously . . . brought sound legal scholarship to bear upon increasingly complex subjects" and "was an effective check against hasty and improper legislation." It was the victim not of its failures but of the politics of the opening decades of the nineteenth century and the partisan attacks of those who claimed to speak in the name of democracy. Prescott and Zimmerman, *Politics of the Veto of Legislation in New York State*, pp. 50–52.

18. See especially Lee Benson, *The Concept of Jacksonian Democracy: New York as a Test Case* (Princeton: Princeton University Press, 1961), pp. 4–8 and passim.

19. These are the categories of Casais, "New York Constitutional Convention of 1821." Casais provides a list classifying each convention delegate; he justifies his four-fold categorization in Chapter III. "Radicals" were supporters of legislative supremacy and the expansion of the suffrage. "Outsiders" were individuals who shared little besides their independence and their dislike for DeWitt Clinton.

20. Young, "A Study of the Constitutional Convention of New York State in 1821," p. 39.

21. Nathaniel Carter, William Stone, and Marcus Gould, *Reports of The Proceedings and Debates of the Convention of 1821* (Albany: E. & E. Hosford, 1821), p. 198 (hereafter cited as *Debates*).

22. Jabez Hammond, *The History of Political Parties in the State of New York*, II, pp. 18–21.

23. Phyllis Field, *The Politics of Race in New York: The Struggle for Black Suffrage in the Civil War Era* (Ithaca, N.Y.: Cornell University Press, 1982), p. 37.

24. Chilton Williamson, *American Suffrage from Property to Democracy, 1760–1860* (Princeton: Princeton University Press, 1960), p. 204.

25. The United States Constitution's veto procedure was in turn a fusion of the methods contained in the 1777 New York Constitution and the 1780 Massachusetts Constitution.

26. *Debates*, pp. 52–53.

27. Ibid., pp. 53, 84

28. Ibid., pp. 53, 59–60, 66, 70–74.

29. Lincoln, *Constitutional History of New York*, I, p. 162.

30. Edward S. Corwin, "The Extension of Judicial Review in New York: 1783–1905," *Michigan Law Review*, XV (Feb., 1917), pp. 284–285.

31. Richard B. Morris, *Select Cases of the Mayor's Court of New York City, 1674–1784*, p. 302.

32. Corwin, "The Extension of Judicial Review," p. 283.
33. 19 Johns. 58 (1821). The Court held that the legislature was not permitted to "inhibit the council from accepting a resignation and appointing a successor," nor could it require the council to inquire into the official conduct of an officer before accepting his resignation (at 59).
34. 7 Johns., 477.
35. Edward Corwin, "The Basic Doctrine of American Constitutional Law," *Michigan Law Review*, XII (Feb., 1914), p. 275.
36. Corwin, "The Extension of Judicial Review . . . ," pp. 292–293, 297.
37. 2 Johns., 162 (Court of Chancery).
38. The Court of Appeals in *Wynehamer v. New York* 13 N.Y. 378 (1856) went out of its way to disavow any appeal to extra-constitutional grounds. See Edward Corwin, "The Doctrine of Due Process of Law Before the Civil War," *Harvard Law Review* 24 (March, 1911, April, 1911), pp. 366ff, 460ff.
39. 13 N.Y., 378 (1856).
40. Ibid., 420.
41. at 399.
42. 98 N.Y., 98 (1885).
43. Ibid., 106–107.
44. For a thoughtful if somewhat polemical corrective to this traditional view, see Frank R. Strong, *Substantive Due Process of Law: A Dichotomy of Sense and Nonsense* (Durham, N.C.: Carolina Academic Press, 1986).
45. Casais, "The New York State Constitutional Convention of 1821," p. 135.
46. Young, "A Study of the Constitution convention of New York State in 1821," p. 89.
47. *Debates*, 1821, pp. 502ff.
48. Ibid., 1821, p. 519
49. Donald Cole, *Martin Van Buren and the American Political System* (Princeton: Princeton University Press, 1984), p. 77.
50. *Debates*, 1821, p. 76
51. See generally James Henretta, "The Rise and Decline of 'Democratic-Republicanism' in New York and the Several States," paper presented in Albany Law School Conference, "In Search of a Useable Past," Oct. 13–15, 1988.
52. The article assumed a definition of militia provided by a variety of acts going back at least to the Duke's Laws of 1665, which defined the militia as all able-bodied men over the age of sixteen. The Federal Militia Act, however, set the age between eighteen and forty-five. 1 Stat. 272, Act of May 8, 1792. The fee for Quaker exemptions was set at ten pounds annually (*Laws of New York*, Chap. 33 (1778), 1st Session.
53. *Debates*, 1821, pp. 577–580.
54. *Laws of New York*, Chap. 1 (1787).
55. *Debates*, pp. 168–169, 171.
56. Ibid., p. 495.
57. 3 Johns., 337.
58. Ibid., 360.
59. A candidate for predecessor would be Art. XXXVII, protecting Native American land rights against fraudulent purchases.
60. *Debates*, pp. 450–455.
61. Ibid., 1821, pp. 456–460; Young,"A Study of The Constitutional Convention of 1821," pp. 110, 137.

62. Lincoln, *A Constitutional History of New York*, III, pp. 33–46.
63. *Debates*, pp. 568–569.
64. Ibid., p. 571.
65. Casais, "New York Constitutional Convention of 1821," p. 145.
66. Casais, "New York Constitutional Convention of 1821," p. 320.
67. Marvin Meyers, *The Jacksonian Persuasion: Politics and Belief* (Stanford: Stanford University Press, 1960), p. 252.
68. Chilton Williamson, *American Suffrage*, p. 195.

Constitutional Changes
1821–1846

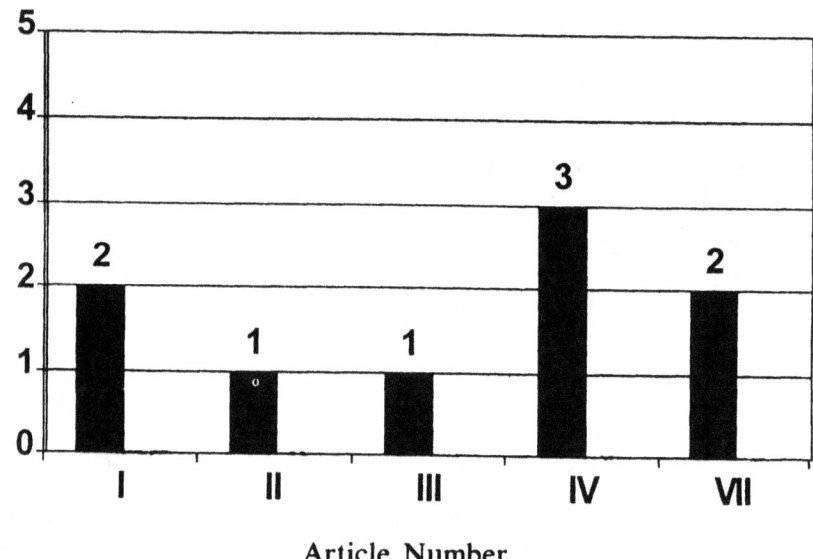

Article Number

*Some proposed amendments affected more than one article. Eight actual amendments were approved; none were rejected.

6

Commerce, Canals, and the Common Man: The Constitutional Convention of 1846

> [The] first constitution ever formed that rested not nominally but, in fact, on a popular foundation.
>
> Churchill Cambreling,
> convention delegate, 1846

CONTINUING SCHOLARLY CONTROVERSIES over the meaning of Jacksonian Democracy notwithstanding, New York did, in fact, experience an egalitarian revolution between 1815 and the Civil War.[1] The liberalization of suffrage in the 1821 Constitution was the first constitutional manifestation of this revolution. Another manifestation was the 1821 convention's decision to build a constitutional amendment procedure into the new constitution. The process of liberalization and democratization did not cease with the adoption of the 1821 Constitution. Of the eight amendments added to that constitution between 1822 and 1846, five expanded popular participation in government. The office of justice of the peace was made elective in 1822; universal white male suffrage was adopted explicitly in 1826; city mayors were made elective in 1833 and 1839; and all property qualifications for holding any public office were abolished in 1846. Prior to the 1846 convention the fundamentals of political democracy were in place, with the significant exceptions of the restrictions on political participation by African-Americans and women. Political democracy was no longer the divisive issue it had been in the revolutionary confederation and early national periods, but the egalitarian impulse had not fully expended itself. Demands came from a variety of quarters to give the people a more direct voice in their government.

By 1846 New York had earned the title "Empire State." No other state had a larger industrial base in the first half of the century.[2] New York had become the commercial hub of the Western Hemisphere. The advent of the railroads and the construction of the Erie Canal were the principal sources of the state's economic success. During this period, the private corporation established itself as the dominant form of business enterprise, and major changes in the economic structure took place. Large-scale enterprises such as banks, life and fire insurance companies, railroads, and factories were associated with an expanding, innovative, dynamic economy. Historically, corporations were quasi-public enterprises regulated by the state and chartered to serve the commonwealth. This notion, still breathing at the beginning of this period, would be moribund by 1850, as a series of steps culminating in the decisions made at the 1846 convention gradually disassociated the state and the corporation.

The detailed policies placed in the 1821 Constitution concerning canal tolls, the sale of the salt springs, limitations on the use of canal revenues, and repayment of canal debt inevitably caused additional accumulations when the necessity of exceptions and adjustments became evident. The constitution fixed the level of duties on the manufacture of salt at the level set by the legislature in 1817. By the 1830s that level required adjustment, necessitating an 1833 amendment giving the legislature the discretion to reduce the tax. A second adjustment, in 1835, allowing the legislature to drop duties when sufficient funds were collected and invested to discharge the outstanding indebtedness.

The state's public works program, of which the canal was the centerpiece, had sharply increased state indebtedness. By the mid-1840s canal debt exceeded $17.5 million; the state had a contingent debt of almost $1.75 million and a treasury debt of $5 million. When the 1846 convention convened, total state debt stood at over $25 million. The construction and maintenance of the canal accounted for more than two-thirds of that amount.[3] The remainder was the result of the state's policy of loaning the credit of the state to corporations. Despite this mounting financial burden, the state legislature imposed no direct taxes between 1826 and 1842. Rather, it relied on loans, which then pyramided; state credit declined, increasing popular disapproval of these grants and pledges. Persistent efforts failed to produce legislation. By 1842 the financial affairs of the state were rapidly approaching a crisis. Governor William Seward in his annual message of 1842 proposed a new financial policy which met with legislative approval. A direct tax was imposed, specifically designated to pay the state's debt. All expenditures on public works projects were suspended until the legislature so provided. This act in effect pledged the tax revenues of the state to its public creditors. Citizens increasingly came to believe that the public credit would not be safe unless the reforms adopted in 1842 were put into constitutional form.

Citizens also attacked corporations, particularly banks and railroads. Popular dissatisfaction arose over the state's policy of lending its credit to these enterprises, and this dissatisfaction was exacerbated by the realization that investors were not personally liable for corporate debts. Critics of private business corporations also faulted the method of incorporation under New York law. The corporate charter was viewed as a special privilege which the legislature granted by special enactment on a case-by-case basis. Although intended to ensure careful investigation by the legislature to determine whether the privilege of corporate status (including limited liability) was warranted, legislative granting of corporate charters actually encouraged log-rolling and appeared to result in the granting of privileges and monopolies to a favored few.

The problems of incorporation by special legislation are well illustrated by the banking system. In the early part of the nineteenth century the legislature passed "restraining" laws which, in effect, made banking a legal monopoly.[4] Jabez Hammond, a contemporary historian, wrote that these laws gave "soulless institutions a power equal to the exclusive power of coining money. . . ."[5] Since only the legislature could grant charter privileges, bank charters and the operation of banks became inextricably linked to the political process, that is to say, to the dominant party in the legislature. Men interested in banking thus became interested in politics, and vice versa. The Albany Regency, the centralized leadership of the Democrats, used the distribution of bank charters and stock in a blatantly political fashion, as did the Whigs under Thurlow Weed.[6] Such complaints about corporations had been a part of public debate since the granting of the first special charters. The 1821 convention responded to some of these early complaints by requiring a two-thirds vote of the legislature on any bill "creating, continuing, altering, or renewing any body politic or corporate" (Art. VII, Sec. 9), but this limitation had little effect on the chartering process. Designed to remove politics from the banking system, this provision had the opposite result. Its only effect was to increase the value of the charters, thus expanding the amount of corruption and money involved.[7] General disgust with this politicization, coupled with the belief that enterprise should be open to all and not just the privilege of politically connected individuals, led to the Free Banking Act of 1838.[8] This act enabled any group with the necessary capital to enter the banking business, thus ending the special incorporation of banks. The Free Banking Act and similar measures were the economic parallels to the democratization of the political arena. By opening enterprise to all and providing equal opportunity, one reinforced and gave stimulus to equalitarian ideals and movements in other sectors of the polity.[9] State indebtedness and the corporation became major issues on the agenda of the 1846 convention.

Special incorporation was part of a larger problem of special or local legislation. Special laws (laws enacted for the benefit of certain individuals or organizations, as opposed to general legislation enacted for the general population) accounted for four-fifths of the legislation passed during the 1840s.[10] These laws clogged the legislative process and were seen as providing special privilege to favored citizens.

The system of land tenure, particularly in counties along the Hudson and in much of the southeastern third of the state, was further cause for discontent. An anti-rent movement originated from the protest of farmers against the anachronistic character of their feudal leases. This system of nominal ownership limited by a variety of conditions was generally referred to as "leasehold." In the worst cases it prevented those who worked the land from ever owning it.[11] The law of July 12, 1782, abolishing the system of entail, permitted certain tenants to hold land in fee simple but did not affect the problem of manorial leases, and subsequent legislation such as the 1787 statute abolishing feudal tenures had been narrowly interpreted by the courts.[12] Agitation escalated into land riots between 1825 and 1846. In Albany County the governor had to summon the militia to restore order. In addition to the violent outbursts, anti-rent advocates were able to mobilize significant political support, organizing anti-rent conventions in 1845 and 1864, which generated support for a constitutional convention.[13]

The reorganization of the judiciary set forth in the 1821 Constitution proved to be too restrictive; the revised state court system was unable to accommodate the growth in population and the economy between 1820 and 1850. Delays and expenses in litigating suits had become intolerable, and the major courts faced backlogs ranging from three to five years.[14] The 1821 convention, swept up in the anti-judicial currents circulating among delegates, adopted a measure allowing legislative removal of all officers holding office "during good behavior" by joint resolution of two-thirds of all members of the assembly and a majority vote of all the members of the senate. This clause encompassed, among others, the chancellor and members of the Supreme Court. This lack of due process, coupled with the fact that removal of judicial officers was permitted without cause, prompted an 1845 amendment requiring that cause for removal be specified and entered into the journals of the two houses, notice be provided, and an "opportunity to be heard in his defense before the question shall be taken upon such removal."

This amendment did not apply to removals begun under the impeachment process, nor did it address the problem of overcrowded courts.

Reform movements of all types proliferated, with the established political parties displaying an increasing tendency to splinter over single issues. Loco-Focos, Barn Burners, the Equal Rights Party, and Hunkers were a few of the many contentious factions dotting New York's political landscape in the 1840s. Several common themes emerged from the cacophony of calls for reform: more popular elections and more control by the people over their government.

Demands for constitutional change began to dominate the political agenda a decade before 1846. As early as 1837 a convention of Friends of Constitutional Reform met at Utica to draft a proposed constitution.[15] Every year from 1841 on, proposals for a constitutional convention were offered by various citizen organizations, but divisions within the Democratic and Whig parties prevented action. By 1845, however, demands for a convention could no longer be ignored. A bill emerged from the legislature and was submitted to the electorate in November 1845. The voters approved the proposal by a majority of almost 200,000. The authorization through referendum was at best extraconstitutional, as there was no provision for amending the document by convention. Despite reservations concerning its power to authorize such a procedure, the legislature went ahead with the process of organizing a convention. The general lack of concern about constitutional authorization for a new convention may be explained by the growing popular demand for a convention and the absorption of constitutional conventions into the political culture of the states. Between 1840 and 1850 fourteen states in addition to New York held constitutional conventions.

Though called by the Whigs, the 1846 convention was organized and dominated by the Democrats, who elected a narrow majority of the delegates. The complexion of the delegates reflected the state's new economic and social order. The convention included among its ranks forty-five lawyers and forty-three farmers. These numbers are in sharp contrast to the occupational breakdown of the 1821 convention: sixty-eight farmers and thirty-seven lawyers.[16] The shift to lawyers at the expense of farmers reflects the increasing complexity and technical character of legal and constitutional reform. Some of the most prominent citizens of the state, such as Martin Van Buren, Horace Greeley, Thurlow Weed, William Seward, and William Marcy, were not delegates. Prominent delegates included Samuel J. Tilden, just beginning his career; Samuel Nelson, who had recently been appointed an associate justice of the United States Supreme Court; and Churchill Cambreling, a member of the U.S. House of Representatives and a former

American minister to Russia. Chosen on the basis of an expanded suffrage, the delegates were undistinguished but competent—the first people's convention.[17]

THE WORK OF THE CONVENTION

Finance

The major reason for the 1846 convention was the financial morass created by the state's canal debt. In 1842 the legislature passed an "Act Providing for Paying the Debt and Preserving the Credit of the State." The bill was referred to as a "stop and tax measure" as it suspended all but essential canal work and provided for a one-mill (0.1%) tax. The general dissatisfaction with the legislature's handling of state finances was exacerbated by the popular view that the legislature was dominated by special interests. This dissatisfaction in turn led the delegates to take a radically altered view of the role the legislative branch should have in the constitutional and political system.

Not content to rely on the 1842 act and fearful that the legislature might repeat its earlier mistakes, the delegates inserted the 1842 policy into the constitution. The canal debt was to be paid out of a sinking fund created from canal revenues. An express sum of money was specified to liquidate the principal and interest on the canal debt. A similar fund was created for reducing the general fund debt. The legislature was forbidden to spend any additional money to enlarge the canal unit until these amounts had been provided. If the sinking fund proved inadequate, the legislature was required to levy taxes to raise the necessary revenue. The legislature was also forbidden to sell or otherwise dispose of the canals or salt springs. These sections sprang from the delegates' wistful hope of removing the burden of the state's debt, particularly debt stemming from canal construction. On the permissive side, provisions were adopted permitting the enlargement of the Erie Canal and the completion of the Genesee and Black Rock canals (Art. VII, Secs. 1–6).

Debt and Taxation

Having addressed the problems created by past mismanagement, the delegates focused on the future, adopting specific procedures and limitations governing the legislature with respect to appropriations, debt, and taxation. Article VII, Section 8 stipulated that no funds could be drawn from the treasury without explicit appropriation by the legislature and that such appropriations could not exceed two years. This provision was modelled on a comparable provision in the United States Constitution. Section 9 of this article barred the legislature from lending the state's credit to any individual, association, or corporation—a practice which had contributed to the state's indebtedness and raised questions concerning the probity of legislators.

The aggregate amount of temporary debt which could be incurred by the state was limited to one million dollars. An emergency exception was added to allow unlimited borrowing to repel invasions, suppress insurrections, or defend the state in war (Sec. 11).

Most remarkable was the provision mandating a popular referendum for the issuance of any long-term bonds for any purpose other than those specified (Sec. 12). Additionally, it required simultaneously with issuance of such bonds that a tax must be levied sufficient to pay interest on and retire the bonds during a period not to exceed eighteen years. The cumulative goal of these measures was to virtually remove the subject of debt from the legislative domain.[18] This provision restricted legislative flexibility with regard to borrowing, necessitating additional amendments to permit borrowing when deemed necessary. On the other hand, loosely drawn language in Section 12 concerning borrowing for "casual deficits" permitted some circumventing of that provision. The one million dollar limit on debt was understood not to apply to temporary borrowings in anticipation of revenues or to borrowings to cover budget shortages. Tax anticipation and budget deficit loans were issued in excess of the limit without any systematic provision for repayment. Given the two decades of financial speculation and disruption which nearly resulted in default by the state on its obligations, the measures adopted by the convention were understandable. The perpetuation of these measures by succeeding constitutional conventions, however, would have profound consequences for the structure and composition of the state's debt.

Two amendments specifically addressed taxation. One (Art. VII, Sec. 13) provided that every law which imposes, continues, or revives a tax shall distinctly state the tax and the object to which it is to be applied. The second (Sec. 14) required that all acts involving taxes or debt shall be taken by the "ayes and noes . . . on the journal, and three-fifths of all members elected to either house shall . . . be necessary to constitute a quorum therein."

The first of these two amendments was never interpreted to mean that every tax had to be earmarked for a specific type of expenditure. The courts of the state have repeatedly ruled that the word "object" meant merely "purpose," and could be broadly defined to mean the support of the general functions of the state.[19] With such a broad interpretation, the provision lost whatever restrictive effects it was originally intended to have.

The other amendment created no problems. Requiring a record of votes and a three-fifths quorum underscored the importance of the financial measures under consideration and therefore encouraged more deliberate action thereon.

The convention made the first attempt to regulate local government debt by constitutional means (Art. VIII, Sec. 9). However, the provision adopted merely made it the duty of the legislature to regulate local fiscal practices by restricting their power to tax, assess, borrow, contract debts, or extend credit. Local governments were, presumably, as likely as the state to abuse their fiscal powers. This amendment came at a time when the growth of cities was creating an urban/rural split in the state.

Corporations

The convention next directed its attention to the corporation. The rise of the corporation raised two issues: monopoly privilege, and the character and role of the corporation in the economy. As one delegate phrased it, convention reformers wished to keep corporations "within the control of the legislature as there was great danger of their becoming formidable and oppressive as they increased numbers and power."[20] But what restraints? Some individuals wished to eliminate the limited liability of the corporation, a move which would have virtually crippled the corporation as a business entity. The committee's initial recommendation proposed making stockholders liable for the debts of the corporation in proportion to their claim on corporate profits, allowing exceptions for insurance companies and railroads, which could not survive without such protection. Debate over this proposal convinced the delegates that a detailed provision might cripple the corporation and prove cumbersome in any case.

The resulting language adopted by the convention says no more than that corporate indebtedness is to be discharged in any way the legislature shall see fit. Since there was, and is, little doubt concerning the power of the legislature to regulate corporate liability, the measures adopted served primarily as recommendations to the legislature that new legislation in this area might be necessary. The situation following the adoption of this section remained unchanged: the legislature was left free to solve the problem of corporate liability. The reasons for these empty gestures are not difficult to fathom. Public agitation and anger concerning monopoly privilege made some action imperative, and a majority of the convention delegates were determined to do something about corporations. The delegates, however, soon realized their inability to draft language capable of prescribing a precise constitutional rule applicable in every case. This realization rendered the assault on corporations by the convention largely symbolic. Anti-corporationist Robert Morris called the convention's action "a tub to the whale," designed to placate the public.[21]

Having decided to accept the corporation under such regulations as the legislature saw fit, the convention prohibited special incorporation acts. The delegates believed requiring general incorporation would provide opportunity and access to all citizens. If business corporations were to gain acceptance as a major force in the state's economic life, access to them must be made more democratic. The door was left open to special incorporation in "cases where, in the judgment of the legislature, the object of the corporation cannot be attained under general laws" (Art. VIII, Sec. 1), but the principle of general incorporation was given constitutional sanction, and subsequent legislatures acted on that principle.[22]

In the same article, the convention provided for banks. The Panic of 1837, and the rash of bank failures accompanying it, made it imperative in the eyes of the delegates to find a constitutional solution. The new constitution banned special charters for banking purposes (Sec. 4). This section absorbed into the constitution the Free Banking Act of 1838, which had taken a major step toward making corporations independent of the state. The constitution barred the legislature from passing laws allowing suspension of payment in specie and made stockholders "individually responsible for the amount of their respective share or shares of stock in any such corporation or association for all its debts and liabilities of every kind" (Sec. 7). Only in the case of banks was the principle of personal liability mandated; indeed, the provision amounted to a form of "double liability."[24]

Limiting the Legislature

Demands for internal improvements initiated a distributive rather than a regulatory public policy. A system of representation that gave priority to local interests made the distribution of resources on a rational basis impossible. A legislative process characterized by special legislation, log-rolling, lobbying, and bribery determined the public policy of the state. A description of this process is provided by a contemporary observer:

> Private bills are commonly drafted by the petitioner, or his counsel; are often read by their titles only, and pass almost of course without amendment. . . . Important changes of general laws, to subserve a par-

ticular though perhaps honest end, are sometimes artfully thrust in by their friends among the matters of little moment, to be hurried through, at the end of a session, without debate, and consequently often without due intelligence of their necessary operation. . . .[24]

Further attempts to reduce special and local legislation resulted in the provision that all such legislation be confined to one subject (Art. III, Sec. 16). The limitation was intended to prevent "log-rolling," the combination of unrelated subjects under one bill to gain sufficient support for the whole. The legislature regularly placed matters of private or special interests in bills of a general nature with general titles, or collapsed provisions in bills with deceptive titles. Two examples will illustrate the nature of this abuse.

The law had long been established preventing a husband from divorcing his wife on the grounds that she treated him cruelly. An attorney petitioned for a bill entitled "An Act for Changing the Time of Holding the General Session and for Other Purposes." Included in the "other purposes" was a rider allowing divorce by a husband on grounds of cruel treatment!

Another case of more momentous consequences involved the chartering of banks. Aaron Burr and his associates wished to charter the Manhattan Company to provide banking facilities for non-Federalist merchants. The state legislature, at the time firmly under Federalist control, was unlikely to accommodate this request. Burr petitioned the legislature to grant a charter for a water company which would furnish an improved water supply to combat the scourge of yellow fever. The incorporation petition requested $2 million; as the entire sum was unlikely to be needed, the petition requested that any surplus capital be used "in any way not inconsistent with the laws and Constitution of the United States or of the State of New York." Under this special charter for water works one of the largest banks in New York was incorporated.[25]

Section 17 appears at first glance to be a home rule provision, as it permits the legislature to confer on county officials powers to deal with essentially local matters; in fact, it was primarily an attempt to relieve the legislature of the massive number of local bills clogging the legislative process. Log-rolling had become a pervasive and unwelcome part of legislative politics. Along with Section 15, requiring majority assent of all members of the legislature rather than a majority of those present, Section 17 was intended to reduce log-rolling substantially if not eliminate it altogether.

The convention placed other limitations on the legislature, forbidding it to sell, lease, or transfer any of the canals or salt springs of the state (Art. VII, Secs. 6, 7).

The 1821 Constitution had decentralized the disbursement of patronage, giving the legislature the greatest degree of control. The 1846 convention eliminated most of the patronage, making practically all state, judicial, and local offices elective. The delegates made elective the offices of secretary of state, treasurer, attorney general, comptroller, canal supervisor, state engineer, and state prison inspectors (Art. V, Sec. 1–4). The new constitution set the term of senators at two years, a reduction of one year. To replace the eight senatorial districts established under the 1821 Constitution, the 1846 Constitution created thirty-two single-member districts. Both the increase in the number of districts and the adoption of the single-member district system were intended to ensure a closer relationship between senators and their constituents and give increased recognition to locality.

The 1846 Constitution's many restrictions on legislative power, in conjunction with changes in the system of representation, reflected a profoundly altered view of the role of the legislature in the polity. No longer was the legislative will identified with the people's will, and no longer could elections alone be relied on to ensure that public policy would be made with rectitude and intelligence. Taken as a whole, the reduction of legislative power was a most striking aspect of the work of the 1846 convention.

Limiting the Executive

Executive power, though not the focus of the convention's attention, did not fare much better. The decision to make most of the major executive officers elective reduced the governor's power over patronage, diminishing the governor's effectiveness as a party leader and making it more difficult for him to exercise any leadership or control over the various departments of the executive branch.

Reorganizing the Judiciary

In addition to making the judiciary elective, the convention completely reorganized the state court system. The convention abolished the Court of Impeachment and Correction of Errors, on which the senate sat, replacing it with a Court of Appeals. This action eliminated the role of the senate in deciding on the constitutionality of legislation.

As late as the 1830s notions of separation of powers and of judicial integrity did not prevent judges from deciding a case in a lower court and then participating in an appeal of that decision as members of an appellate court. The Court for the Correction of Errors in *Re Members of the Court of Errors* (1830) declared that the chancellor might decide to take part in a decision he participated in when sitting as a circuit judge.[26] The legislature had determined that no judge of any appellate court to which a writ of error was returnable shall participate in any case or matter determined by him when sitting as a judge in any other court. The Court of Errors believed this to be an encroachment on the powers of the chancellor as conferred by the constitution. The legislature could not add to the limitations on the chancellor's power as prescribed in the constitution. This practice, and the Court's decision sustaining it, were the reasons for Article VI, Section 3, which explicitly prohibited judges to sit in review of their own decisions.

The convention abolished the Court of Chancery. The new Court of Appeals became the state's court of last resort, "a central court with power to review the judgements of lower tribunals, and thus preserve harmony in judicial decisions" (Art. VI, Sec. 2). A new Supreme Court was established, with jurisdiction at law and equity. The court consisted of thirty-two judges from eight judicial districts elected for terms of eight years (Art. VI, Secs. 3, 4). A county court system was also created and, for the first time, the surrogates court was given constitutional status (Sec. 14).

Cities

Discussion of municipalities at the convention arose in the context of two issues: local debt and general incorporation. Concern over expensive public improvements and demands for reforms in assessment procedures were also salient features of the 1846 convention. Henry C. Murphy, formerly mayor of Brooklyn, informed the delegates that he had "long since come to the conclusion" that municipal corporations had "usurped" their powers. Local laws of special privilege are enacted because no one in Albany "except the representatives from the locality cares what it contains" and such measures "are passed without examination because they "affect only a particular community."[27] The issue of municipal power, Murphy asserted, was "one of the most important questions" before the convention. In response the convention established the first committee to address the issue of cities at a New York convention, the Select Committee on Municipal Corporations.[28] That committee recommended that local assessment for improvements be approved by those assessed and future debts be enacted and approved by a majority of voters.[29] Rural delegates concerned more with state finance, and unwilling to tamper with municipal affairs, rejected these recommendations, adopting instead a clause calling on the legislature to curb local expenditures.

The general incorporation movement affected more than the private corporation. It was a response to the onerous and increasingly impossible burden of passing social and/or local legislation. The issue touched a variety of constitutional questions, including the role of a state legislature and of local governments.

In an attempt to free the legislature from what were increasingly perceived as unnecessary and burdensome tasks, New York passed a general municipal incorporation law in 1837. Prior to 1800 incorporation and local self-government were deemed privileges. With the 1837 law the New York State legislature abdicated responsibility for grants of municipal privilege, and for a large part of the state's subsequent history the question of self-government for nascent urban centers would be decided not by county officials or central legislative authority, but by the will of local voters.[30] That permissive legal structure may not have fragmented and fractured the state's political map but it did provide the avenue by which diverse social, ethnic, and cultural interests could achieve that balkanization.[31]

Despite the general incorporation laws, the New York legislature continued to pass special legislation concerning municipalities. In so doing it generally deferred to the wished of the local delegation unless the bill involved partisan issues. This posture of deference provided access to extra-legal actors as well as to city decision-makers. Such a system allowed for flexibility and reform—excessive flexibility, from the perspective of early advocates of municipal home rule.[32]

Grievances and Rights

The convention addressed various issues concerning land ownership, the suffrage, and individual rights. When the convention convened and delegates approached the issue of anti-rent agitation over agricultural leases, little controversy remained. The cumulative impact of legislation beginning in the 1780s and continuing through 1846, combined with the disintegration of the leasehold system under withering criticism and the availability of abundant lands at more favorable terms, had practically eliminated the problem.[33] The convention reaffirmed the legislation and added a provision limiting the duration of agricultural leases to twelve years, thus removing the last vestiges of the old feudal system of land tenure in New York. The delegates made their actions prospective, refusing to disturb any arrangement already made. As a result, the long-range solution adopted at the convention did little to relieve the plight of those tenants who were still bound by the leasehold.[34]

As universal white male suffrage had been achieved before the convention met, and agitation for women's suffrage had yet to acquire sufficient momentum to produce any impact in the political arena, the convention focused on African-American suffrage. All the delegates could achieve on this issue was separate submission of a constitutional amendment providing for equal suffrage for African-Americans. Voting patterns on this issue repeated the pattern in 1821, with Democrats overwhelmingly opposed to any change and Whigs generally favoring liberalization.[35] There were various reasons for the failure of the convention to remove the racial qualifier from the suffrage provision. The issue was a politically explosive one, with potentially devastating consequences for delegates and their respective parties. Some delegates openly asserted the inferiority of African-Americans. Others presented forceful defenses of suffrage for all races.[36] A majority of both parties favored elimination of the property qualification, but for opposing reasons. Democrats desired its elimination in the belief that the absence of any property qualification would lessen the chances of passage. Whigs also favored elimination, but on the grounds that there was no justification for this racial discrimination. This intersection of positions as the parties traveled in opposite directions accounts for the otherwise illogical and inconsistent decision to allow the vote to African-Americans who satisified the property requirements specified in the 1821 Constitution. Whatever their personal feelings, the issue was not of high priority for most delegates, and they put the needs and welfare of the party above commitment to equal suffrage. The decision to send the question to the electorate illustrated the convention's caution and the unwillingness of the delegates to take an unambiguous stand on this potentially explosive issue.[37] Its rejection by a 223,834 to 85,306 vote suggests that the fence-sitting of the delegates was a prudent if not principled stance.

The convention broadened the popular basis of representation by eliminating "paupers" from the excluded classes. The provision continued the exclusion of "aliens and person of color not taxed." These exclusions appear to have been the result of a compromise. Basing representation on population would have increased representation in New York and Kings Counties, where a large number of aliens and African-Americans resided, but to have linked representation to suffrage alone would have minimized their voices in the legislature. Despite the rhetoric regarding principles of equality, most of the arguments appear to have been rationalizations.[38] Aliens and "colored not taxed" were excluded because, unlike women, paupers, children, lunatics and felons, their distribution was not uniform throughout the state. That fact, and not arguments about fairness, seemed to be dispositive.

The delegates devoted some attention to questions of individual rights, adding protection against excessive bail or cruel and unusual punishment and unreasonable detention of witnesses (Art. I, Sec. 5). The prohibition against clergymen serving in public office was eliminated. That provision was inserted in the 1777 document at a time when the suspected threat of ecclesiastical interference or control appeared greater than it did in 1846. Support for its continued existence lingered, as the thirty-three votes to retain it attest, but with its raison d'etre gone the prohibition struck delegates as an "odious distinction," one that put "a large class of citizens, of the highest character, on a footing with the felons condemned to state prison."[39]

The Constitution of 1821 prohibited the taking of private property without just compensation. In 1846 limitation on the power of eminent domain was expanded. The convention was told that just compensation was not forthcoming because unjust methods of determining what was just were being used.[40] Needing little convincing, the delegates inserted a clause requiring that compensation shall be ascertained by jury or "by no less than three commissioners appointed by a court of record . . ." (Art. I, Sec. 7). Subsequent legislatures chose to rely on commissioners to circumvent the jury alternative altogether. Although some delegates may have felt betrayed, the jury provision most likely was inserted for symbolic reasurrances, as delegates realized that these decisions required technical expertise and experience.[41]

A proposal requiring full free schooling failed. Opponents objected on two grounds: a preference for a combination of community funding and tuition charges, and a belief that community funding takes "A's property without his consent and applies it to the benefit of B, which is unconstitutional."[42]

Future Constitutional Revision

The most innovative and democratic device adopted by the convention was a reshaping of the amending process. The 1821 Constitution permitted amendment only by action of the legislature. As noted above, any proposed amendment required a majority vote of the legislature, a second enactment by a two-thirds vote in the next legislature, and final ratification by a majority of the electorate. The 1846 convention eliminated the two-thirds requirement, making the amendment process completely majoritarian (Art. XIII, Sec. 1).

An even more striking affirmation of popular sovereignty was the convention's adoption of a provision requiring that, every twenty years, the legislature must put before the voters the question: "Shall there be a convention to revise the Constitution and amend the same?" (Art. XIII, Sec. 2). This generational revision echoed Thomas Jefferson's belief that constitutions and laws should bind only the generation enacting them, and that constitutions or statutes therefore should expire every twenty years.[43]

The 1846 Constitution was approved overwhelmingly, by a vote of 221,528 to 92,436. The special amendment allowing equal suffrage for African-Americans was rejected by a similar margin.

The Political Theory of the 1846 Constitution

The 1846 Constitution has been called the "People's Constitution" with good reason.[44] No previous constitutional convention in New York had done as much to involve the people directly in the process of governing, and none had been so democratically chosen. It was not dominated by brilliant or outstanding personalities; rather, it consisted of ordinary public officials, party activists, and citizens. However, the measures adopted by the convention, and not its formation or composition, were the primary reasons for the appellation "people's convention." The decisions of the delegates to make nearly all administrative and judicial offices elective, reduce senatorial terms to two years, require single-member senatorial districts, and mandate the need to secure popular approval, in a referendum, of all debt measures over a million dollars amounted to a radical shift from the republican principle of representation to the democratic principle of participation. Even the amendment process, the fundamental basis for the government, was made a majoritarian act of the people.

This drive for direct involvement of the people manifested itself in all branches of the government, including the judiciary. Beyond making all justices elective, the Court of Appeals was to be a "half and half" court, with half its judges elected directly by the people and the other half elected from members of the Supreme Court. This provision made it possible for laymen to be elected to the highest court in the state. The Judiciary Committee drafted this provision with full knowledge of this fact. The chair of that committee, Charles Ruggles, commented on this possibility:

> The presence of a portion of laymen in that court, if such should be elected . . . may in many cases be useful. It may serve to correct the tendency which is said to exist in the minds of professional men, to be led away by habits of thought, from the just conclusions of natural reason into the track of technical rules, inapplicable to the circumstances of the case and at variance with the nature and principles of our social and political institutions.[45]

Here, in slightly different form, is the tension found in the 1821 convention between the "common sense" of the virtuous independent republican citizen and the "judicial refinements" of the experts. The provision is a dramatic example of the democratic ideology at work.

The great difference between the political theory of the 1846 Constitution and that of the 1821 Constitution is the absence in the 1846 document of the counterbalance of the Federalist theory of separation of powers and checks and balances. The convention moved the state from its reliance on the omnipotent legislature to a more sophisticated conception of government organization, including a suspensive executive veto, limits on legislative power, and a popularly elected judiciary with limited terms. By the middle of the nineteenth century New Yorkers had come to realize the importance of three separate branches, each with sufficient power to resist the encroachments of the others. Unlike the balancing connected with Federalist constitutional theory, this balancing aimed at creating three branches of government entirely dependent on the will of the people and thus capable of resisting improper actions by the other branches. Convention delegates realized that legislative decisions concerning state finances went unchecked by the other branches and were rarely subject to popular approval. Popularly elected judges would enforce constitutional prohibitions on legislative power, and the executive, with a strengthened veto, would protect popular interests. The decision requiring submission of the question of a constitutional convention every twenty years is consistent with the convention's theory that balance and independence could be achieved only by placing final control in the hands of the people.

This movement away from the radical Whigs' identification of legislative will with popular will characterized other state constitutional changes between 1820 and 1855. Twenty-three states substantially revised their constitutions between 1840 and 1855.[46] In any event, in New York, various restrictions placed on the legislature in 1846 did not shift powers to the executive and the judiciary for the purpose of checking legislative power; the transfer was from the government directly to the people, diminishing the power of all three branches. Thus, the 1846 Constitution is the most democratic constitution New Yorkers have adopted.

Although the judiciary was made elective and thus, in theory, open to laypersons, the convention's decision to divest the senate of its power to pass on the constitutionality of laws gave the Court of Appeals the position of highest court in the state, augmenting the status and authority of the court system. As long as the senate was part of the constitutional court, it was unlikely that laws which the senate had passed would subsequently be declared unconstitutional. In the seventy years between 1777 and 1847, only three laws were declared unconstitutional by the Court of Impeachment and Correction of

Errors.[47] The abolition of both the Council of Revision and the Court of Impeachment left the Court of Appeals in a position to exercise the power of judicial review more vigorously than its predecessor. Unclear, however, is the extent to which this development was anticipated or countenanced by the delegates.

The 1846 Constitution represents the apogee of participatory democracy in New York. All judicial officers, as well as the attorney-general, secretary of state, treasurer, comptroller, state engineer and surveyor, canal commissioners, the clerk to the Court of Appeals, sheriffs, county clerks, district attorneys, and all city, town, and village officers were to be chosen by popular election, except as otherwise provided for by the constitution. Although further restrictions were placed on the legislature, and the suffrage was expanded to African-Americans and women by individual amendments in 1874 and 1917 respectively, the general direction of constitutional change after 1846 was to reverse this devolution of power to the people. This new dynamic in constitutional revision, first manifest at the 1867 convention, was propelled by reform movements identified with making government more effective and responsible.

The 1846 Constitution: An Assessment

The long list of restrictions on legislative power adopted in 1846, typical of other state constitutions in the mid-nineteenth century, diminished the ability of the political system to govern and marked a shift in the role of government in New York. From the turn of the century, the government had taken an active role in regulating and stimulating the economy.[48] That role led to abuses by the legislature which provided the basis for the movement to restrict its power. For example, special incorporation laws, whereby the legislature incorporated firms individually, and which created monopolistic practices, were replaced by general incorporation laws. Monopolistic concentrations were mitigated, but the 1846 convention had taken another step in effacing the ideal of the corporation as a quasi-public instrument. At the same time that the economy was developing into a rational, integrated market system, with the corporation as its driving force, the political system was being decentralized. As L. Ray Gunn has declared:

> The active, intimate, palpable connection between the political system and the socio-economic environment gave way to a passive, supervisory, formalized system. . . . The goal of such an arrangement was to give "utmost latitude" to individual action and industry. . . .[49]

To be sure, a political culture deeply suspicious of power and authority would not have countenanced direct state control of the economy, but a tradition of active regulation and encouragement of the economy had developed in the first half of the nineteenth century. The significance of the 1846 convention was its retreat from this tradition and its redefining the role of the government in society, ensuring that the transformation of the socio-economic order of New York would take place under the umbrella, but not the active direction, of the government.[50]

The 1846 convention was the high-water point in the move to divest the legislature of what had come to be thought of as essentially local duties. The various limitations on the exercise of legislative power had the effect of reducing the administrative functions of the legislature. The 1846 Constitution specifically authorized the legislature to delegate more responsibility to local units.[51] These provisions had been preceded by a series of statutes enlarging the duties of county boards of supervisors, including the power to levy and collect taxes.[52] Pursuant to the authorization to delegate more responsibility, the legislature in 1849 enacted a statute giving the boards certain legislative powers including that of creating new towns, dividing existing ones, purchasing real estate needed for public purposes, and, within specified limits, levying taxes and borrowing money.[53] Although intended to reduce the workload of the legislature and remove it from the business of special and local legislation, the effect was to boost the powers and activities of local governments, laying the groundwork for future calls for more local self-government.

Along with its long list of restrictions on legislative power, the 1846 Constitution continued the tendency, evident in the 1821 Constitution, of providing constitutional solutions to new problems created by economic expansionism. Similarly, the new constitution reflected the continuing success of attempts by various groups and regional interests to have their goals more permanently protected by ensconcing them in the constitution. As in 1821, one immediate result of this transformation in the ideas of what a constitution should and should not do was the lengthening of the document. The 1777 Constitution contained approximately 6,600 words, including the Declaration of Independence which was incorporated into its preamble. By 1846, the length of the state's constitution had more than tripled, to 20,400 words.

NOTES

1. The major critic of the notion of Jacksonian Democracy, Lee Benson, agrees that an egalitarian revolution took place. Benson, *The Concept of Jacksonian Democracy*, pp. 336–337.

2. Harry Carman and August Baer Gold, "The Rise of the Factory System," in Alexander Flick, ed., *History of the State of New York*, VI, p. 193.
3. Lincoln, *A Constitutional History of New York*, II, p. 165.
4. *Laws of New York*, Chap. 117 (1804); Chap. 236 (1818).
5. Hammond, *Political Parties in New York*, II, p. 489.
6. Benson, *The Concept of Jacksonian Democracy*, pp. 47–49.
7. Bray Hammond, *Banks and Politics in America From the Revolution to the Civil War* (Princeton: Princeton University Press, 1957), pp. 578–579; Jabez Hammond, *The History of Political Parties in the State of New York*, I, p. 337.
8. *Laws of New York*, Chap. 260 (1838).
9. Benson, *The Concept of Jacksonian Democracy*, p. 13.
10. L. Ray Gunn, *The Decline of Authority: Public Economic Policy and Political Development in New York, 1800–1860* (Ithaca, N.Y.: Cornell University Press, 1988) pp. 186–187.
11. Edward P. Cheyney, "The Anti-rent Movement and the Constitution of 1846," in Flick, ed., *History of the State of New York*, VI: pp. 291-292.
12. One notable exception was the case of *De Peyster v. Michael*, 6 N.Y. 467 (1852), which held that the law in question prohibited all restraints on alienation. This ruling, however, came after the convention had constitutionalized these policies.
13. Patricia McGee, "Issues and Factions: New York State Politics From the Panic of 1837 to the Election of 1848" (Ph.D. Diss., St. John's University, 1970), pp. 149–154.
14. [John Bigelow], "History of Constitutional Reform in the United States," *United States Magazine and Democratic Review*, vol. 18 (1846), p. 405. Statements regarding the plight of the judiciary dot the convention records. Two sources for the debates of the convention are available: W. G. Bishop and William Attree (reporters), *Reports of the Debates and Proceedings of the Convention for the Revision of the New Constitution of the State of New York, 1846* (Albany: Evening Atlas, Printer, 1846), and S. Croswell and R. Sutton (reporters), *Debates and Proceedings in the New York State Convention for the Revision of the Constitution* (Albany: Argus Co., 1846), hereafter referred to by the names of the reporters.
15. *Address and Draft of a Proposed Constitution Convention of Friends of Constitutional Reform, Utica, 1837* (New York: published by the convention, 1837).
16. Lincoln, *Constitutional History of New York*, II: p. 108.
17. Dougherty, *Constitutional History of the State of New York*, pp. 162–163.
18. Gunn, *The Decline of Authority*, pp. 185–186.
19. Special Legislative Committee on Revision and Simplification of the Constitution, Staff Report No. 14 (1958), *State Taxation*, p. 73.
20. Bishop and Attree, *Debates and Proceedings*, p. 223.
21. Ibid., pp. 738–739. Murray Edelman provides a framework for understanding the role of symbolic reassurance in politics in his *The Symbolic Uses of Politics* (Urbana: University of Illinois Press, 1964).
22. Gunn, *The Decline of Authority*, p. 186.
23. Bray Hammond, *Banks and Politics in America From the Revolution to the Civil War*, p. 559n.

24. William H. Gardiner, "Revisions of the Laws of New York," *North American Review* XXIV (1827), pp. 199–200.

25. New York State Constitutional Convention Committee, *Problems Relating to Legislative Organization and Powers*, VII (Albany: J. B. Lyon, 1938), pp. 69–70 (known as the *Poletti Reports*, after its chair, Charles Poletti).

26. *Re Member of the Court of Errors*, 6 Wendell 158 (1830).

27. Crosswell and Sutton, *Debates*, pp. 738–739.

28. Ibid., pp. 41–42.

29. Ibid., p. 463.

30. Jon Teaford, *City and Suburb: The Political Fragmentation of Metropolitan America, 1850–1970* (Baltimore: Johns Hopkins Press, 1984), p. 7.

31. Ibid., pp. 9–10.

32. Jon Teaford, *Unheralded Triumphs: City Government in America, 1870–1960* (Baltimore: Johns Hopkins Press, 1984), p. 8.

33. Cheyney, "The Antirent Movement and the Constitution of 1846," pp. 316–317.

34. Lincoln, *Constitutional History*, II, p. 115.

35. Phyllis Field, *The Politics of Race in New York: The Struggle for Black Sufferage in the Civil War Era* (Ithaca, N.Y.: Cornell University Press, 1982), pp. 54–56.

36. Bishop and Attree, *Debates and Proceedings*, pp. 1027–1036.

37. Field, *The Politics of Race in New York*, p. 37

38. Bishop and Attree, *Debates and Proceedings*, pp. 383–391, 467–468.

39. Ibid., p. 430.

40. Ibid., p. 118.

41. Ibid., p. 983.

42. Thomas Finegan, *Free Schools: A Documentary History of the Free School Movement in New York State* (Albany, 1921), pp. 256–262. In 1849 the legislature passed a law to the same effect, but that law was rejected in a referendum in 1850. New York would not attain this goal until the Free School Law of 1867.

43. Letter to Samuel Kercheval, July 16, 1816, *Thomas Jefferson Writings*, ed. Merrill D. Peterson (New York: Library of America, 1984), p. 1402. Other states shared this enthusiasm for Jefferson's idea of generational revision. In one form or another it was adopted, among others, by New Hampshire (1792), Ohio (1802), Indiana (1816), Michigan (1850), Maryland (1852), and Massachusetts (1873). At present eight states provide for submission of the convention question every twenty years; one state, every sixteen years.

44. Edna Jacobsen, "New York's Constitution A Hundred Years Ago," *New York History* 28 (1947), p. 192.

45. *Debates and Proceedings*, pp. 371–372. Other courts, e.g., Chancery, also declared the act unconstitutional.

46. Parkinson, p. 228.

47. Lincoln, *Constitutional History* II, p. 146. While it was in existence (that is, from 1777 through 1821), the Council of Revision did veto bills on grounds of unconstitutionality. Frank Prescott and Joseph Zimmerman, *The Politics of the Veto of Legislation in New York State* (Washington, D.C.: University Press of America, 1980), p. 51, provides a statistical breakdown of the vetoes of the council.

48. Carter Goodrich, *Government Promotion of American Canals and Railroads, 1800–1890* (New York: Columbia University Press, 1960). Karen

Daniels, "Towards the Empire State: New York Poltitics and Economic Growth, 1800–1815" (unpublished Ph.D. diss., State University of New York at Buffalo, 1985) shows that both Republicans and Federalists did a great deal to stimulate economic growth, though with little discussion of the question of the proper role of government in the economy. Apparently, it was taken for granted that the state had an important role in stimulating and regulating economic growth.

49. Gunn, *The Decline of Authority*, p. 188.
50. Ibid., p. 195.
51. Ibid., p. 200.
52. *Laws of New York*, Chap. 314 (1838). Gunn analyzes these statutes, seeing them as nineteenth-century attempts to make explicit and formal a definition of political community (pp. 203–204).
53. *Laws of New York*, Chap. 194 (1849).

7

The First Failure: The Constitutional Convention of 1867

> To remold the organic law of the first Commonwealth of the world, Empire in name and Empire in fact.[1]
>
> William Wheeler,
> convention president

THE 1846 CONSTITUTION was twice amended between 1847 and 1866. A number of amendments involving the judiciary, African-American suffrage, gubernatorial succession, and prohibition were proposed, but failed to pass. The one major change effected by constitutional amendment during this period concerned the state's canals. The 1846 provisions compelled the state to adopt a pay-as-you-go policy with regard to canals, but the detailed proscriptions and prescriptions soon outlived their usefulness as the financial posture of the state changed. In 1851, barely five years after the adoption of a new constitution, the need for new measures permitting the enlargement of the canal system was recognized. Standing in the path of that project were the constitutional proscriptions on debt assumption and canal policy. Governor Washington Hunt recommended, and the legislature adopted, the first of a long series of attempts by the government to evade the debt restrictions in the constitution. The legislation authorized the issuance of canal revenue certificates, but the state would be under no obligation to redeem them beyond what might be provided by canal revenues. The validity of this statute was challenged in *Newell v. People* (1852). The Court of Appeals, unwilling to close its eyes to the obvious subterfuge, held that the statute contravened the provision barring assumption of debt without a referendum, and the provision regulating the disposition of canal revenues.[2] A constitutional amendment adopted in 1854 eliminated the obstacle posed by *Newell*, but other provisions of the 1846 Constitution continued to obstruct the fashioning of a flexible canal policy. A steep drop in canal revenue, combined with a large increase in the expenses of the government, prompted demands for a new constitutional convention.

The most unusual of these demands was an 1858 petition to hold a convention which would relieve the people from the financial burden of supporting the government by vesting the power of the state government in the president, vice-president, and directors of the New York Central Railroad. This bill appears to have been taken seriously: it passed both houses of the legislature! The people rejected the call for a convention by just over 6,300 votes. The petition reflected both the popular enthusiasm for the railroads and the low esteem in which the government was held.

By the mid-1860s the Radical Republicans, who now included in their ranks reformist Republicans and former Democrats, dominated New York state politics. Led by Governor Reuben Fenton, they succeeded in pushing through a variety of reforms concerning labor, housing, education, and social problems in New York City.[3] Eager for a constitutional convention to provide the capstone of their post-war reconstruction program, Republicans pushed for a convention in 1865, a year earlier than required by the constitution's every-twenty-year clause (Art. XIII, Sec. 2). This bill failed in the senate because a provision in the 1846 Constitution (Art. VII, Sec. 12) prevented the submission of any bill or amendment when a law asking approval for debt assumption by the state was also on the ballot, as was the case that year.[4]

By 1866 the perennial canal question had acquired new complexities. The process of awarding contracts for canal work was repeatedly plagued with bid-rigging and other forms of fraud. These fraudulent activities were attributed to a group called the "Canal Ring." In addition, a legislative investigating committee discovered that $7 million in public funds had been squandered because contracted work had not been completed and, in some cases, not even begun.[5]

Other issues claimed the public's attention as components of the task for constitutional revision. In his call for a convention, Governor Fenton cited judicial reform as the foremost problem.[6] Other reformers stressed the problems of cities and metropolitan government, debt and taxation, and official corruption.

Radical Republicans, firmly in control of the legislative and executive branches, placed the convention question on the ballot. By a vote of 352,364 to 256,364 the electorate supported the call for a constitutional convention—the first to be convened as a result of the every-twenty-year requirement of the 1846 Constitution. A technical challenge almost prevented the convening of the convention, despite the broad voter support. Because the number of votes cast was not a majority of the total eligible voters in the state, as arguably required by Article XII, Section 2 of the 1846 Constitution, a question arose about the sufficiency of the vote. The legislature ended the immediate controversy by determining that a sufficient number of votes had been cast. Though Republicans were committed to eliminating the property qualification for African-Americans, those who failed to meet that requirement were not permitted to vote for delegates.

Convention delegates were chosen according to a new plan of representation. The bill authorizing the convention stipulated the election of thirty-two at-large delegates, with four elected from each of the thirty-two senatorial districts, for a total of 160—an increase of thirty-two over the 1846 convention. In an effort to diminish partisanship and provide for minority representation, electors were permitted to vote only for their first sixteen choices to fill the at-large positions. This procedure guaranteed sixteen at-large seats for each political party. The impact of the Civil War was manifest in the requirement for each delegate to take an oath of loyalty to the Union.[7] The voters chose ninety-seven Republicans and sixty-three Democrats. Radical Republicans organized the convention and appeared to be in a position to finish the task of putting their stamp on New York State.

The convention held its first session June 4, 1867, adjourning on February 28, 1868. Among the delegates were a number of distinguished New Yorkers: William Wheeler, president of the convention, who ten years hence became vice president of the United States under Rutherford B. Hayes; Samuel J. Tilden, a delegate at the 1846 convention and subsequently the Democratic candidate for president of the United States in 1876; Horace Greeley, editor of the *New York Tribune*, later the Liberal Republican presidential candidate in 1872; Andrew Dickson White, soon to become the president of Cornell University; and Theodore Dwight, the state's foremost legal scholar. Although lawyers predominated, educators, businessmen, journalists, and statesmen were represented. Charles Lincoln, with his usual penchant for praise, hailed it "a gathering of great men."[8]

The Work of the Convention

If one issue symbolized the era it was an issue on which Republicans stood prepared to insist. That issue was equal rights for African-

Americans. William Wheeler, in his acceptance speech as the convention's president, affirmed that goal as a solemn obligation, and the Committee on Suffrage recommended elimination of the discriminatory property qualification.[9] The real debate took place over whether this question should be submitted to the voters separately from the rest of the constitution. Opponents of the measure shrewdly argued that it had been submitted separately in 1846 and again in 1860 (and had been rejected both times). To submit the constitution as a whole would jeopardize the work of the convention and deprive the voters of a clear voice on the issue. Despite this argument, and some vintage racist comments by delegates, the initial vote opposed separate submission.[10]

Democrats refused to give up. They hammered the Republicans with blatantly racist attacks aimed at kindling white prejudice in the electorate. Although the attacks caused anxiety among Republicans, initially they refused to reverse their position. The nerve-shattering factor was the election returns from Connecticut, Vermont, California, and Maine, which suggested a voter reaction against Radical Republican policies and raised the possibility that the African-American franchise issue might cause a similar reversal of Republican fortunes in New York.[11]

The delegates revealed their faltering courage in deciding to adjourn the convention until after the November elections. The ostensible reason for the adjournment was to secure additional time for the convention to complete its work. In fact, the decision was shaped by Republican fear that voters would defeat the constitution because of opposition to the article on suffrage, and might turn against the Republican party.[12] Republican losses in the 1867 election further demoralized and divided the party. When the convention resumed session on November 12, the delegates adopted a plan under which the judiciary article, the suffrage article, and the remainder of the constitution would be submitted separately to the voters.

African-American suffrage was not the only franchise issue facing the convention. The delegates reduced the district residency requirement to ten days. The former thirty-day residency requirement had disenfranchised many seasonal workers from New York City, as well as Methodist ministers assigned new parishes (Art. II, Sec. 2).

The convention declined to recommend women's suffrage "however defensible in theory" because "public sentiment does not demand, and would not sustain, an innovation so revolutionary and sweeping. . . ."[13] The delegates rejected a proposal for reducing the minimum voting age to eighteen, but also repudiated a literacy requirement, because, as the committee put it, "men's relative capacity is not absolutely measured by their literary acquirements."[14]

The 1867 convention also made additions to the Bill of Rights. The delegates approved a search-and-seizure provision modelled on the Fourth Amendment (Art. I, Sec. 9), as well as a provision allowing defendants to confront hostile witnesses (Art. I, Sec. 6). The convention also approved juries of fewer than twelve in the justices court.[15] This action was necessitated by the noted *Wynehamer* case, which held that trial by jury required a common law jury of twelve.[16] A right to peaceably assemble and petition the government was inserted (Sec. 10). Prior to this action no such protection appeared in any New York constitution, and with the rejection of the proposed constitution, no constitutional protection would be afforded New Yorkers in this respect until the 1894 Constitution. Finally, the delegates approved an amendment authorizing the legislature, by general law, to permit parties to construct drains and ditches on the land of others, under proper safeguards and with monetary remuneration, when such drainage was necessary. The provision was a response to the needs of farm interests, especially those who owned swampy land which was unproductive as long as they were unable to drain it. Some delegates objected to this proposal because it amounted to a taking of private property for private purposes, but the convention majority was more interested in making land productive than with guaranteeing property rights which might inhibit such productivity (Art. I, Sec. 7).

The convention also guaranteed the right to fish in any of the international waters bordering the state (Art. I, Sec. 29). This article was necessitated by poorly drafted legislation aimed at protecting the birds and fish in the waters of the state. Supporters claimed that without this protection the fishermen of New York, but not other states, would be barred from fishing these waters. Although the legislation had been redrafted to eliminate the offending provision, the fishermen and their supporters at the convention wanted the extra security of a constitutional provision.[17]

The Branches of the Government

The Legislature

Major restructuring of the legislature was recommended by the Committee on Legislative Reorganization, but most of these recommendations were rejected by the convention. The senate would continue to have thirty-two districts, each electing one senator. The major change affecting the senate involved an extension of the term of office from two to four years, staggered so that only half the members would stand for election at one time.

The assembly was to be composed of 139 members, an increase of eleven, chosen from counties for one-year terms. The convention returned to the county as the unit of representation, as established by the 1821 convention, abolishing the district system of the 1846 Constitution. The eleven members were added to reduce the unrepresented fraction which resulted from distributing 128 seats among counties rather than districts.

The convention continued the trend, in evidence since 1846, of limiting legislative discretion, adding more than fifteen new restrictions. These can be grouped into three categories: Bill of Rights (Art. I, Secs. 1, 9, 19); debt and taxation (Art. VIII, Secs. 13, 15); and maladministration, corruption, and policy restrictions (Art. III, Secs. 5, 14, 16, 17, 24, 25; Art. V, Sec 6; Art. VIII, Secs. 14, 17; and Art. X, Sec. 1).

The 1846 provision against local or private bills was expanded, forbidding the legislature to pass bills changing the names of persons; laying, working, or discontinuing public or private roads; and involving the sale, mortgaging, or leasing of the real property of minors or the disabled. In an effort to tighten the section limiting local bills to one subject, the convention added "that if the title contains only one subject the law shall be valid as to that, and void as to all other subjects" (Art. III, Sec. 14). The legislature was prohibited from auditing private claims or accounts against the state or passing special laws connected with those claims (Sec. 16). The legislature was also prohibited from enacting statutes granting rights to operate street railroads in any city, town, or incorporated village without the consent of local authorities and the owners. In addition, the legislature was prevented from authorizing the consolidation of railroad corporations owning parallel or competing lines. These measures appear to have been aimed at reducing the potential for abuse stemming from the increasingly close interactions between railroads and the legislature. A determination to eliminate corruption connected with the awarding of canal contracts induced the convention to prohibit the legislature from granting any extra compensation to public officials, agents, or contractors, or diminishing the compensation of those officials, except judicial officers, during their terms of service. Delegates felt that public officials should not be in a position of exercising their authority under the prospect of salary increases or decreases.

The 1846 Constitution specified salary compensation at three dollars a day, not to exceed three hundred dollars per session, excluding mileage, which was separately specified. Delegates to this convention specified the salary at one thousand dollars plus ten cents per mile for traveling expenses (Sec. 5). Interestingly, it authorized the legislature to provide for deductions for non-attendance!

The Executive

The major issue the delegates faced in reviewing the structure of the executive branch was the veto power. Beginning in 1847 governors began signing bills into law after the legislature had adjourned—a practice upheld by the Court of Appeals in *People v. Bowen*.[18] Some thought the court's opinion in *Bowen* applied only to the ten-day period mentioned in the constitution in connection with the veto (Art. IV, Sec. 8, 1846 Constitution). In 1867 the governor signed a bill into law three months following the adjournment of the legislature. The convention responded by limiting the time which a governor had to sign a bill to ten days, excluding Sundays (Art. IV, Sec. 10). The problem stemmed from the escalating tendency of the legislature to pass a flood of legislation at the close of the session, presenting bills to the governor immediately prior to adjournment, thus making it difficult for the governor to give thorough attention to each bill. The governor's power to call the legislature into extraordinary session was delimited. The proclamation calling the session was required to stipulate the particular object or objects of the session. The legislature, in turn, was prevented from adopting any law at that session not related to the objects stated in the proclamation (Sec. 6). The convention strengthened the governor's veto power by requiring a two-thirds vote of all members elected, rather than of all members present, for a successful override of a governor's veto (Art. IV, Sec. 10), but rejected a proposal granting the governor an item veto.

Although they considered adopting the short ballot and granting the governor the power to appoint all members of the executive branch, delegates rejected that far-reaching attempt to make the governor master of his own house. They did adjust the elections of the secretary of state, comptroller, treasurer, and attorney general to coincide with the election and term of the governor. They also agreed to give the governor the power to appoint the Board of Prisons; the offices of state engineer and surveyor were consolidated under the Office of Superintendent of Public Works, to be appointed by the governor (Art. IV, Sec. 5). One of the most innovative provisions concerning government organization called for the centralization of canal administration. The canal was operated by a canal board, a contracting board, a state engineer, a surveyor, and a canal commissioner and appraiser. The latter three offices would be abolished; canal administration would be vested in an Office of Superintendent of Public Works, who, along with the commissioners of the Canal Fund, would be responsible for the operation of the canal. This centralization of canal administration is one of the earliest attempts at administrative consolidation in New York.

The Judiciary

The convention devoted the greatest attention to the judiciary. The 1846 Constitution had established a Court of Appeals and divided the intermediate appellate courts into eight districts. The objective was to depoliticize the appellate function and promote harmony by centralizing ultimate jurisdiction. The drafters of the constitution left it to the legislature to define and delimit this jurisdiction. Initially, appeals were limited, but the trend during this period was toward broadening the role of appellate courts, and appellate caseloads rose accordingly. By 1865 the Court of Appeals (created by the 1846 convention), with fifteen hundred inherited cases, was four years in arrears.[19] The backlog and the annual changes in the members of the Court of Appeals mandated by the 1846 Constitution made it difficult for the court to achieve permanency and continuity, or for it to perform its duties with dispatch.

The 1867 convention proposed a Court of Appeals of six associate justices and one chief justice, each selected by popular vote for terms of fourteen years. The fourteen-year term was derived from the average time actually served by judges in the federal system, who served during good behavior.[20] In doing so, the convention eliminated supreme court judges from the court and nearly doubled their terms. At the first election, each elector was permitted to vote for the chief justice and a maximum of four associate justices, thus enabling the minority party to select at least two judges. Mandatory retirement age was extended from sixty to seventy years. (Art. VI, Sec. 2, 13). The major dispute centered on whether fourteen years was sufficient to enable judges to gain the independence and experience requisite to judicial office. Lengthy and learned arguments were presented on both sides.[21] A related issue was whether to allow eligibility for re-election. It was believed by certain delegates that re-eligibility might tempt judges to neglect their duties at the end of their term as they prepared for the election campaign. Others thought that under normal circumstances a judge whose service was reasonably satisfactory would be re-elected without extraordinary effort.[22] To prevent the Court of Appeals from beginning with a backlog of cases, the convention created a Commission of Appeals (Sec. 4), empowered to decide cases transferred to it by the court. When this commission began operating in 1870, 800 cases were transfered from the docket of the old court—an indication of the magnitude of the old court's backlog.[23]

The term for Supreme Court judges was extended from eight to fourteen years, with each judge elected for a full term. The convention enlarged and specified the county court's jurisdiction in monetary terms. The provision was added to offset the effects of the decision in

Kundolf v. Thalheimer in which the Court of Appeals held that county courts were not courts of general jurisdiction, thus limiting the legislature's power to expand their jurisdiction.[24] To reduce the inconsistency among appellate courts, the number of appellate districts was reduced from eight to four.

In the past, the legislature had acted directly to allow, and to fix the terms of, claims against the state. This system proved unsatisfactory: the legislature was simply unequipped to give intelligent consideration to such claims. The process was thus open to abuse, and many disputes were settled in favor of dubious claimants.[25]

For the first time a Court of Claims was created (Art. V, Sec. 8). The court would consist of three judges appointed by the governor, with senate approval. It was not incorporated in the judiciary article—a decision of some importance, as only the judiciary article was approved by the voters. A Board of Claims was created in 1883 and a Statutory Court of Claims was established in 1897. In 1949 the court was established as a constitutional court of record.

There was sentiment within the state and among the delegates for a non-elective judiciary. Rather than recommend a non-elective system, the convention proposed a later submission of the question after the constitution had been in operation, giving the public time to decide whether they wanted an elected or appointed judiciary. In 1873 the electors overwhelmingly voted to retain an elective judiciary. The structure of the appellate judiciary proposed by the 1867 convention is similar to the one currently operating in New York.

Public Policies and the Constitution

Canals

As the canal system involved many aspects of public policy, ranging from questions of debt to executive organization, the convention appointed two major committees to report on the canals: a Committee on Canals and a Committee on the Finances of the State, Public Debt, Revenues, Expenditures and Taxation, and Restrictions on the Powers of the Legislature in Respect Thereto.

The administration of the canal system had been the subject of recent investigations in response to allegations of fraudulent bidding practices in the awarding of contracts. One particularly disturbing abuse was designed to evade the "lowest bid" requirement. Administrators would reject the lowest bid on grounds of informality—meaning that the bid did not meet technical legal requirements. The contract would then be awarded to the highest bidder. Bidders would collude in order to defeat the purpose of the low-bid requirement. In response to this subversion of the low-bid requirement, the convention adopted a provision precluding rejection of a bid for informality unless opportunity for correction was allowed (Art. V, Sec. 7). To strengthen procedures in general, the Committee on Canals also added a requirement that no changes in specifications could be made prior to or after the execution of the contract unless approved by the Commissioners of the Canal Fund and the Superintendent of Public Works (Art. V, Sec. 4).

The duplication of agencies also fostered the growth of fraudulent practices and was part of the reason for the centralizing of canal operations. Provision was made for the payment of the old canal debt, totalling $21,375,522, from canal revenues and an increase in the sinking fund for that purpose. Upon discharge of the debt, canal revenues were to be used to reimburse the treasury for funds advanced from monies raised by taxation.[26] The delegates recognized the crucial connection between the canal system and the state's debt when they included in the same article the canal provisions and general provisions dealing with debt and state finance. In addition, the convention simplified the canal article and eliminated unnecessary language.

Cities

For the first time in the history of New York constitutional conventions, the delegates appointed a Committee on Cities, Their Organization, Government and Powers. Between 1846 and 1867 New York City became the hub of commerce, population, and wealth and consequently the focus of a variety of city and state political interests and factions wishing to shape the character of the city. By 1867 the problems of New York City could no longer be ignored.

The 1846 Constitution managed two provisions concerning city-state relations. The first invited the state to intrude on city affairs by making it the duty of the legislature to provide for organization of cities and incorporated villages and to restrict their financial practices so as to prevent abuses connected with debt and assessment practices (Art. VIII, Sec. 9). It was a mild first response to the growth of cities, at a time when cities began to undertake extended public works projects. The language was precatory and did not require or recommend specific steps.

Prior to the 1850s the state often passed various measures involving city affairs at the behest of local officials or reformers. State involvement intensified in the 1840s as the state appointed a variety of commissions governing diverse aspects of city life.[27] Increasingly, this state intervention was directed at controlling municipal expenditures. Added to the tensions developing between the city and state was the fact that New York was becoming a "foreign" city. Sixty percent were native-born in 1845; by 1855 50% were foreign-born. This shift gave rise to the Know-Nothing Party in the mid-fifties. By mid-century, New York had become a polyglot Democratic stronghold, vibrant and unruly, wet and wicked, dirty and dynamic.[28]

In 1855 the Whig Party was absorbed by the Republican Party, which proceeded to capture state government. It was this political division, rooted in two cultures—city versus state, rural versus urban, white Protestant versus ethnic Jews and Catholics—which would profoundly alter the course of constitutional history in New York for the next hundred years. Established city elites, frightened as "their city" became a city of others, turned to Albany for assistance. This assistance took many forms, including controls on city finances and morality measures involving liquor regulation, corruption, and prostitution.

The tendency to run to Albany was not without its critics. Mayor Jacob Westervelt cautioned the City's Common Council: the inevitable result of such actions would be a "city subject to the control of the state."[29] In 1856, with Republicans in full control of state government, Governor John A. King informed the legislature that "the municipal affairs of the city will undoubtedly require and receive a large share of your time and attention."[30] Republicans proceeded to do just that, extending and enhancing the power of the state over the city. In the 1860s Governor Reuben Fenton continued these policies. From the Republican perspective New York was a city wallowing in corruption and unable to provide basic services—both ills resulting from control by a corrupt Democratic Party machine.[31] Governor Fenton sponsored a series of measures that included the formation of a Metropolitan Police Force, Health Board, and Fire Department.[32] These intrusions would have been impossible without support from municipal taxpayer groups and reformers. The reform of assessment procedures and the elimination of corruption seemed more important than concerns about the implication of such intrusion for city home rule. The most egregious example of this state policy was the creation of a Metropolitan Police Force in 1857. The legislature disbanded the inefficient, undisciplined, and highly politicized municipal police force and created a metropolitan force which would operate in New York City as well as several nearby counties. The legislature took political control of the police force from the mayor and placed it under the control of police commissioners appointed by the governor, and required the city to pay the expenses for the new force.[33] The law was challenged in *People ex rel. Fernando Wood v. Simeon Draper et al.* on the grounds of a violation of Article X, Section 2.[34] In sustaining the law the court reasoned that the legislature had created a special district which transcended municipal boundaries, and was free to do so when, in its judgment, local authorities were not providing sufficient protection for life and property.

King's appointees—three old Whigs, an ex-Know Nothing, and a Radical Democrat—raised concerns about whether the state's takeover was aimed at legitimate reform or political control. Whatever the motives, the measure unquestionably struck deeply into the city's ability to select its own officials. The law also precipitated the first New York City Police riot. When members of the municipals confronted metropolitans on the steps of City Hall, a melee ensued, resulting in several serious injuries. Only with the timely assistance of the militia did the metropolitans prevail and compel Mayor Fernando Wood to bend to the authority of the state.[35]

The second provision was an amalgamation of provisions in the 1777 and 1821 Constitutions and two amendments from 1833 and 1839 concerning the choice of local officers (Art. X, Sec. 2). It stipulated that all local officials not otherwise provided for in the constitution shall be chosen by local electors or local governing agencies. It has been interpreted as an early, if limited, home rule right.[36] Although there is no indication that such was its intention, it did, in fact, "create a very definite legal right—the right to local selection of city officers."[37]

The state employed a variety of techniques to circumvent this provision. It created special commissions with the power to implement various municipal public projects. When this practice was challenged, the appointments were upheld on the grounds that the section applied only to officers "intrusted with the performance of permanent functions of the city government" and did not apply to officers who performed temporary functions.[38]

A second limitation sprung from the provision which allowed the state to determine the mode of selection of "all officers whose office may hereafter be created by law." This clause was construed to include local as well as state offices, and was the clause which provided the state with the basis for the creation of the Metropolitan Police Force in 1857. Finally, the provision was interpreted to permit state appointment of any officer of any city if the function of said officer had not been performed by a local officer prior to 1846.[39] The state, with judicial sanction, reduced significantly the efficacy of the provision. At the 1867 convention it was asserted that

> of the entire amount raised for the annual support of the city of New York more than three-fourths—seven dollars out eight . . . are disbursed by those who hold their appointment under state authorization and who

are in no way responsible to the people of the city, if indeed they are responsible to anybody for the amount of their expenditures.[40]

Such was the state of city-state relations at the opening of the 1867 convention. Providing relief from "inter meddling of the legislature" was a principal element of the convention's agenda.[41]

The committee's initial report would have allowed virtually complete home rule power for the cities. In the debate on this proposal it became evident that the delegates were unwilling to allow cities such independence. The severity of urban social problems, the stranglehold the Democratic Party had on New York City, and the perception that New York was unable to handle its affairs competently were the major factors in the convention's ultimate decision to reject significant home rule powers. Miles Townsend of Rensselaer County (Troy) protested, asserting that home rule would put power "into the hands of the worst men that God ever suffered to live in a civilized country."[42] Though reluctant to grant significant home rule power to the municipalities, the delegates were willing to approve measures ensuring increased efficiency in these municipalities. Ira Harris, chair of the Committee on Cities and a strong supporter of home rule powers, articulated the problem:

> While a great diversity of opinion exists as to what shall be done, all agree in one thing; that municipal governments in this State are exceedingly imperfect and inefficient [and] the interference of the legislature has at length reduced the city government to a condition of political chaos.[43]

Cities were instructed to elect a mayor, who, as chief executive officer, would be accorded increased powers to appoint and remove subordinates, thus providing a modicum of responsibility and leadership in city government. Members of city councils were prohibited from holding any other offices (Art. VII, Secs. 4, 5). The convention authorized the legislature to pass "general laws"—laws encompassing all cities, not just one or a few—to give these provisions effect. The delegates denied the legislature the power to pass "special laws"—laws tailored to one or a few cities—except where the object of such an act "cannot be obtained by such general laws" (Art. VII, Sec. 6). Professor Francis Lieber of Columbia College proposed that city comptrollers should be appointed by the legislature or the governor, with a proper inspection over them.[44]

The first attempt by a New York constitutional convention to deal with the cities revealed a conflict between the impulse toward good government and reform, on the one hand, and the impulse toward local autonomy or self-government on the other.[45] The tension between these two values in the context of New York City would emerge in every subsequent constitutional convention.

The amount of public corruption had reached serious proportions by the 1860s. A special committee appointed by the convention to investigate testimony about bribery of the legislature labelled the crime as one of "deep turpitude, of growing prevalence, and dangerous tendency."[46] The result was a completely new article (Art. XIII), dealing exclusively with bribery of public officials, which added a constitutional dimension to the fight against public corruption. Section 2 stipulated that the briber would not be subject to punishment if the bribe was accepted, making it clear that the article was aimed at ensuring the honesty of the public official rather than the citizen. This section also provided for the admissibility of testimony by the person offering the bribe. District attorneys were specifically directed to prosecute such offenses, under penalty of removal by the governor (Art. XIII, Sec. 4).

Delegates opposing Article XIII argued that it was unnecessary because the legislature undoubtedly possessed the power to enact similar provisions. Proponents contended that the legislature could not be relied on to pass such legislation; even if it could, it might pass laws "through which fraud can drive a coach and four."[47] Finally, the convention added to the state's oath of office a clause intended to address the problem of corruption at elections; failure to take the oath or violation of same meant removal from office (Art. XIV, Sec. 1).

The convention passed a series of other important measures. For the first time in New York's history a proposed constitution provided for completely free common schools (Art. IX, Sec. 2) and for the support of Cornell University (Art. IX, Sec. 1). The state's relationship to Cornell was similar to relationships between other state governments and the land-grant colleges established under the Morrill Act of 1862. The proposed constitution required that real and personal property be subject to a uniform rule of assessment and taxation (Art. VIII, Sec. 15). This section was added to correct inequities created by the different methods of taxing realty and personalty. For example, under the previous system of taxation a merchant who purchased goods for five thousand dollars, and who owed three thousand dollars on that amount, received a tax abatement on that obligation, whereas a farmer who purchased land for the same amount and owed a similar debt received no tax abatement.[48] The proposed constitution included an article (XI) devoted solely to prisons, creating a new board of prisons to oversee the state's penal institutions.

To remove any ambiguity as to whether the calling of a convention required a majority of those voting or a majority of the eligible voters (the obstacle on which the 1867 convention nearly foundered), the convention specified that only a majority of those actually voting was required (Art. XIV, Sec. 4). Given the notoriously low turnouts on convention votes throughout New York's history, this decision would remove a key obstacle to the calling of future constitutional conventions.

The convention ended as it began—in a dispute which prevented it from even setting a date for submission of the proposed constitution. Not until 1869 did the legislature agree to submit the proposed constitution to the voters. In the process, it further subdivided the way the voters would consider the various sections of the constitution, removing the article on taxation for separate consideration. The statute setting up the convention had specified that the convention submit its work to the people at the November 1867 election. Since the convention failed to achieve that deadline, the legislature had to determine whether any of the convention's actions following that date were valid. This problem was resolved by voting retroactive approval of the extended session—all to no avail, however, as the electorate rejected all but the judiciary article, approving that provision by the slimmest of margins, 247,240 to 240,442.

The Political Theory of the 1867 Convention

> It was a period of political theories not drawn from the experience and the teachings of the past, but which had their origin in the fertile region of political speculation and were attractive from their novelty and plausibility. Among these was the theory that public officers of every class should be elected by the people, and for a very short terms, that they might always be kept under constant sense of their responsibility to the power which created them, a theory which had its foundation in an honest desire to secure faithful and efficient officers, but which, in its practical operation, has been attended with consequences which, if imagined, or suggested, would have been treated as absurdly improbable.[49]

This reflection by delegate Charles Daly on the motivating force at the 1846 convention also indicated the problems perceived by most delegates to the 1867 convention. The accomplishments of the convention can be summed up as a reaction, first, to the extreme decentralization effected by the Constitution of 1846 and second, to the 1846 convention's view that the remedy for political evils was more—and more frequent—elections of public officials.

With the debatable exception of African-American suffrage, little in the 1867 constitutional proposal can be called an extension of democracy. Much of the document is a return to Federalist political theory as embodied in the United States Constitution. The restructuring of the legislature is a good illustration of the 1867 convention's reaction to the 1846 convention's attempt to put policy-making as close to the people as possible. Senators' terms of office were lengthened to four years. The express intents of this change were to free the senators from local prejudice and to attract a superior caliber of men to the office.[50] Similar arguments are found in James Madison's Federalist essays.[51] By moving from the district to the county as the unit of representation, the 1867 convention enlarged assembly districts. Again, the delegates argued that enlargement would attract candidates of higher quality. Article III, Section I allowed voters to select a candidate from any part of the state, thus broadening their choice and presumably providing a better range of choices. The 1867 convention also strengthened the governor's veto power and his ability to appoint some executive officers, and achieved some degree of administrative consolidation in the interest of government efficiency and integrity. The delegates extended judicial terms of office from eight to fourteen years, and consolidated appellate court districts. As in 1846, the 1867 convention imposed restrictions on the legislature, but unlike 1846, the executive and judicial branches, not the people, were the chief beneficiaries of the limits on legislative power.

The 1867 convention did not make radical or dramatic moves, and to the extent that its work had any consistent theme or purpose, it was the rejection of the decentralization and diffusion of power characteristic of the 1846 Constitution. One exception was the move to grant some minimal home rule powers to cities. Otherwise the delegates were unable to achieve a consensus or articulate a theory for any bold moves in restructuring the relations between the governor and the executive branch, or to redistribute power between the state and local governments.

The 1867 Constitution: An Assessment

The 1867 convention was the longest in New York's history, at nine months, nearly four times as long as its predecessor. It produced thirteen volumes of materials: five volumes of proceedings and debates, five volumes of documents, a two-volume manual, and a one-volume journal. $250,000 was initially allotted for convention expenses, but actual expenditures were closer to $500,000. This is in marked contrast to the 1846 convention, which produced one volume of debates, two volumes of documents, and a one-volume manual. What accounts for these dramatic increases?

First, this was the first time that everything said and done at a constitutional convention was recorded. Previously reporters produced summaries of the debates and proceedings. The record of the 1867 convention includes every type of motion, from the profound to the trivial: parallel to motions on impartial suffrage were motions to remove a partition to allow more light and air into the chamber.[52]

Second, New York's social and political order had become more complex, making attempts to address problems more difficult and time-consuming.

Third, the convention's sheer size was instrumental in delaying its proceedings and swelling the size of the record of its business. There were thirty additional delegates in 1867—meaning, other things remaining equal, additional speeches to report, more calls for votes, and more motions to debate.

Fourth, the 1867 convention was particularly disputatious. It began its proceedings with trival quarrels over whether the sergeant-at-arms and his eight doorkeepers should also double as convention postmaster and help in the seating arrangements of delegates. The convention had scarcely begun when one of the strongest supporters of the convention, delegate L. Harris Hiscock, was shot and killed by a man who believed that Hiscock had abused his wife. The convention even debated how to mourn Hiscock and whether the murder should be called an assassination.[53]

The judgment of the press on the convention was not favorable. Newspapers such as *The New York Times*, *The New York Herald*, and *The New York Tribune* and journals of opinion such as *The Nation* all lamented the convention's lack of progress and judged its accomplishments unworthy.[54] These negative judgments were harsh and premature. One of the major reasons the convention met was to reform the judiciary, and the convention managed to agree on a plan that ultimately was approved by the voters. The delegate's decision to submit the suffrage article separately was inconsequential in retrospect, as the constitution was rejected without it. This point gains added force in light of the voters' approval in 1874 of a constitutional amendment giving African-Americans the vote on equal terms with whites. The ratification of the Fifteenth Amendment to the United States Constitution almost certainly invalidated the state's constitutional provision imposing a discriminatory property qualification for African-American voters, but there is no record of any formal challenge to that provision.

Scholars and political observers offered a range of explanations for the failure of the 1867 Constitution: fear that it was a vast scheme for centralization and usurpation of power,[55] submission of the proposed constitution to the voters at an inopportune time,[56] the voters' rejection of African-American suffrage,[57] and partisan opposition and indifference unrelated to the constitution's merits or deficiencies.[58] The loss of control by the Republicans in 1868, the disillusionment with Republican policies in general and with African-American suffrage in particular, and the determined opposition of the Democrats account for the constitution's rejection in 1869. What would have happened if the convention had submitted its work in November 1867 (the originally scheduled date), before the Democrats captured the governorship? If the timing of the constitution's submission was crucial to its defeat, then the convention would have to shoulder most of the responsibility for the failure. The delegates could have completed their work in the allotted time if they had not tolerated absenteeism of an almost scandalous degree, and if they had not adopted the practice of adjournments from Friday to Tuesday. On more than one occasion the convention could not conduct its business for lack of a quorum.[59]

If the criterion for judgment is the adoption of a constitution, then the 1867 convention was a short-term failure but a long-term success. Most of the significant proposals adopted at the 1867 convention eventually were incorporated in the constitution: home rule, some executive consolidation, prohibition against search and seizure, provisions addressing bribery in public office, a court of claims, free instruction in public schools, and the current structure of the Court of Appeals. For the next forty years, reformers developed both organizational structures and coherent theories to launch and sustain a crusade for state government reorganization and municipal reform. In addition, the recommendation requiring only a majority of those voting, rather than of those eligible to vote, to sustain a call for a constitutional convention found its way onto the reformers' agenda, ultimately gaining a place in the 1894 Constitution. The 1867 convention also set a precedent for future constitutional assemblies by submitting its work in parts.

Whatever valid charges can be leveled at the chamber door of the convention, lack of foresight is not one of them. The people of the state eventually recognized the convention's wisdom, paying it a final tribute by adopting, in one form or another, most of its recommendations.

Notes

1. Reports of the *Proceedings and Debates of The Convention for Revision of the Constitution of the State of New York, 1867–1868*, 5 vols. (Albany: Weed Parsons & Co., 1868), I, p. 19. Hereafter cited as *Proceedings and Debates* 1867.
2. 7 N.Y. 9 (1852).
3. For full discussion of these reforms see James C. Mohr, *The Radical*

Republicans and Reform in New York During Reconstruction (Ithaca: Cornell University Press, 1973), Chaps. 2-6.

4. Ibid., p. 203.

5. Henry W. Hill, *An Historic Review of Waterways and Canal Construction in New York State* (Buffalo: Buffalo Historical Society, 1908), p. 155.

6. Address to the Legislature, January 2, 1867, in *Messages and Papers of the Governors*, V, pp. 746-748.

7. This requirement was subsequently voided by the Court of Appeals in *Green v. Shumay*, 39 N.Y. 418 (1868).

8. Lincoln, *Constitutional History*, II, p. 246.

9. *Proceedings and Debates*, 1867, I, pp. 19-20.

10. Ibid., I, p. 349.

11. Mohr, *The Radical Republicans*, pp. 238ff., gives careful examination to these election returns.

12. Mohr analyzes the convention vote to adjourn, as well as the Republican motives (ibid., pp. 248-263.

13. *Proceedings and Debates*, 1867, I, p. 178.

14. Ibid., p. 179.

15. Justices' courts were justice of the peace courts and were not considered courts of record.

16. 13 N.Y. 378 (1856). While the convention was meeting the case of *Dawson v. Horan*, 51 Barb. 459 (1868) was decided, modifying that part of *Wynehamer* which prompted this amendment. Dawson was reaffirmed in *Knight v. Campbell*, 62 Barb. 16 (1872).

17. *Proceedings and Debates*, 1867, V, p. 3555.

18. 21 N.Y. 517 (1860).

19. Henry Cohen, *The Powers of the New York Court of Appeals* (New York: Baker, Voorhis and Co., 1934), p. 120.

20. *Proceedings and Debates*, 1867, III, p. 2173.

21. Ibid., III, pp. 2366-2426.

22. Ibid., III, p. 2374.

23. Francis Bergan, *The History of the New York Court of Appeals, 1847-1932* (New York: Columbia University Press, 1985), p. 117.

24. 12 N.Y. 593 (1855).

25. Ernest H. Breuer, *The New York State Court of Claims: Its History, Jurisdiction and Reports* (Albany: New York State Library Bibliography Bulletin No. 83, 1959), pp. 14-15.

26. Lincoln, *Constitutional History*, II, p. 402.

27. These measures are examined in Jeff Hoyt, *Abuse of Power, New York and the Formation of Municipal Law, 1846-1866* (New York: Garland Press, 1987), pp. 266-277.

28. See Edward K. Spann, *The New Metropolis: New York City, 1840-1857* (New York: Columbia University Press, 1981).

29. Annual Message of Mayor, January 4, 1854 as quoted in the *New York Daily Times*, January 4, 1854, p. 3.

30. Annual Message of Governor, January 6, 1857. Lincoln, ed., *Messages From the Governors*, I, p. 26.

31. New York was regarded as the filthiest city in the world. Mohr, *The Radical Republicans*, p. 61.

32. Hoyt, *Abuse of Power*, pp. 268-279.

33. *Laws of New York*, Chap. 569 (1857).

34. 15 N.Y. 532 (1857).

35. James F. Richardson, *The New York Police, Colonial Times to 1901* (New York: Oxford University Press, 1970), pp. 82–108.
36. McBain, *The Law and Practice of Municipal Home Rule*, p. 3.
37. Ibid., p. 34.
38. *Greaton v. Griffin*, 4 Abb. Pr. (New Ser.) (N.Y. 310) (1968).
39. McBain, *The Law and Practice of Municipal Home Rule*, p. 38.
40. *Proceedings and Debates*, 1867, IV, p. 2928.
41. Ibid., IV, p. 2927.
42. Ibid., IV, p. 2953.
43. Ibid., IV, pp. 2926–2927.
44. Francis Lieber, *Changes Proposed in the Constitution of New York* (1867), p. 84.
45. *Proceedings and Debates*, 1867, IV, pp. 2926–2928.
46. Lincoln, *Constitutional History*, II, p. 380.
47. *Proceedings and Debates*, 1867, I, p. 502.
48. Ibid., V, p. 3759.
49. Ibid., III, p. 2359.
50. Dougherty, *Constitutional History of the State of New York*, pp. 211–213.
51. See *The Federalist Papers*, especially Numbers 10 and 62.
52. *Proceedings and Debates*, 1867, I, p. 25.
53. Ibid., I, pp. 27–29.
54. Homer Stebbins, *Political History of the State of New York, 1865–1869* (New York: Columbia University Press, 1913), Chap. 6, passim.
55. Finla Crawford, "Constitutional Development, 1867–1915," in Flick, ed., *History of the State of New York*, VII, p. 205.
56. Dougherty, *Constitutional History*, p. 206.
57. Mohr, *The Radical Republicans*, p. 274.
58. Lincoln, *Constitutional History*, II, p. 420–422.
59. *Proceedings and Debates*, 1867, I, p. 164; III, pp. 1958–1959.

8
New Modes of Constitutional Revision: The Birth of the Constitutional Commission, 1868–1894

THE FAILURE of the proposed constitution at the polls did not lessen agitation for constitutional reform, as the need for such reform was generally recognized. Governor John T. Hoffman directed attention to the corrosive impact of money on the electoral system, advocating the adoption of strong constitutional measures to arrest this corruption.[1] An amendment addressing electoral corruption was passed by two successive legislatures as required by the constitution, but was not submitted to the voters.[2]

In his annual message to the legislature in 1872, Governor Hoffman focused on the need for general constitutional revision. Although he believed another convention inexpedient, he was not confident the legislature could accomplish the necessary changes.[3] The constraints of ordinary business made it unlikely that the legislature could successfully undertake the kind of comprehensive reform he deemed necessary. It was more suited to piecemeal change—to patching, not restructuring, the document. Summoning the legislature into extraordinary session was another alternative. In all probability that would have required a second special session, and since Hoffman believed the legislature an inappropriate agency, whether in special or regular session, he chose a constitutional commission, a procedure unprecedented in the state's constitutional history. Under his proposal the commission would consist of thirty-two eminent citizens chosen by the governor from each political party. The commission would report its recommendations to the legislature for consideration. Governor Hoffman seized this opportunity to recommend a number of substantive reforms, including executive reorganization and consolidation, restructuring the senate, home rule, measures to remedy electoral corruption, and canal reorganization.[4]

The legislature approved his call, creating a commission of thirty-two members to be selected from judicial districts, four in each, by the governor and the senate.[5] Initially, the legislature directed the commission to propose amendments to the constitution, providing that "no amendment shall be proposed to the sixth article thereof [judiciary article]." This latter was presumably inserted because of the extensive revisions of that article by the 1869 amendment. That restriction, however, was removed the following year in an amendment to the authorization.

The commission met at Albany on December 4, 1872, adjourning on March 15, 1873. Its final report was presented to the legislature later that month.

SUFFRAGE

The commission rejected petitions abolishing suffrage restrictions based on gender, but, with little fanfare, recommended the removal of property requirements for African-Americans. This change was largely a matter of propriety and form as the Fifteenth Amendment, passed in 1870, almost certainly negated the old property requirement based solely on race. The legislature adopted this proposal and the voters ratified the amendment in 1874.

A provision was added that allowed qualified citizens the right to vote on all questions "submitted to the vote of the people of the State."[6] The former provision permitted electors (voters) to vote for officers of the state, leaving open the possibility that additional requirements could be added for participation in referenda. For example, measures increasing taxes or issuing bonds could be restricted to taxpayers or property owners. The legislature approved this measure, but, inexplicably, omitted the phrase "of the state," meaning that the proscription on additional requirements would apply to all referenda, local as well as state-wide. Nonetheless, the final decision from the Court of Appeals upheld additional requirements when local referenda are in question, arguing that the requirements apply only to general elections relating to the affairs of the entire state. The Court noted that it has always been the policy of the state "to limit the right of suffrage in such elections,"[7] giving little significance to the fact that the phrase "of the state" did not appear in the document.

The commission reviewed the issue of electoral corruption extensively. The impact of money on elections, particularly in the form of bribery, had long been recognized as a problem of major proportions. A variety of amendments had been introduced in the legislature, the convention of 1867 devoted extensive attention to it, and Governor Hoffman's annual messages of 1871 and 1872 contained recommendations for reform. The commission's recommendations would have made it a crime for office-holders to receive money or promise of favor for the purpose of influencing the vote or wagering on the outcome of elections. The provision barring from voting any one who makes a bet on the results of an election was not aimed at gambling per se, but at preventing evasion of the companion section prohibiting the buying of votes for cash. Warren Moscow, a long-time reporter on state politics, quipped that without that bar to betting, those interested in buying votes "would have lost a large number of two and five dollar bets that they never expected to win anyway."[8] The proposed amendment no longer left it to legislative discretion to pass laws excluding those convicted of bribery from the suffrage. The elaborate definition of bribery in the provision is not only vivid testimony to the open electoral fraud which characterized New York politics after the Civil War, but also to the frustration created by the failure of previous attempts to correct the problem. The line between a candidate's promise to voters and an offer of inducement constituting a bribe is a fine one, as the case of *People ex rel. Bush v. Thorton* (1881)[9] indicates. A candidate's pledge that he would accept only half his salary if elected was held to be a bribe of the electors! A voter, challenged under these provisions, was required to swear under oath that he or she was innocent of such practices before being allowed to vote.

Concern with the manifest corruption of the electoral process was reflected in various recommendations made by the commission. To ensure the "purity of office," any attempt to bribe a public officer was designated a felony. The legislature had previously passed a statute to this effect,[10] but that legislation had proved ineffective, partly because of the way immunity was granted under the law. The commission's recommendation contained a remarkable provision allowing the briber immunity from civil and criminal liability if "he shall testify to the giving or offering of such bribe."[11] This measure, first offered at the 1867 convention, was defended on the grounds that it was better to convict one than none, and that the criminality of the briber was less than the criminality of the corrupt official. If the bribe was not accepted, the attempted bribe became a felony.

Officials were required to swear that they had neither offered money nor any valuable compensation to any person for giving or withholding the vote for the office to which they were elected. However, an amendment removing from office anyone swearing falsely, or refusing this oath, was defeated. Nonetheless, in 1902, when the governor removed a sheriff from office for falsely swearing, that action was sustained by the Court of Appeals on the grounds that the removal power was a purely executive one, and not subject to judicial review.[12]

To ensure vigorous enforcement, another provision was added granting the governor authority to remove any district attorney who failed to faithfully prosecute anyone charged with violating the bribery provision. The state would absorb the cost of any prosecutions.

A recommendation directed at preventing multiple office-holding was also, at least in part, an anti-corruption measure, as its aim was to limit the possibility of corrupt officials expanding their influence. All these measures were approved by the legislature and ratified by the people in 1874.

THE LEGISLATIVE BRANCH

The commission recommended radical restructuring of the senate. Thirty-two senators would be chosen, four from eight large districts, with terms of office extended to four years. The commission intended this chamber to have a reflective role rather than a representative one. The primary function of the assembly was to express the wishes of local constituencies, the senate to reflect on the proposals of the assembly, subjecting them to the wisdom, experience, and independence that a body so constituted would provide. It was believed that the larger districts created by this plan would attract more experienced, more talented individuals free from narrow, parochial interests. Four-year terms would be sufficient to provide senators the independence to scrutinize carefully the frequently "ill-digested" and "special" legislation constantly generated by the assembly. The image of the state senate was similar to that expressed in the *Federalist Papers*: a body which would check unnecessary, unwise, and badly drafted legislation; a body which would provide wisdom, experience, and steadiness to the process.[13] The legislature rejected these proposals.

These proposals represent the last attempt by a constitutional body to reflect on and present a coherent justification for a second chamber. Such reflection did not take place with the adoption of the 1777 Constitution. Subsequent developments, including the adoption of similar suffrage requirements for both bodies and the increase of senate districts from four to thirty-two, eliminated any differences originally intended and made the raison d'etre for a second chamber even more problematic. The issue would be raised again at the 1915 and 1938 conventions, but no action would be taken.

Dissatisfied with the restrictions in the 1846 Constitution concerning multiple office-holding, the commission added city office-holders to the list of those prevented from taking their seats as legislators. This inclusion was precipitated by the audacious "Boss" Tweed, who was simultaneously a state senator and Commissioner of Public Works for New York City.

In a move designed to strengthen local governments, the commission proposed requiring the legislature, by general law, to confer upon boards of supervisors of counties such further powers of local legislation and administration as the legislature deemed appropriate. Prior to this provision, governing boards were entirely dependent on the state legislature. This amendment gave these boards constitutional status. The duties and powers could be exercised by common councils or boards of aldermen in cities whose boundaries were coterminous with a county. The stipulation that such powers be conferred on these boards only by general laws was directed at the evils incident to the use of special legislation noted in other proposals recommended by the commission.

THE EXECUTIVE

The commission recommended an extension of the governor's term to three years, made the eligibility requirements for the governor and lieutenant-governor identical, fixed the governor's salary at $10,000, and provided "a suitable and furnished executive residence" for his use.[14] The lieutenant-governor's salary was fixed at $5,000, and he was prohibited from receiving any other compensation for duties performed under the constitution.

The governor's power to convene extraordinary sessions of the legislature was expanded by a provision preventing the legislature, in special session, from acting on any subject save those presented by the governor. The commission ended a controversy over an issue which had confounded the conventions of 1821, 1846, and 1867, viz., the number of legislators necessary to override a veto. The commission recommended that the number be two-thirds of the elected members, not of those present. Of greater significance was the recommendation granting the governor an item veto over appropriation bills. The governor was restricted to a ten-day limit to sign a bill and was given thirty days to sign a bill after the final adjournment of the legislature.[15]

The commission recommended the creation of two new state offices, a superintendent of public works and a superintendent of prisons. The former would replace the canal commissioner and the latter the prison inspectors. These officers would be appointed by the governor with the approval of the senate. Unlike the other amendments adopted by the legislature and ratified by the voters in 1874, these were rejected by the legislature. Recommended again by the governor in 1875, they became law in 1876.

The Legislative Process

The 1846 Constitution required all private and local bills to embrace no more than one subject, that subject to be stated in the title of the bill. The provision had two purposes: to restrict log-rolling by preventing the accumulation of unrelated subjects in one bill, and to allow adequate review of the contents of the bill under consideration by the legislature and the people, thus preventing fraudulent insertion of items unrelated to the title of the bill. The clause proved only partially successful. The growth of special legislation continued unabated. The 1867 convention strengthened the language forbidding laws to be amended or revised by reference to their titles only (Art. III, Sect. 14). The 1872 commission also made further recommendations to tighten the language, but these were rejected by the legislature, leaving the section as it stood in 1846.

A second recommendation would prevent the legislature from enacting laws by reference; that is, it forbade the incorporation, by mere reference to some existing statute, of a clause affecting public or private interest to any extent not disclosed on the face of the act itself. The abuse addressed is obvious. Bills voted on by legislators often contained material by reference which, if fully known, would not have obtained passage. Such bills fail to disclose their scope and content. The courts have not construed this provision to make all referential legislation impossible. Rather, they have construed the clause in line with the evil it was intended to remove.[16] Three more "truth in legislation" proposals were recommended by the commission but rejected by the legislature. The first would have required three readings for every bill, no two of which were to be on the same day, with the printing and distributing of all bills to legislators at least one day prior to the vote taken on final passage. A second proposal required that no bill could be passed without the assent of a majority of members elected to each house. A third proposal prohibited the introduction of all private or local bills within the final ten days of the session without the consent of three-fourths of the legislature. The congested rush of business at the close of a session undoubtedly fostered practices which made it difficult, if not impossible, for legislators to determine what they were voting on, let alone to give bills ample consideration. The first two of the three proposals were later placed in the constitution by the convention of 1894.

A major concern of the commission was the disturbing increase in the volume of legislation generated, particularly special laws granting privileges to individuals and to municipal and private corporations. The problem was recognized as early as the 1820s. As one commentator noted:

> a legislative committee would rarely know what it was doing when it was considering a charter, but it could not escape the knowledge that it was giving to someone something which he very much wanted and was willing to pay for it.[17]

The 1846 convention adopted a series of measures restricting the granting of charters by special legislation and limiting private and local bills to a single subject. It continued the 1821 Constitution's provision requiring a two-thirds majority for any law appropriating funds for local or special purposes. These provisions did not stem the flood of special legislation. The convention of 1867 also gave thorough and detailed consideration to this topic.[18]

In his 1872 message to the legislature, Governor Hoffman proposed a measure which would have required the legislature to use general statutes in a wide variety of subjects. He noted that from 1852 to 1872 the legislature had passed an average of 500 bills per session; that figure had risen to 1,000, making deliberation impossible. Three-fourths of these enactments were special laws. Hoffman also noted that he had used his veto to combat the twin evils of privilege-granting and ill-drafted legislation.[19] However, a governor could not singlehandedly solve these problems. What was needed was uniformity, a resort to general laws whenever possible, and restrictions on the use of special laws. The commission followed the proposals of the 1867 convention, and recommended the prohibition of private or local laws in fourteen categories, including: changing the names of persons; locating or changing county seats; incorporating villages; granting to any corporation, association, or individual the right to lay railroad tracks or any exclusive privilege, immunity, or franchise; allowing the legislature to grant railroad franchises to occupy public streets by general law; and that such franchises cannot be authorized by general law without the consent of local authorities and the owners of one-half the value of the abutting property. It was hoped that such a specific delineation of subject matter would reduce the pressure on legislators from interested parties to pass bills that provided private benefit, and prevent legislators from passing on legislation in areas in which they were neither well-informed nor competent. In addition, a policy of legislation by general laws would reduce the sheer volume of legislation or, at the very least, reduce its rate of growth. The section failed to have the full impact intended, as the courts allowed the term "general law" to apply to less than all places or persons in the state.[20]

In addition to placing further limitations on the legislature, these measures had as a further objective a more open legislative process, on the not unreasonable assumption that openness and knowledge would inhibit questionable practices and reduce corruption and favoritism.

The commission recommended an exemption be granted from the sections dealing with legislation by reference and subject matter not to be addressed by special law to a Law Revision Commission, created by the legislature in 1870. Commission members may have believed that such a commission would not be subject to the same problems and pressures as the legislature and that such a restriction would merely have the effect of making their work more difficult. There was some question as to whether this amendment would apply only to this commission or to future commissions. The convention of 1894 continued this provision and the courts have applied it to subsequent commissions.

The Constitution and Government Debt

The 1846 Constitution authorized the legislature to restrict the powers of local government to tax, borrow money, contract debt, or loan credit (Art. VIII, Sect. 9). The hope was that debt mismanagement would be corrected by legislation. The legislature did, in fact, enact laws pursuant to this mandate.[21] However, the restriction in these statutes proved too severe, making it extremely difficult to incur any debt. Local government avoided these restrictions by petitioning the legislature for special legislation authorizing them to incur debt for specific amounts, durations, and projects.[22] Thus, the first serious attempt to restrict local debt ended in disaster. It prompted a flood of special legislation—a flood which gave rise to constitutional limitations that otherwise may have been unnecessary.

Expenditure and debt increased rapidly during and after the Civil War. Local government continued to receive special authorization for streets, water supply, sewers, and support of railroads. The 1867 convention unsuccessfully entertained motions to curb these abuses. Localities continued to lend their credit and make direct grants to private corporations. Included with railroads were charitable organizations with religious affiliations, which were receiving money with essentially no controls or restrictions. The problem was aggravated by the activities of the Tweed Ring in New York City. Between 1866 and 1872 the Ring increased the city's indebtedness from $36 million to $107 million, from 6% of the assessed evaluation to over 10%. By manipulating the books, Tweed and his associates concealed this fact from the public.[23] Large portions of this money were siphoned off to finance the Ring's activities and compensate supporters.

The commission gave high priority to this problem in its deliberations. The data gathered showed debt to have reached upwards of 25% of the assessed valuation in some localities.[24] The commission concluded that it was absolutely imperative to "impose some restraint upon the power of municipalities to incur debt."[25] and recommended that local governments be prohibited from giving their money or property, or loaning money or credit "to or in aid of any individual, association or corporation" and from owning stock or bonds in any private association. It did not prohibit local governments from providing "aid or support of the poor as may be authorized by law." Debt could be issued only in furtherance of local, public purposes. That recommendation, with minor alterations, was adopted by the legislature and ratified by the people in 1874. It marks the first time New York inserted direct restrictions on local borrowing in its constitution.

The commission also suggested similar limitations for the state. The 1846 sections on state debt did not prevent the legislature from abusing it fiscal powers. Prohibited from loaning its credit, the legislature resorted to direct grants, among others, to aid private corporations and associations. The new provision would prohibit the state from giving or loaning its money or credit (but not property) "to or in aid of any association, corporations or private undertaking." Exempt from these restrictions were aid to education, support for the blind, deaf, and dumb, and juvenile deliquents. These amendments were adopted in 1874.

Prior to the adoption of the gift and loan restrictions on state and local governments, the only constitutional limitation on the disposition of state and local funds was the requirement of a public purpose. That requirement is rooted in the due process clauses of the national and state constitutions. At the state level it finds additional support in Article I, Section 7 (eminent domain) and Article XVI, Section 1 (taxation). For the state to use its power of eminent domain or taxation to take money or property from one and give it to another for a private purpose violates due process of law. However, the due process clause has not been a significant limit as neither federal nor state courts have used the public purpose test to nullify state actions. Although the public purpose doctrine has not been repudiated, and continues to operate, at least in theory, as a restraint on use of public funds in areas not covered by these provisions, the gift and loan provisions have eclipsed that doctrine in New York. Adjudication over the scope of the gift and loan provision has been extensive, but, outside the eminent domain area, there is no court of appeals decision in this century striking down the appropriation of public funds on the grounds of a lack of a public purpose.

Corporations

Corporations had been the subject of the 1821 and 1846 Constitutions. The two-thirds requirement for special chartering of a corporation in the 1821 Constitution was intended to discourage their development. However, that provision only increased the need to resort to special laws and increased the group of people who had to be influenced. The 1846 Constitution devoted a separate article (VIII) to corporations, establishing the policy that would remain, with some modifications, until well into the twentieth century. The 1867 convention, fearful of the power of the railroads in the state, and believing that allowing the legislature discretion to incorporate by special law was the primary source of legislative corruption, recommended prohibiting special act incorporations, with exemption provided for scientific, literary, and benevolent organizations.[26] The 1872 Commission restricted the power of the legislature to enact special legislation regarding a series of topics, including special laws incorporating villages, grants to lay railroad tracks, special privileges, immunities or franchises, and forbidding exemptions from taxation on real or personal property. These specific subsections of the amendment were directed at restricting the legislature's ability to grant favored treatment to the corporation.

The commission also addressed the issue of banking corporations. The constitutional limitation relative to special charters for banking purposes was held not applicable to special charters for savings banks, trust companies, or safe desposit companies. They were not considered organized for "banking purposes" under Article VIII, Section 4. Over two hundred special charters were granted to savings banks.[27] This provision ratified what was already contained in statutory law.[28] It did not require that banks be chartered by general laws, only that there be uniformity in defining their powers, rights, and liabilities. The commission insisted that charters to savings banks be effected by special law, thus giving the legislature flexibility in determining localities and numbers needed.[29]

Institutions for savings were forbidden to possess any capital stock; trustees were forbidden to share in profits or loans or to use the association's money or property. These associations were regarded as benevolent institutions serving the poor of the community. That profits should be dispersed in the form of dividends on capital stock, or as payments to trustees, was considered unseemly.[30] In addition, delegates worried that stockholders with a strong monetary interest might maneuver savings institutions into dangerous speculation, causing bank failures and loss of savings by those "least able to bear the loss."[31] Actuated by a desire to make large profits and declare impressive dividends, some savings banks had taken risks inconsistent with the nature of their business, causing severe financial injury to depositors.[32] This not unreasonable fear was not confined to the nineteenth century.

CANALS

A number of the lateral canals were no longer productive, and were, in fact, a burden on the state. The section preventing the state from selling any part of the canal was modified to allow sale of these burdensome canals. The Canal Commissioner's office was abolished and replaced by a Superintendent of Public Works. This was a pivotal provision in reducing canal administration and consolidating executive functions. Considering the evasion of the lowest-bid requirement of the 1854 amendment, the commission added a provision disallowing extra compensation to any contractor. If, through unforeseen cause, the terms prove unjust or oppressive upon application of the contractor, the contract may then be cancelled.[33] An amendment mandating the establishment of a sinking fund to discharge canal debts, kept separately and safely invested, encountered no opposition and was adopted in 1874. A proposal placing a time limit on claims for damages arising out of construction, maintainence, or repair of the canals also was accepted.

Upon receiving the commission's extensive changes in the consitution, some legislators thought a special session would be necessary. After some discussion with Governor John A. Dix, who intimated his disinclination to call such a session, legislative leaders agreed that enough discussion had been allotted to the amendments, which were essentially identical to those debated and proposed by the 1867 convention. The legislature made minor alterations and in the November 1874 election the electorate gave its approval to all eleven amendments. So ended a chapter in the state's constitutional history which witnessed the creation of a new mode of constitutional reform. Not surprisingly, in 1875, the state would resort to a second commission.

Home Rule

The term "home rule" appeared officially in 1886 when Governor David B. Hill vetoed a measure he considered a violation of "home rule for cities."[34] When the principle involved in home rule first made its appearance is more difficult to determine. If home rule may be said to derive from local election of local officers, then home rule was present in the 1777 Constitution, which contained provisions confirming local election of local officials.[35] The 1821 Constitution extended elections to county, town, city, and village officers (Art. IV, Sec. 15). The 1846 Constitution provided that all county, city, town, and village officers whose election or appointment is not specified therein should be elected by electors of the respective localities or appointed by authorities thereof (Art. X, Sec. 2).

The convention of 1867 proposed a measure of home rule power to municipalities, and the 1872 commission recommended significant home rule powers. The former was rejected by the voters, the latter by the legislature.

Municipal reform of the city was promoted by a coalition which drew its membership from two cosmopolitan elites: descendants of the established mercantile and land-holding classes, and a younger group of professionals aspiring to elite consciousness. This dynamic arose out of the breakdown of traditional channels of patrician leadership and the consequent blurring of the status lines between classes, both precipitated by rapid urbanization and industrialization. Dedicated to fiscal stability, to running a municipal corporation in a manner similar to a business corporation, with efficiency in government as their central value, and believing that partisanship has no place in municipal government, this reform coalition would provide momentum for municipal reform proposals for the following half-century.[36]

Upon assuming the governorship in 1875 Samuel Tilden made municipal reform the centerpiece of his administration. In a special message to the legislature on municipal reform he urged the appointment of a commission to report on appropriate legislation and constitutional amendments regarding municipal reform.[37] The legislature created this commission, whereupon the governor appointed twelve prominent citizens. Before the commission issued its report, a new governor, Lucius Robinson, reinforced the message of Tilden in his annual message to

the legislature in January 1877. He noted the almost "chaotic condition
... of the government of the city of New York," and the fact that $85
million of that city's debt was the direct result of action by the state
legislature.[38] The *Report of the Commission to Devise a Plan for the
Government of Cities in the State of New York* was presented to the
legislature on March 6, 1877. The committee thoroughly examined
various aspects of municipal affairs such as organization, governance,
and indebtedness. The report suggested the following as causes of
the problem:

1. Incompetent and unfaithful governing boards and officers . . .
2. The introduction of state and national politics into municipal affairs . . .
3. The assumption by the legislature of the direct control of local affairs.[39]

The commission proposed the following solutions:

1. Separation of municipal from state and national politics. The commission believed that partisan politics had little or no role in the management of cities and that sound business principles and practice ought to be the basis for municipal governance.
2. Delegation of the entire business of local administration to the people of the cities. The state role should be reserved for passing general laws under which local affairs are to be administered.
3. Appointment of a chief executive officer for cities with general supervisory powers, including power to appoint and remove, and a Board of Alderman possessing legislative power for the municipality.
4. A board of finance chosen by electors who own property or pay taxes of specified amounts depending on the size of the city. These boards should be responsible for monitoring the fiscal affairs of the cities.
5. Restrictions on indebtedness and taxation aimed at creating a "pay-as-you-go" policy.
6. In line with the non-partisan assumptions, the commission recommended serious thought be given to proportionate representation of political minorities on city governing boards.

The recommendations were approved by the legislature in 1877, but
action by a second legislature was not forthcoming. The legislature
was not anxious to approve a plan restricting suffrage on the basis of
property ownership or an individual's status as a taxpayer. Legislators
were also influenced by the fact that these amendments would restrict,
in significant ways, their power to intervene in the affairs of municipali-

ties. With the specter of a boss-ridden New York City haunting them, few were willing to grant even a modicum of autonomy to cities.

Other home rule measures were unsuccessfully introduced. Indeed, the major change affecting local governments during the 1880s was an amendment drastically limiting the borrowing and taxing powers of local governments.

In 1876 an amendment was approved creating the office of Superintendent of Public Works to administer the canal. 1882 marked a milestone in the constitutional history of the canal. An amendment that year abrogated canal tolls. Competition from the railroads and the elimination of the old canal debt fostered a free canal movement in the state. This amendment was the culmination of that movement. Henceforth, canal expenses were to be paid from legislative appropriations. A final amendment that same year added the Black Rock Canal to the sale prohibition clause.

The Commission of Appeals was terminated in 1873, but the new Court of Appeals had already become overburdened. A constitutional amendment in 1872 continued the commission for an additional two years from the date of its expiration. It could accept no more than 500 cases annually from the Court of Appeals. That commission terminated in July 1875, having resolved one thousand cases in the five years of its existence.[40] The first commission assisted in reducing the case load of the high court, but could not address the causes of case backlog, and the court's problems became progressively more troublesome. Getting an appeal heard could require as long as two years. In response, the legislature, in 1887, adopted a concurrent resolution amending the constitution to provide for a second division of the court. The resolution was repassed in 1888 and approved at the polls that same year. It provided that "whenever and as often as there shall be an accumulation of cases on the calendar of the Court of Appeals that the public interests require a more speedy disposition thereof," the court shall certify that fact to the governor, who would then designate seven Supreme Court justices to act as associate Court of Appeals judges, forming a second division of the Court of Appeals.[41]

The second commission on appeals differed in significant respects from the first. The seven members were composed entirely of Supreme Court judges designated by the governor (the first commission's membership was drawn primarily from judges of the old Court of Appeals). The designations by the governor were temporary, ending when the Court of Appeals decided the court was no longer necessary. The governor was given the power to replace any member of the second division and designate another Supreme Court justice. That power, as one student of the court has noted, was a rare—perhaps unique—

example of gubernatorial power over the judicial branch.[42] Promptly following approval of the amendment in 1888, the court certified to the governor that a second division was needed, and one began functioning in March 1889. It was appointed again in January 1891 and completed its labors in October 1892, ending New York's constitutional experiment with two high courts.

The failure of the state legislature to address the problem of escalating local debt was noted by two governors, Lucius Robinson, a member of the Constitutional Commission of 1872, and Alonzo Cornell. Both cautioned against the dangers of a large local debt structure, but neither issued a call for constitutional amendments. Municipal debt mushroomed in New York; the net bonded debt for New York City tripled between 1868 and 1873. Boss Tweed and his myrmidons were blamed for this problem, but of greater significance was the city's unrealistically optimistic view of its financial future and its willingness to mortgage the city for public works and other improvements.[43] Other cities—Chicago, Boston, Cincinnati—also experienced a rise in indebtedness. The deflation in the wake of the Panic of 1873 saw a sharp drop in the assessed valuation of taxable property, a decline which threatened to cripple the cities. Support for reform, however, was gaining momentum both within and without the legislature. In 1881 a comprehensive amendment was introduced and passed. With some modifications this amendment was reintroduced in the 1882 legislature, passed, and approved by a subsequent legislature and ratified by the people in 1884.

The amendment limited local indebtedness to 10% of the assessed property valuation in cities with populations in excess of 100,000, prevented those cities whose debt was reduced below the maximum allowable from borrowing, exempted water debt issued for a period of twenty years, required a sinking fund for the retirement of that debt, and permitted issuance of certificates of indebtedness in anticipation of collection of taxes. The measure was a direct response to calls from citizen groups formed to establish some limitations on municipal indebtedness. The cities had certainly provided ample ammunition for amendment supporters. Governor Robinson, in his annual message of 1879, lectured cities in the following language:

> They played with debt, and courted taxation as if for pastime. Many towns almost buried themselves with bonds, issued for railroads which have never been built, and covered their farms with mortgages for which they received no consideration.[44]

Only four cities had populations over 100,000 in 1884: New York, Brooklyn, Buffalo, and Rochester. These four were targeted because their increases in debt and property tax levies were more pronounced and affected more people.[45] Similar constitutional limits were placed on cities in other states.

The amendment also contained a tax limit clause, apparently as an afterthought. Its origins are obscure and it was little debated. The amount of taxes raised in any one year could not exceed 2% of the assessed valuation of real and personal property of any municipality. The tax limitation apparently was to work in tandem with the debt limitation. A city which had borrowed to the limit would be prevented from "going on a spree" by charging additional capital expenditures against the tax levy.[46]

The amendment had some serious defects which were to hamper its long-term effectiveness. It failed to distinguish gross debt and net debt, i.e., debt remaining after deductions from the gross debt of the sinking fund accumulations. It did not make clear whether it referred to bonded indebtedness only, or to other forms of debt. It exempted bonds issued for water projects but limited their terms to twenty years, too brief a span for financing water works, rendering the exemption practically useless. Finally, New York City suffered discrimination because the 10% debt limit applied to the combined county and city debt, whereas in the other cities it applied separately to their city and county debt, effectively granting those communities a 20% debt limit.[47]

The immediate result was to force cities to exercise more caution in borrowing. The long-term effects, however, were quite different. Debt limits were soon avoided by the expedient of raising assessed valuations. With regard to tax limitation, one study of New York City concluded that the limit "had no effect whatsoever on the City's fiscal operations during the first thirty-five years, neither contributing to sound management as intended, nor inadvertently interfering therewith."[48]

With the adoption of the 1884 amendment the constitutional framework governing debt and tax policies of state and local governments was in place. Additions and subtractions would be made, but that constitutional framework would be the constitutional policy of the state for the next century.

The Judiciary Commission of 1890

For the third time in less than twenty years the state relied on a commission to address pressing issues of constitutional reform. The constitutional commission of 1890 had its origin in the failure of the legislature and governor to agree on a bill to convene a constitutional convention. In 1886 the electorate, pursuant to the every-twenty-year provision of the 1846 Constitution, overwhelmingly approved the calling of a constitutional convention by a vote of 574,992 to 30,766. Facing the prospect of a prolonged deadlock, and with a manifest need for judicial reform, the legislature in April 1890 authorized the creation of a commission consisting of thirty-eight members divided among the eight judicial districts of the state. The members were to be appointed by the governor with the approval of senate, with no more than half coming from any one political party. Its jurisdiction was limited to revisions of the judiciary (Art. VI).[49] This was the first constitutional commission created by the legislature, though the statute itself was drafted by the Committee on Law Reform of the New York State Bar Association.[50] The model was obviously the 1872 commission and an equally prominent group of lawyer judges was appointed, including Joseph Choate; George F. Danforth, former chief judge of the Court of Appeals (chair of the commission); and William B. Hornblower, nominated by President Cleveland in 1893 to serve on the U.S. Supreme Court. The commission convened in Albany on June 3, 1890, held its final meeting on January 23, 1891, and submitted its final report to the senate on March 4 of that year.

The major issue confronting the commission was the burdensome caseload of the Court of Appeals, which resulted in persistent delays. The commission had three alternatives: enlarge the court, divide the court in similar fashion to the Commission on Appeals, or limit its jurisdiction. The commission rejected the divided court approach. That approach, employed in 1872 and 1888, in effect created two final courts of appeals in the state. Co-ordinate courts would inevitably mean divergent opinions and uncertainty as to the law of the state. A second alternative, enlarging the court to fifteen members, was also rejected, although it had strong support in the legislature and among members of the bar.[51] Commissioner William Hornblower opined that a larger court becomes a "town meeting . . . [a] debating society," lacks "consistency" and the elements of "individual responsibility and homogeniety."[52] The commission provided four general terms (later renamed appellate divisions) of the Supreme Court, consisting of five judges each, four of whom constituting a quorum. They would be charged to hear appeals from all the circuits, special terms, and from local courts. A unanimous decision of the appellate division could go to the Court of Appeals only if it was requested by the court (certified), or if leave to appeal was granted by the appellate division, or if it fell within a narrowly specified category of cases. The commission's recommendations involved a set of assumptions about the role of appellate courts in the judicial system of the state. Appellate courts had two major functions: to apply the law previously established by the legislature and to correct any major errors committed by lower courts, and to decide new questions of law and provide guidance for courts in the future. The first function primarily concerned individuals, whereas the second involved the community at large. The greatest portion of cases handled by the appellate division will fall into the first category and should rarely be carried beyond the first appellate level. The second is the primary function of the Court of Appeals, and the cases coming to it should be restricted largely to those in that category.[53] The commission submitted other recommendations, including an increase in the number of Supreme Court justices and abolition of the Superior Court of New York City.

The commission's report to the legislature came too late for full consideration at the 1891 session. Moreover, the legislature was not in agreement with the commission's proposals on the Court of Appeals. It adopted a resolution for an amendment to the constitution which would have enlarged the Court of Appeals, leaving its jurisdiction intact. In 1892 Democrats gained control of both the legislature and the governorship, thus ending the impasse over the selection of delegates to the convention. The legislature decided that the commission's recommendations should be addressed at the convention. The 1894 convention, to the surprise and chagrin of the Democratic legislature, was controlled by Republicans and gave the commission's recommendations more consideration than they received in the chambers of the legislature.

The Constitutional Commission as a Constitutional Innovation

The convening of a constitutional commission whose work was successfully received established a new and valuable instrument for effecting constitutional change. Governor Hoffman's reasons for resorting to a commission rather than a convention are instructive. He believed a convention neither "necessary" nor "the best means by which to attain the end" of constitutional reform. A commission of eminent citizens would achieve as good, if not better, results than the larger body. It would afford the opportunity of full debate and the benefit of input from the press and public. Furthermore, the governor believed that amendments agreed on by such a commission would almost certainly "secure the popular approval."[54] Here we have, in embryo, what would become the case for forming commissions in the future: talented, experienced, thoughtful citizens deliberating on a single task, in a group small enough for ordered, intimate discussion, but large enough to entertain a representative range of alternatives. Since its work had to be considered by the legislature and ratified by the people, little if any popular control over the process was lost. In terms of focus, size, and expertise, the state seemed to have stumbled on an effective tool to accomplish needed constitutional reform.

By the turn of the twentieth century, the value of the constitutional commission had been established. Such commissions could be employed for a variety of purposes and structured in a number of different ways. They have been recommended by the governor and appointed by the legislature (Constitutional Commission of 1872); recommended and appointed by the governor (Tilden Commission, 1875), and they have functioned as preparatory commissions created in anticipation of impending conventions. Since 1867 legislatures have directed that information relevant to conventions be prepared and presented to the delegates. The full import of such preparatory commissions was not realized until the 1915 convention. Beyond the immediate impact of that commission's work on that convention's decisions, its careful and thorough research would continue to shape the contours of constitutional change for the next quarter century. The use and development of constitutional commissions would continue throughout the twentieth century.[55]

Notes

1. Message to the legislature, January 26, 1871, Lincoln, ed., *Messages From the Governors*, VI, pp. 263–264.
2. Lincoln (*Constitutional History*, II, p. 466) speculates that this failure was related to the fact that a proposal was under consideration by the legislature to create a constitutional commission.
3. *Messages From the Governors*, VI, p. 393.
4. Ibid., VI, pp. 393–404.
5. *Laws of New York*, Chap. 884 (1872).
6. *Journal of the Constitutional Commission of the State of New York, 1872–1873* (Albany: Weed Parsons & Co., 1973), p. 338 (hereafter *Journal*).
7. *Esler v. Walters*, 56 N.Y. 2d 306 (1982), at 314.
8. Warren Moscow, *Politics in the Empire State* (New York: Alfred A. Knopf, 1948), p. 225.
9. 25. Hun 456 (1881).
10. *Laws of New York*, Chap. 539 (1853).
11. *Journal*, p. 474.
12. *In Re Guden*, 171, N.Y. 529 (1902).
13. James Madison, Alexander Hamilton, and John Jay, *The Federalist Papers*, ed. Isaac Kramnick (New York: Penguin Books edition, 1987), Numbers 62–66.

14. *Journal*, p. 215.
15. This proposal was discussed at the 1867 convention; see p. 123 above. The amendment overruled *People v. Bowen* 21 N.Y., 517 (1860).
16. *People ex rel. Everson v. Lorillard*, 135 N.Y., 285 (1892).
17. As quoted in the *Poletti Reports* (1938), VII, *Problems Relating to Legislative Organization and Powers*, p. 76.
18. *Proceedings . . . Constitutional Convention, 1867*, II, pp. 1379–1381; III, pp. 2102–2128; IV, pp. 2777–2785; V, pp. 3603–3609, 3683–3685.
19. *Messages and Addresses of the Governors*, VI, p. 399.
20. Galie, *The New York State Constitution*, p. 91.
21. *Laws of New York*, Chap. 420 (1847); Chap. 603 (1853).
22. Temporary Commission on the Revision and Simplification of the Constitution, *Constitutional Debt Limits for Local Governments*, Staff Report No. 32 (Albany, 1960), pp. 10–11.
23. Temporary Commission . . . , *Constitutional Tax Rate Limits*, Staff Report No. 31 (Albany, 1959), p. 12.
24. *Journal*, Appendix I, pp. 5–63.
25. Ibid., Appendix I, p. 5.
26. 1867 Convention, *Documents*, V, No. 185.
27. *Poletti Reports* (1938), VII: *Legislative Organization and Powers*, p. 538.
28. *Laws of New York*, Chap. 213 (1869).
29. *Journal*, pp. 429–430.
30. *Poletti Reports* (1938), VII: *Legislative Organization and Powers*, p. 542.
31. *Journal*, p. 429.
32. Dougherty, *Constitutional History*, p. 239. The existence of the extensive statutory provisions of the Banking law, General Corporation Law, Stock Corporation Law, and the General Associations Law, coupled with the view that the material was not appropriate for constitutional stature, led the Inter-Law School Committee (The Problem of *Simplification of the Constitution* Leg. Doc. (1958) No. 57, Chapt. 10); and the Temporary State Commission on the Revision and Simplification of the State Constitution, (Staff Report No. 23, *Private Business Enterprise* (1959), p. 30), to recommend that sections 1–4 of the current article be removed.
33. See the discussion on this point in the 1867 convention, p. 126 above.
34. "Veto Message to the Legislature," April 14, 1886, *Messages From the Governors*, VIII, p. 212. The Constitutions of 1777, 1821, and 1846 all contained provisions which bore on the issue of home rule, though none provided home rule in the sense in which that term was used by its proponents in the last quarter of the nineteenth century. The meaning of home rule depends on the context in which it is used. Broadly conceived, it refers to the ability of local government to perform functions and activities traditionally undertaken by these governments without undue interference by the state. Home rule powers refer to the constitutional and statutory powers to enact local legislation and carry out the duties and responsibilities of the local government. See *Local Government Handbook*, 4th ed. (Albany: State of New York Secretary of State, 1987), pp. 53–58. The 1777 Constitution (Art. XXXVI) expressly validated and continued the charters of bodies politic granted by the King of England and confirmed the central appointment of mayors of the cities, with the legislature specifically authorized to alter that system.

35. Temporary State Commission on the Constitutional Convention, *Local Government*, Report No. 13 (Albany, 1967), p. 69.
36. Martin J. Schiesl, *The Politics of Efficiency: Municipal Administration and Reform in America: 1880–1920* (Berkeley: University of California Press, 1977), pp. 6–24.
37. *Messages From the Governors*, VII, p. 844.
38. Ibid., VII, p. 30.
39. *Report of the Commission*, pp. 9–16. Assembly Doc. No. 68 (1877).
40. Francis Bergan, *The History of the New York Court of Appeals, 1847–1932* (New York: Columbia University Press, 1985), p. 119.
41. In the interim, the legislature appointed a constitutional commission on the judiciary to address the deeper problems causing the delays.
42. Bergan, *The History of the New York Court of Appeals*, p. 133.
43. The Tweed Ring undoubtedly made these projects costlier than they might otherwise have been. Teaford, *Unheralded Triumph*, p. 285.
44. *Messages From the Governors*, VII, p. 298.
45. *Constitutional Tax Rate Limits*, Staff Report No. 31, p. 19.
46. Ibid., Staff Report No. 31, p. 19.
47. *Constitutional Debt Limits*, Staff Report No. 32, p. 23–24.
48. *Constitutional Tax Rate Limits*, Staff Report No. 31, p. 39.
49. *Laws of New York*, Chap. 189 (1890).
50. Bergan, *The History of the New York Court of Appeals*, p. 136.
51. Ibid., p. 139.
52. William Hornblower, "Appellate Courts," *Columbia Law Times* V (March, 1892), p. 155.
53. This understanding is laid out more fully in Hornblower, "Appellate Courts," pp. 151–159. See also J. Hampden Dougherty, *Constitutional History of the State of New York*, pp. 326–327.
54. *Messages From the Governors*, VI. p. 393.
55. More information on the history of these commissions in a comparative context is presented by Robert Williams, "The Role of the Constitutional Commission in State Constitutional Change," Temporary State Commission on constitutional Revision, Gerald Benjamin, ed., *The New York State Constitution: A Briefing Book* (Albany: Nelson A. Rockefeller Insitute of Government, 1994), pp. 73–79. These developments will be chronicled in subsequent chapters.

Constitutional Changes
1847–1894

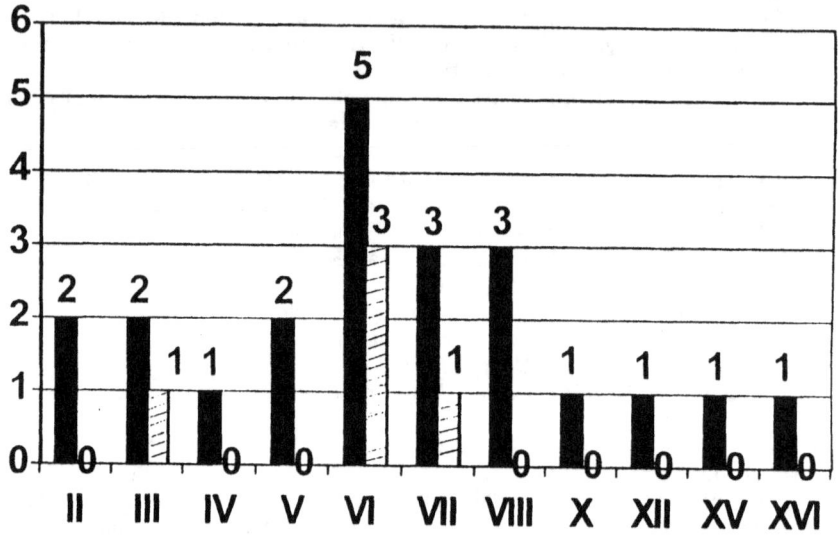

Article Number

Approved (22)   Rejected (5)

*Some proposed amendments affected more than one article.

9

On the Threshold of the Twentieth Century: The Constitution of 1894

BETWEEN 1846 and 1894, the Empire State's pre-eminence grew at a rapid pace. The nation's leader in commercial and financial activity had within its borders the largest city in the country. These signs of progress were accompanied by a host of problems, most of which can be categorized under three headings: canals, corruption, and cities. In addition, the judiciary—which had been the object of numerous amendments, a constitutional convention in 1867, a constitutional commission in 1872, and a judiciary commission in 1890—remained in need of reorganization.

In accordance with the every-twenty-year requirement clause of the 1846 Constitution, the question of whether the voters wished to call a convention to revise and amend the constitution was placed on the ballot in 1886. The voters approved the proposal for a second time, in this instance by an overwhelming majority of 574,993 to 30,766. Despite this unambiguous mandate for constitutional revision, a convention was not convened until 1894.

The eight-year delay in convening a constitutional convention can be explained by examining the partisan divisions within New York State's government during these years. Democratic Governor David B. Hill disagreed with the Republican-dominated legislature over the procedure for selecting convention delegates. Hill proposed election of delegates from the state's congressional districts, which had been redistricted by the Democrats in 1883, while Republicans proposed delegate election from assembly districts, which had been redistricted by the Republicans in 1879.[1]

The deadlock was broken in 1892, when the Democrats gained control of both the executive and legislative branches of the government. Parties had monopolized the delegate selection process since 1821. In his annual message to the legislature in 1887 Governor Hill suggested an alternative to the party responsibility theory and the non-partisan approach to the selection of delegates. Anticipating aspects of contemporary pluralist and interest group theories of democracy, he suggested that

> so far as is possible, the various interests in the state should be represented in the convention, which should include not only the adherents of the two principal parties, but the prominent representatives of the prohibition, license, woman suffrage, labor reform, and anti-monopoly sentiment as well as those identified with any other special interests of importance, desiring changes in the organic law of the state, thereby rendering it emphatically the people's convention as contemplated by the constitution.[2]

Doubts were expressed as to the constitutionality of appointed delegates, and the act was replaced with one making no provision for direct representation of interests.[3] The issue of minority representation raised by the governor is of significance not only because it provides a picture of those minorities deemed important enough to deserve formal recognition, but also because it suggests that parties are at best imperfect representatives of all the important and legitimate interests in the polity.[4] The delegate selection process adopted was similar to the one employed in 1867, with five delegates (four in 1867) chosen from each senate district and fifteen at-large delegates. Confident of victory, they disregarded the governor's earlier plan to ensure minority representation for groups such as women, labor, and those favoring prohibition. Conversely, Republicans were so sure of defeat that they did not bother to nominate many party regulars who would otherwise have been candidates. Instead, their nominations included distinguished figures such as lawyers Joseph Choate and Elihu Root and an unusually large number of independent Republicans.[5] The Republicans secured 83 of the 160 district seats and all fifteen at-large delegates. The landslide was increased when the convention unseated six Democrats and the sole labor delegate, and replaced them with Republicans. Several deaths and a resignation reduced the final total to 171: 104 Republicans and 67 Democrats.[6] Lawyers constituted 80% of the delegates, with journalists a distant second. Joseph Choate was elected president of the convention.

In retrospect, two events explain this stunning reversal in the fortunes of the Democratic Party. The economic depression of 1893 was particularly severe in New York, causing heavy unemployment, especially among the urban poor.[7] Even more significant were the various scandals plaguing the Democratic Party. Exposés of Democratic corruption reported in newspapers and magazines, the increasing strength of the independents, and skillful Republican manipulation of the issues shaped the membership of the convention. Furthermore, the corruption issue provided the basis for the loose alliance between Republicans and independent reformers that was to dominate the work of the convention.

Republican dominance raised the real possibility of a partisan convention producing a partisan constitution. But Republicans were divided between rural traditionalists, fearful of the growing power of the cities with their swelling immigrant populations, and independent, reform-minded Republicans who believed that the party had to come to grips with developments that were changing the character of the state. Reformers were further divided between upstate and New York City delegates. These divisions foreshadowed the profound impact New York City would have on the decisions of the delegates at the 1894 convention, and would also prevent independent-progressive Republicans from attaining most of their more forward-looking proposals.[8] They had the additional result of producing a convention less partisan than it might otherwise have been. Republicans recognized the value of an alliance between party regulars and independent Republicans, and consciously cultivated that alliance.[9] The election of Joseph Choate, former president of the New York Bar Association and president of the Union League, reflected the strength of the independent Republicans. The felicitous coincidence of interests had reformers, regulars, and some Democrats uniting in support of a number of amendments, not always for the same reasons.[10]

THE WORK OF THE CONVENTION

Article I, Bill of Rights

The 1821 convention had adopted a formal Bill of Rights (Art. VII), but it included provisions that were not matters of rights, such as the prohibition against lotteries. The 1846 convention moved this article from VII to I and added a provision removing the suffrage from anyone convicted of bribery or any infamous crime. At present, Section IX of this article gathers together the right to assemble with rules governing divorce, lotteries, pool selling, and bingo. Three proposals were added to this article. The first of these concerned drainage of agricultural land—hardly a subject for a bill of rights.

Delegates approved an amendment which would allow the legislature, by general laws, to permit, under proper safeguards and with compensation, the construction of drains and ditches on the land of others when such drainage was deemed necessary to make the land productive. Legislative attempts to allow farmers to improve their land in this fashion were curtailed by court decisions which limited such actions to public health concerns.[11] Farmers pressed for this measure which would supercede these court decisions and enable them to "properly improve their land."[12] The use of eminent domain to improve property when such improvement was perceived as a means to economic prosperity was not unusual in the nineteenth century, as its use by the railroads attests. This argument was made explicitly at the convention.[13]

A second change, prohibition against gambling, appeared in the 1821 Constitution's ban on lotteries. The policy of restricting gambling activities, however, predates the state's existence, going back to 1720.[14] The Constitution of 1846 continued this prohibition. The convention in 1894 added the phrase "pool-selling, bookmaking or any other kind of gambling" and directed the legislature to pass appropriate laws to prevent offenses against any of these provisions (Art. I, Sec. 9). The additions were a reaction to passage of the Ives Pool Hall Law1,[15] which permitted racing and pool-selling from May to October of each year. This act and the lax attitude of the legislature toward gambling aroused the ire of numerous delegates at the convention. Republican delegate-at-large Edward Lauterbach summarized the sentiments of many when he stated that it was time to consider the subject "in the light of ethics, morality and propriety, so that the State itself, awakening to a consciousness of the iniquitous policy which itself has pursued, shall conduct itself decently, and not indecently."[16] The proposal passed overwhelmingly by a vote of 109 to 4. The anti-gambling amendment was consistent with the convention's overall goal of eliminating corruption and immorality in public life.

The convention apparently did not intend to eliminate all gambling, and the courts so held, permitting casual gambling.[17] As noted, the legislature did not share the anti-gambling sentiments of the delegates. Their first "appropriate law" was a statute reducing the offense from a crime to a civil offense.[18] Not content with this rebuke of the convention's mandate, it passed the Percy-Gray Law.[19] This statute, ostensibly aimed at enforcing the anti-gambling provision, had the effect of permitting licensed gambling at racetracks. Racetrack gambling was a felony everywhere except at the tracks themselves, where the only penalty was forfeiture of the amount waged or lost, which could be recovered in a civil action. This legislation appeared inconsistent with the spirit if not the letter of the constitution, but in *People ex rel. Sturgis v. Fallon* (1897) the Court of Appeals held that it was beyond judicial province to declare a statute in violation of the constitution because it was deemed by the court not sufficient to prevent such offenses. That duty was committed to the legislature, and measures in furtherance of that goal were at the discretion of the legislature.[20] A later case held that the constitutional provision was not self-executing and therefore required legislative action in order to make gambling a crime.[21] Eventually the legislature adopted an approach more in line with the provisions, and repealed the Percy-Gray law. The 1894 convention was the high-water mark of anti-gambling sentiment in New York State. Subsequent amendments would have the effect of relaxing the prohibition.

The final change to this article created a right to recovery in wrongful death cases. The amendment prevented the legislature from abrogating a right of action to recover damages for injuries resulting in death (Art. I, Sec. 8). This section was prompted by attempts of various groups, especially railroads, to limit recoverable damages for wrongful deaths. In response to this pressure, the legislature had placed a five-thousand-dollar limit on such damages.[22] A strong undercurrent of anti-railroad sentiment was evident at the convention. It was believed that railroads were exerting too much influence on the state legislature. As Steuben County delegate William Nichols commented, "There are some offenses against public morals, some abuses so flagrant, so hopeless of correction by the legislature of this state, that it becomes the duty of the sovereign convention to provide for them. . . ."[23]

SUFFRAGE AND THE ELECTORAL PROCESS

The convention adopted only one provision directly affecting the suffrage article. That amendment required full citizenship for ninety days before the right to vote could be exercised. The Committee on Suffrage, acting on allegations that Democrats were naturalizing immigrants in large numbers just before elections, had recommended a sixty-day waiting period. On the floor a motion was made to extend that period to six months. Moderate Republicans led by Elihu Root, along with Democratic support, were able to block this motion.[24]

The growing strength of the women's suffrage movement made it inevitable that this issue would be addressed at the convention. Indeed, a symposium of nineteen individuals who spoke on various aspects of the question was held before the convention at a special evening session. Lincoln reports that the convention received 600,000 petitions on behalf of women's suffrage. The Committee on Suffrage reported a women's suffrage amendment adversely, but a long and thoughtful debate took place on the floor.[25] In the end, the suffrage amendment was defeated by a vote of 58 to 98, a vote which compares favorably with the 9 to 133 vote at the 1867 convention. The vote shift reflected both the strength of the suffrage movement and the persuasive power of full debate and argument.

A literary test proposed by the committee was prompted by Republican concerns about the growing immigrant population, with its potential impact on traditional Republican values and the likelihood that the immigrants would become affiliated with the Democratic Party. Although defeated on the floor of the convention, the measure had gained support since its initial appearance at the 1867 convention, where it had died in committee, and continued to gain support, becoming part of the constitution in 1921.

The move to extend the suffrage to women in 1917 reflected the growing strength of the women's movement, just as the restriction on suffrage implied in the literary requirement reflected an anti–immigrant sentiment which would persist through the twenties.

A majority of delegates were in full sympathy with C. A. Fuller's position: "If politics are to be purified . . . it must be done by this constitutional convention. . . ."[26] The convention adopted a series of measures aimed at reforming and purifying the political process and reducing the role of political parties in the electoral process.

To "secure purity" and "absolute impartiality in the conduct of elections" the convention required all election boards to represent equally the two parties receiving the highest vote in the last state election.[27] In practice, that meant the Democratic and Republican parties. Town meetings and villages were exempted from the requirement (Art. II, Sec. 4), an exemption that provoked bitter responses from city delegates who labelled it a blatantly anti-city measure. A variety of defenses were offered in its behalf, some embarrassingly weak, including "antiquity." It was argued that without the exemption, partisanship would be injected into village elections where none had existed.[28] The provision constitutionalized the statutory policy of the state, thus giving constitutional recognition to political parties for the first time. Reformers were ambivalent about the measure. Some thought that curtailing electoral fraud was worth the price of constitutional recognition for parties, while others had their doubts. In either case, it was evident that bipartisanship was not synonymous with nonpartisanshp: granting the dominant parties a monopoly on the election boards meant excluding independents from various boards, ensuring that all the spoils would go to the two major parties.[29]

The measure which reformers considered most important was the separation of city elections from state and national elections (Art. XII, Sec. 3). Its rationale rested on the assumption that party affairs had less relevance to city affairs than to state or national affairs. There was no Democratic or Republican way of paving the streets. As one delegate put it: city administration involves only questions of "right and due administration." Like the bipartisan boards proposal, the requirement applied only to cities over 50,000 in population. The exemption for smaller cities, which generally held their elections in the spring in any case, was inserted to win support from delegates from the smaller municipalities.[31]

A third measure mandated personal voter registration in cities with populations exceeding 5,000. The exemption for rural areas angered city delegates, who viewed it as an attack on the political morality of city dwellers. No doubt convention delegates had New York City and that city's Tammany machine in mind when they approved this proposal. Supporters of the exemption argued that it was unfair to require farmers to travel long distances to register, and that rural voters were so well known to one another that fraud was all but impossible. One Democratic delegate replied: "there is more corruption to the square inch in the country than was ever heard of in the city," which suggests the animosity these exemptions engendered in city delegates.[32]

The use of the recently introduced voting machines raised a number of technical problems as well as the question as to whether their use would be "voting by ballot" as required by the 1846 Constitution. The adopted provision explicitly provided for secrecy of the ballot and allowed the use of the voting machine (Art. II, Sec. 5). Since secret voting by ballot or machine required the elector to read the ballot, it has been suggested that the amendment constituted a de facto literacy test.[33]

In line with the convention's determination to purify the political process, an amendment forbidding a public official from accepting free transportation passes "for himself or any member of his family" over the line of any common carrier was adopted. The specific problems seemed an unlikely prospect for constitutional status, but delegates believed that the legislators were unlikely to adopt such a prohibition.[34] Both the corporation official offering the bribe and the public official accepting were deemed guilty of a misdemeanor. Additionally, the public official would be required to relinquish his office. Like the 1874 bribery amendment, corporation employees agreeing to testify would be offered immunity. Delegates believed that the public official was the more serious offender for accepting the bribe and that the officials who accepted such passes were primarily responsible for the corruption created by such offers.[35]

In another attempt to decrease partisan influence and to improve government service, delegates added a provision calling for a standard of "merit and fitness" to determine appointments in state and local government, and the use of competitive examinations "insofar as practical" (Art. V, Sec. 8). Attempts at civil service reform were not unprecedented. Legislation aimed at such reform was passed in 1883, 1884, and 1893.[36] An investigation in the early part of 1894 revealed the weaknesses of the civil service system.[37] The need to constitutionalize and invigorate these legislative efforts rested on delegate's perceptions that the legislature would persist in carving out exemptions for various positions and even entire divisions or departments from the examination requirements. The proposed amendment provided an avenue for evasion by the inclusion of an "as far as practical" phrase in the amendment. Allowing the actual implementation to the legislature ensured that little that was unacceptable to party regulars would be adopted. Finally, the preferences given to Civil War veterans, however laudable, was an obvious deviation from the merit principle.

The reception of this amendment was anything but cordial. Governor Frank S. Black, in his first address to the legislature, asserted that "civil service would work better with less starch" and recommended what he called a plan with more "common sense."[38] The legislature adopted his recommendation in 1897 with the passage of the Black Civil Service Law.[39] The legislation allowed choice from all eligible candidates on the list rather than confining the selection to those highest on the list. The Black Law was repealed in 1899 with the passage of the White Law, so named for its sponsor, Senator White. The provisions of this law, as amended, constituted the basis for civil service classification in the state until the major recodification and revisions undertaken in 1958.[40]

THE LEGISLATURE

The most controversial action taken at the convention was the revision of the apportionment plan. Prior to the 1894 convention the only other constitution to apportion the assembly was the first constitution of 1777. All other apportionments were accomplished by the legislature. The 1777 Constitution provided for an assembly of seventy members chosen annually by counties "justly apportioned to the number of electors in said counties" (Art. V). The legislature was to make adjustments as necessary every seven years. The introduction of new counties afforded an opportunity to deviate from a strict adherence to mathematical equality.[41] The convention of 1801 regulated the number in the assembly at 100 and allowed for two additional members every year, to a maximum of 150. The legislature was required to apportion members among counties "as nearly as may be, according to the number of electors found in each county by the census directed to be taken in the present year." The 1821 Constitution set the number of assemblymen at 128, to be elected annually. That number remained fixed until 1894. The 1821 Constitution specifically provided that every county "shall be entitled to one member" (Art. I, Sec. 7), a provision that all but guaranteed malapportionment of the assembly. The 1846 Constitution made single-member districts mandatory, but the division of counties into assembly districts was placed with boards of supervisors, not the legislators (Art. II, Sec. 5). The only other change affecting the apportionment of the assembly was the change of the population base used for purposes of apportioning representation. The 1821 Constitution changed the base from electors (voters) to "inhabitants excluding aliens, paupers, and persons of colour, not taxed" (Art. I, Sec. 7), and the 1846 Constitution removed the class of paupers from the exclusions. An 1874 amendment broadened the population bases by eliminating persons of color not taxed, leaving "inhabitants, excluding aliens."

The Senate

The 1777 Constitution provided for twenty-four senators apportioned among "four great districts" of two or more counties, with senators "justly apportioned to the number of senatorial electors in the districts" (Art. XII). Provision was made for a census, increases in size, and reapportionment every seven years "subsequent to the termination of the present war." The convention of 1801 fixed the senate size at thirty-two, where it remained until 1894. These senators were to be apportioned "as nearly as may be, according to the number of electors qualified to vote for senators." In 1821 the state was divided into eight districts. The 1846 Constitution extended the recognition given localities by increasing the number of districts to thirty-two, to be apportioned "as nearly as may be of an equal number of inhabitants, excluding aliens and person of colour not taxed, and consisting of convenient and contiguous territory . . ." (Art. III, Sec. 3). Each district was the constituency of a single senator. Notwithstanding this recognition of localities, it should be noted that the county was never recognized as a political unit or community entitled to separate representation in the senate until the Constitution of 1894.

Over the years New York City multiplied in size, and as the senate was fixed at thirty-two members, any additions for the city meant losses for the rural areas. The 1846 Constitution limited the legislative power to apportioning those counties that received two or more senators, a limitation most likely aimed at removing the temptation to gerrymander district lines.[42] The counties surrounding and including New York City were allowed fifteen of the thirty-two senators in 1892. The continued disproportionate increases in New York and Kings Counties, which would merge with Queens and Richmond Counties into Greater New York in 1897, provided all the motivation needed by Republicans, especially rural Republicans, to make apportionment a central issue at the 1894 convention.

Senate districts remained equitably apportioned between 1821 and 1846. The 1846 Constitution authorized the senate to apportion senators to counties entitled to more than one senator and gave it the power to divide these counties into single-member districts (Art. III, Sec. 4). Both of these decisions resulted in population differences among senate districts, but these differences were the results of redistricting limitations imposed by the constitution. The deviations were the consequence of the rule found in Article II, Section 4, prohibiting the division of any county, unless such county was "equitably entitled to two or more senators." This rule compelled the legislature to create districts unequal in population. The percentage variations between the smallest and largest districts ranged from 58% in 1879 to 42% in 1892.[43]

The 1872 Commission recommended removing "persons of colour not taxed" to make that section consistent with the proposed 1874 amendment which would eliminate the property qualification as a condition of African-American suffrage. The legislature approved the change for the assembly provision, but rejected the revision for the senate, leaving the population base for apportioning the senators reading: "inhabitants excluding aliens and persons of colour not taxed . . . ." The census of 1875 and 1892, however, did not exclude them. The Court of Appeals in *People ex rel. Carter v. Rice* sustained this inclusion, holding that since the same ratio existed between white and untaxed African-Americans, no injury was shown and the inclusion was immaterial.[44]

The express objectives of the majority of the Committee on Legislative Organization and Apportionment of the Convention of 1894 was to "remedy the gross inequalities and injustice of the Apportionment Act of 1892.[45] Nowhere, however, was partisanship more in evidence than on the question of apportionment.

The new apportionment increased the number of senators to fifty, an addition of eighteen from the 1846 Constitution. In so doing the convention accomplished one of its major goals: to restore rural areas to the representation they held under the 1846 Constitution.[46] In theory, each senator would represent 2% of the population (Art. III, Sec. 4). Counties would be awarded one senator for each 2% of the population they contained. However, this general principle was modified in a number of ways. Counties allocated four or more senators were required to have a full ratio (2%) for additional senators; no county could have more than one-third of all senators; and "no two counties or the territory thereof as now organized which are adjoined counties, and which are separated by public waters shall have more than half of all senators" (Sec. 4). The first modification has worked to the detriment of Erie County and the counties of New York City; the other two restrictions have had no effect as the conditions that would trigger them have never been met. These rules assured that New York City could never control the senate.

The convention increased assembly size from 128 to 150 and divided the sixty counties of the state into three groups: those with one assemblyman (every county with the exception of Hamilton, which was grouped with Fulton, was guaranteed at least one assemblyman); those with two assemblymen; and the ten largest counties with more than two (Art. III, Sec. 5). Most of the middle group did not contain sufficient population to justify two assemblymen. The decision to represent acres, not people, was roundly criticized by Democrats, but to no avail.[47]

The Legislative Process

The convention resolved the question of whether the senate could elect a temporary president regardless of the ability of the lieutenant-governor to perform the duties of president of the senate. The adopted amendment provided the senate that power. Henceforth the senate would have two presidents or presiding officers: the lieutenant-governor, elected by the people, and a temporary president elected by the senate from among its members (Art. III, Sec. 10).

Every convention since 1821 had passed amendments aimed at making the legislative process more open and effective. The delegates in 1894 approved two provisions with this goal in mind. The first would require that all bills be presented to the legislature at least three days prior to final passage (Art. III, Sec. 15). Delegates hoped this would open the process to all members of the legislature and prevent bills from being rushed through unread and undigested. Also adopted was a prohibition against riders to appropriation bills (Art. III, Sec. 22). The convention documented the use of riders that would never have been enacted on their own merit.[48] Frequently, these items were not indexed and could not be located within the bills without a careful reading of the entire bill. Since the governor's item veto power was restricted to items of appropriation of money, and since these riders were not part of a provision for a specific item, the governor was forced to accept the rider or veto the entire appropriation bill.

The Executive

The convention made only two changes of any consequence in the executive article. Having separated municipal elections from state and national elections, it was necessary to alter the governor's term. The existing three-year term meant elections would be held in odd-numbered years, thus periodically coinciding with municipal elections. The choice was between a two-year and a four-year term. In selecting the two-year term the convention retreated from the movement, evident since the Civil War, to enhance the powers of the executive (Art. IV, Sec. 1). On the other hand, state officials were to be elected at the same time as the governor and for the same term, thus strengthening the governor's ability to administer the executive branch.

The second change involved gubernatorial succession. In case the president of the senate, when called upon for some reason to act as governor, was incapable of so acting, the office was to devolve upon the speaker of the assembly (Art. IV, Sec. 7).

The Judiciary

Attempts to cope with the increasing volume of cases coming to the Court of Appeals had been made by the convention of 1867. The creation of a second division of that court to decide a portion of these cases solved the immediate problem, but did not address the root causes. The Judiciary Commission of 1890 recommended restructuring the appellate division and limiting the jurisdiction of the high court to certain well-defined cases. The legislature received these proposals coolly, but the delegates embraced them. Four appellate divisions of the Supreme Court were established, creating the intermediate appellate court system that remains essentially unchanged to this day. Thirty judges were added to the Supreme Court for the purpose of reducing delays in bringing cases to trial. Rejecting both the second division approach and the approach favored by the legislature of enlarging the Court of Appeals, the delegates limited the jurisdiction of the Court of Appeals to review of questions of law, except in capital cases, and added that except for such cases, appeals could be brought as a matter of right only from final determinations of the appellate division. The appellate division was authorized to allow interlocutory appeals on questions of law that it believed the Court of Appeals ought to review (Art. VI, Sec. 7). The new article also authorized the legislature to further restrict that court's jurisdiction if deemed necessary, as it did in 1898, 1899, and 1900. Nevertheless, the problem of calendar delay persisted. By the start of the 1915 convention the Court of Appeals was 600 cases in arrears.[49] Further constitutional relief would have to wait until the convening of the Judiciary Convention in 1921.

POLICY ISSUES

Education

An article (Art. XI) on education was added by the convention of 1894. It contained three sections. The first directed the legislature to provide for the maintenance and support of free common schools for all the children of the state, the second section constitutionalized the Board of Regents, and the third prohibited the use of public property or money in aid of denominational schools.

Section 1 not only recognized what had been state policy for some time, but also conferred on education the status of a fundamental constitutional value. Although it gave great impetus to state support for education in New York, this section has not been interpreted to require the state to equalize expenditures among the school districts of the state.[50] It covers handicapped, delinquent, neglected, and dependent children, but it does not impose upon the state a duty to see that each pupil receives a minimum level of education; rather, the state is required to provide minimal acceptable services, in contrast to unsystematized delivery of instruction.[51]

With the adoption of Section 2, New York established the first state system of education in the country. Two authorities were established: a Board of Regents of the University, having jurisdiction over higher education, and the Superintendent of Common Schools (public schools), heading a department of the same name. This section provided partial constitutional status to the Board of Regents, insulating it from capricious legislative action and partisan politics.[52] This section did not unify higher and elementary education in New York. That step was taken by the legislature in 1904 when the Department of Public Instruction was consolidated with the University, unifying control of higher and elementary education in the state. In 1925 constitutional status was given to this arrangement by an amendment to Article V, Section 4, providing that the Regents shall be the head of the Department of Education with the power to "appoint and at pleasure remove the Commissioner of Education to be the chief administrative officer of the department." By these actions all the educational work in the state was put under the legislative direction of the Board of Regents and the executive direction of the Commissioner of Education.

The last section, forbidding aid to sectarian educational institutions, gave rise to lengthy and divisive debate. Prior to this amendment it was not uncommon for religious and secular instruction to be combined in public schools. After a thorough review of education in the state, Charles Lincoln concluded that in the "first half of our state history there seemed to be no objection to combining religious and secular instruction in public schools."[53] This provision, popularly known as the "Blaine Amendment" after Senator James Blaine, who proposed a similar amendment to the national Constitution, was precipitated by a proposal in the 1893 legislature to provide Catholics with a pro-rata share of state school aid. The lines were drawn, and there is little doubt that they were drawn on religious grounds. Two committees addressed the issue: the Committee on Education and the Committee on Charities. A complete ban on aid proved more difficult to achieve than proponents had expected. Testimony from various religious groups presented before the Charities Committee regarding the extent of their support for charitable institutions, along with the impact of withdrawing such aid, including the additional financial burden placed on the state, had delegates seeking a compromise. Realizing there was no possibility of obtaining aid for parochial schools, Catholic delegates conceded that point and focused on retaining the aid to charitable institutions under their jurisdiction.[54] A compromise was achieved by the leadership, whereby aid to sectarian educational institutions, except for "examinations and inspections," would be prohibited, and aid to charitable institutions would continue. When this accommodation was threatened by supporters of a complete ban, President Choate and floor leader Elihu Root successfully invoked party discipline and the compromise was adopted.[55]

The force of the language in the amendment suggests a prohibition more stringent than that required by the Establishment Clause of the First Amendment, and, in fact, the immediate result of this amendment was to shut down a number of cooperative arrangements between parochial and public schools. However, the pressure for various forms of aid did not cease with passage of this amendment. What did disappear was the consensus that had fostered the provision. In the face of its stringent prohibition, the New York State legislature and the Court of Appeals have permitted a more accommodating approach to the aid question. The subsequent history of this provision provides vivid evidence of how a changing political consensus can affect the understanding and interpretation of a constitutional provision.[56]

Canals

A perennial topic since the 1821 Constitution and one of the major policy issues of the nineteenth century, the New York canal system, by 1894, no longer possessed the economic or constitutional importance it had once enjoyed. Nevertheless, significant divisions remained between those who believed constitutional action on canals was unnecessary and those who desired specific directives for further canal development. The result was a provision stating that canals shall be improved in ways the legislature shall deem appropriate. As the legislature unquestionably already possessed this power, this amendment is best seen as giving symbolic reassurance to supporters of canal development by placing in the constitution a directive indicating the state's continuing commitment to canal development (Art. VII, Sec. 10).

Conservation

Unlike canal policy, conservation policy was new to convention deliberations in New York. As with many other constitutional provisions, this amendment had its origins in legislation.[57] Concern over the destruction of the state's forests, and the consequences of that destruction for the health and well-being of the state, led to the adoption of a provision setting aside the Adirondack and Catskill Forest Preserves, to be kept "forever wild" forest land (Art. VII, Sec. 7). The provision, adopted without a single dissenting vote, was a laudable attempt to ensure that the state's great natural resources would not be sold off to commercial developers or otherwise dissipated. The very stringency of its language, however, has frequently interfered with legitimate and important uses of the land, such as scientific forestry. Not surprisingly, this provision has been amended fifteen times to accommodate other uses.

The convention created a State Board of Prisons, a Commission on Lunacy, and a State Board of Charities (Art. VIII, Sec. 11). These agencies were responsible for the supervision and inspection of their respective clienteles. Constitutionalizing these agencies, however, added no new functions that were not previously being performed, beyond centralizing administrative control; rather, they reflected a judgment by the convention as to the permanency of the state's obligation.

Home Rule

The question of home rule, the extent to which municipalities are free to decide their own affairs without legislative interference, had been the subject of extensive discussion at the 1867 convention, the Constitutional Commission of 1872, and the Tilden Commission on the Cities in 1875, all with no constitutional result. The first constitutional home rule provisions in the nation were produced during the depression-stricken 1870s.

The state legislature retained ultimate authority to bestow or deny any municipal power and to determine municipal structure.[58] Generally, these decisions were a response to the judgment of the local delegation. For the most part, "state assemblies and senates rubber stamped hundreds of local bills."[59] The major exception to this deference occurred when a bill became a partisan issue. Nowhere in the state did this exception apply with greater force than in New York City. Repeated state interference in that city's affairs reflected the overlapping of party and geographic lines, with upstate New York predominantly Republican or anti-Tammany Democratic and New York City the citadel of the Tammany machine. These partisan and factional rifts reduced the deference generally accorded a city's request.[60] In 1891 a special committee of the senate investigating municipal problems listed first among the difficulties the "too frequent yielding on the part of the legislature to the importunities of representatives of the various cities for the passage of local bills."[61] In addition to the partisan rift, confusion existed regarding which functions were local in nature and which were performed by the locality for the state.

The origins of the movement for home rule are thus inextricably bound up in this ambivalent relationship of city to state. The earliest home rule provision in the country, adopted in the 1870s at least in part in response to the depression of that decade, did not emphasize liberating the city from state control. The goal was to "block ceaseless costly change . . . [and] halt the constant amendments granted by indulgent politicians in the local delegations."[62] The goal was to diminish the power of local lobbyists serving special city interests, and to limit what was considered irresponsible use of state lawmaking power. In New York the amendment of 1874 placing limitations on special and local legislation reflected this objective, as did the recommendations of the Commission of 1872 requiring a general law for the creation of cities, a provision its supporters hoped would relieve the legislature from the swarm of local bills which consumed so much legislative time. The initial target of home rule supporters was excessive lawmaking, whether by state or local governments. By the close of the nineteenth century that concern had shifted from a focus on the excess of lawmaking to a suspicion of state lawmakers.[63] In the 1890s the situation was complicated by the simultaneous rise of a trend toward state administrative supervision of city governments. The increasing need for professional expertise meant that in areas such as water supply, sewerage, finance, and education, "state administrators were assuming for the first time coercive authority over urban governments."[64] Trained professionals repeatedly called for coercive action by the state, particularly in the area of health, and the legislature responded.[65] Supervision in other areas soon followed, including education and urban finance.

In the context of these divergent trends—home rule and administrative centralization, the political and geographical rift between upstate New York and New York City, and the confusion as to which functions were local and which were performed by localities for the state—the 1894 convention addressed the question of the state's cities.

On issues such as electoral reform, independents and Republican regulars found common ground. On the question of home rule, independents made common cause with nonpartisan groups like the City Club of New York, the Alliance of Citizen's Associations, and a coalition of good-government groups called the Committee of Twenty-One. The recommendations of the Committee of Twenty-One were submitted to the Committee on Cities. That committee, though mildly predisposed to home rule, greeted these proposals with scepticism; one delegate, Tracy Becker (R.-Buffalo), referred to club members as "theoretic gentlemen."[66] Nonetheless, the committee did recommend adoption of some moderate home rule powers for the cities. Even these moderate proposals did not survive the withering attack made on them by rural Republicans and Democrats, who considered the proposals a sham. Caught in this cross-fire, urban moderate Republicans were unable to sustain a coherent alliance, and most of the committee proposal was gutted on the convention floor. The convention did approve two constitutional innovations concerning home rule. One provided for a "suspensory" local "veto." "Laws relating to the property affairs or government of cities" were divided into general and special city laws. General city laws were defined as those which related to all cities in one or more of the three classes of cities, according to the level of population. First class included all cities of 250,000 population or more (only New York was in this class); the second, cities of 50,000 but less than 250,000; and the third class, all other cities (Art. XII, Sec. 2). Special laws were those which related to a single city or to a number of cities, but not to all those contained in their class. A bill for a special law had to be submitted to the mayor of the city, who then had fifteen days to certify whether or not the city accepted the law. Upon acceptance the bill was then submitted to the governor for action; if rejected, the legislature could override the governor's veto by a majority vote. This suspensory veto did not apply to any general laws passed by the legislature.

Both measures had as their purpose reducing interference in city affairs by special legislation, and they had their intended effect. Between 1902 and 1914 there were 524 instances in which the legislature, by failing to re-enact statutes, allowed city vetoes to stand.[67] The suspensive veto provision was unquestionably beneficial to New York City. It gave a measure of freedom from proactive legislatures, but almost no opportunity for positive local action. Home rule in that sense would have to wait until the Home Rule Amendment of 1923. The classification of the cities into three population categories was intended to ensure that legislative action would be by general law, and yet sufficiently tailored to meet the needs of cities whose problems were likely to be similar by virtue of their similar sizes. It was also believed that legislation passed by general law was less likely to be intrusive and arbitrary than special laws.

Such was the extent of municipal home rule. Though viewed by many as woefully inadequate—Democrats thought it "composed of stale wind and foul water"—it was the first time a measure of home rule was explicitly granted constitutional status.[68]

The ambivalence of Republican moderates on the issue of home rule hindered their ability to form a coherent plan. Seeking a measure of autonomy for cities, they stopped short of genuine home rule, which, in Manhattan, would likely have meant Tammany rule. Accepting final control in Albany, however, meant that the modernization of municipalities favored by Republican moderates would not materialize.[69]

Local Finance

The convention did little concerning the regulation of municipal finance. The Panic of 1893 and the depression which followed was essentially a business depression. Cities had by then refinanced their debt at much lower interest rates, and their conservative fiscal policies had shielded them from the effects of the economic downturn. Cities like New York and Buffalo were able to issue municipal bonds at favorable interest rates and embark on permanent improvements in their services and aesthetics.[70]

Given this remarkable turnaround, in less than twenty years, in the financial picture of the cities, what is remarkable is not the fact that the convention took little action concerning municipal finance, but that so much discontent surfaced at the convention concerning the conditions of the cities. The answer resides in "the politics of purity" which permeated the convention debates. Graft and corruption may have had little impact on the bond markets, but it was grist for countless Sunday sermons. Cities had achieved a degree of financial stability and the capacity to provide a full range of service functions, but they did so by a process that offended many. The venality and corruption that were an inevitable concomitant to operating a fragmented governmental structure in a pluralistic democratic environment were unacceptable to reform groups, social elites, Protestant ministers, and the growing body of professionals. The messy mainstays of urban politics—bargaining, compromise, and accommodation—were a response to the fact that no one group ruled the city unchallenged, not the social elite, the Plunkitts of Tammany Hall, the new administrative experts, or the reformers. For all their flaws, "American city governments did work." The political system that effected these results seemed far from the "unsullied, republican virtues glorified in the school books of nineteenth century America and hardly accorded with the high moral standards preached from the Protestant pulpits on Sundays."[71] A generation of New Yorkers, bred on those texts and imbued with the message of those sermons, came together at the 1894 convention to reaffirm that vision.

The Militia

The convention made extensive changes in the militia article and did so with little controversy. The article was in need of revision, having remained essentially unchanged since the 1821 Constitution. The unratified constitution of 1867 contained significant changes, including a division of the militia into an active (national guard) and a reserve force, conscientious objection status on other than religious grounds, and a definition of who constituted the militia (Art. XXI, Sec. 1). No definition of the militia had appeared in the 1821 or 1846 Constitutions. The convention adopted the definition found in federal law: all able-bodied men between eighteen and forty-five who were citizens and residents of the state, subject to such regulations and exemptions as may be made by the federal government or the state legislature. This clause indicated the extent to which the militia article is dependent on federal requirements.

Section 2 authorized the legislature to allow aliens and non-residents to volunteer in the active forces. The conscientious objection clause was eliminated on the grounds that the exemption had been incorporated into federal and state law.[72]

Section 3 divided the militia into an active (national guard) and a reserve force. This clause was the first to recognize a naval branch of the militia. It was inserted because there was some doubt as to whether the legislature had the constitutional authority to maintain a naval militia. A minimum of 10,000 men, armed, equipped, disciplined, and ready for active service, were to be maintained. The legislature was required to provide sufficient appropriation for this force. The specifications of a minimum size left some discretion to the legislature, but ensured that the legislature could not eliminate or reduce to insignificance the national guard of the state.

Sections 4, 5, and 6 dealt with election and removal of militia officers. They prescribed which officers the governor was to appoint, viz., chiefs of staff, with all other officers chosen as the legislature shall provide. This change eliminated the detailed specifications of officer selection found in previous constitutions, as well as the requirement that officers be elected by those under their command. In *People v. Molyneux* the Court of Appeals held that senate consent was required in the appointment of major-generals.[73] The governor as commander-in-chief was to commission all officers. This provision was the last surviving clause of the 1777 Constitution. Removal of officers took place by senate action on recommendation of the governor, sentence of court martial, finding of an examining board, or absence without leave for more than six months. The new militia article was implemented in 1898 with the adoption of a military code.[74]

Other Issues

All amendments proposed by labor or socialist groups were rejected, with the exception of an amendment prohibiting the competition of free prison labor. The state had long used the contract labor system. Attempts were made to restrict this system in the 1880s, and strong support existed for its abolition when the convention met. The amendment accomplished three objectives: it provided employment for convicts within the prison, prohibited the sale of products from convict labor on the open market, and required the state and its political subdivisions to purchase the products of inmates. The section combines punishment and reformation of the offender with reimbursement to the taxpayer for the expenses of prosecuting and incarcerating the criminal, while removing what delegates saw as a legitimate grievance of labor.

The growing strength of the prohibition movement was manifest at the convention. A proposal forbidding the legislature to grant licenses to traffic in intoxicating liquors was reported favorably by the Committee on Legislative powers. That measure, however, was referred back to the committee and no further action was taken.

Amending the Constitution

The delay in holding the convention reduced to twelve years the time remaining before the every-twenty-year provision would place the question of a convention on the ballot. The convention decided to have the question next placed on the ballot in 1916 (Art. XIV, Sec. 2). The delegates intended, as far as possible, to make the process of selecting future delegates self-executing, eliminating the need for legislative action in the process. To accomplish this objective the convention delegates specified the date of the next convention and detailed the procedures to be followed in selecting convention delegates. Concern over the number of votes cast on amendments at the convention resulted in a provision requiring all amendments passed at future conventions to be by majority of the elected delegates rather than of those present and voting.

A final controversy involved a court challenge to the convention's decision to accept the credentials of some delegates and to reject those of others in districts where results were disputed. A suit was initiated by a rejected candidate who obtained a writ of prohibition from the Supreme Court restraining the convention from interfering with the delegate's right to his seat. The convention presented a report on this conflict between convention and judicial authority, which concluded that no judicial, legislative, or executive official possessed the authority to interfere with the exercise of power and the performance of the duties which the people have enjoined upon the convention. The committees voted to forward this report to the judge. The case was heard before a another Supreme Court judge who denied the application for the writ and vacated the proceedings already instituted.[75] To prevent the possibility of similar challenges in the future, delegates added a clause specifying the powers of the convention on these questions.

The convention addressed the possibility of coincident submission of amendments. Since Article XIX provides for two modes of amendment, one by the legislature and one by constitutional convention, the possibility existed that two amendments or revisions on the same subject could be submitted simultaneously. In that event the amendment submitted by the convention, if approved by the voters, would supercede the amendment proposed by the legislature. This choice is consistent with the view that the convention is a constituent body chosen for the specific task of amending the constitution and is by that fact closer to the sovereign will of the people than is the legislature.

The Political Theory of the 1894 Constitution

Though meeting in the midst of a severe depression, the constitutional convention adopted a constitution that left the role of the government in the economy essentially unchanged. The delegates seemed unaffected by the economic conditions and by the demands for social and economic reform. The general focus and concerns of the delegates were on governmental reorganization and a cleansing of the electoral process. Two-thirds of the approximately forty amendments offered involved the structure of government and the electoral process. Twenty-two of the twenty-five amendments eventually adopted concerned the government or the political process.[76] The delegates did engage in constitutional reform, enlarging participation while restricting legislative power, that is, securing liberty against authority. The actions and attitudes of the delegates reflected the general American distrust of governmental power. Given a choice between policies which promoted private enterprise and regulation of that enterprise, the delegates clearly preferred the former. They expected government assistance in their enterprises, but distrusted its actions and continually made attempts to reduce its authority.[77] Frustration with the social and economic dislocations as well as abuses of power associated with the rise of industrial capitalism had not yet reached the point where new political response was required.

The 1894 convention and the constitution it produced marks the apex of the movement to place restrictions on the exercise of governmental power, particularly the power of the legislature. This movement has generally been understood as part of a broader laissez-faire ideology which derived from Adam Smith, among others. The period between 1821 and 1894 is traditionally seen as one in which constitution-makers created a constitutional order that left the government in essentially a passive role, allowing maximum lattitude for individual enterprise while inconsistently providing support for this enterprise. That view appears to be one regularly expressed by delegates, legislators, and governors. Governor Roswell P. Flower's response to Samuel Gompers's plea for government assistance seems to epitomize this outlook:

> In America the people support the government; it is not the province of the government to support the people. Once recognize the principle that

the government must supply public work for the unemployed, and there will be no end of official paternalism.[78]

This understanding of New York State's constitutional and political tradition is not without difficulties. For one, it fails to explain what appears to be an inconsistent approach by the judiciary toward economic regulation: striking down regulations on substantive due-process grounds, but, more frequently, sustaining social and economic regulation.[79] Just as significant is the failure of this view to explain the character and purpose of the variety of restrictions imposed on legislative power by constitutional delegates throughout the century.

The ideology of Americans in the nineteenth century was not laissez-faire.[80] The extensive regulatory policies adopted under the police power and the significant public assistance to private enterprise are inconsistent with such an ideology. The combination of assistance and passivity is best seen—as Jame Willard Hurst and others have— as promoting greater release of individual and group energies.[81] The ideology was one rooted in a tradition which permitted regulation or assistance in the name of the public good or commonweal. Correspondingly, it was an ideology which prohibited the adoption of policies designed or seen as advancing the parochial interests of individuals or groups. The application of substantive due process, first by state and later by federal courts, was not a judicial creation out of whole cloth of a new doctrine; nor was it merely a tool used by pro-business judges to prevent the state from adequately dealing with social and economic problems. Recent scholarship has demonstrated that substantive due process was part of the English common law tradition and had as its chief functions providing a sword against private monopoly and a shield against monopoly granted by public (government) dispensation.[82]

In this light, the American political tradition concerning the exercise of governmental power is better expressed by saying that governmental power should not be used to benefit one group at the expense of another; government policy should promote equality before the law. This belief was reflected not only in state court decisions but also in the numerous provisions of the 1846 and 1894 Constitutions that aimed at preventing special or local legislation. Their purpose was not to prevent action in the public interest either in the form of regulation or assistance. They were directed, as the convention records amply demonstrate, toward ensuring governmental action in the general interest. The danger of special or private local legislation was that it engaged the exercise of governmental power to assist one group or class at the expense of another group or class. Only where the regulation or assistance was manifestly in the public interest was legislative action permissible.[83]

This ideology assumed that a commercial republic would not create the conditions for social dependency, which in turn could provide a basis for groups to justify special claims to assistance from the government, and that if such pockets of dependency did develop, the existence of the frontier would provide a safety valve, enabling them to become free and independent citizens once again.[84]

A careful examination of the Constitution of 1894 reveals precisely this intent. The legislature was not to be used to provide advantages to individuals, groups, or corporations. Pressure from all quarters, if measured by the sheer volume of special legislation approved, let alone introduced, was intense and irresistible.[85] Such pressures explain the persistent and oftimes cumbersome attempts of delegates to combat this evil.

With the advent of urban industrial America came the creation of a number of groups with no immediate prospects for pulling themselves up by the proverbial bootstraps, and with no safety valve. The legislature took unprecedented actions in response to their vulnerability and to an increasingly coercive market mechanism. The attempts by the judiciary, state and national, and by the constitution-makers at the conventions of 1846 and 1894, to sustain this eighteenth- and nineteenth-century understanding of constitutional government did not succeed. Their efforts could no longer bear the weight of a new social and economic order. The conditions of the free and independent citizen assumed by the American tradition no longer existed and were not likely to re-emerge without significant governmental intervention.

The ultimate failure of these attempts to sustain this understanding of the role of government in the face of an increasingly incompatible environment should not blind us to the real intent: to prevent government from becoming a vending machine for those in a position to make use of it. The problems of special or partial interest legislation did not vanish with the abandonment of the distinctions and devices favored by nineteenth-century constitution-makers. Twentieth-century New Yorkers, recognizing the need for limits on the exercise of governmental power, would explore and adopt other means to combat this problem.

Assessment

President Choate's judgment on the character of the convention's work can be substantiated. Of the approximately four hundred proposals submitted to the committees, thirty-three were adopted. The number of new sections was not significant, and the changes that were effected addressed problems that required immediate solutions. The overall approach of the convention was to discourage undue experimentation. The delegates devoted a large portion of their time and energy to electoral reform, in particular to what they viewed as the corrupting impact of urban machine politics. The boldest inititatives taken concerned the judiciary, apportionment, and electoral reform. The delegates made significant commitments to education, conservation, and the separation of church and state. They continued to place restrictions on legislative power: no fewer than thirteen new provisions removed subjects from the discretionary power of the legislature.

The philosophy of the 1894 convention, which may be summarized as "conserve where possible and change to preserve," is defined as much by what the convention did not do as by what it did. The delegates made no attempt to deal with the problems of the haphazard growth of government boards and agencies; there was no attempt to delineate an administrative theory which might have sustained proposals for executive reorganization and an executive budget.

The proposal for woman's suffrage was vigorously debated and received more votes than in the previous convention, but was defeated nonetheless. Proposals for anti-trust regulation, pensions for the elderly, a right to organize for labor, and the banning of child labor failed to advance beyond the committee. The philosophy of government identified with progressivism was not manifest at this convention, and it did not address in any way questions of economic reform, thus leaving the government's role in the economy unchanged. In the midst of a depression and with the growth of monopolies and corporate abuse, the convention adhered to the traditional understanding of constitutional reform. The middle-class professionals who constituted the overwhelming majority of delegates did not define reform to include economic issues. To the extent that they went beyond governmental reorganization and electoral reform, they did so to regulate public morality.

The apportionment rules adopted by the convention would be the rules governing the apportionment of the state legislature until federal courts found them in violation of the national Constitution in the mid-1960s. These rules consistently discriminated against urban areas and the Democratic Party. To the extent that they shaped the contours of party strength in the senate and assembly, they also shaped the public policy of the state in the first half of the twentieth century.

The so-called "Blaine Amendment," which required a more rigorous separation of church and state than that required by the national establishment clause, would be a latent explosive planted in the document. When the convention of 1967 recommended a constitution without that provision, the bomb would explode.

The 1894 convention manifested, to a degree greater than at any previous time in New York's history, the tension between urban and rural New York. This tension is most clearly evident in the arguments over apportionment, but it is also obvious in the suffrage amendments, the dual registration system for urban and rural areas, the separation of city from state and national elections, and the delegates' unwillingness to grant any significant home rule power to the cities. The vision of a rural republic, Protestant and Republican, and that of an urban democracy, ethnic and Democratic, provided the ideological and cultural context for many of the delegates at the convention.

The convention succeeded in providing some protection for traditional New Yorkers against a new order emerging from a combination of immigration, urbanization, and industrialization. The concern of many Republicans to preserve a New York they believed was slipping away, combined with the inability of independent and city Republicans to unite on a coherent response to this emerging order, accounts for the lack of theoretical coherence at the convention.

Notes

1. Samuel T. McSeveney, *The Politics of Depression: Political Behavior in the Northeast, 1893–1896* (New York: Oxford University Press, 1972), pp. 63–64, and Lincoln, *Constitutional History of New York*, III, pp. 3–25, provide a full discussion of this dispute.

2. Annual Message, January 4, 1887. *Messages From the Governors*, VIII, pp. 309–310.

3. *Laws of New York*, Chap. 8 (1883).

4. Arthur F. Bentley, *The Process of Government* (Chicago: University of Chicago Press, 1980); David Truman, *The Governmental Process* (New York: Alfred E. Knopf, 1951).

5. Richard McCormick, *From Realignment to Reform: Political Change in New York State, 1893–1910* (Ithaca: Cornell University press, 1981), pp. 52–53.

6. Sketches of the delegates can be found in the *Convention Manual of Procedure, Forms and Rules For the Regulation of Business in the Sixth New York State Constitutional Convention, 1894* Pt. I, vol. 2: *Delegates Manual and Introduction* (Albany: The Argus Co., 1984).

7. McSeveney, *Politics of Depression*, pp. 33–35.

8. Robert Crosby Eager, "Governing New York State: Republicans and Reform, 1894–1900" (Ph.D. Diss., Stanford University, 1977), p. 52.

9. See, e.g., the remarks of delegate Frederick Holls, as quoted in Eager, "Governing New York State," pp. 8–9.

10. Richard McCormick, "Shaping Republican Strategy: Political Change

in New York State, 1893-1910," 2 vols. (Ph.D. Diss., Yale University, 1976), p. 54.

11. *People ex rel. Pulman v. Henion*, 64 Hun. 471 (1892); *Matter of Ryers*, 72 N.Y. 1 (1878) and Galie, *The New York Constitution*, pp. 50-51.

12. *Revised Record of the Constitutional Convention of the State of New York . . . 1894*, 5 vols. (Albany: The Argus Co., 1900) IV, p. 1050 (hereafter cited as Rev. Rec. 1894.

13. *Rev. Rec. 1894*, IV, p. 1050. See also Morton Horwitz, *The Transformation of American Law, 1780-1860* (Cambridge: Harvard University Press, 1977), Chap. 3.

14. *Colonial Laws of New York*, Chap. 411 (1721).

15. *Laws of New York*, Chap. 479 (1887).

16. *Rev. Rec. 1894*, IV, p. 1126. Lauterbach was a New York City lawyer and president of Alabama Great Southern Railway.

17. *People v. Laude*, 81 Misc. 256 (1913).

18. *Laws of New York* (1895), Chap. 570-571.

19. Ibid. (1895), Chap. 572.

20. 152 N.Y. 1 (1897).

21. *People ex rel. Collins v. Mclaughlin*, 128 A.D. 599 (1908).

22. *Laws of New York* (1849) Chap. 256.

23. *Rev. Rec. 1894*, III, p. 126.

24. Ibid., IV, pp. 462-478.

25. Lincoln, *Constitutional History*, III, pp. 81-83.

26. *Rev. Rec. 1894*, III, p. 129.

27. Ibid., III, pp. 110-111 .

28. Ibid., III, pp. 244-246, 537-545.

29. McCormick, "Shaping Republican Strategy," I, pp. 67-68.

30. *Rev. Rec. 1894*, II, p. 111. Of course, Democrats saw the matter differently. Nonpartisanship, according to the Democratic *New York Sun*, was a "catch phrase" for reducing or eliminating Democratic control of the large cities, where Republicans were a minority. McCormick, "Shaping Republican Strategy," I, p. 62, fn. 19.

31. McSeveney, *The Politics of Depression*, p. 69.

32. William Veeder, Brooklyn, *Rev. Rec. 1894*, III, p. 947.

33. McCormick, "Shaping Republican Strategy," I, p. 58.

34. *Rev. Rec. 1894*, III, pp. 124-126.

35. Ibid., IV, pp. 488, 503.

36. *Laws of New York*, Chap. 354 (1883); Chap. 410 (1884).

37. New York State Temporary Commission on the Revision and Simplification of the Constitution, Staff Report, *Civil Service*, No. 20, 1958, p. 6.

38. Annual Message, January 6, 1887, in *Messages From the Governors*, IX (Albany: J. B. Lyon, 1909), p. 749.

39. *Laws of New York* (1897), Chap. 428.

40. Ibid., (1897), Chap. 370.

41. New York State Temporary Commission on the Revision and Simplification of the Constitution, Staff Report No. 33, *Legislative Reapportionment* (1960), pp. III-5.

42. Ibid., pp. II-5 n. 16.

43. Ibid., pp. II-9.

44. 135 N.Y. 473 (1892).

45. *Rev. Rec. 1894*, III, p. 344.

46. Ibid., III, p. 347.
47. Relevant parts of this debate are found in *Rev. Rec. 1894*, III, pp. 1002–1021, 1046–1054; IV, pp. 31–37, 65–96.
48. Ibid., II, pp. 599–601.
49. Temporary State Commission on the Constitutional Convention, Staff Report No. 12, *The Judiciary* (1967), p. 111.
50. *Levittown Union Free School District v. Nyquist* 57 N.Y. 2d 27 (1982) Cf. *Robinson v. Cahill* 303 A. 2d 273 (N.J., 1973) (requiring equal expenditures on state constitutional grounds).
51. *Wiltwych School for Boys Inc. v. Hill*, 11 N.Y. 2d 182 (1962); *Donohue v. Copiague Union Free School District*, 47 N.Y. 2d 440 (1979).
52. Galie, *New York State Constitution*, p. 233.
53. Lincoln, *Constitutional History*, III, p. 563.
54. Eager, "Governing New York," pp. 38–39; McSeveney, *The Politics of Depression*, pp. 73–75.
55. John Webb Pratt, *Religion, Politics and Diversity: The Church-State Theme in New York History* (Ithaca: Cornell University Press, 1967), p. 255 n. 68.
56. Temporary State Commission on the Constitutional Convention, Staff Report No. 10, *Individual Freedoms* (1967), pp. 26–31, provides a summary of the state judiciary's treatment of this clause between 1894 and 1967.
57. Lincoln, *Constitutional History* III, pp. 391–429, gives thorough coverage to this legislative history.
58. The doctrine that municipal corporations owe their origin and derive their powers wholly from the legislature was confirmed by national and state courts. *Atkin v. Kansas*, 191 U.S. 207 (1903), citing the opinion of Judge Dillon's rule in *City of Clinton v. Cedar Rapids and Missouri River R.R. Co.*, 24 Iowa 455 (1868). As the New York Court of Appeals expressed it: "In the absence of express restrictions placed in the constitution upon its legislative powers, the legislature may create, destroy, enlarge or restrict, combine or divide municipal corporations." *LaGuardia v. Smith*, 228 N.Y. 1 (1942).
59. In some cases the yielding came as a result of outright bribery, as when, in the late 1860s, Boss Tweed bribed state legislators to obtain a new city charter. See Ernest Griffith, *A History of the American City*, 4 vols. (New York: Praeger Publishers, 1938–1974), III, *The Conspicious Failure, 1870–1900*, p. 72. Teaford, *The Unheralded Triumph*, p. 8. The title of these works suggest their differences as well as the revisionist character of Teaford's argument.
60. Teaford, p. 95.
61. Griffith, *A History of American City Government*, III, *The Conspicious Failure 1870–1900*, p. 217.
62. Teaford, p. 111.
63. Ibid., p. 121.
64. Ibid., p. 123.
65. *Laws of New York*, 119 Sess. (1887); 11th Sess. (1888); 12th Sess. (1889).
66. *Rev. Rec. 1894*, II, p. 253, 352–356.
67. McBain, *Law and Practice of Home Rule*, p. 103.
68. *Rev. Rec. 1894*, IV, pp. 985, 982–993.
69. Eager, "Governing New York," pp. 28–32.
70. Teaford, *Unheralded City*, pp. 284–293.
71. "For all their flaws American city governments did work," Ibid., p. 311.

72. It is likely that recent interpretations of the First Amendment's Free Exercise clause would require states to grant such an exemption. See *Welsh v. United States*, 398 U.S. 333 (1970).
73. *People v. Molyneux*, 40 N.Y. 113 (1869).
74. *Laws of New York* (1898), Chap. 212.
75. Lincoln, *Constitutional History*, III, pp. 666-670.
76. McCormick, "Shaping Republican Strategy," I, p. 55.
77. Richard L. McCormick, *The Party Period and Public Policy American Politics from the Age of Jackson to the Progressive Era* (New York: Oxford University Press, 1986), pp. 216-217.
78. As quoted in McCormick, *From Realignment to Reform*, p. 57.
79. See Melvin Urofsky, "State Courts and Protective Legislation During the Progressive Era: A Reevaluation," *Journal of American History* 72 (1985), pp 63-91; Kermit Hall, *The Magic Mirror: Law in American History* (New York: Oxford University Press, 1989), pp. 238-243.
80. Frank Bourgin, *The Great Challenge: The Myth of Laissez-Faire in the Early Republic* (New York: George Braziller, 1989); Arthur Schlesinger, Jr., *The Cycles of American History* (New York: Houghton Mifflin, 1986), Chap. 9.
81. James Willard Hurst, *Law and the Conditions of Freedom in the Nineteenth Century United States* (Madison: University of Wisconsin Press, 1956), pp. 3-32.
82. Frank Strong, *Substantive Due Process of Law: A Dichotomy of Sense and Nonsense* (Durham: Carolina Academic Press, 1986), p. 82 and passim.
83. Howard Gillman, in his *The Constitution Besieged: The Rise and Demise of Lochner Era Police Powers Jurisprudence* (Durham: Duke University Press, 1993), pp. 10-16, has argued this point persuasively, based on a study of federal court decisions regarding government regulation. He demonstrates that federal judges were not so much promoting laissez-faire as upholding a long-standing constitutional prohibition against "class legislation."
84. Gillman, *The Constitution Besieged*, p. 21.
85. Alexis De Tocqueville provides an insightful analysis of the inevitability of this kind of group pressure for government assistance. *Democracy in America*, J. P. Mayer and Max Lerner, eds., trans. George Lawrence (New York: Harper & Row, 1966), II, p. 672.

10

The Progressive Movement and the Constitutional Convention of 1915

> ... This convention has risen above the plane of partisan politics.
>
> Elihu Root,
> convention president,
> Closing Address[1]

THE 1894 CONSTITUTION specified 1916 as the year when the question of holding a convention would be submitted to the voters. Democratic governor Martin Glynn argued for submission in 1914, as 1916 was a presidential election year, but Democratic control of both houses of the state legislature undoubtedly influenced Glynn's decision. Holding a constitutional convention two years prior to the specified date would guarantee Democratic control, enabling the party to rewrite the invidious apportionment provision inserted by Republicans in 1894 to ensure rural Republicans would not be out-voted by urban Democrats.

In December 1913 the legislature voted to move the date of the referendum on holding a convention to April 1914. In that election, voters approved the call for a convention by the slim majority of 153,322 to 151,969. The total vote cast in the election, 310,444, was less than half the vote totals of each of the two previous referenda in 1866 and 1886. Comparing this figure with the 1,611,672 votes cast for candidates in the 1912 gubernatorial election makes the contrast even more arresting. Holding the referendum in the spring contributed to the unusually low turnout. This limited turnout prompted calls for a constitutional provision forbidding the summoning of a convention or the ratification of amendments by minorities of the electorate.[2]

For the third time in as many conventions, Republicans emerged with a majority of delegates, electing 116 to the Democrats' 52. No Progressives were elected. What could account for this reversal in

Democratic fortunes? Between 1912, when Democrats began promoting a convention, and 1914, when the actual vote occurred, the Democratic Party was rocked by internal divisions over the impeachment and conviction of Governor William Sulzer. Sulzer's removal was the only successful impeachment of a governor in New York history.

New York's first impeachment law was placed in the 1777 Constitution. That law reflected its English origins, but colonists had transformed the process from a weapon for chastising corrupt officials into a vehicle for expressing grievances against imperial rulers. Following independence from colonial rule and the establishment of a republic, impeachment was viewed as a protection against the abuse of power.[3] Such protection was balanced by a similarly strong desire to transform the process from a partisan act to a legal one. A number of due process measures were included in the 1777 Constitution to ensure that this immense power in the hands of the legislature would not be used for partisan political purposes. From the beginning, the attempt to achieve both objectives created a constitutional ambivalence and a likelihood that it would be little used. Ironically, the first successful impeachment and conviction of a governor would be immersed in partisanship.

In an attempt to limit further partisan use of this power, impeachment charges were restricted to "high crimes and misdemeanors," presumably following the national Constitution (Art. II, Sec. 4). Though the convention reduced the number of votes necessary for impeachment from two-thirds to a majority, it retained the two-thirds vote required for conviction. The 1846 Constitution removed the definition of an impeachable offense altogether. Convention delegates complacently assumed that its embodiment in statutory law, and the unlikehood of its use, made it unnecessary to retain the definition. Another group of delegates found it difficult to furnish a definition encompassing all impeachment offenses, and concluded that such an attempt was beyond the scope of a constitutional provision.[4] The convention also removed the phrase "in office," thus leaving open the question of when an impeachment proceeding was applicable. This decision was embodied in Section 12 of the Code of Criminal Procedure in 1881. An Assembly Judiciary Committee in 1853 was asked to consider this question and related issues. The committee concluded that an impeachable offense did not include acts committed when the official was not an officer of the state.[5] Governor Sulzer's impeachment and conviction overruled the decision of the Assembly Committee.

Sulzer was elected to office in 1912 by a large popular vote. He was a progressive populist Democrat loosely associated with the Tammany machine. Upon assuming the governorship he announced plans to expose and eradicate corruption and elevate standards of official integrity. He abolished various no-show Democratic jobs and refused to fill positions with men recommended by Tammany boss Charles Murphy. He offended Republicans as well as Democrats by recommending that direct primaries replace party conventions in nominating public officials.[6] This display of independence, as well as his tendency toward reckless, impulsive action and flamboyancy, alienated Sulzer from many party regulars, particularly Murphy. In retaliation for Sulzer's disregard of his wishes, Murphy pressed his influence with the state legislature to initiate impeachment proceedings against the governor.[7] Articles of impeachment were instituted on grounds of filing false campaign receipts and expenditures, diverting those funds for personal use, bribing witnessess testifying before a legislative commission, and bribing an assemblyman to secure his vote for one of the governor's bills. Sulzer was convicted for filing false reports on campaign expenditures and on one count of suppressing evidence, but exonerated on the five other charges. Even his supporters admitted the campaign irregularities, arguing that these offenses did not approach the level of impeachable offenses.[8]

Sulzer's impeachment raised fundamental questions regarding the impeachment clause. Had it failed to prevent its use for partisan purposes? Although the grounds for impeachment were specified statutorily as "willfull and corrupt conduct" in office,[9] the Frawley Committee—the joint legislative committee established to hear the impeachment charge—broadened the standard to include "high crimes and misdemeanors" thus including acts committed while a candidate for office.[10]

The trial raised other important issues. Should members of the Frawley Committee, which proposed the impeachment of Sulzer, be disqualified from sitting on the Court of Impeachment? If not, the effect would be to allow some individuals to be both indictors and judges. Presiding Judge Edgar Cullen ruled against the motion to remove these senators. The second issue concerned whether the legislature could properly consider impeachment during a special session called by the governor explicitly for another purpose. Cullen ruled that the provision prohibiting the legislature from acting on unrelated subjects when called into special session did not apply to the power of impeachment, as this power was exclusive to the legislature (Art. IV, Sec. 4). This interpretation was upheld by the court in *People ex rel. Robin v. Hayes.*[11]

The third issue concerned the impeachment of a governor for conduct prior to tenure in office. The Court of Impeachment was divided on this issue. There was strong sentiment for the position that the acts of a candidate could not be separated from the acts of the official.

Others believed the statutory provision limiting offenses to those committed in office could not bind the court; only the constitution could. As the legislature was not permitted to enlarge the provisions of the constitution, neither could it abridge them.[12]

Sulzer's conviction raised serious questions about the lack of definition and the deficiencies in due process in the constitutional provision concerning impeachment. New York law currently allows impeachment for misconduct when in office, committed in a prior term of office and while a candidate for office.[13] The constitution fails to define who is subject to impeachment and under what standards, thus providing opportunity for abuse.

Sulzer's removal from office on October 17, 1913, caused an eruption of anti-Tammany sentiment. In the November 1913 elections Republicans gained control of the assembly, and in the election of 1914 they captured the governor's mansion when Charles Whitman soundly defeated Martin Glynn. This anti-Democratic fervor extended to the voting for convention delegates, with Republicans claiming all fifteen at-large seats and 116 of the total seats.

The delegates at the 1915 convention can fairly claim the distinction of being the most qualified and experienced group of delegates to sit in any constitutional convention held in New York.[14] Among the Republican delegates were Elihu Root, former secretary of war, secretary of state, United States Senator, and a veteran of the 1894 convention; Henry L. Stimson, former secretary of war; Seth Low, president of Columbia University and former mayor of both Brooklyn and New York City; Jacob Schurman, president of Cornell University; George Wickersham, former United States attorney general; Louis Marshall, a leading constitutional scholar of the day; and John Lord O'Brien, a former United States Attorney. The Democratic delegates included Alfred E. Smith and Robert F. Wagner, both of whom were beginning their political careers, and Morgan J. O'Brien, a prominent leader of the Democratic Party and former state Supreme Court Justice. Although various professions were represented, three of every four delegates were lawyers. The judgment of Stanley Isaacs, a leader of the Progressive Party, that the convention "was controlled by the most conservative people in the Republican Party allied with the most conservative people in the Democratic Party" was seconded by conservative Republican leader and delegate William Barnes.[15]

More was at stake in the call for a constitutional convention than the political maneuvering of the parties. Between 1895 and 1915, scholars, reformers, and some politicians began to focus on state government and, in particular, on the question of state government reorganization. They had three goals: administrative consolidation, executive appointments of major administrative offices, and an executive budget.[16] The movement for constitutional reform was given a boost when, in 1906, Charles Evans Hughes, one year prior to his election as governor, endorsed the goal of state reorganization. Hughes made that goal a principal theme of his administration. In his inaugural address in 1909 he remarked: "While the governor represents the highest executive power in the state, there is frequently observed a popular misapprehension as to its scope. There is a wide domain over which he has no control or slight control."[17] Though his efforts on behalf of reorganization legislation were unavailing, Hughes's commitment inspired other prominent Republicans to take up the cause. Prior to his removal from office, William Sulzer, Hughes's successor as governor, gave the movement for reform further impetus by appointing a Committee of Inquiry, which recommended administrative reorganization.[18]

Contributing to the momentum for constitutional reform was the growing popularity of one of its key components, the idea of the short ballot. The "short ballot" was the shorthand term for the transformation of key state offices from elective to appointive, vesting the appointment power in the governor and the legislature. The Progressive Party endorsed the idea of the short ballot, and by 1914 all three parties had a short ballot plank in their platforms.[19]

A second major constitutional issue was the question of home rule. The 1894 Constitution offered only token efforts to provide more autonomy for cities, and most observers agreed that the steps were inadequate.

In sum, those seeking to understand the constitutional reform movement in New York in the Progressive Era should remember that it was actuated by the desire both for reform and for partisan political advantage. The unexpected Republican victory in the convention election provided the party an opportunity to achieve its two key goals: first, effectuating state reorganization proposals initiated by Governor Hughes; second, using this campaign for government reform as an avenue to modernize the Republican Party, bringing it in line with the Progressive era.[20]

The Work of the Convention

The legislature directed that information relevant to the convention be prepared and presented to the delegates. This was not the first time such information had been prepared. In 1867 and 1894 previous legislatures enacted similar directives, but in both cases there were delays in presenting the materials to the delegates. For the 1915 convention, the legislature, determined to do better, wrote into the law that the New York State Constitutional Convention Commission should supply "research materials . . . to such delegates, before the opening of the convention."[21] The comprehensiveness and quality of these preparatory materials established New York as "the first state to lay a solid research foundation for a constitutional convention."[22] The government agency authorized to prepare this material, the Department of Efficiency and Economy, relied heavily on the New York Bureau of Municipal Research, a newly formed private organization dedicated to producing research on government organizations. The Bureau of Municipal Research assigned to this work two of its most promising employees, Charles A. Beard, later to become a world-renowned historian and political scientist, and Frederick Cleveland, an acknowledged expert on budgetary matters.[23] The report issued by the Bureau was the first complete description of a state government ever prepared.[24] Because the Department and the Bureau practically merged in preparing this report, its recommendations naturally embodied the goals of the administration reorganization movement. This massive pro-reform pre-convention preparation, in conjunction with the early commitment of convention leaders to such reforms, enabled the forces supporting a restructuring of government to arrive at the convention well prepared.

The pro-reform forces also brought to the convention a parade of well-known scholars and experts in government organization, including President Frank J. Goodnow of Harvard University, a former professor of government, and former U.S. President William Howard Taft, then a professor at Yale Law School, both appeared before the Committee on Finance. The testimony of these men played a central role in the convention's decisions to reorganize the executive branch and provide for an executive budget.[25] This remarkable effort made the delegates the most informed of any state constitutional convention up to that time.[26]

The convention convened on April 4, 1915 and adjourned on September 4, 1915. It considered over 700 measures, adopting thirty-three. The delegates elected Elihu Root as convention president, guaranteeing that reform-minded Republicans would control the convention's key committee chairmanships.[27] Root shrewdly attempted to depoliticize the reform proposals by including major Democratic figures in all consultations. The result was that all thirty-three measures adopted had the support of a majority of Republicans and Democrats, and most of the measures carried by overwhelming majorities.[28] The progressive Republicans' close cooperation at the convention earned them the sobriquets "House of Lords" and "Federal Men," the latter epithet referring to their national experience in Washington and their cosmopolitan outlook.

The major goal of the convention leadership was to reform the executive branch. To replace the approximately 169 separate department bureaus, commissions, boards, and committees, many with overlapping functions, the convention substituted seventeen departments. They were placed into three categories. The first class—the attorney general, the state's chief law officer, and the comptroller, the state's chief fiscal officer—were to remain elective officers, because delegates thought that the particular functions they performed required independence from the governor (Art. VI, Sec. 2). The second group of departments comprised those whose duties were not purely administrative but shared some judicial or legislative powers. These included the department of education, the public service commission, the labor and industry commission (newly created), and the department of conservation (newly created); they were to be directed by commissioners whose terms of office were not to exceed the governor's and whose removal was made more difficult than that of officers of purely executive departments (Art. VI, Secs. 2, 13, 15, 16, 17). The Department of Education would be administered by the University of the State of New York with the head of the department appointed by the Board of Regents (Secs. 2, 14). The third class encompassed the purely executive agencies. Ten agencies were so designated. Each was to be headed by a single person appointed by the governor and serving at his pleasure. The legislature was prevented from adding new departments, but could assign new functions to any of the seventeen existing departments (Art. VI, Sec. 3). The delegates failed to achieve complete administrative consolidation but took a significant step toward that goal. The impact of the short ballot idea was also evident. The offices of secretary of state and treasurer were eliminated as elective offices (Art. VI, Secs. 2, 4, 6), and the offices of state engineer and surveyor were abolished.

The second major goal of the reformers was the reconstruction of the state's budgetary process. At the time of the convention, the legislature made appropriations without any plan or study as to the needs of the state or sources of potential revenue. The governor was left with the task of fitting legislative expenditures with revenues. Under the new Article V, the plan for the budget would be prepared by the governor in advance, after consultation with department heads, and then be submitted to the legislature for its approval. The governor and the department heads had the right—and the duty, when requested—to appear before the legislature to be heard with respect to the budget (Art. V, Sec. 1). The legislature was granted the power to reduce or eliminate items on the budget but prohibited from increasing any item except those concerning the legislature or judiciary. However, the convention provided the legislature with some power to add expenditures after the executive budget had been acted on by both houses.

The convention introduced two other changes in the executive branch. The lieutenant governor would act as governor in cases of vacancy or during impeachment proceedings (Art. VI, Sec. 5), and his salary was raised from ten to twenty thousand dollars (Art. IV, Sec. 1).

The delegates changed little in the legislative branch. The apportionment article was continued (Art. III, Secs. 4, 5); this was a stinging defeat for the Democrats, as one of the principal reasons for calling an early convention was to change this provision. The salaries of legislators were raised from $1,500 to $2,500 (Art. III, Sec. 8).

The delegates dropped the provision in the 1894 Constitution prohibiting members of the legislature from receiving any civil appointment within the state from the governor, the legislature, or city governments. They hoped that allowing such appointments would be an added inducement for the best and the brightest to devote themselves to the service of the state, while allowing them to continue their careers in public life. The convention also added a number of new restrictions on legislative power, as noted below.

The judiciary, subject to major change at every convention since 1821, received further important modifications. The legislature was directed to adopt a simple code of laws and was prohibited from altering that code for five years; thereafter, the legislature could institute only those changes previously approved by a commission organized to report on needed revisions (Art. VIII, Sec. 6). The purpose of this restriction was twofold: to prevent frequent changes in the law and to ensure that such changes as were made had a well considered basis. To reduce congestion, the delegates adopted three reforms. First, they authorized the Court of Appeals to add members from the Supreme Court until its backlog of cases had been eliminated (Art. VIII, Sec. 8). Second, they specified and limited the types of cases that court could hear, and granted the legislature the power to institute further restrictions (Art. VIII, Sec. 9, 11). This reform presaged the adoption at the federal level of the Judiciary Act of 1925, which granted the Supreme Court the power to control the largest portion of its caseload through the use of the writ of certiorari. Third, they permitted the legislature to enlarge or restrict the jurisdiction of the appellate term (Art. VIII, Sec. 3).

The convention abolished the practice of many state judges of appointing lawyers as referees to assist them in recording testimony and reporting on the facts, and of compensating them on the basis of cases processed (Art. VIII, Sec. 8). The referees were replaced with salaried commissioners, who were forbidden to practice law while serving as commissioners. The delegates reasoned that this change would eliminate any temptation to process cases too quickly and the possibility of outside influences.

The convention authorized the legislature to confer on inferior courts the power to try misdemeanors without a jury trial and to establish juvenile courts (Art. VIII, Sec. 22). This is the first constitutional recognition of the need to treat youthful offenders in courts separate from those used to adjudicate adult felons, and one of the earliest constitutional provisions dealing with the adoption of a juvenile justice system (an idea originating in 1899 in Cook County, Illinois).

Home Rule

The second major item on the convention's agenda was home rule. Significant home rule powers were granted to cities. Each city would have exclusive power to manage, regulate, and control its property affairs and municipal government (Art. XV, Sec. 3). The grant also included the power to amend the city charter. The state legislature was prohibited from passing legislation concerning the property affairs or government of cities except as such laws are general—that is, applying to all cities of the same class (Art. XV, Sec. 4). The convention also conferred a measure of home rule on the counties of the state by restricting the use of special laws relating to most counties except on request of the governing bodies of those counties (Art. III, Sec. 25).

Suffrage

The suffrage article (II), a perennial topic at New York constitutional conventions since 1777, was altered in two ways. The delegates provided for special registration for those who, by virtue of their occupation, would be absent during regular registration periods (Art. II, Sec. 4), and agreed to submit a constitutional amendment granting the vote to women, acknowledging the controversial character of this proposal by agreeing to submit it as a separate amendment.

Individual Rights

The convention proposed several amendments to the state's bill of rights. Individuals accused of crimes punishable by five years or less ("minor felonies") could waive their rights to a grand jury indictment and jury trial. The purpose of this proposal was to prevent a defendant from languishing in jail for months in areas of the state where the grand jury would not be in session for months at a time.[29] It was a curious form of logic that propelled delegates to allow defendants to surrender procedural rights to avoid delays that were beyond their making. The amendment was necessary because the Court of Appeals had determined the right to a jury trial could not be waived. It is a precursor to the eventual acceptance of an individual's right to waive constitutional rights to facilitate a plea of guilty for consideration (Art. I, Sec. 6). The convention also inserted a right to appeal from the minor or magistrates courts—a right not guaranteed by the 1894 Constitution (Art. I, Sec. 6).[30] Finally, the delegates adopted an equal protection clause similar to and probably modeled on the one found in the Fourteenth Amendment (Art. I, Sec. 6).

Delegates also sought to provide added protection for individual rights in the context of the taking of private property by any civil division of the state. At the time, years could pass between the taking of property by a civil division of the state and payment of compensation to the property owner, a delay delegates sought to eliminate.[31]

Taxation

Taxation was the subject of a new article (Art. X). In an attempt to restrict log-rolling, the convention required that the state legislature could not grant exemptions from taxation except by general laws enacted by two-thirds of the members of both houses (Art. X, Sec. 1). For the first time, the state was granted power to provide for the supervision, equalization and review of assessments (Art. X, Sec. 2). A real estate assessor would be chosen locally, but the legislature was authorized to provide for assessment of all property of designated public service corporations (Art. X, Sec. 3). This allowed for centralized assessment of property of public service corporations (for example, railroads) which encompassed various tax districts and also prevented wealthy individuals from claiming two different residences and "swearing off" their taxes (Art. X, Sec. 3).[32]

Canals and State Debt

The delegates debated extensively the issues of canals and state debt. They overhauled the expensive and uncertain system of supplying sinking funds for the retirement of state debt. This reform was rooted in the startling expansion of state debt from almost nothing in 1893 to $186 million in 1915. The bulk of this debt was connected with the canal system and highways. Figures were introduced to demonstrate that if serial bonds had been issued to retire the canal debt instead of long-term bonds as required by the existing system, the state would have saved $46,677,000 in interest.³³ The delegates authorized the issuance of serial bonds under two limitations: first, all such serial bonds should not exceed fifty years, and, second, no debt was to be authorized exceeding the estimated life of the improvement being financed (Art. IX, Sec. 4).

As to the state's canal system, the convention expanded the constitution's coverage to include the Barge Canal and the canal terminals, thus protecting them from sale (Art. IX, Sec. 10). By defining the canal system for the first time, delegates intended to prevent court determinations as to which sections were useful and which were not.³⁴ The convention also mandated that the canals should be improved in such manner as the legislature shall provide and that debts may be authorized for that purpose (Art. IX, Sec. 12).

Welfare

The convention added two specific welfare measures to the constitution. The delegates extended the section dealing with workmen's compensation to embrace compensation for injuries or deaths resulting from occupational diseases of employees (Art. I, Sec. 19), and prohibited manufacturing in tenements, also known as "sweatshops" (Art. III, Sec. 29). (This latter reform was doubtless inspired by the tragic and infamous 1911 Triangle Shirtwaist Company fire, which killed dozens of young women who could not escape from the factory because it lacked proper fire escapes.) These reforms should not be taken to suggest that the 1915 convention was much more receptive to social welfare measures than the 1894 convention had been. The delegates rejected proposals for old-age pensions and various other amendments favorable to labor.

The final draft of the constitution was accepted by a vote of 118 to 33. The changes were submitted to the voters as a package containing four separate amendments: women's suffrage, legislative apportionment, taxation, and debt for canal improvement.

The constitution was defeated by a large majority, 400,423 (for) to 910,462 (against). Various explanations have been offered for this resounding defeat. To begin with, support for holding the convention was tenuous, the margin of support, a slim 1,353 out of a strikingly small total turnout of 310,444. Some have focused on the convention's decision to submit most of its work as a single package.³⁵ Tammany and upstate political bosses helped seal the fate of the document by persuading convention reformers to combine all proposed amendments into a single package. Distaste for one or two of the unimportant but unpopular amendments created a coalition of diverse groups aligned in opposition to the proposed constitution. This fact, along with a quiet mobilization of Tammany and upstate machines, resulted in the defeat of the constitution.[36] Labor was incensed because the convention rejected all eight pro-labor proposals submitted to it.[37] The Progressive Party opposed the constitution mainly for political reasons, including the apprehension that its adoption would threaten the Progressive Party in New York.[38] Tammany Hall opposed the document largely because of its apportionment and home rule provisions, which, they claimed, were not broad enough. Finally, upstate Republicans opposed the constitution because they disliked the allegedly dictatorial powers it conferred on the governor, and the salary increases provided for the governor and the legislature. In sum, the voters defeated the constitution because it was too radical for some and too conservative for others.[39]

The Political Theory of the 1915 Constitution

If the conventions of 1867 and 1894 exhibited little theoretical coherence, the same cannot be said about the 1915 convention and the constitution it produced. Explicitly, and for the most part consistently, it followed a coherent philosophy of government. That philosophy can be summarized by three values: expertise, efficiency, and economy.

The convention's emphasis on expertise was evident in the provision that the civil law could be amended only at the recommendation of a commission of experts, in the constitution's general resort to nonelective department heads, and in the design of a budgetary process dominated by policy planners and budgetary specialists. The delegates' concern for efficiency was manifest in the constitution's provisions authorizing non-jury trials for misdemeanors, the individual's right to waive grand juries and trial juries, the limiting of appeals, and the general tendency to streamline the organization and functions of the state government. Finally, the delegates hoped the new constitution's emphasis on expertise and efficiency would combine with specific provisions, such as the proposed budgetary reforms and the reductions in the number of state agencies and boards, to achieve economy in government.

The variety of new restrictions placed on the legislature, such as the ban on creating new departments, on increases in the governor's budget, and on additions to civil codes, removed policy discretion from the control of the legislature and placed it within the authority of the governor and the bureaucracy. The delegates justified these limitations in the name of responsible government and efficient and expert policy-making.

The constitution was framed in a decade in which "reformers played a major—if not decisive—role in New York's government and politics."[40] The business firm was the apparent model for the delegates' advocacy of centralized authority in the hands of a single executive. The model of democracy implicit in the convention's work assumed a reliance on experts to minister to the government and to propose policies, with voters electing the governor and an elected legislature ratifying the policies originating from the governor's office.

The model of government set forth in the 1915 Constitution represented a departure from the traditional notions of separation of powers and divided government and was consistent with the ideas of the leading thinkers of the Progressive Era, who extolled the British system where the ministry provided a unified executive and administrative leadership legitimated by the approval of Parliament. From this perspective, the removal from the constitution of the provision disallowing legislators from receiving any civil appointments from the governor, the legislature, or any city government, acquires special significance. This change would have had the effect of collapsing the rigid barriers separating the executive and legislative branches, creating the equivalent at the state level of a British cabinet government. The power to appoint legislators as members of the cabinet would create powerful bonds between the two branches and directly enforce party responsibility.

Charles Beard, one of those instrumental in preparing research material for the convention, provided additional light on the intent underlying many of the 1915 convention's proposed reforms:

> In breaking down the rigid separation of the governor and his cabinet from the legislature and admitting them to the floor of the house—a system of interpellation may be established which will contribute powerfully to efficient and responsible government and will open up undreamt possibilities in politics.[41]

The Constitution of 1915: An Assessment

The proposed 1915 Constitution would have made New York "the first state that ever has undertaken to frame the financial measure of its constitution around the budget idea."[42] Charles Beard claimed that the document established "a degree of responsible government hitherto unknown in American politics."[43] Although rejected by the voters, the proposed constitution and the preparatory work accompanying it provided the educational foundations for constitutional reform for the next twenty years. By 1927, through the work of Governor Alfred E. Smith, Robert Moses, Belle Moskowitz, and others, amendments were adopted providing for executive consolidation, the short ballot, and an executive budget. Of the thirty-three changes recommended in 1915, a majority had been adopted by 1935, including women's suffrage, home rule for the cities, and provisions concerning the judiciary. The accomplishments of the 1915 convention paved the way for those later successes. Its proposals presaged the shift of power in state government from the legislative to the executive branch, providing affirmative grants of power to the executive. However, its move toward a parliamentary democracy has not taken hold in the constitutional culture of New York.

At a reunion dinner of the delegates to the 1915 convention, Elihu Root gave a fitting assessment of their work: "I think it makes but little difference whether a man gives his life and his service to laying the foundation and building up the structure, or whether he is the man that floats a flag on the battlements and cries, 'Victory'."[44]

Notes

1. *Revised Record of the Constitutional Convention of the State of New York, 1915*, 4 vols. (Albany: J. B. Lyons, 1916), IV, p. 4380 (hereinafter referred to as *Rev. Rec.*).
2. Dougherty, *Constitutional History of the State of New York*, 2d ed., p. 377.
3. Peter Hoffer and N. E. H. Hull, *Impeachment in America, 1635-1805* (New Haven: Yale University Press, 1984), pp. xi, 59-67.
4. Croswell and Sutton, *Debates and Proceedings, 1846*, p. 436.
5. Lincoln, *Constitutional History*, IV, p. 603.
6. Annual Message to the Legislature, January 1, 1913. *Public Papers of William Sulzer, Governor, 1913* (Albany: J. B. Lyon, 1914).
7. *Proceedings of the Court for the Trial of Impeachments: The People of the State of New York by the Assembly Thereof Against William Sulzer as Governor, 1913*, 2 vols. (Albany: J. B. Lyon Co., 1913), hereafter *Court for the Trial of Impeachments*. See Jacob Friedman, *The Impeachment of Governor William Sulzer* (New York: Columbia University Press, 1939) for full treatment.
8. See "Tammany and the Sulzer Case," *The American Review of Reviews*, XLVIII (1913), pp. 531-533.
9. *New York Code of Criminal Procedure*, Sec. 12 (1913).
10. *Court for the Trial of Impeachments*, I, pp. 46-47.
11. 163 A.D. 725 (1914).
12. *Court for the Trial of Impeachments*, II, p. 1596.
13. This conclusion is based on the analysis of cases found in *New York's Impeachment Law and the Trial of Governor Sulzer: A Case for Reform* (Albany: New York State Senate Judiciary Committee, 1986), pp. 31-38.

14. Frederick C. Tanner, Republican state chair, thought the personnel of the convention "the highest class—both from the point of experience and ability—that has ever been held to pass on constitutional questions," *The Oral History of Frederick C. Tanner*, 2 vols. (New York: Columbia University Press, 1950) I, p. 140.

15. As quoted in Thomas Schick, *The New York State Constitutional Convention of 1915 and the Modern State Governor* (New York: National Municipal League, 1978), p. 40.

16. Schick, *1915 Convention*, pp. 15–27, chronicles the rise of this reform movement and its impact on the convention.

17. See his inaugural address in *Public Papers of Charles E. Hughes, Governor*, 1909 (Albany: J. B. Lyon, 1910), pp. 8–9. The two parties of the state, particularly the Republican party led by Boss Thomas C. Platt, though not the originators of this system, seized the opportunity to thwart responsible leadership and diffuse authority. See Harold Gosnell, *Boss Platt and His New York Machine* (Chicago: University of Chicago Press, 1924), p. 215. In 1872 Governor John T. Hoffman provided a "sweeping and prescient discussion of the need for constitutional reform" which would make "the governor responsible for every branch of the actual administration of the state's affairs," as quoted in [Robert Kerker], *The Executive Budget in New York: A Half Century Prespective* (Albany: New York State Division of the Budget, 1981), p. 8.

18. Schick, *1915 Convention*, pp. 25–26.

19. Ibid., 26.

20. Gerald McKnight, "The Perils of Reform Politics: The Abortive New York State Constitutional Reform Movement of 1915," *The New York Historical Society Quarterly* 63 (1979), p. 212.

21. *Laws of New York*, 1914, Chap. 261.

22. Albert L. Strum, *Methods of State Constitutional Reform* (Ann Arbor: University of Michigan Press, 1954), p. 109.

23. Schick, *1915 Convention*, pp. 43–44.

24. Ibid., p. 44.

25. Finla Crawford, "Constitutional Developments, 1867–1915," in Alexander Flick, ed., *History of the State of New York*, VII, *Modern Party Battles* (1935), pp. 229–230.

26. McKnight, "Perils of Reform Politics," p. 215.

27. Ibid., p. 214.

28. In his closing address, President Root compiled the lopsided votes on the major proposals at the convention. *Rev. Rec.*, IV: 4381.

29. Ibid., IV, p. 4046.

30. Ibid., IV, p. 4171.

31. Ibid., IV, pp. 4046–4047.

32. Ibid., II, pp. 1861–1862, 1866–1874.

33. Ibid., II, pp. 1257–1262.

34. Ibid., I, pp. 1059ff.

35. Schick, *1915 Convention*, pp. 119–125.

36. Robert Caro, *The Power Broker: Robert Moses and the Fall of New York* (New York: Vintage Books, 1975) p. 97.

37. Finla Crawford, "Constitutional Developments, 1867–1915," VII, p. 235.

38. McKnight, "Perils of Reform Politics," pp. 218–219, cites other political reasons for Progressive opposition.

39. Gilbert Giddings Benjamin, "The Attempted Revision of the State Constitution of New York," *The American Political Science Review* 10 (1916), p. 42.

40. David Ellis, et al., *A History of New York State*, rev. ed. (Ithaca, N.Y.: Cornell University Press, 1967), p. 376. The role of the reformers is well chronicled in [Kerker], *The Executive Budget in New York*, Chap. 1, "The Progressive Consensus on Executive Responsiblity."

41. Quoted in Benjamin, "Attempted Revision," p. 43.

42. New York Bureau of Municipal Research, "The Budget Idea in the United States," *Municipal Research*, No. 69 (January, 1916), p. 64.

43. Charles A. Beard, "The Budgetary Provisions of the New York Constitution," *The Annals of the American Academy of Political and Social Science* 62 (Nov., 1915), p. 68.

44. Held on December 17, 1926 in New York City. Copy of Address in Henry L. Stimson Papers, Yale University, New Haven, Ct. Quoted in Schick, *1915 Convention*, p. 133.

11

Re-establishing the Government: Constitutional Development, 1915–1938

THE CONSTITUTION adopted in 1894 and revised in 1938 remains the Constitution of the State of New York in the waning years of the twentieth century. This constitution represents the culmination of nineteenth-century constitution-making and nineteenth-century ideas regarding the nature and function of a constitution. It did not address issues that were raised by an expanding industrial state, including the role of the state in promoting the economic and social welfare of the citizenry, the role of labor in the economy, the efficiency and effectiveness of the state's executive branch, pressure for additional home rule powers for cities, and relief from constitutional tax and debt limitations. The failure of the 1915 constitutional convention left these issues to be addressed by constitutional amendments.

ARTICLE I

Two minor adjustments were made to Section 7. The 1894 convention permitted owners of undrained land to invoke eminent domain to improve their land. The Court of Appeals limited the usefulness of this provision by declaring that assessments for the improvements could be made only on the landholders whose land was being drained. An amendment in 1919 permitted assessments on any property benefiting from the drainage. As there was some doubt as to whether this use of eminent domain was for a public purpose or use, the amendment declared that drainage of such land was a public use.

A 1913 amendment gave cities the authority to make "excess condemnations" of property in the construction of public improvements. The purpose was to protect cities from protracted litigation over the question of damages to land adjacent to such sites. Such damaged land would be of little use to the city or the property owner after litigation.

Proponents of the change believed it would be less costly in the long run to take the whole parcel of land and then later sell or use what remained.[1] The amendment also removed any constitutional barriers created by court decisions, holding that private property could be taken only for public improvement.[2] In 1927 this clause was again amended to authorize the legislature to include counties as well as cities in the provision.

The 1846 procedure for determining compensation when private property is taken for public purposes was amended in 1913 to provide a new and additional alternative, "a Supreme Court with or without a jury but without a referee" (Sec. 7). The commissioners appointed to hear such cases had become patronage appointments with little knowledge of real estate values. In addition, they were recompensed on a per diem basis, thus encouraging delay. This amendment was designed to eliminate "the unconscionable delays and chicanery attendant on a politically controlled commissioner system."[3] In 1933 this clause was again amended. In proceedings affecting property in New York City to be acquired by the city, compensation was to be determined by a term of the Supreme Court consisting of one or more justices, but without a jury. The goal of this revision was to familiarize such a court with compensation cases, thus promoting uniformity and consistency.[4]

Section 2 of the article protecting the right to trial by jury was the subject of two amendments. It was amended in 1935 to allow less than unanimous verdicts in civil cases. The amendment was intended to reduce disagreement and to promote fairer verdicts and sounder expressions of jury will. Under the unanimity rule, the unyielding juror was given the power to extract compromises that would not occur otherwise. The amendment was necessary to counteract the strong judicial tradition in the state supporting unanimous verdicts.[5] Two years later a waiver of a jury trial was permitted in non-capital cases. Under this amendment the right to jury trial, long considered so fundamental and essential that its waiver by the defendant was prohibited, yielded to desires to reduce trial expenses and to allow defendants to avoid the adverse effects of publicity and prejudice that usually accompany sensational trials.

The most important change in Article I during this period involved an issue which reflected, on the state level, a battle between a judiciary bent on protecting the public against what it saw as special or class-based legislation and the attempts by the legislature to remedy serious social and economic problems.[6]

In 1910, after thorough consideration of the problem, the New York legislature passed a Worker Compensation Law, making New York the first state in the nation to adopt a comprehensive worker's compensation law.[7] In *Ives v. South Buffalo Railroad*, the Court of Appeals, in a unanimous ruling, declared that the statute violated federal and state due process.[8] Specifically, the court argued that the statute deprived employers of their right to trial by jury, since these claims would be paid on a no-fault basis. The police power was not broad enough to permit the state to require employers to compensate employees when the employer was without fault in the occurrence of the injuries. This decision provoked angry criticism, and prompted submission to the legislature of an amendment to the constitution, which passed in 1912 and 1913 and was ratified by the people in 1913. The following year the legislature re-enacted the statute.[9] A second challenge to the law brought a different response from the court. With minimal reference to the recently passed amendment, the court reversed its earlier decision, finding that neither state nor federal due process was violated by the statute.[10]

The swiftness of this reaction suggests the extent to which a political consensus had formed on this issue, and the extent to which the court's understanding of constitutional limitations on legislative action, however firmly rooted in history, was in conflict with the popular understanding.

The gap between the judiciary and the legislature over the power of government to regulate the economy was evident when the state passed legislation requiring contractors engaged by the state to pay wages and ensure similar working conditions to those in the locality where the work was being done. In *People v. Coler*[11] the Court of Appeals struck down that legislation, precipitating a response in the form of a 1905 amendment to Article XII, Section I permitting the legislature to regulate and fix the hours of work and wages and salaries of employees of any division of the state.

Subsequent repudiation of the philosophy underlying the Coler decision by the state's judiciary makes the importance of this amendment contingent on the unlikely possibility that the court will return to a narrow view of state police power.

Article II: Suffrage

At the turn of the twentieth century, universal male suffrage had been achieved. Woman suffrage, though debated at the 1867, 1894, and 1915 conventions, had not been achieved in the state or at the federal level. In 1917, two years after voters rejected a similar proposal, an amendment was passed granting women the vote in state elections. Although the marshaling of forces in favor of woman suffrage had been taking place since the mid 1800s, the margin of victory, 703,129 to 600,776, suggested that the males of the state were anything but unanimous on the question. The amendment also added a provision that "a citizen by marriage shall have been an inhabitant of the U.S. for five years." This provision refers to the practice of obtaining citizenship by marriage, a procedure that was subsequently rendered inoperative by federal legislation passed in 1927 (Cable Act).[12] The act stated that "no woman would be entitled to naturalization . . . if her citizenship originated solely by reason of her marriage." This amendment was the last significant expansion of suffrage by state action in New York. Initially the state judiciary did not give an expansive reading to the decision to grant women the right to vote. In *Matter of Grilli* a state court held that although women are qualified to vote they may not sit as trial jurors until the legislature so provides.[13]

In 1919 voters ratified a provision which allowed the legislature to provide a means for citizens to vote whose business took them out of the state or their county of residence. Absentee voting was expanded twice: absentee rights were extended to residents of soldier's and sailor's homes in 1923 and again in 1929 when residents of veterans' bureau hospitals were granted a similar right. Absentee voting proposals had not received much support in the state until after the 1915 convention and were largely a response to dislocations caused by World War I.[14]

An amendment ratified in 1921 limited the suffrage to those who, except for physical disability, were "able to read and write English." The 1867 and 1915 conventions considered, but rejected, a literacy test. As immigration increased, support for a literacy requirement in English gained popularity, no doubt fueled by the patriotic fervor unleashed by World War I. Precise figures are unavailable on the number disenfranchised by this amendment, but the Staff Report on Suffrage, prepared by the 1965 Temporary Commission on the Constitutional Convention, estimated the figure at 100,000.[15] Amendments to the Federal Voting Rights Act of 1965 suspended all literacy tests until 1975, when the suspension was made permanent. New York's literacy requirement was held to be in violation of the national Constitution insofar as it disenfranchised Puerto Ricans whose native tongue was Spanish.[16] Legislation implementing this provision was deleted from the recompiled election law in 1977. The literacy clause of the New York Constitution is currently inoperative.

Article III: The Legislature

Nine amendments on a variety of issues were adopted during this period. A perennial amendment question concerned salaries, as any change in compensation required a constitutional amendment. Although voters regularly rejected proposed amendments increasing salaries of government officials (four were rejected between 1885 and 1938), in 1927 voters approved a $1,000 salary increase for legislators, making their annual salaries $2,500 (Sec. 6).

In 1931 Sections four and five were amended to permit the use of the federal census in place of the state census unless the former proved inadequate for the state's purposes. This change enabled the state to eliminate the expenses of what was essentially a duplication of the federal survey.

An important amendment in 1937 extended the term of office for assembly members to two years. This modification was justified on the grounds that assembly members would "never get away from the polls" or from the influence of "active private interest groups detrimental to the public interest."[17] With this change the terms of office for senate and assembly members were made identical, eliminating one of the few remaining differences between the two houses. The provision came just three years after the adoption of a Nebraska amendment establishing a unicameral legislature. In 1937 twenty-three states introduced unicameral legislature proposals. Similar recommendations had been made by the 1872 Constitutional Commission and by a minority report of the Committee on Legislative Reorganization at the 1915 convention. This proposal, resurrected periodically by reform groups, has not garnered much support in New York.

The voters also added to the list of subjects on which private or local bills were prohibited the granting to any person, association, or corporation an exemption from taxation on real and personal property (Sec. 18, 1909). This limitation was one the legislators wished to place on itself as it would relieve them from the burden of having to consider the flood of requests for special exemptions.

The last five amendments addressed Sections 26 and 27 and provided a degree of home rule for counties. These amendments are examined under the home rule section of this chapter.[18]

Articles IV and V:
The Executive and Civil Officers and Departments

No articles underwent more change in the two decades prior to the 1938 convention than Articles IV and V. Comprehensive reorganization of the executive branch, the short ballot, the executive budget, and a four-year gubernatorial term were all accomplished between 1925 and 1938.

The movement for executive reorganization in New York has traditionally been traced to 1906, when gubernatorial candidate Charles Evans Hughes committed himself publicly to reorganization.[19] A forceful and persuasive call was featured in his inaugural address.[20] Subsequent governors also pledged themselves to the goal. Governor Sulzer appointed a Committee of Inquiry which submitted a variety of recommendations for streamlining the executive branch.[21] Investigations of state government conducted for the 1915 constitutional convention revealed that it was both irresponsible and unresponsive. Instead of a logical system there was historical accumulation. "From the point of view of democracy it is unsuccessful and from the point of view of business management it stands universally condemned." This conclusion from the report prepared by the Department of Efficiency and Economy for the 1915 convention would be repeated in every subsequent study.[22] The proposals made at the 1915 convention were defeated, along with the rest of the proposed constitution. Executive disorganization, however, continued apace. By 1919 it was estimated that the government was a miscellany of 187 offices, boards, commissions, and other agencies.[23]

Despite the defeat of the 1915 constitution, support for the recommendations of the convention continued. The 1918 election of Alfred E. Smith as governor seemed to be another reversal to the cause for reform. Although he had supported the recommendations of the Bureau of Municipal Research at the convention when Tammany opposed the proposed constitution, Smith campaigned against it. Whatever other political aspirations Smith entertained, he was a loyal son of Tammany.[24] Prior to his victory, however, Smith had determined to alter the image of the Democratic Party, and Tammany boss Charles Murphy, recognizing the need for the party to be seen as one of social progress and social ideals, supported Smith. That support enabled Smith to capture the governorship, setting in motion forces that would re-establish and modernize the government of New York.

Smith made modernization a major goal of his administration from his first message to the legislature in January 1919 to the completion of his reform efforts in 1926. As a former member of the state assembly, speaker in 1917, and minority leader at the 1915 convention, Smith understood state government as well as anybody. He engaged individuals recommended by Belle Moskowitz, a brilliant reformer who had supported his campaign by reaching out to independent progressive Republicans and women, recently enfranchised by a state constitutional amendment in 1917. One of these reformers was Robert Moses, a former member of the Bureau. Moses would play an active and significant role in engineering constitutional reform and, indeed, changing the face of New York over the next half-century. At the suggestion of Moskowitz, Smith called for the creation of a Commission for Reconstruction of State Government.[25] Confident that the legislature would fund the commission, Smith appointed its members and Moskowitz began hiring staff. However, Smith's political acumen failed him. Republicans who controlled the legislature suspected the commission would provide Smith with a program to run on in 1920, and they were miffed by Smith's failure to consult with them on the appointments to a bi-partisan commission. His request for a modest $75,000 was turned down. In response, commission members announced that they would raise their own operating funds. With this inauspicious birth the commission began its work on January 10, 1919 with Belle Moskowitz as executive-secretary and Robert Moses as chief of staff. Its report was released in October of that year. The recommendations were along the lines followed by the 1915 convention. In forceful and emphatic tones it set forth the Progressive philosophy in general, and, in particular, the philosophy of the Bureau of Municipal Research. This included an executive budget, a four-year term for the governor, power to appoint heads of all major departments, consolidation of all administrative departments, and logical reorganization of related offices and work.[26] Most of these recommendations could be accomplished by statute. However, three required constitutional amendments: the creation of sixteen departments, with provisions that all future agencies would be placed in one of those sixteen; the executive budget; and extension of the governor's term to four years. Smith, Moses, and Moskowitz set about organizing the campaign for their adoption. The legislature passed most of the statutory reforms and gave first passage to the department consolidation amendment.

In 1920 Smith lost the governorship to Nathan Miller, who opposed the amendment's repassage. The Citizen's Committee on Reorganization in the state government was dissolved. Re-elected in 1922 by 387,000 votes, the largest plurality any gubernatorial candidate had ever achieved, Smith headed back to Albany, taking Moses with him. In 1925, amendments consolidating executive departments and shortening the ballot were approved. The first provided for legislative assignment of executive functions to twenty departments (Sec. 2) and permitted legislative reduction of the number of departments, but prohibited statutory creation of any new departments. The legislature was permitted to create temporary commissions for special purposes (Sec. 3). All department heads, with the exceptions of the attorney general and the comptroller and the heads of Departments of Education, Agriculture, and Marketing, were to be appointed by the governor (Sec. 4). The offices of secretary of state, treasurer, state engineer, and surveyor were made appointed posts (Sec. 1). The governor's term was extended to four years in 1932. Since the amendment required implementing legislation, Governor Smith and the legislature agreed to create a bipartisan citizen's group to study the structure of the government and submit recommendations to the legislature. The commission was popularly known as the Hughes Commission, after its chair, Charles Evans Hughes. The final report of the commission, issued in February 1926, was accepted by the legislature without reservation. Reorganization was a reality. New York became the first state to implement administrative reorganization by constitutional change.

The 1915 convention gave considerable attention to the subject of administration reorganization and a state budget, adopting a comprehensive program of fiscal reforms.[27] Although the budget amendment was rejected in 1915, Governor Whitman decided it was within his power to prepare and submit a budget and a consolidated appropriations act. The submission engendered immediate opposition: he was accused of usurping legislative power. In the end the governor had to concede that the legislature could do what it wished with what were merely compilations of tentative proposals. Realizing that some order or budget planning was necessary, the legislature passed the Sage-Maier Bill.[28] This statute effected some improvements in the system, but fell short of what Governors Whitman or Smith would accept. The Hughes Commission submitted detailed weaknesses of this system and recommended a consolidated budget system with accountability and control regarding expenditures.[29] In addition to presenting a coherent statement of the executive responsibility and consolidation creed, the Hughes Commission recommended the adoption of an executive budget system:

> The only way in which the true order of procedure can be fully established and the governor relegated to his true function of proposing a budget and the legislature deposing of the budget, is by the passage of a constitutional amendment.[30]

The recommendations of a commission jointly created by the legislature and the governor, led by the well respected Charles Evans Hughes and supported by former Republican Governor Nathan Miller and Assembly Speaker H. Edmund Machold, a former opponent of the idea, could not be ignored. They were adopted by the legislature and approved by the voters in 1927.

New York belatedly joined the ranks of executive budget states. However, unlike the majority of other executive budget states, New York lodged its budget system in the constitution, and the extent of its reorganization was still considered, a decade later, to be "the most extensive administrative reorganization yet undertaken by any state government."[52] Section 1 of the amendment mandated department heads to prepare financial estimates in accordance with the governor's instructions and to appear at the governor's budget hearing. Representatives of the Senate Finance and Assembly Ways and Means Committees were invited to attend the estimate revisions hearings. The presiding officers of each house were required to submit the budget requirements for the legislature; the comptroller must transmit the estimates of the financial needs of the judiciary to the governor, who must include these estimates in his budget without revision. This provision was intended to preserve the integrity and independence of each of the three branches. The governor is then obliged to submit a complete budget of proposed expenditures and estimated revenues. Within thirty days of submission of these estimates, the governor is empowered to amend or supplement the budget and, at any time before adjournment, with the consent of the legislature, may amend the original appropriations bill. The legislature "may not alter an appropriations bill except to strike out or reduce items therein." It may add items of appropriations, provided such items are stated separately and distinctly from original items in the bill and they must each refer to a single object or purpose. This enables the governor to arrange the appropriations in lump sums or as discrete items as necessary. The legislature can eliminate or add items, providing the additions can be clearly recognized. The appropriation bills, having passed both houses, become law immediately without further action by the governor. However, the governor is granted veto power over appropriations for the legislature and judiciary, and over the items added by the legislature to his original bill or bills. This veto can be overridden in the manner prescribed in the constitution. The legislature is forbidden to consider further appropriations until those submitted by the governor have been acted upon. Such further appropriation can only be in the form of separate bills, each for a single project or object, and are subject to the governor's approval and veto power.

The first executive budget was submitted to the legislature in January 1929. It contained a number of lump-sum appropriations which were to be spent as the governor directed. The legislature challenged the governor's power to control these lump sum appropriations, and appended to the bill a provision requiring the approval of legislative leaders of the segregation of these items. The issue went to the Court of Appeals after the appellate division decided in favor of the legislature. In *People v. Tremaine*[31] the court sustained the governor's interpretation on four major points: the legislature's attempt to grant finance committee chairs authority to approve segregation of lump sum items was tantamount to a civil appointment and prohibited by the constitution; IV-A limited legislative authority to strike out or reduce recommended appropriations or add separately stated items referring to a single purpose or object; since the clause added by the legislature was neither an appropriation relating to a single purpose or object it was an invalid exercise of legislative power; the legislature could not circumvent the governor's veto power over items of appropriation or "other items in the bill" by attaching conditions to segregation provisions.[32]

The integrity of the executive budget was preserved and the case confirmed the shift from complete legislative control to executive responsibility, one of the most significant state developments in the twentieth century.[33]

A balanced budget is not specifically mandated by the constitution. Governors Whitman and Dewey, among others, took the position that a balanced budget was implied in the section (9) limiting temporary borrowing. That section appears to bar submission of a second unbalanced budget. In the first quarter century no unbalanced budget was submitted, and the requirement was considered to be constitutional. Further support for a balanced budget interpretation is found in Section 2 which mandates that revenues "which he [the governor] may deem necessary to meet proposed expenditures" be factored into the budget. Recent decisions of the Court of Appeals have limited the force of this requirement without specifically denying it constitutional status. In *Wein v. Carey* (1977) the court determined that the requirement of a balanced budget proposal does not mean that a balanced budget will in fact result. Two successive deficits were insufficient to prove that "improper manipulation" of budget estimates of revenues and expenditures had occurred.[34] In *Oneida County v. Berle* (1980) this decision was reaffirmed. The obligation to submit a balanced budget did not necessarily entail the duty to maintain a balanced budget. The governor's duty to present a balanced budget did not include the power to impound funds to avert a deficit.[35]

The impact of these changes on state government were immense. The released executive energy enabled governors to provide effective and forceful leadership. Smith made the point in his own inimitable fashion:

> When the the Governor wants to talk about the state hospital he will have one man to talk to. When he wants to talk about public parks, he will have one man to talk to and the same way when he wants to talk about agriculture, charties and education.[36]

New York had become the "great classic of the reorganization movement."[37]

Article VI: The Judiciary

The restructuring of the judiciary by the 1894 convention proved inflexible in a number of ways. Just five years following the adoption, two amendments were adopted. The first authorized the governor, upon application of the Court of Appeals, to assign up to four additional judges to that court to serve until the calendar was reduced below two hundred cases; the second authorized the governor to make temporary designations to the appellate division when certified by any division that such judges are needed. A 1905 amendment authorized the legislature to increase the number of Supreme Court judges for any judicial district, subject only to a limitation based on population. This amendment marked a departure from the previous constitutional practice of fixing the number of judges in the constitution, thus requiring periodic amendments when increases were necessary. It also permitted the legislature to create new judicial districts. Eight years later the legislature was authorized to increase the number of county court judges within defined limits by specified population ratios. The last amendment before the major revisions adopted as a result of the Judiciary Convention of 1921 occurred in that year. It authorized the legislature to establish children's courts and courts of domestic relations. The recognition of the latter two courts in the constitution reflected the growing importance of these areas of the law and the need for judicial specialization.

The defeat of the proposals submitted by the 1915 convention, including those concerning the judiciary, had little to do with the judiciary article. There was general agreement that the judicial article required further attention, and that gradual change would not provide the systematic revision required. In this context the legislature created an institution unprecedented in New York constitutional history: a constitutional convention devoted solely to a single subject, the judicial system.[38] The Judiciary Convention of 1921 was composed of one judge from the Court of Appeals, designated by that court; one justice from each of the appellate divisions, designated by the respective divisions; one supreme court justice from each district, chosen by the other justices in the district; the attorney-general; three senators appointed by the president of the senate; three members of the assembly, appointed by the assembly speaker; and one attorney from each of the nine judicial districts, with a least ten years of active practice in the courts of New York, to be appointed by the governor—for a total of thirty members. The convention convened on May 10, 1921, and adjourned on December 5, 1921. It appointed an executive committee of nine, which held fifteen public sessions and prepared a report which it presented to the convention on November 5, 1921.[39]

The convention accepted the recommendations of the executive committee with the exception of those on the Court of Claims. Membership of the Court of Appeals was to remain unchanged: one chief judge and six associate judges, with no more than four justices of the Supreme Court to serve as additional associate judges when needed. The principle change regarding the Court of Appeals concerned jurisdiction. The court would continue to be "essential and always a court of law," meaning that its primary functions should be applying the law as established by the legislature and correcting major errors committed by the lower courts. Its power to review facts was enlarged to include, along with criminal cases involving the death penalty, cases in which the appellate division made a new finding of facts. On the other hand, the convention recommended repeal of an 1884 provision (Sec. 9) which precluded review by the Court of Appeals of unanimous decisions of the appellate division when evidence sustaining the factual finding existed. Appeals would be taken from the appellate division in certain specified cases only with permission of the latter. The result was that the right of appeal was not entirely dependent on the discretion of the appellate division or the Court of Appeals. The motivation of the convention was not so much to expand or restrict the jurisdiction as it was to fix that jurisdiction in the constitution, free from "annual tinkering with by the legislature."[40]

The revisions, with minor changes, continued the structure of the Supreme Court and the appellate division. For the first time, appellate terms were granted constitutional status, but were not organized as permanent courts. To ensure flexibility and obviate resort to further amendment, the judiciary convention accorded the appellate division power to discontinue such terms if necessary. Terms of judges in county and surrogate courts were extended to fourteen years, and county court monetary jurisdiction was increased from $2,000 to $3,000. The convention made a series of recommendations for consolidating New York City courts. Service as a delegate to a constitutional convention was exempted from the prohibition on judges serving in any public office. All the recommendations were accepted by the legislature and were ratified by the people in 1925.[41]

In addition to being a new and effective mechanism for achieving constitutional reform, the convention was significant for its accomplishments. The 1921 convention's recommendations were the sole recommendations on the judiciary accepted by the voters in this century. The work of the 1915 convention, on which the judiciary convention built, was rejected at the polls; the judiciary article submitted separately by the 1938 convention was similarly rejected, as was the work of the 1967 convention. The structure established in 1925 was the last systematic revision of the judiciary article until the adoption of a unified court system thirty-five years later.[42]

Article VII: State Debt

The state debt article was barely touched at the 1894 convention. There was no general fund debt at the time the convention was deliberating and the total debt of the state had been declining precipitously since 1846, decreasing from $24,735,080 to $2,320,660 in 1896.[43] That was to change radically between 1900 and 1938, during which time more than one billion dollars of borrowing was authorized. This expansion of debt was facilitated by a number of constitutional amendments which liberalized borrowing. Two of these proposals were passed in 1905, one liberalizing debt restrictions and the other providing a new way of repaying the state debt. The first extended the maximum maturity of bonds from eighteen to fifty years (Sec. 4). By reducing the size of annual payments over the course of the total amount of interest to be paid, this amendment encouraged borrowing. The amendment also permitted the submission of a debt proposal and a constitutional amendment (but not another debt question) simultaneously. A new Section 11 provided an alternative method of financing the sinking fund installments, enabling the state to provide the necessary installments from the general revenue rather than imposing a special property tax. The legislature did in fact repeal the property tax, and transferred the burden of making sinking fund payments to the general fund.[44]

Section four was again amended in 1909. The new provision limited how and when the state's debt was to be repaid. Supporters hoped the amendment would limit opportunity for "juggling with the funded debt for political or ulterior purposes."[45]

As debt continued to increase, attention was focused on repayment plans. In 1920 three major changes in the debt structure were added to the constitution (Secs. 2, 4, 5, 11). The authorization for casual deficits of one million dollars was deleted and replaced with a clause allowing unlimited borrowing, with tax anticipation notes to be repaid in one year (Sec. 2). The amendment authorized the state to execute all future long-term borrowing by serial bonds divided into equal annual installments not to exceed the life of the project, and in any event no longer than fifty years. It allowed the state to substitute serial bonds for outstanding sinking funds, provided that completion costs did not exceed the original debt. The amendment also adjusted the management of the current sinking funds (Sec. 5). Finally and most remarkably, the amendment made annual appropriations for interest and retirement of the debt absolutely mandatory on the legislature, inserting a powerful prophylactic against any possible default. The comptroller was authorized to pay the debt service in the event the legislature failed to act. With the adoption of this provision the state, in effect, surrendered its sovereign right to repudiate its debts. Bondholders were granted the right to enforce bond contracts with the state in judicial forum.[46]

In 1936 the legislature appropriated only enough funds to cover nine months of debt service for the 1937 fiscal year, intending to appropriate funds for the remaining three months in the next session. The comptroller intervened and impounded funds for the additional three months.[47]

Section 3, which allowed unlimited accumulation of debt to repel invasions, suppress insurrections, or otherwise defend the state, was amended in 1929 to include unrestricted debt to suppress forest fires. The addition was prompted by concern over the constitutionality of the conservation law revision permitting the state to obtain temporary loans to suppress forest fires.[48]

Five amendments to Article VII were authorizations to borrow money for a variety of projects. In 1905 the state embarked on a massive highway construction program, prompting a constitutional amendment which approved authorizing the state to issue $50 million worth of bonds for a term of fifty years to finance the program. The wording of the amendment permitted the authorization to become a revolving one, enabling the state to issue new bonds for highway development without referendum, as otherwise required by Section 2. Voters approved, by referendum, a law authorizing $45 million in bonuses to veterans of World War I.[49] The law was challenged as a violation of Article VII, Section 1, which prohibits the state from giving or loaning its money or credit to individuals, associations, corporations, or private undertakings. The Court of Appeals in *People v. Westchester County National Bank*[50] held that "The state proposes to give its credit to the soldiers and sailors not to satisfy any obligation that it owes them, but as a gratuity. The act is therefore prohibited. . . ." To reverse the effect of this decision and validate the proposed bonuses, a 1923 amendment authorizing the proposed bonds was approved.

During the 1920s a major portion of the state's needs had to be financed by means of loans. The country was experiencing a wave of prosperity. Public and private credit was expanding as real estate prospered and people demanded a variety of improvements from their state and local governments. Proposals for bond issuances were increasing so rapidly that it became difficult for the state to arrange separate submissions. The constitution permitted only one submission per year (Sec. 4). To surmount this difficulty a new section (15) was inserted, providing for the annual issuance of $10 million in bonds for years following adoption, to support the financing of public improvements through appropriations by the legislature. Bonds issued under this amendment were also exempted from the requirement that they be approved by the electorate. This authorization could have been obtained by a referendum approving the debt, but a constitutional amendment was favored for two reasons: the bond issue could be for a term of fifty years, rather than the eighteen then specified in the constitution, and it gave the state revolving authority to borrow for ten years without seeking electorate approval each year. This amendment, which took effect in January 1926, was, in the words of the *Poletti Report*, a "very radical departure from the referendum requirement maintained in the Constitution of 1846."[51]

The rapidly expanding highway system criss-crossing the state created an alarming increase in the number of accidents at railroad (grade) crossings, intensifying public pressure to eliminate these hazards. In 1925 an amendment authorized the issuance of up to $300 million in bonds for removal of these crossings. The amendment specified that 50% of the expenses of the program would be borne by the railroad companies, with the remainder divided between the state and the towns, cities, and villages. This amendment was altered in 1927 to include counties, and the allocation of costs between state and localities was left to the legislature. Although a grade crossing removal project began and some progress was made, approximately two-thirds of the bond allocation remained unused by the late 1930s.[53] The slow pace of grade elimination generated dissatisfaction with the approach embodied in the 1925 and 1927 amendments. Consequently, the 1938 convention would alter considerably the allocation of expenses between the government and the railroads.

Article VIII: Local Debt and Tax Limitations

The interval between 1895 and the beginning of the Great Depression witnessed extensive municipal public works projects. Such projects would have been impossible under a fair reading of the debt and tax limitations placed in the Constitution in the final quarter of the nineteenth century. Cities discovered ways to circumvent these restrictions. One such technique was the simple expedient of raising the assessed valuation of taxable property, thus raising the tax base used to determine debt limits.[54] In other cases, particularly with regard to debt limitations, the only way to finance public improvements was through a constitutional amendment liberalizing the debt restrictions. Between 1895 and 1927 six amendments were passed, creating exemptions for cities wishing to undertake public works projects.[55]

One of the six was necessitated by the consolidation of New York City in 1897. When the city enlarged its boundaries by annexing all or part of the surrounding counties, it found itself in excess of its debt limitations, making it impossible to finance any city improvements for some time. The dilemma was created partly by the 1894 Constitution, which required the city to include within its debt-incurring power the debts of the incorporated counties. To avoid this disconcerting prospect, an 1899 amendment provided that when a city absorbs all or part of several counties, the debt-incurring power of those counties ceases, but their existing debt would not be charged against the city's debt. The effect of this amendment was to allow the city to understate the full extent of its debt liabilities. In addition, the legislature allowed the city to include the assessed value of certain tangible property, thus increasing the tax base used to determine debt limitations. These measures enabled New York City to incur growing amounts of debts.

Four of the amendments were necessary to correct the myopic language of the 1884 amendment, which exempted debt for water projects but allowed only a twenty-year term for the bonds, making the exemptions practically useless. To rectify this error and to allow cities to borrow for water projects, amendments were passed exempting New York City in 1905, all second-class cities in 1907, all third-class cities in 1909, and Buffalo, Syracuse, and Rochester in 1917. The addition of these four amendments made Section 10 practically impossible to decipher. A 1927 amendment reduced the accumulation of impenetrable verbiage to one simple, comprehensive sentence.

New York City's decision to construct and operate subway lines in the 1890s created more debt for the city than any other single project. Between 1905 and 1908 the city reached its debt limit two or three times, causing suspension of the project. By 1908 the city's debt margin could not sustain the project. A decision to raise assessed valuations sharply proved insufficient to support the extension of the subway system being contemplated. An amendment was sought and successfully adopted in 1909 which exempted subway bonds and dock construction from the city's debt limitations. Unfortunately, the subway loan did not prove even partially self-supporting; thus, the new bonds failed to qualify for the new exemption. The amendment specified that the exemption would apply only to bonds that were not a burden on the taxpayer. As a result the city obtained only $50 million from the amendment, a "one-time shot-in-the-arm" rather than the continuing support necessary to finance subway construction.[56] In 1927 another amendment exempted $300 million in bonds for transit construction in New York City, and $5 million for Syracuse for its special assessment debt.

Conservation and Canals

All these exemptions were intended for revenue-producing improvements only. Debt limits for non-revenue producing projects remained under the 1884 and 1894 restrictions.

Prior to the 1938 revisions, both conservation and canals were included in the local debt and tax limitation article. Five amendments affecting the conservation provision (Sec. 7) and four concerning canals (Sec. 8) were adopted within this period.

In 1917 an amendment permitted use of up to 3% of the forest preserve land for municipal water supply reservoirs, canals, and regulation of stream flows. Amendments in 1918, 1927, and 1933 authorized state highway construction within the preserve. In 1931 a new section (Sec. 16) was inserted, mandating an eleven-year reforestation program: The legislature "shall appropriate" specific sums for the purchase of land beyond the forest preserve for reforestation. The initial allocation of one million dollars would be increased by $200,000 each succeeding year. These lands were exempted from the prohibition in Section 7 prohibiting cutting, removing, or selling trees. The amendment enabled the state to put to effective use abandoned agricultural land.[57] These mandates were, by and large, disregarded as a result of the financial exigencies created by the depression. Other amendments proposing recreational use and water power development within the preserve were rejected in 1923 and 1932.

The amendments to the canal section involved changes in the exemptions to the general prohibition against selling, leasing, or disposing of the canal system. In 1918 part of the canal in Utica was exempted to permit street improvements. In 1921 two similar—but not identical—amendments were submitted which exempted sections of the canal between Rome and Mohawk and reinstated the prohibition on the sale of the Utica section. Ambiguities created by these overlapping amendments remained unresolved until 1933 with the adoption of a third amendment. Like its conservation counterpart, this section contained a welter of exemptions and additions, making future exemptions and additions likely.

ARTICLE XII: HOME RULE AND THE CITIES

The provisions of the 1894 Constitution failed to satisfy the larger cities. Moreover, the demands made on cities would multiply in the first third of the twentieth century. The 1915 constitutional convention considered the issue extensively, but those efforts would not bear fruit at the polls.[58]

The 1894 provisions did have the immediate effect of reducing special city legislation passed without the approval of the cities in question, but it did not stop special legislation.[59] The classification of New York as the only city in the first class allowed special legislation for that city under the guise of a general law. In addition, the court gave an expansive reading of the police power, enabling the state to pass general laws which applied to separate cities.[60] Some relief was provided by a 1907 amendment adjusting the population of cities for classification purposes. A city in the first class would be one with 175,000 or more inhabitants; second class designated 50,000 but less than 175,000; and third class included all other cities. Additionally, the amendment altered the phrase "property, affairs, or government" in the 1894 Constitution (Sec. 2) to read "property, affairs of government. . . ." This change has had no impact on subsequent interpretations of the phrase as the courts, the legislature and nearly all commentators have ignored it. The reason for the change is unclear, but it is unlikely to have been inadvertent.[61]

A Home Rule Act adopted by the legislature in 1913 spoke of every city as having the "power to regulate, manage and control its property and local affairs," but the courts chose not interpret this clause as providing home rule, at least in the sense of enabling cities to amend their charter provisions.[62] In addition to the restrictive readings given these provisions by the courts, and the legislature's use of a fictitious classification system to circumvent the special law procedure of the 1894 Constitution, the 1894 clause had a critical defect as far as home rule was concerned. That flaw was stated succinctly by Professor Howard McBain: "It gives a large measure of freedom from positive interference but almost no measure of opportunity for constructive local action."[63]

Persistent criticism and pressure for reform eventually resulted in a Home Rule Amendment, approved in 1923. With its adoption the suspensive veto over special legislation was eliminated, as was the population classification of cities. To qualify as "general" a law could not be special or local "either in its terms or effects." The state legislature was prohibited from passing any special legislation concerning the "property, affairs, or government" of cities except on message from the governor affirming a state of emergency, and then only with the concurrence of two-thirds of both houses of the legislature. Outside the "property affairs or government" no restrictions were placed on legislative powers. Just as significant was Section 3, which endowed cities with actual legislative power. Cities could adopt and amend local laws not inconsistent with state laws in a specified number of distinctly local matters, and the legislature was authorized to confer upon cities further powers as it deemed expedient.

Proponents of city home rule in the 1920s focused on protecting cities from special legislation, under the assumption that a truly general law could not threaten city home rule. Legislative abuse was less likely to occur if laws were applied to all cities of the state. Logically, sixty cities could assert more pressure on the state legislature than one or two. Finally, reformers reasoned that if the legislature could legislate for cities only by general laws, it would be compelled to grant home rule to cities.[64]

When New York City, acting pursuant to this grant, adopted a local law providing for city acquisition and operation of surface transportation lines, the Court of Appeals struck down the law as ultra vires, beyond the grant of local legislative power provided by Section 3 of the article. Judge Benjamin Cardozo argued that cities were not authorized to adopt local laws relating to their property affairs or government, but only to adopt such laws with regard to the matter specified in Section 3. The court noted a gap between Section 2 and Section 3. Section 2 protected cities against special legislation but was not a grant of home rule power, whereas Section 3, which was a grant of home rule power, did not contain the power necessary to sustain this law.[65] In 1928 the legislature amended the City Home Rule Law to narrow the gap between Sections 2 and 3, giving cities power to act in the area of their property affairs or government, including the subjects noted in Section 3.

One year later the Court of Appeals delivered what is considered by most commentators the crippling blow to city home rule. In *Adler v. Deegan*[66] the court upheld a Multiple Dwelling Law which was applicable solely to New York City. It was designed to remedy problems with tenement housing, such as unsanitary and unsafe slum dwellings. If the law related to the property affairs of the government of the city and was not general in scope, then it had to be declared invalid since it had not been the subject of an emergency message from the governor and a two-thirds vote of the legislature. The court, obviously sympathetic with the law, found that the area was one of "state concern," that it was a health law, not related to the property affairs and government of a single city. In justifying what appears to be a decision counter to the plain meaning of this phrase Judge Frederick Crane wrote: "When the people put these words in Article XII of the Constitution they put them there with a Court of Appeals definition, not that of Websters Dictionary."[67] Crane's view was that the words "property affairs of government" were taken from the 1894 Constitution by the drafters of the home rule amendment with the intention of preserving their technical meaning, viz., the meaning of the phrase as interpreted by the judiciary between 1894 and 1923, making those precedents binding on the post-home rule amendment court.[68] Judge Cardozo's concurrence recognized as untenable the argument that this law was unrelated to the affairs, property, or government of the city; he developed an approach that would become the standard for future cases: "if the subject be in a substantial degree a matter of state concern, the legislature may act, though intermingled with it are concerns of the locality."[69] The crux of that ruling was that matters of state concern are beyond the purview of home rule as a shield, with the judiciary deciding what are matters of state concern.

By the time of the 1938 constitutional convention the home rule provision of the constitution had been limited by judicial decisions and a variety of legislative enactments addressing serious social and economic problems, problems which seemed to make the concern for local autonomy a secondary consideration at best.

The Adler case was not the only court decision raising questions about the extent of city home rule. The rise of public benefit corporations, known as authorities, also threatened the autonomy of cities. In *Robinson v. Zimmerman* the court sustained a statute creating a sewer authority in Buffalo.[70] Traditionally, ownership and operation of a sewer system was subject to city jurisdiction. Nonetheless, the statute establishing the authority was passed by a simple majority, without an emergency measure—arguably contrary to the requirements of Section 2 of this article.

The problem of home rule for cities was not the only dimension of home rule addressed by constitutional amendment. Counties also received a measure of protection. Prior to these amendments the constitution authorized the legislature to permit boards of supervisors to exercise powers of local legislation and administration (Sec. 17). In 1874 this provision was altered to read: "the legislature shall, by general law confer upon boards of supervisors . . . such further powers of local legislation and administration as the legislature shall deem expedient" (Sec. 23). This prohibited certain types of private and local bills, and encouraged passage of general law (Sec. 18).

Two amendments applied solely to Nassau and Westchester Counties, two of the most populous counties in the state. Both attempted to grant these counties a measure of home rule. A 1921 amendment permitted the legislature to prescribe special forms of government for these two counties subject to approval by the electorate at a general election. Although both counties attempted to revise their forms of government under this amendment the voters within the counties rejected these plans. A subsequent amendment in 1929 concerning these two counties was more specific and extensive in granting them a measure of local autonomy and establishing the procedure under which the legislature must act when passing special legislation regarding the two counties.[71]

In 1935 these amendments were superceded by the adoption of a county Home Rule Amendment (Sec. 26). It called on the legislature to provide alternative forms of government for counties outside of New York City, and for submission of the plan chosen to the voters for approval. The approval was subject to a "split referendum," requiring approval in every city with 25% of the county population, and in the part of the county outside of such cities. Behind this requirement was a desire to give both rural and urban residents a voice in determining the type of government under which they wished to live. Towns were especially worried about the possibility of large-scale transfers of their functions to the counties if reorganization could take place by a simple majority.

The amendment, though intended to parallel the city home rule amendment of 1923, differed from the latter in two important respects. Unlike the city home rule act, the county amendment vested no direct constitutional power in the counties to adopt and amend local laws, however, the legislature is explicitly empowered to provide for the exercise of such power. A second crucial difference lies in the fact that the county home rule amendment authorized the legislature to specify the optional forms of government from which counties are to choose, while the city amendment allowed cities, within the scope of the act, to exercise their own choices.

The attempt to achieve county home rule is complicated in as much as counties are intermediate governmental units between the state and municipal government. Any attempt to expand their powers involves sensitive questions regarding the relationship between county powers and functions and town, village, and city functions. It raises "basic questions about the structure and distribution of powers of local government within the county."[72]

The 1935 amendment significantly advanced the ability of local officials and voters to reorganize county government and operate it as they saw fit. The legislature has enacted numerous statutes providing counties with a range of options for the organization of their governments.[73]

The emergence of an active state, one taking a more direct role in the maintenance of the social order, was related to the rise of a progressive consensus on the need for effective and responsible government. That consensus emerged in the 1915 constitutional convention, though its acceptance proved too much for the electorate to accept, at least in its entirety. Elites from a variety of quarters, such as government, business, and the academy, recognized that the constitutional structure of the state as it had evolved in the nineteenth century would not enable the state to play an active and effective role in managing a social order characterized by a dynamism seldom witnessed in world history, let alone the history of the state or nation.

The first third of the twentieth century was a period in New York's constitutional development in which the values of efficiency and effective government replaced the nineteenth-century constitutional tradition which had emphasized democratization, decentralization, and the delimitation of governmental power. Executive reorganization, the short ballot, and an executive budget system, as well as a four-year term for the governor, were effective in shifting the balance from decentralization and democratic participation to a more centralized and efficient governing apparatus. The governor would be the fulcrum: popularly elected, providing energy and direction, and equipped with the tools for effective governance. It may be more accurate to say that there was a shift from a decentralized, locally oriented, legislatively based representation to a centralized, state-oriented, executive-based representation. That shift would be the central defining feature of New York's governmental system into the 1980s. The legislature would continue to provide a district-oriented focus, but its role in shaping the policies of the state would be radically altered, if not significantly diminished.

Notes

1. *Poletti Reports* (1938), VI, *Problems Relating to the Bill of Rights and General Welfare*, pp. 145–146.
2. E.g., *Bennett v. Boyle*, 40 Barb. 551 (1864).
3. Lewis Orgel, *Valuation Under Eminent Domain* as quoted in *Constitutional Convention Committee Reports*, Vol. 6: *Bill of Rights and General Welfare*, pp. 129–130.
4. Orgel, *Valuation Under Eminent Domain*, pp. 133–134.
5. *Cancemi v. People*, 18 N.Y. 128 (1858); *People v. Cosmo*, 205 N.Y. 91 (1912).
6. Howard Gillman, *The Constitution Besieged* (Durham: Duke University Press, 1993), pp. 32–45.
7. *Laws of New York*, Chap. 635 (1910), known popularly as the Wainwright Law.

8. 201 N.Y. 271 (1911).
9. *Laws of New York*, Chap. 41 (1914).
10. *Matter of Jensen v. Southern Pacific Railroad Co.*, 215 N.Y. 514 (1915). *White v. New York Central Railroad Co.* 216 N.Y. 653, aff'd 243 U.S. 188 (1917).
11. 166 N.Y. 1 (1900).
12. 8 U.S.C. 368 (1927).
13. 110 Misc. 45 (1920).
14. *Poletti Report*, VI, *Problems Relating to Bill of Rights and General Welfare*, p. 169.
15. Temporary Commission on the Revision and Simplification of the Constitution, *Suffrage and Elections*, Staff Report No. 30, p. 23.
16. *Katzenbach v. Morgan*, 384 U.S. 641 (1966).
17. *Public Papers of Governor Herbert Lehman, 1935* (Albany: J. B. Lyon, n.d.), p. 231.
18. One, in 1899, exempted New York City from the provision (Sec. 26) requiring boards of supervisors in each county. It was occasioned by the consolidation of five counties into greater New York in 1897.
19. Thomas Schick, *The New York State Constitutional Convention of 1915 and the Modern State Governor* (New York: National Municipal League, 1978), p. 24.
20. *Public Papers of Charles Evans Hughes, 1910* (Albany: J. B. Lyon, n.d.); pp. 25–26.
21. Schick, *Constitutional Convention of 1915*, pp. 25–26.
22. New York State Department of Efficiency and Economy and Bureau of Municipal Research, *Constitution and Government of the State of New York* (Albany, 1915), p. 58.
23. New York State Reconstruction Commission, *Report to Governor Alfred E. Smith on Retrenchment and Reorganization of the State Government* (Albany, 1919), p. 6.
24. Robert Caro, *The Power Broker, Robert Moses and the Fall of New York* (New York: Vintage Books, 1975), p. 127.
25. Annual Message from the Governor, January 2, 1919, *Public Papers of Alfred E. Smith, 1919* (Albany: J. B. Lyon, 1920), pp. 30–31. The impact of Belle Moskowitz on New York politics and government through her role as Smith's closest advisor is fully told in Elizabeth Israels Perry, *Belle Moskowitz Feminine Politics and the Exercise of Power in the Age of Alfred E. Smith* (New York: Oxford University Press, 1987). Perry provides a detailed account of Moskowitz's role in the birth of the commission, pp. 119–139.
26. *Report to the Governor*, p. 23.
27. *Journal of the Constitutional Convention of the State of New York, 1915* (Albany: J. B. Lyons, 1915), pp. 384–403.
28. *Laws of New York*, Chap. 130 (1916).
29. *Report of the State Reorganization Commission, February 26, 1926* (Albany, 1926), pp. 4–5.
30. Ibid., p. 11.
31. 52 N.Y. 27 (1929).
32. 52 N.Y. 27, at 49–50. Fuller treatment of this case can be found in *The Executive Budget in New York State* (Albany: New York State Division of the Budget, 1981), pp. 48–52.
33. The integrity of the executive budget was reaffirmed in *People v. Tremaine*, 281 N.Y. 1 (1939). The legislature had consolidated the line item in Gover-

nor Lehman's budget into lump sums and rearranged and redefined the items, making across the board cuts in the consolidated items. The Court of Appeals ruled that the legislature had no authority to alter the budget bills of the executive and must act on them as submitted. In reaching this decision the court concluded that the constitution mandated item-budgeting and that appropriations are to be itemized, "so far as practicable or possible" (at 10).

34. 41 N.Y. 2d. 498, at 504–505 (1977).
35. 49 N.Y. 2d. 515 (1980).
36. as quoted by Caro, *Power Broker*, p. 261.
37. Leslie Lipson, *The American Governor From Figurehead to Leader* (Chicago: University of Chicago Press, 1939), p. 90.
38. *Laws of New York*, Chap. 348 (1921).
39. The records of the convention's executive committee are incomplete. Minutes for only three of the sessions are preserved at the New York State Library. The text of the executive committee's report is reprinted in Volume IX of the *Poletti Reports* (1938), *Problems Relating to Judicial Administration and Organization*.
40. Remarks of William Guthrie, chair of the Executive Committee, *Minutes of the Executive Committee*, as reprinted in *Poletti Reports* (1938), IX, *Problems Relating to Judicial Administration and Organization*, p. 177.
41. The convention recommended an opening clause vesting the judicial power of the state in the courts to parallel similar clauses in the executive and legislative articles. The legislature did not accept this recommendation.
42. The 1920 amendment embodied essentially the same proposals made at the 1915 convention. *Journal of the 1915 Constitutional Convention, Report of the Committee on State Finance*, p. 321.
43. Figures taken from New York State Temporary State Commission on the Constitutional Convention, *State Finance*, Staff Report No. 8, 1967, p. 76.
44. *Poletti Reports* (1938), X: *Taxation and Finances*, p. 129.
45. *Report of the Committee of Inquiry to Governor Sulzer*, Senate Doc. (1913), No. 57, pp. 105–106.
46. The 1920 amendment embodied essentially the same proposal made at the 1915 convention, *Journal, 1915 Convention, Report of the Committee on State Finance*, p. 321.
47. Temporary Commission on Constitutional Convention, *State Finance*, 1967, pp. 85–86.
48. *Seventeenth Annual Report of the Conservation Department*, Leg. Doc. (1928) No. 38, p. 198.
49. *Laws of New York*, Chap. 872 (1920).
50. 231 N.Y. 465 (1921).
51. *Poletti Reports* (1938), X, *Taxation and Finances*, p. 94.
52. A. E. Buck, *The Reorganization of State Government in the United States*, as quoted in *The Executive Budget in New York State*, p. 41.
53. *Constitutional Convention of 1938, Journal* (Albany: J. B. Lyon, 1938), pp. 207–210.
54. *Poletti Reports* (1938), X, *Taxation and Finances*, pp. 234ff.
55. The rejected 1915 Constitution also included provisions liberalizing debt restrictions.
56. Temporary Commission on the Revision and Simplification of the Constitution, *Constitutional Debt Limits for Local Government*, Staff Report No. 32 (1959), p. 46.

57. *Report of the Joint Legislative Committee on Natural Resources*, Leg. Doc. (1953), No. 69, p. 98.

58. *Rev. Rec., 1915*, II, pp. 1961-2037, 2087-2176; III, pp. 2940-2982, 3708-3726.

59. Harold McBain, "Home Rule for Cities," in *New York Constitutional Commission, The Revision of the State Constitution* (New York, 1915), pp. 6-7.

60. *People ex rel. Einsfeld v. Murray*, 149 N.Y. 267 (1896).

61. The one commentator who noticed this change was W. Bernard Richland, "Constitutional Home Rule in New York," *Columbia Law Review* 54 (March, 1954), I, pp. 323-324. Richland argues that the change should have had a direct bearing on a key argument that the Court of Appeals was to use in the landmark *Adler v. Deegan*, 251 N.Y. 467 (1929) case, discussed below, p. 290. The court argued that the phrase was to be interpreted as it appeared in the 1894 Constitution. Subsequent revisions reverted to the disjunctive "or."

62. A subsequent statute, the Optional City Government Law of 1914, Chapter 444, applicable to the second and third cities, allowed these cities to choose among a set of optional forms of governance for adoption by way of local petition and referendum.

63. McBain, *The Revision of the Constitution*, p. 10.

64. Temporary State Commission on the Constitutional Convention, *Local Government*, Staff Report No. 13, 1967, p. 72.

65. *Browne v. City of New York*, 241 N.Y. 96 (1925).

66. 251 N.Y. 467 (1929).

67. Ibid., 473.

68. This decision has been subjected to sharp criticism, e.g., Richman, "Home Rule in New York," I, pp. 329-331.

69. 251 N.Y. 467, at 491.

70. 268 N.Y. 52 (1935). See below, pp. 246, 248.

71. One other amendment to Article III, Section 27, authorized the legislature to confer on county auditors or other fiscal officers such powers as the legislature shall deem expedient.

72. Temporary Commission on the Revision and Simplification of the Constitution, *County Government*, Staff Report No. 15 (1959), pp. 138-139.

73. E.g., The Optional County Government Law, *Laws of New York*, Chap. 862 (1937); Alternative Government Law, *Laws of New York*, Chap. 545 (1954).

Constitutional Changes
1895–1937

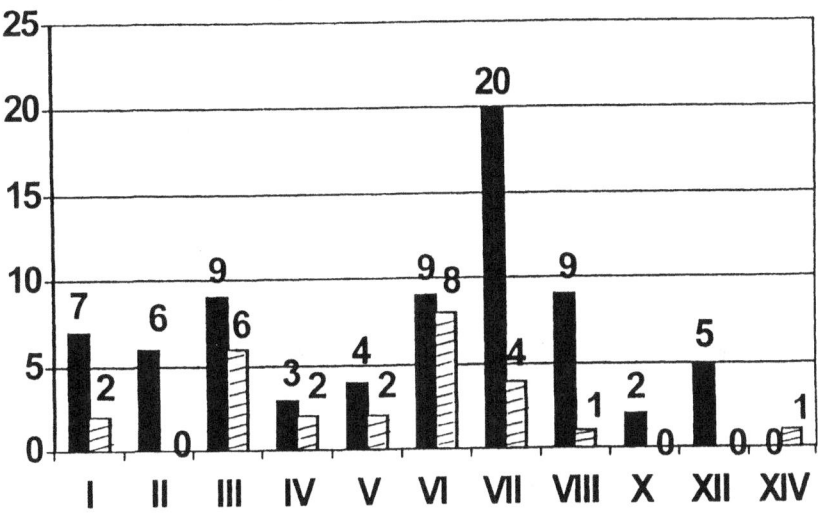

■ Approved (76)   ▨ Rejected (26)

*Some proposed amendments affected more than one article. Sixty-nine amendments were approved, twenty-four rejected.

12

Constitution-Making During the Depression: The Constitutional Convention of 1938

WITH A BITTER CONTEST for the presidency between the incumbent, Democrat Franklin D. Roosevelt of New York and Republican challenger Alfred Landon of Kansas, and a governor's election, the question of a constitutional convention would have failed to appear on the 1936 ballot had it not been for the provisional twenty-year requirement. The reform groups of the state had voiced little demand for a convention, mainly because they had previously achieved their major goals. Between 1915 and 1935, executive reorganization, the executive budget, and home rule for the cities had been adopted by constitutional amendments. The major political parties, neither of which included the issue in their state platforms, had other reasons for their lack of enthusiasm for a new constitution. A new constitutional convention meant a new reapportionment provision. The state legislature had been unable to agree on reapportionment since 1925, thus silently ratifying the gerrymander embodied in the 1894 Constitution. Tammany Democrats opposed any convention, as reapportionment would mean the loss of power to the outlying boroughs of New York City, and they feared modification of the single-member district system. Non-Tammany Democrats, in a rare display of agreement with their adversaries, were not as confident of their political position, and thus were unsure of gaining control of a convention if called two years hence.[1]

Some notable individuals and groups did support the call for a convention. Democratic Governor Herbert Lehman advocated a convention, as did New York City Mayor Fiorello H. LaGuardia, the American Labor Party, and the Citizen's Union of New York, which issued a position paper recommending a constitutional convention.

The proponents' case for a new convention can be summarized thus:

although the process of piecemeal amendment had been successful in effecting specific reforms, it had created a massive document with obsolete provisions and sections, lacking overall consistency. Moreover, the legislature was either handicapped in, or disqualified from, dealing with certain issues such as apportionment and home rule. Finally, even if the proposals suffered defeat at the polls, the accomplishments of a constitutional convention would focus the people's attention on problems of government and provide a full agenda of proposals for legislative consideration.[2]

The strongest case against the calling of a convention was presented in the editorial pages of *The New York Times*. Its list of arguments focused on the absence of leadership. The voters

> have had little guidance from the usual sources: the rival platforms are silent on the subject, campaign speakers have had nothing illuminating to say about it, civic bodies have given it only casual and belated consideration. There is no organized propaganda behind this particular referendum. . . ."[3]

The voters decided in favor of a convention by the slim margin of 1,413,604 to 1,190,275. The total vote on the convention question was 3,000,000 less than the total vote in the governor's race, providing additional evidence for the proposition that in New York the question of calling a constitutional convention usually has been decided by an active minority of the electorate.

Six identifiable party or factional groups emerged from the Depression and in reaction to the New Deal. Upstate Republicans, the most conservative of the factions, did not oppose the New Deal publicly; rather, they attempted to slow the pace and extent of government regulation. New York City Republicans had developed a degree of independence from the upstate branch of the party, and frequently supported independent and reform measures and candidates, like Fiorello LaGuardia. The Democratic Party was divided among New York City Democrats, who supported the New Deal, Tammany Democrats, at best tepid toward Franklin Roosevelt and his reforms, and upstate Democrats, who were supportive of the national New Deal and New York's "Little New Deal" fostered by Governor Herbert Lehman. Finally, the American Labor Party, founded in 1936 and closely aligned to the labor movement, fully supported the New Deal. This party had grown rapidly between 1936 and 1938, polling 274,924 votes in the 1936 fall election.[4]

When the process of delegate selection began, the Democratic Party appeared to have the advantage. With the re-election of Governor Lehman the Democrats gained control of the state senate. The American Labor Party was strong enough to be courted by both Democrats and

Republicans in the delegate selection process. Realizing this, and fearful of a Democrat-controlled convention, Republican leaders immediately began galvanizing party regulars throughout the state, conjuring the specter of a convention controlled by "radical New Dealers." Conversely, Democrats, preoccupied with the mayoralty race, were not as active or well-organized with delegate selection. Thus, for the third consecutive time, as in 1894 and 1915, the final result was a Republican delegate majority. Of the 153 district delegates, the Republicans captured 84, the Democrats 68, and American Labor 1. The fifteen at-large seats were closely contested; Republicans garnered eight seats and Democrats seven. The deciding factor was the decision of the Labor Party to divide its support between the two major parties. Kenneth F. Simpson, Republican chairman of New York County, convinced the maverick Republican Mayor Fiorello La Guardia to exert his influence with the American Labor Party to obtain its backing for Republican delegates to the convention.[5] The seven Democratic at-large delegates won with the support of the American Labor Party. If American Labor had supported all fifteen Democrats, and if this support had been equally effective, the convention would have comprised 84 Republicans, 83 Democrats, and 1 American Labor delegate.[6]

Prominent delegates included former Governor Alfred E. Smith and U.S. Senator Robert F. Wagner, both delegates at the 1915 convention, and Robert Moses, who had achieved a reputation as the state's "Caesar of parkways and bridges." Two-thirds of the delegates had been active in politics as party officials, public officials, or both. Seventy percent of the delegates were lawyers—slightly less than the three-out-of-four ratio at the 1894 and 1915 conventions; approximately thirty of these delegates were drawn from the judiciary. For the first time in New York, women served as delegates to a state constitutional convention. The convention delegates were composed of men and women of diverse experience in politics and government, as well as varying degrees of expertise in specialized fields.

Once again, proponents of the convention recognized that the task of revising a constitution required information on all aspects of the constitution and its history, as well as the problems connected with its operation. Governor Lehman proposed to the legislature the creation of a commission to assist the delegates in accumulating such data, as was done in 1894 and 1915. Expressing a twentieth-century version of the Whig understanding of the virtuous citizen pursuing the public good, he suggested that the convention should be "directed by leading experts in state government."[7] The legislature rejected this request, arguing that such material would constitute interference with the people's convention. It is at least as likely that assembly Republicans opposed Lehman's proposal because they feared that his request was a way of promoting a "must list" for constitutional reform.[8] Governor Lehman thereupon appointed an "unofficial committee" to provide information for the delegates. The committee was under the direction of Judge Charles Poletti, later lieutenant-governor and governor. It produced twelve volumes: five reference volumes, and seven volumes devoted to problems related to the bill of rights, taxation and finance, and issues of home rule and local government. Despite the haste in gathering this material, the work of the Poletti Committee remains a comprehensive source of reliable information on the constitutional tradition of New York.

The Work of the Convention

Frederick E. Crane, a member of the Court of Appeals, was elected president of the convention, with prominent Republicans occupying the remainder of the key posts. Chief Judge Crane commanded bipartisan respect as a jurist. He was determined to lead the whole convention rather than a merely partisan majority. The attendance of Alfred E. Smith created a dilemma for Democrats and for the convention, as he had become a bitter opponent of Roosevelt and the New Deal. He remained, however, one of New York's great governors and the quintessential Democrat. Republicans considered offering him the post of vice president of the convention, but decided that he was too much of a Democrat. Democrats, conversely, believed that his insurgency made him too unreliable to be offered an operational position. A compromise was reached by creating a new post, honorary president. Operational leadership of the Democratic delegates was given to Senator Robert Wagner.[9]

The convention held its opening session on April 5, 1938 and adjourned on August 26, 1938. Its work was shaped by three factors: the predominance of lawyers, organization along party lines, and the impact of interest groups. The significance of the latter was recognized by the delegates when they incorporated into convention rules sections of the statute law requiring registration of all lobbyists and itemized statements of expenditures. Compliance with these rules was minimal and enforcement practically non-existent. The "futility of the gesture" was due to the fact that many of the delegates thought the rule silly, and that much of the lobbying was done through public agencies or through unpaid respresentatives of private groups, both exempt from the requirements.[10] In adopting these rules the 1938 convention was the first convention in New York State to formally recognize the role

Bill of Rights

The convention made a number of changes in Article I. The boldest innovation was the addition of a "Labor Bill of Rights." It contained three parts: a declaration that labor was not to be considered as a commodity or an article of commerce, a limitation on hours of labor and payment of the prevailing wage rate in public works, and a guarantee to labor of the right to organize and bargain collectively. Like other parts of the constitution, this provision was based on statutory enactments. The provision declaring that labor was not a commodity is found in the Clayton Anti-Trust Act (1914) and in the state equivalent, the Donnelly Act.[11] The first paragraph exempted labor unions from the state's anti-trust law, previously used to restrict organized union activity. The second part constitutionalized a policy which had a long history in the state. By 1894 the regulation of wages and hours, and the prevailing wage-rate requirements, had become state law. An early attempt to apply the law to municipalities was declared unconstitutional, but a constitutional amendment nullified that decision in 1905.[12] The desire to tranform public policy into constitutional policy, thereby affording it permanency and status and immunizing legislative action from adverse court review, were two major justifications offered for its inclusion.

The third paragraph followed the pattern of the first two, placing in the document a policy previously recognized by the legislature and the judiciary. New York was a leader in recognizing bargaining agreements and the right to picket. However, this right does not prevent the state from declaring strikes by public employees illegal, nor does it prevent the state from refusing supervisory personnel the right to organize and be recognized for collective bargaining purposes.[13] Much of the protection in this section is currently provided by federal labor law. The occupancy of the field by federal law has pre-empted this section as well as other state labor law, giving it primarily a stand-by character.[14] The importance of these sections, aside from their symbolic value, lies in its potential, should federal policy radically change.

The delegates also adopted a provision prohibiting discrimination against an individual's civil rights on the basis of race, color, or creed (Sec. 11). This section marks the first appearance of an equal protection clause and protection against discrimination in the New York Constitution, although there had been anti-discrimination statute law. The first sentence is the state equivalent of the Fourteenth Amendment's equal protection clause, and New York courts have held the protection provided by this clause to be no broader than that of the federal counterpart.[15] The second section is potentially more far-reaching. It prohibits the state or private individuals and corporations from subjecting individuals to discrimination in violation of their civil rights on the basis of race, color, or creed. A straightforward reading of this clause suggests that by extending the Fourteenth Amendment's state action requirement to include private action, the protection provided by this provision exceeded the protections afforded by the national amendment. The first major test of its scope came in *Dorsey v. Stuyvesant Town Corporation* in 1949.[16] The Court of Appeals in *Dorsey* limited the expanse of the clause, reasoning that the civil rights mentioned in the section refers solely to those elsewhere declared, referring to the convention debates where it was asserted that the civil rights referred to were those "found in the Constitution, in the Civil Rights Law, and in the statutes."[17] The clause is not self-executing; for its protection to operate, legislation is necessary. While the concept of state action has undergone some expansion by the Court of Appeals since *Dorsey*, that court has not expanded its reach much beyond that of the Fourteenth Amendment and has adopted the three-tiered scrutiny test used by the Supreme Court when applying the equal protection clause.[18]

A third addition to the Bill of Rights prohibited unreasonable searches and seizures (Sec. 12). Prior to 1938 no guarantee against search and seizure was present in the state constitution. A proposal at the 1867 convention was rejected along with the document. Since the Fourth Amendment to the national Constitution was not applied to the states until 1949, New York was without constitutional protection against unreasonable searches and seizures for most of its existence.[19] The language of the section is identical to that of the Fourth Amendment, with the addition of a paragraph governing the use of wiretapping. Debate at the convention focused on two issues: wiretapping, and whether a clause should to be added requiring exclusion of evidence gathered in violation of this protection, i.e., an exclusionary rule. Lehman Democrats, led by state senate majority leader John Dunnigan, Judge Charles Poletti, and Judge Edward Weinfeld, were convinced of the necessity of an exclusionary rule to protect privacy rights in criminal cases and to deter police misconduct. Governor Lehman addressed the convention on June 13. He focused on the need for a search and seizure provision and an accompanying exclusionary rule, stating: "I am of the firm conviction that the constitutional convention now assembled in New York has no more important task before it than strengthening the Bill of Rights."[20] The response of opponents was immediate. They requested that a speech delivered two days earlier to the District Attorney's Convention in Cooperstown in New York by Thomas E. Dewey, former prosecutor and district attorney for New York County, be entered into the record.[21] Dewey had a reputation as an aggressive prosecutor of organized crime. He attacked the exclusionary rule as a handcuff on law enforcement which benefited only criminals. The Lehmanites retaliated by proposing a number of exclusionary amendments. Dunnigan, an architect from the Bronx and chair of the Civil Rights Committee, led supporters of the rule; Dewey and Mayor Fiorello LaGuardia led the Republican opposition outside the convention. Dewey and his supporters at the convention retreated from their opposition to a search and seizure clause and Dunnigan yielded on the need for warrants for all wiretaps.[22] Dewey's willingness to support a search and seizure provision, coupled with his rousing speech against the Dunnigan exclusionary rule, carried the day and the convention rejected the rule. The debates were both intensive and of high quality; they comprise one of the most enlightening discussions of civil liberties in the annals of New York's constitutional history.[23]

Until *Mapp v. Ohio* in 1961, where the Supreme Court applied the exclusionary rule to the states, the chief difference in the two sections concerned the exclusionary rule, with the federal courts applying the rule and the state courts rejecting it.[24] In *People v. Richter's Jeweler's Inc.* (1943)[25] the Court of Appeals held that the refusal of the 1938 convention to adopt the rule left the common law rule of admissibility unchanged.

The policy of the state courts in the succeeding quarter of a century followed the Supreme Court, interpreting the state clause to mean what the Fourth Amendment was interpreted to mean. Recently, the Court of Appeals has pursued an independent path, holding in a series of decisions that the state clause provides greater protection against unreasonable searches and seizures than is provided by the Supreme Court's interpretations of the Fourth Amendment.[26]

The second paragraph is an application of the principle in the first section to the specific area of wiretapping. However, although specifying "probable cause" for such taps, as required by the Fourth Amendment, the section specifies "reasonable cause," and mentions only two types of electronic surveillance: telephone and telegraph. Statutes adopted under this provision allowed any supreme or county court judge to issue a warrant, and any police officer to the rank of sergeant to apply for one. The constitutional provision as written did little more than authorize eavesdropping, and the statute passed pursuant to this section was declared unconstitutional in *Berger v. New York*,[27] casting doubt on the validity of this constitutional provision. New York has subsequently revised its statutes to conform to *Berger* and the requirements of the Federal Omnibus Crime Control and Safe Streets Act of 1968.[28] The provision of the national and state statutes are more demanding than the requirements of the constitutional provision.

With regard to the right to trial by jury, the convention strengthened the requirements concerning its waiver. The guarantee of trial by jury appeared in the Charter of Liberties and Privileges of 1683. It is protected by two distinct sections, Article I, Section 2 and Article VI, Section 18 of the current constitution. The first provision for waiver was adopted in 1846 and allowed waivers of jury trials by mutual agreement in civil cases. Prior to 1930 the Court of Appeals adhered to a principle that such waivers were unacceptable in criminal cases.[29] A 1937 amendment permitted waiver of the right in non-capital cases. Behind this amendment was the desire to reduce trial expenses and allow the defendant to avoid the adverse affects of publicity and prejudice on a jury in sensational cases. The "no waiver" philosophy remains evident in the explicit prohibition against any such waiver in capital cases. To ensure that the waiver was made knowingly, intelligently, and voluntarily, the 1938 convention inserted a clause requiring the waiver to be by written instrument in open court. This standard anticipated by thirty years the one adopted by the Supreme Court.[30] The chief issue concerning the waiver is whether the right is absolute or whether a judge has any discretion in denying the waiver. The right to a waiver is not absolute and a judge may refuse to accept a waiver if the request is made in bad faith or if a defendant is not fully aware of the consequences of the choice.[31]

Not all the additions to Article I had the purpose or the effect of expanding rights. The convention inserted a provision mandating the removal of any public official who refused to waive immunity when summoned to testify before a grand jury regarding his/her official conduct (Sec. 6). This constituted a significant qualification to the protection against self-incrimination, providing prosecutors a powerful weapon for obtaining evidence of official misconduct. The prosecutor may seek to compel any public official to testify before a grand jury about conduct in public office under penalty of loss of employment. The official may also be required to sign a waiver of immunity, again under penalty of loss of job for refusal. Such testimony could then be used in subsequent criminal prosecutions. This section was occasioned by the Seabury Investigations of public officials, many of whom refused to answer questions concerning their office, citing the right against self-incrimination.[32] The clause was amended twice more, in 1944 and 1958, to make it applicable to other offices held by the official under investigation, and to the conduct in any office held within five years of the grand jury call. All this changed when the Supreme Court challenged the validity of these waiver provisions. The Court ruled that imposition of any sanctions which made the assertion of the right costly was a violation of the Fifth Amendment.[33] The state has been allowed to dismiss one who, though not required to waive immunity, refused to answer questions specifically, directly, and narrowly related to the performance of his or her duties.[34] Most of this section no longer retains the force of law and remains inoperative as long as *Garrity* and *Broderick* stand.

Delegates also made it clear that the power of the grand jury to investigate official misconduct could not be superceded or impaired. This provision was adopted in response to an attempt by the governor and legislature of Pennsylvania to restrict the power of the grand jury to investigate public corruption. That attempt, which took place barely a month before the convention met, alarmed the delegates. Phillip Halpern (R.-Buffalo) eloquently expressed convention sentiment:

> The function of grand juries in the investigation of the misconduct of public officials is one of the most important functions served by the grand jury system today. The existence of an independent agency drawn from the citizenry at large for that purpose is one of the most estimable features of the American system of government. . . .[35]

Two of the boldest proposals adopted at the convention concerning rights were embodied in Article XVII, "Social Welfare" and Article XVIII, "Housing." Both reflect the convention's attempt to adjust the constitution to new social conditions created by the Depression.

Article XVII established an affirmative social right which any individual may demand from the government. It required the state to assume a major role in the field of social welfare. The police power certainly gave the legislature all the authorization needed to pass such legislation, but by placing the authorization in the constitution, the state elevated the status of its commitment to the needy, thus removing all doubts regarding the use of public funds for such purpose.

The article contained five sections. Section I contains a broad mandate: "The aid, care and support of the needy are public concerns and shall be provided by the state and by such of its subdivisions. . . ." The clause was left intentionally vague. The Committee on Social Welare wished to place an enabling clause in the constitution, realizing that, in its absence, legislation of this type would be of doubtful constitutionality.[36] Although the section contains no mandate to the legislature, its impact can be seen in the shift from local to state financing of health-related activities.

Health-Related Expenditures in New York*

Date	State Expenditures	Local Expenditures
1938	5,800,000	23,400,000
1958–1959	23,314,000	35,135,000
1964–1965	77,000,000	64,900,000

Figures compiled from The Temporary Commission on Revision and Simplification of the Constitution, Staff Report No. 24, *Health and Welfare* (1958), p. 82; Temporary State Commission on the Constitutional Convention, Staff Report No. 11, *Welfare, Health and Mental Health* (1967), p. 56.

In *Tucker v. Toia* (1977) the Court of Appeals determined that it is the judiciary's duty to see that the legislature does not "shirk its responsibility."[37] The courts, however, have granted the legislature wide discretion in establishing criteria for determining need and establishing programs to assist those in need. The clause does not mandate that public assistance be granted to an individual in every instance, nor does it require that the state always meet in full measure all of the legitimate needs of each public assistance recipient.[38] The elaborate statutory law in New York has made public welfare an institutionalized feature of state government.

Section 2 continued the state Board of Social Welfare as a constitutionally mandated body, delineated that board's power, and authorized it to make rules and regulations subject to legislative control for the effective pursuit of its duties. The detailed enumeration of the board's powers to visit and inspect, reiterated in Section 6, were intended to overcome a Court of Appeals decision in 1900 which drastically limited the board's powers to visit and inspect.[39]

Section 3 established the protection of health as a matter of public concern and directed the legislature to make provision for that protection and promotion. Section 4 mandated state care for those suffering from mental disorder or defects and inspection of such institutions. Section 5 authorizes the state to provide maintenance and support of a system of corrections encompassing prisons, parole, and probation, and provides for a state commissioner of corrections whose agency was given the responsibility to visit and inspect those institutions.

Article XVIII was the first constitutional affirmation of a public role for housing and related programs. It signalled a recognition by the delegates of the importance of decent housing and neighborhoods in a constitutional democracy and the state's obligation to assist the cities in achieving those goals. The first section provided, in broad language, sufficient authority to enable the government to meet the housing needs of New Yorkers into the twenty-first century. However, the subsequent nine sections are crowded with detailed, cumbersome language and restrictions which blur the clear authorization found in Section 1. The phrase "low-income housing" has been interpreted liberally by the courts and the legislature to denote housing built for those who cannot cause unaided private enterprise to build housing to satisfy their limited rent-paying ability. Such an interpretation permits the state to build housing for middle-income groups. A 1965 amendment added nursing homes to this category.

Section 2 enumerates the powers of the legislature in carrying out this mandate. Basically, it amounts to a series of exemptions to the limitations on state and local governments found elsewhere in the constitution, particularly in Articles VII and VIII, which deal with state and local finance. This section exempts legislative efforts in pursuit of housing goals from the limits in Article VII, which prohibits the loaning of state money or credit to individuals or public corporations. In the absence of this exemption, the latter provision would have restricted attempts to promote housing development. Section 3 includes an exemption from the requirement that the electorate approve all debt over one million dollars. This section authorized the borrowing of up to $300 million without electoral approval and also granted other exemptions from the limitations in Article VII. Section 4 provided exemptions from the debt limitations on cities, towns, and villages in Article VIII. Sections 5–9 address such matters as excess condemnation and acquisition of property to effectuate the goals set forth in Section 1. The final provision, Section 10, is a supremacy and enabling clause which makes clear that the provisions of this article were intended to supercede other sections of the constitution that might otherwise be in conflict with them. In anticipation of court decisions interpreting the inclusion of some powers to mean the exclusion of others not mentioned, delegates added that the article "shall not be construed as imposing additional limitations."

The cumbersome and confusing language of the provisions has required the legislature and the judiciary to contort and strain the provisions to keep them abreast of changing housing needs. The article did not include counties within its compass, and the restrictions on cooperation with private enterprise have limited its flexibility and effectiveness. More comprehensive ideas of community development have made the narrow assumptions concerning housing embodied in the article obsolete. The article confines the state and localities to the redevelopment and clearance of blighted areas; comprehensive development would involve programs to conserve and improve areas experiencing a decline before they deteriorate into slums, and to do so on a community-wide basis.

Suffrage

In dealing with suffrage, the convention authorized the legislature to provide for permanent registration (Art. II, Sec. 6), which the legislature eventually accomplished, thus superceding the dual registration systems for rural and urban areas first established in the 1894 Constitution.

The Legislature

The delegates made two significant changes in the organization and structure of the legislature. An apportionment provision was drafted which maintained the Republican advantage guaranteed by the language of the 1894 Constitution. It was a foregone conclusion that the Republicans would not relinquish their electoral advantage. The Democrats denounced the unfairness and inconsistencies in the proposed apportionment provision but conceded that its adoption was inevitable. As one delegate expressed it, "Every one of you admits that the proposal stinks to high heaven, but every one of you says 'Well, we got the votes, we might as well put it over'."[40] The reapportionment measure (Art. III, Sec. 5) was the most partisan measure passed by the convention.

The reapportionment amendment was essentially the creation of the state Republican organization. State chair William S. Murray and New York County chair Kenneth Simpson were in Albany working closely with convention leaders on this issue.[41]

The principal features of the proposed reapportionment were as follows: senate membership to increase from 51 to 53 members, assembly membership from 150 to 159 (Art. III, Sec. 2). The distribution of the seats increased slightly. New York City's representation in the senate increased to 45%, but its representation in the assembly slightly decreased, to 40%. The ability of the city to gain ascendancy in the assembly was limited by a provision guaranteeing minimum county representation (Sec. 5C). The city was similarly limited in the senate by a clause stating "Counties wholly within the boundaries of a city shall not have together more than one-half of the total number of senators" (Sec. 5B). This clause replaced a similar 1894 provision that produced the same effect, i.e., that of ensuring that New York City could not obtain a majority in the senate. In the event the legislature failed to reapportion, a commission selected from judicial districts of the state, chosen by Supreme Court justices in each district, would decide. The result of such a selection would be an overwhelmingly Republican commission (Sec. 5F). Possessed of a clear majority of the state's population, the city by the mid-forties held only 25 of the 56 seats in the senate and 67 of the 150 seats in the assembly. A legislative reapportionment in 1944, by a legislature under Democratic control, added five seats to the senate to benefit suburban counties adjacent to New York City. That same year, in the first election held under the new and ostensibly fairer division of legislative seats, Democrats managed to win only 21 senate seats and 55 assembly seats.[42]

The convention made two other adjustments to the legislature. The delegates voted to ban proportional representation, labelling it un-American (among other things). The measure was viewed as an attack on New York City, where proportional representation had been employed (Art. II, Sec. 9). Proportional representation gave some minority groups a forum and degree of access to the city's governmental decision-making apparatus that they had not enjoyed under previous representational systems.[43] But New York City Democrats had smarted under the system; in 1937, the first year of its operation, Democrats captured only fourteen seats, with the Republican-Fusion ticket winning six and the American Labor Party independently taking five. Upstate Republicans, fearful of its adoption in their cities, had reason to align with New York City Democrats. Governor Al Smith suggested the basis for their informal alliance in his own inimitable fashion:

> Of all the wild eyed crazy nonsensical things that has ever afflicted the city of New York, I certainly think there is nothing that equals proportional representation . . . I urge my upstate brethren to be very careful and see that it never gets into their election or into their bailiwicks. . . .[44]

Response to the ban from New York City and, surprisingly, upstate areas was overwhelmingly negative.[45] Delegates retreated from their decision to include the proposal in the constitution and instead they voted to submit the issue as a separate amendment, a decision that would prove fatal.

The convention voted to increase the term of senators to four years (Art. III, Sec. 1). The senate had long sought a four-year term, but its efforts were blocked by the sotto voce opposition of the local leadership in both parties, who feared longer terms would give senators too much independence. The extension of senate terms was a quid pro quo with the governor and assembly, both of whom had their terms extended in 1937 to four and two years, respectively. The electorate rejected this term extension along with the reapportionment provisions.[46]

The Executive

Silently ratifying the constitutional revolution that had occurred between 1915 and 1935, the delegates made only minor changes in the executive branch. The 1938 convention continued the earlier succession provisions, with one exception. In the event that the office of governor became vacant and no lieutenant-governor was in office, the temporary president of the senate, or the speaker of the assembly, if there were no temporary president of the senate, would serve as governor only until the next election, such election occurring not less than three months after the office became vacant. The amendment failed to clarify whether a lieutenant-governor was to be chosen as well as a governor. A 1945 amendment removed this doubt by specifying that both were to be chosen at such an election. In 1949 another amendment provided that the lieutenant-governor-elect would succeed in the event of the death of the governor-elect prior to taking the oath of office. In 1963 a recodification of the succession provision was approved.

The convention paved the way for greater use of lump sum appropriations by deleting the constitutional requirement that the governor had to submit a budget consisting of "clearly itemized" estimates and adding language which allowed the governor to include in his budget any information deemed proper. The Convention Committee on State Finance and Revenue, its sponsor, believed that the "Governor should have a free hand in submitting recommendations and information in the budget. . . ."[47]

The convention effected one change concerning the comptroller's office. This office had been a constitutional office since 1821. A 1925 amendment reorganizing the departments of the state specified the duties of the office, forbidding assignments to the comptroller of administrative functions inconsistent with the auditing functions of that office. The 1938 convention accorded the comptroller a significant financial responsibility, viz., authority to approve, in advance, all disbursements made by the state, thus mandating a centralized pre-audit.

The Judiciary

The delegates subjected the judiciary to a number of partisan and non-partisan changes. The non-partisan changes included new provisions that allowed more flexible assignment of judges to assist where congestion was the greatest (Art. VI, Secs. 15, 16), expanded the reviewing power of the Court of Appeals (Art. VI, Sec. 7), and authorized removal of state judges following a hearing (Art. VI, Sec. 10).

The first of the two partisan revisions approved by the convention allowed judicial review of all agency decisions upon both the law and the facts of the case. This proposal was an anti-New Deal measure aimed at curbing the growing power of the so-called alphabet agencies at the state level and limiting the growth of administrative—as opposed to common—law. Its supporters, including many bar association groups, expressed profound fear of administrative tyranny.[48]

The other partisan revision of the judiciary divided the second judicial district into two districts, making ten districts altogether. The reason appeared to be a contest over partisan control of judicial selection. As the Democrats controlled judicial selection in the second district, its division of the new district would give control to the Republicans. As Justice Harlan Rippey of the New York Court of Appeals remarked: "There is no one who would be willing to admit, unless he wants to stamp himself as a hypocrite, that there is any reason on earth for these amendments except political reasons. . . ."[49]

State and Local Finance

The 1938 convention continued the process of gradual liberalization of the restrictions placed on the legislature by nineteenth-century constitution-makers. Simultaneously, the convention delegates tightened limitations on the use of state credit and imposed additional restrictions on local debt and taxation.

The convention added public corporations to the list of those to which the state could not give or lend its credit. The Committee on State Finances furnished two reasons for this addition: to make explicit what the committee claimed was implicit in the word "corporation," and to prevent cities or public authorities from relying on the state for assistance when they were unable to sell their securities. It was believed that state credit should be reserved for the state, with only those exceptions set forth in the constitution.[50] The provision does not prevent the state from giving its money, as opposed to its credit, to assist municipal or other public corporations. A clear distinction is made between lending money and lending credit, a distinction based on the fact that granting the state's money does not create the dangers of collapse, insolvency, and crisis associated with the abuse of credit. However, in *Wein v. State* (1975) the Court of Appeals did allow the state to use its short-term credit (tax and revenue anticipation notes) to fund an emergency appropriation for New York City.[51] The court believed the temporary obligations of these funds, secured by committed revenues and not capable of being "rolled over" into long-term debt, were not in conflict with the established constitutional prohibition against the long-term commitment of the state's credit.

The convention added six exemptions to the restrictions in Section 8, as follows: "aid and care and support for needy"; "health and welfare services for all children"; protection against unemployment, sickness, and old age; assistance for the physically handicapped (already present in the 1894 Constitution); and certain low-income housing and slum clearance (in Art. XVIII). These exceptions reveal in striking fashion the tension between the delegates' desire to guard against misuse of state money and credit and their recognition that the state has an important role to play in providing for its less fortunate citizens. Indeed, the exceptions were interpreted not only as permissive, but as a "way to recognize the responsibility of the State for the aid, care and support of persons in need . . . and enable the State itself, if the Legislature so desires, to administer all forms of relief directly."[52]

When the convention focused its attention on local finance, it created an entirely new article (VIII). Section 1 is the local government equivalent of Section 1 of Article VII. It prohibits local entities from loaning their money or credit to any individual, association, corporation, or private undertaking. Exemptions were granted for the health and welfare of all children and for aid, care, and support of the needy and of the institutions which provide that care and support. Counties were allowed to incur debt to advance to a town or school district "the amount of unpaid taxes returned to it." Conversely, deep concern was expressed regarding the difficulties experienced by New York City and other cities with the management of their debts. Support existed for the view that if the debt restrictions had been tighter and more specific and applicable to all local governments, not just cities and counties, these difficulties might have been avoided. The attempt to define and elaborate the debt provisions resulted in a text seven times longer than the previous provisions on "Local Finance" and consisting of twelve sections. The overall purpose of this article was summarized by the chairman of the Committee on Cities, Harold Riegelman:

> . . . this proposal is intended to strengthen the credit of the municipalities of the State by applying reasonable and moderate preventives against abuse of their credit. The more wisely we safeguard that credit, the less the tax-payers will have to pay in interest charges.[53]

Eleven of the sections relate to local debt; one concerns tax rate limitations. School districts were made subject to the restrictions on local governments: gifts of loans of credit to, or in aid of, public corporations were explicitly prohibited; and gifts and loans of municipal money, property, or credit to "private undertakings" were prohibited.

Section 2 spelled out in detail the conditions under which debts could be incurred. All indebtedness was to be backed by the full faith and credit of the issuing government; future long-term borrowing, except borrowing by New York City for transit and certain other purposes, was to take the form of serial bonds payable in annual installments. The debt could be paid in unequal installments, but could not extend beyond the life of the improvements, and in no case could they exceed forty years. These debts could be refunded only with the approval of the state comptroller and under such conditions as prescribed by that office, but in no case for more than twenty additional years. Appropriations for debt were to be made annually by the borrowing authorities, and in the event of failure by an authority to make such appropriations, the chief fiscal officer was required to set aside, from the first available revenues, the amount required to make the payment due. This latter provision, in effect, granted bondholders the first claim on all available revenues.

Section 3 prohibited the creation of any new overlapping, independent taxing and borrowing districts or entities such as metropolitan districts. Exceptions were permitted for school districts, fire districts, and other specified districts. Existing tax units could not incur debt without the consent of the locality, any of whose property is subject to that taxation or assessment by these taxing units. Finally, any debt incurred would be included in determining the debt limitations of the locality, unless such debt would otherwise have been exempted had it been undertaken by the locality itself. This section would prevent, for example, the creation of a sanitary district unless the town or county where the district is located was willing to pledge its full faith and credit to payment of the indebtedness created by the district. The Committee on Taxation and Finance claimed that this section would not affect "the future creation of public benefit corporations, generally known as authorities, which do not have taxing power . . . nor . . . the future creation of special districts where the town itself incurs the debt."[54] Nevertheless, strong sentiment existed in opposition to the proliferation of these special districts and authorities which had begun to appear around the state. The Committee's concern was that such units

> seriously complicate the governmental structure of the State . . . diminish both the direct administrative and financial responsibility of the normal units of government of the State . . . prevent control of the aggregate amount of debt which may be locally incurred, and they may cause an excessive burden of taxation on real property for which the normal units of government are in no way responsible.[55]

Section 4 included towns and villages under the debt limits adopted in 1884. In place of the uniform rate of debt for all cities and counties of 10% of real estate valuations, different debt limits were set for different classes of local government, running from 10% for New York and Nassau County to 8% for towns and villages. The new limits were to be phased in over a ten-year period. The general effect of the provision was to reduce the borrowing power of localities, and the clear intent of these added restrictions was to balance the "insistent demand for a drastic reduction in the debt limit of localities" against the need to maintain "the ability of the localities to render necessary services."[56]

The base on which the percentage debt limit would be calculated was also altered. In place of the assessed valuation of real estate for the latest single year, a five-year moving average was adopted. As the committee explained it: "in times of depression, when borrowing is least objectionable, the ability to borrow is not reduced too drastically and, in times of rising values, when borrowing should be curbed, there may be a lag in the expansion of the borrowing capacity. . . ."[57]

Sections 5, 6, and 7 collected scattered debt exemptions and added some new ones. Section 5 provided general exemption for temporary debt, self-sustaining projects, water supply, and the funding of non-actuarial pension plans. The reason for this last exemption was to make it possible for municipalities to place unsound pension plans on an actuarially sound basis. Since this would require contracting debts, exempting such debt would give local governments an incentive to take the step. Section 6 continued exemptions for New York City, Syracuse, Rochester, and Buffalo, and added a new one granting the City of New York an additional $350 million in exemption for rapid transit construction. Section 8 extended to towns and villages the protective provisions made for counties and cities, viz., that any indebtedness valid at the time of its inception shall not be made invalid by any provision of this article. Section 9 continued the 1899 amendment terminating the debt-incurring power of counties merged with, or absorbed by, any city. Section 11 allowed local government to exempt temporary debts incurred to finance capital improvements. It allowed local governments to make appropriations for capital expenditures or improvements for which they otherwise might borrow and to exclude taxes raised for these appropriations from the tax limits specified in Section 10. This provided local governments with a significant exemption, because real property taxes for capital expenditures could be raised without constitutional limit. The purpose was to encourage local governments to finance projects on a "pay-as-you-go" basis without restriction by tax limit.

The debt sections of the article combined basic provisions for debt regulation and limitation, with numerous specifications aimed at making the provisions as complete and detailed as possible, in the hope that misunderstandings or evasions would be minimized.[58]

Section 10 addressed the topic of local taxing power. Most delegates believed that constitutional tax limits and constitutional debt limits were closely linked. Four convention committees had jurisdiction to examine aspects of debt and tax limitations: the Committees on Cities, on Counties, on Towns and Villages, and on State Finance. These committees agreed to act jointly on these matters through their chairs. The largest part of the report and the debates were taken up with the debt provisions. The section on taxes appeared at the end and amounted to no more than 5% of the entire text.

The convention adopted four major changes in tax limitations. Previously adopted tax limitations were applied to all cities and villages, providing uniformity across the state. Delegates justified the extension on the dubious and unstated assumption that since it had worked as expected in cities under the restriction, it would work on all other local entities as well.[59] It is likely that delegates, having extended debt limits to all localities, believed the same should apply to tax limitations. There is some indication that the national campaign then being waged by the National Association of Real Estate Boards was a crucial factor in getting the limitation inserted into the document.[60] The basis on which the limits were calculated was changed from annual assessed value to a five-year average of assessed value. As with the debt restriction, this alteration was intended to eliminate rapid fluctuations in borrowing and taxing power.[61] It was prompted by the rapid decreases of assessed values brought on by the depression. The last two changes were exemptions allowing the raising of money for education.

Even before the convention met, the Court of Appeals in *Robertson v. Zimmerman* (1935) approved the exclusion of the bonded indebtedness of a sewer authority, the bonds of which were paid solely from revenues generated by the authority (with no liability on the part of the city), from calculation of the city's debt.[62] The decision encouraged the creation of similar authorities throughout the state.

These authorities or public benefit corporations are separate, autonomous corporations operating locally or state-wide outside the operating departments of the state. They share certain common characteristics: they are created by a special act of the legislature; possess broad administrative autonomy; usually finance themselves through bond issues, user fees, or tolls; and operate outside the normal constitutional and statutory restrictions of state government. The most prominent contemporary examples are the New York Thruway and New York City Transit Authority.

By 1938 the state had thirty-three such authorities. Their use has enabled municipalities to fund projects without encumbering their constitutional and statutory debt limits. There is some evidence that tax and debt limitation have encouraged municipalities to resort to these entities. These developments and the prospect for continued unregulated development of authorities provided the motivation for the revisions of Article X on corporations. A new section (5) explicitly stated that "No municipal or other corporation [with enumerated exceptions] . . . possessing the power (a) to contract indebtedness and (b) to levy taxes or benefit assessments upon real estate . . . shall hereafter be established or created except by special act of the legislature." This first paragraph implicitly recognized the value of these authorities, but required that they originate in a special act of the legislature, thus ensuring that the legislature pass directly on the establishment of each new authority. Without state approval, it was argued, local authorities would multiply unnecessarily. The establishment of these public benefit corporations was considered an exercise of sovereign power that should not be delegated.

The paragraph reflects the convention's ambivalence over these entities. They posed serious dangers by enabling localities to "evade debt limitations of the Constitution," but, as Abbot Low Moffat, chair of the State Finance and Revenues Committee, pointed out, "frequently authorities have proved of inestimable value, and probably the most satisfactory way of handling a given problem." Former Governor Alfred E. Smith, speaking in opposition to any restrictions on these authorities, claimed the article would "paralyze the one method we have discovered of getting work done expeditiously and without overtaxing our people."[63]

The second paragraph required municipal voter approval at a referendum for the establishment of such public corporations. If the voters believed it necessary to contract indebtedness in excess of the debt limits, they ought to do so by voting directly on that question. The provision also would prevent the state from transferring municipal utility services from local government and into a public benefit corporation without referendum approval of the voters. This provision was intended, in some degree, to overrule the legitimizing consequences of *Robertson v. Zimmerman*. It has not been as effective as supporters had hoped. A vivid example of its circumvention, as well as the complex financial maneuvering involved in the creation of these corporations, is found in the establishment of the Water Finance Authority of New York City.[64] The Water Finance Authority, a financing device, is a public benefit corporation created by state law. Its sole function is to issue bonds to raise capital for investment in the city's water and waste systems. Fees are collected by another single-purpose public benefit corporation, the New York City Water Board. A third agency, the Department of Environmental Protection (DEP), operates the two systems. Though separate legal entities, these two authorities, created in 1984, are completely interdependent. No bonds could be issued without the fee collection of the Water Board, and both depend on the DEP for the operation of the water and waste systems. Why the need for two authorities? Prior to 1984 there was a Board of Water Supply, a line agency of city government. That agency was exempt from the constitutional debt limit of the city. However, since its bonds were considered general obligation bonds of the city in the view of the credit markets, its bonds received no more favorable reception in the market than did city bonds. By creating a legally separate Water Authority able to issue revenue bonds backed by the revenues from water and sewer fees and not anchored in the full faith and credit or taxing power of the city, "city government was able to raise over $8 million for the ten-year water and sewer systems capital improvement program, without limiting credit available for borrowing for other purposes."[65] The provision of the constitution in question, Article X, Section 5, reads, in part, "no such public corporation . . . shall hereafter be given both the power to contract indebtedness and the power, within any city, to collect rentals, charges, rates or fees . . ." unless the electors of the city approve such a grant by a majority vote. In establishing a second authority, and dividing the two powers mentioned in the clause between the agencies, and linking them by financing and rebate agreements, city lawyers argued that the referendum requirement could be avoided, and it was.

Despite the efforts of the 1938 convention to limit the proliferation of these authorities, municipalities continued to rely on them. As distinct legal corporations, separate from the general government, they are not subject to the referendum requirements or debt limitations imposed by the constitution on state and municipal borrowing. They also avoid the briar patch of laws, administrative rules, personnel problems, and politics that often inhibit quick action and bring large municipalities to a standstill.[66]

The fact that these entities were not responsible to the electorate or to the normal political processes prompted a third paragraph which authorized the comptroller of the state to supervise their finances in ways similar to the auditing of the regular state departments. This power, however, did not include the authority to audit all vouchers prior to payment, nor to void those vouchers absent from that pre-audit.

The last paragraph prevents the state from assuming any liability for the debts of these authorities. Every statute establishing these entities to 1938 had, in fact, contained such a disclaimer of liability. Despite such disclaimers the Court of Appeals in *Williamsburgh Savings Bank v. State* (1926) suggested that the state would be liable for such debts, and this clause was intended to preclude such liability.[67] Towns were exempted from this limitation because they could establish water and sewer systems and the like only by creating special districts.

Taxation

Until the 1938 convention only three measures concerning the power of the state to tax were found in the constitution. Two dealt with legislative procedure and were adopted at the 1846 convention. The third, adopted in 1901, prevented the granting of tax exemptions by private or local bill (Art. III, Sec. 17, current constitution). A taxation article was approved at the 1915 convention, but failed along with the rejected constitution. The 1938 convention adopted a completely new article on taxation (Art. XVI). The major premise of this article is announced in its opening section: "The power of taxation shall never be surrendered or contracted away . . ." and "any laws which delegate the taxing power shall specify the types of taxes which may be imposed thereunder and provide for their review" (Sec. 1). The first clause prevents tax policies from becoming contracts between the state and corporations; the second prevents the legislature from passing blanket enabling acts empowering cities to impose taxes at their discretion, as had occurred in the 1930s. The prohibition is, in fact, a limitation on local government as it requires the legislature to exercise more control when delegating taxing power to the cities. Delegates wanted to ensure that local taxing policies were consistent and not in competition with state policies. Attempts by New York City to limit taxpayer access to court for review of tax decisions led to the clause guaranteeing administrative or judicial review.

Paragraph two required that exemptions from taxation be granted only by general law and gave constitutional status to what heretofore had been statutory exemptions for private religious and charitable institutions. Section 2 required the legislature to provide for the supervision, review, and equalization of assessments. Despite this provision, underassessment of property values continued. However, the section had the effect of centralizing tax assessment policies, though local officials retained significant control over this process. The section also prohibits assessments at levels higher than full value. In practice, property assessments have been far below full value despite a statute mandating full value assessment. The state has established a Board of Equalization and Assessment, charged with the duty of establishing an equalization rate to be used in the distribution of state financial aid, but its powers are limited by the provisions of the home rule article (Art. IX).[68] Full assessment of property value was required after the Court of Appeals, in *Hellerstein v. Assessor of the Town of Islip* (1975), ordered full-value assessment, though the state subsequently repealed the statute on which that decision was based.[69]

In another example of the convention's rejection of a court holding, the delegates allowed counties to advance delinquent taxes owed to villages and then collect those taxes themselves, overruling the decision in *Pelham v. Village of Pelham* (1915).[70] This paragraph also settled a dispute between town and village assessors, allowing, it was hoped, a more orderly and efficient system of municipal tax collection. The provision is permissive, not mandatory.

The two sections illustrate the tension between promoting the goals of efficiency and order, which necessitates some centralization, and the home rule principle of local control, which promotes decentralization.

Sections 3 and 4 were placed in the constitution to preserve New York's—and particularly New York City's—role as the financial and banking capital of the nation. Section 3 located intangible property such as money and securities in the domicile of the owner of said property, unless it is used by the owner to conduct business in New York. This was designed to assure non-residents and out-of-state corporations that they could keep their intangibles in the state without fear of legislative imposition of taxes. This section also prohibited taxation of undistributed profits. Section 4 prohibited discriminatory taxation of out-of-state corporations. It was precipitated by a proposed New York City tax on banks and banking deposits, and the resulting fear that such taxes would discourage out-of-staters from placing their money in city banks. It was believed that such taxation would encourage banks to become part of the national banking system, thus weakening the dual banking system.

Section 4 removed any doubts created by the wording of Article XIII, Section 7 and Article VI, Section 25a (compensation for public officers and judges, respectively) regarding the constitutionality of taxing wages, salaries, and other compensation of state employees. The pensions of state employees were exempted from taxation.

Home Rule (Article IX)

After expending much time and energy on the home rule issue, the convention, with a few notable exceptions, reaffirmed the principles established by the 1923 amendment.

The gubernatorial emergency message procedure was deleted. Hereafter a special law would require a special request from the mayor concurred in by the local legislative body or, absent mayoral approval, two-thirds of the local legislative body and the concurrence of two-thirds of both houses of the state legislature. With the governor's emergency message procedure removed, retention of the two-thirds requirement seems anomalous. Together, the two were attempts to protect the municipality against unwanted legislation. Under the new request procedure such a requirement served only as an obstacle to city requests for local legislation.

Home rule was extended to counties, excluding the five counties of greater New York City, and the legislature was directed to extend it to villages prior to July 1, 1940. With regard to counties, a special law relating to one county required a home rule request from the Board of Supervisors or county executive and concurrence of the board, a certificate of necessity from the governor establishing the basis for the request, and the concurrence of both houses of the state legislature (Sec. 2d). As to villages, a special law (one not relating to the property affairs of government of all villages) required a home rule request from its chief executive concurred in by the local legislative body, or a message of necessity from the governor providing the basis for necessity, and the concurrence of both houses of the legislature (Sec. 16).

Express power was vested in cities to enact local laws concerning their property affairs or government (Sec. 12). Two dimensions were provided. Cities were granted the power to adopt and amend local laws not inconsistent with the laws of the state relating to their property affairs and government. In addition, cities were granted the power to adopt and amend local laws not inconsistent with the laws of the state, whether or not these laws relate to their property affairs or government in respect to specified subjects on distinctly local matters (Sec. 12). Although the section substantially enlarged local legislative power, its exercise was limited by the requirement that such exercise be in conformance with "the laws of the state" which permitted special laws in all areas of state concern. An expansive reading by the judiciary of what is of state concern would negate the potential impact of this section.

The 1938 convention expanded the local legislative powers of cities, but it did not intend to go beyond the principles established by the 1923 amendment. Indeed, there was strong support for the judiciary's narrow reading of the phrase "property, affairs or government" and its correspondingly expansive understanding of matters of state concern.[71]

CONSTITUTIONAL POLICIES

Canals and Conservation

The convention instituted changes in the canal and conservation articles. The Barge Canal was protected against sale or disposal by the state, but the sale of land and terminals unessential to the operation of the canal was permitted (Art. XV, Secs. 1, 2). The convention also made changes in constitutional provisions dealing with conservation issues. In 1931 an amendment had specified that certain funds were to be spent by the legislature for acquiring new forest lands. At the time of the 1938 convention, only a fraction of that money had been appropriated or spent. It was the opinion of most legislators that the state's responsibility to deal with problems posed by the Great Depression pre-empted conservation. The 1938 convention eliminated the dollar amount but retained the general policy commitment (Art. XIV, Sec. 3). The delegates also authorized the legislature to acquire land beyond the "Blue Line" (the Adirondack and Catskill Parks) and such land was exempted from the restrictions found in Section 1. This measure would permit reforestation, with legislative approval.

Education

The convention amended the provision relating to the common school fund, the literature fund, and the United States desposit funds. Henceforth, revenues garnered from the three funds would be used for common schools and libraries. This change eliminated aid to academies, the predecessors to high schools and normal schools, or teachers' colleges. (These academies flourished in the nineteenth century, but by the 1930s had dwindled to a handful, most having developed into colleges or become public high schools.) The practice of using deposit funds for libraries was constitutionalized. The 1894 provisions mandating $25,000 in appropriation were eliminated and made part of the capital of the common school fund. Such appropriations were thought financially unnecessary in light of the generous support which the state made available for public schools (Art. XI, Sec. 3).[72]

The 1938 convention also adopted a wide range of miscellaneous provisions designed to address discrete problems of state and local governance. State employees, concerned that their pensions would be subject to legislative manipulation, successfully petitioned the delegates for an amendment making membership in a pension or retirement system of the state a contractual relationship entitled to constitutional protection (Art. V, Sec. 7). State and local governments may increase the benefits connected with those plans, but they may never be diminished. The clause was included at the request of, and for the benefit of, the civil service workers of the state and its subdivisions. A few delegates complained that the proposal constituted a raid on the state's treasury, but there was little organized opposition either at the committee hearings or on the convention floor. The decision appears to have been made for an immediate political gain on the part of the delegates. Democrats, more vulnerable to pressure from the civil service groups, voted 66 in favor to 1 opposed; Republicans divided almost evenly, 45 to 42.[73]

The convention furnished some relief to the railroads from the expense of eliminating grade crossings. The legislature had enacted legislation mandating the elimination of all grade crossings and requiring railroads to assume 50% of the cost. Whether due to the poor financial conditions of the railroads or their unwillingness to comply, little or nothing had been accomplished. After vigorous debate, the convention agreed to compel the railroads to pay for the benefits received from the improvements but also provided that, in any case, such payments could not exceed 15% of the total costs (Art. VII, Sec. 14).

Amendments

The convention altered the procedure concerning future amendments to the constitution. Delegates approved a requirement that any amendment passed by the legislature was to be submitted to the attorney general for an opinion regarding its impact on other sections of the constitution (Art. XIX, Sec. 1). They also prohibited submission for a constitutional convention to the voters during a national or state election year, thus fixing 1957 as the next automatic submission year under the every-twenty-year clause (Art. XIX, Sec. 2).

When the convention adjourned on August 26, the delegates agreed to submit their work in nine parts. Part one was an omnibus proposal of fifty amendments considered "non-controversial," including various changes eliminating obsolete language and providing a more logical and orderly arrangement of the document. Parts 2 through 9 set forth eight proposals to be submitted separately to the electorate: reapportionment; grade crossing elimination; low-rent housing; judicial reform, including the creation of the tenth judicial district and judicial review of administrative agencies; the rights of labor; proportional representation; state funding for social welfare purposes; and permission for New York City to incur indebtedness to unify the transit system. In the referendum to approve or reject the convention's proposals, the Democratic Party platform supported all but the reapportionment, judiciary, and proportional representation amendments. The Republicans approved all except the proportional representation proposal. The voters rejected three of the eight: the reapportionment, judiciary, and proportional representation amendments, the three most partisan proposals.

THE POLITICAL THEORY OF THE 1938 CONSTITUTIONAL CONVENTION

The 1938 convention was not given to bold innovations. In part, the delegates' moderation was rooted in their lack of any mandate for significant constitutional change; in part, it was due to the Republican control of the convention. The Democrats, divided into pro and anti New Deal factions, could not generate united opposition. Where the delegates added new material of any significance to the constitution, such as the labor bill of rights, housing, social welfare, and taxation, they were adding to the constitutional policies previously enacted by the legislature.

If one consistent theme emerges from the convention, it was the willingness of a majority consisting of Democrats and Republicans to recognize the role of government in providing for the social and economic welfare of its citizens. This consensus on government responsibility is in sharp contrast to the views of the 1894 and 1915 conventions. Until 1938, the New York Constitution was virtually mute on such issues. The change in political philosophy, evident in the work of the 1938 convention, was largely a product of the Great Depression and the New Deal. The earlier nineteenth-century ideology limited the exercise of governmental power to those policies clearly providing benefits for all and not for one or more groups at the expense of the others. It assumed that the commercial republic would not create conditions of permanent or semi-permanent social dependency, in turn providing a justification for groups to make special claims to assistance from the government. The decision of the delegates at the 1894 convention were in many respects a reaffirmation of this philosophy. By 1938 the dominance of industrial corporations, and the inability of the economy to sustain growth and full employment without falling into cycles of inflation and depression, made continued adherence to the earlier creed untenable. The document produced by the 1938 convention gave constitutional recognition to a political theory which expected the government to play an active role in maintaining steady growth of the economy and providing a variety of welfare programs for those in need. However attractive the earlier republican tradition, it could not survive the rapid and momentous changes ushered in with the twentieth century.[74]

Although the delegates accepted welfare-state liberalism, they did not espouse anti-business or anti-private enterprise positions. The convention's proposals included several which were supportive of business interests, including sections in the taxation article intended to encourage capital accumulation, and the grade crossing amendment, providing relief to the railroads. Moreover, the convention rejected proposals which would have given the state authority to own and develop all the power resources adjacent to the St. Lawrence and Niagara Rivers. Convention delegates, representing a combination of business and labor groups, defeated a proposal to ban all billboards on scenic highways and parkways, as well as a proposal to establish a compulsory automobile accident insurance system similar to worker's compensation.

The 1938 Constitutional Convention: An Assessment

The 1938 constitutional convention, though ostensibly organized and operated on a non-partisan basis, was controlled by the Republicans. On at least three issues, party considerations were dominant: reapportionment, the new judicial district, and the ban on proportional representation. On the other issues, upstate versus urban cleavages cut across party lines. Although partisan considerations were evident throughout the work of the convention, the parties did not claim responsibility for the convention's actions; thus, there would be little accountability for the results. The absence of a party position on many of the issues, and the resulting lack of direction, allowed interest groups to assume a major role at the convention. Their activity was public, pervasive, and intense. They were permitted to testify and submit briefs before the formal public hearings held by the convention. They flooded the convention with "petition, remonstrances, communications—resolutions regarding constitutional revision."[75] A number of the groups had the additional advantage of delegates who were members or supporters of the groups' goals, and were willing to introduce their proposals at the convention. It is fair to say that no convention in New York's history was subjected to as much pressure from interest groups as the 1938 convention. It is not surprising that the two full-length studies of the convention focus on the role and impact of these groups, with one study concluding: "The constitution . . . is a major pressure front under modern circumstances."[76] On all but one of the measures which were not party questions, the outcome of the convention's deliberations was consistent with the position of major groups which backed or opposed the measure.[77] Although it achieved some success in pruning a number of obsolete provisions, e.g., Article VIII, Section 8 (concerning bill holders and insolvent banks) and Article I, Sections 11–14 (concerning allodial land tenures and limitations on land leases and grants), the convention nevertheless managed to increase the size of the document by over 15,000 words.

The convention began with the goal of streamlining the 1894 document. The increased length of the constitution cannot be attributed to attempts to place additional restrictions on governmental power. It is, rather, attributable to the expansion of governmental activities in fields heretofore thought to be the province of the private realm. The new articles represented successful attempts by interest groups and the new social forces they represented to gain constitutional recognition of their policies and goals.

The convention managed to create a single comprehensive article on local tax and debt; however, that structure had lasted only ten years when, in 1949, substantial revisions were necessary. Rather than achieving their intended effects, i.e., protecting against abuse of taxpayers' money, these limitations have encouraged some unsound fiscal practices and resort to a variety of devices such as the public benefit corporation to circumvent these restrictions. The convention established affirmative social rights which the individual may demand from the government, e.g., Article XVII (social welfare), Article XVIII (housing), and Article I, Sections 17–18 (rights for labor and workman's compensation). These articles compare favorably with the United Nations' Declaration of Human Rights (Art. 25, Sec. 1), adopted a decade after these provisions were included in the New York Constitution.

The leading students of the 1938 convention have characterized its accomplishments as "middle-of-the-road conservatism."[78] This judgment is valid if it means that the delegates did not undertake a rewriting of the 1894 Constitution or that they failed to inaugurate a new social democracy. Delegates did reject a proposal which would have declared state ownership of power sites along the Niagara and St. Lawrence Rivers inalienable and that development of those sites be restricted to public corporations and other agencies of the government. However, by committing the state to a new set of social responsibilities with regard to labor, welfare, housing, and health insurance, the revised constitution was more progressive than either the United States Constitution or the decisions of the United States Supreme Court. Although the substance of most of the convention's constitutional provisions had been embodied previously in statutory law, the elevation of these subjects to constitutional status had the effect of furnishing legitimacy and permanency to the state government's new responsibilities, removing doubts about their constitutionality and giving the state Court of Appeals an invitation to activism not otherwise available. From this perspective, it is misleading to label the work of the convention conservative. It would be more accurate to identify the guiding spirit of the 1938 convention as "positive liberalism": the belief that the state has the obligation to promote the welfare and protect the rights of as many people as possible.[79]

What is remarkable is that a constitutional convention controlled by Republicans and a minority bloc of anti-New Deal Democrats approved measures so unmistakeably liberal in character. A recognition of the power of party and pressure should not obscure the fact that delegates recognized the real problems facing New York and embodied the felt need of the time in responding to them.

NOTES

1. Wilbert L. Hindman, "The New York Constitutional Convention of 1938: The Constituent Process and Interest Group Activity" (Ph.D Diss., University of Michigan, 1940), pp. 3-8.
2. These arguments are quoted in Hindman, "The Convention of 1938," p. 10.
3. *The New York Times*, October 27, 1936, p. 24. Editorial opinion around the state was generally unfavorable.
4. These categories are developed more fully by Hindman, "The Convention of 1938," pp. 18-21.
5. Moscow, *Politics in the Empire State*, p. 75-76.
6. Hindman, "The Convention of 1938," suggests some reasons for the American Labor Party's decision to split their support, as well as the reasons for Republican successes.
7. as quoted in Hindman, "The Convention of 1938," p. 47.
8. *New York Times*, June 9, 1937, p. 6.
9. Hindman, "The Convention of 1938," p. 73.
10. Ibid., pp. 82-83.
11. *Laws of New York*, Chap. 804 (1933); Chap. 12 (1935).
12. *People ex rel. Rodgers v. Coler*, 166 N.Y. 1 (1901).
13. *City of New York v. DeLury*, 23 N.Y. 2d 175 (1968).
14. Supreme Court decisions have also contributed to this supercession, especially *EEOC v. Wyoming*, 460 U.S. 226 (1983); *Garcia v. San Antonio Metro Transit Authority*, 469 U.S. 528 (1985).
15. *Matter of Esler v. Walters*, 56 N.Y. 2d 306 (1982).
16. 299 N.Y. 512 (1949).
17. *Revised Record of the Constitutional Convention of the State of New York*, 1938, 4 vols. (Albany: J. B. Lyon, 1938), IV, pp. 2626-2627 (hereafter cited as *Rev. Rec., 1938*).
18. Galie, *The New York Constitution*, pp. 57-58.
19. There was, however, statutory protection going back to 1828, *Revised Statutes*, Pt. I, Chap. 4 (sec. 11).
20. *Rev. Rec.*, I p. 337.
21. Ibid., I, p. 368. An informative discussion of the debate over issues in the context of Dewey's rise to prominence can be found in Lawrence Fleischer, "Thomas E. Dewey and Earl Warren: The Rise of the Twentieth Century Urban Prosecutor," *California Western Law Review*, 28 (1991-1992), pp. 26-31.
22. Ibid., I, pp. 407-408.
23. Ibid., I, pp. 336-40; 406ff.
24. *People v. Defore*, 242 N.Y. 13 (1926).
25. 291 N.Y. 161 (1943).
26. See the cases discussed in Galie, *The New York Constitution*, pp. 58-62.
27. 388 U.S. 41 (1967).
28. *New York Criminal Procedure Law*, Sec. 700.15 (4). (McKinney, 1984).
29. *People v. Cosmo*, 205 N.Y. 91, at 97 (1912).

30. See *Boykin v. Alabama*, 395 U.S. 238 (1969).
31. *People ex rel. Rohrlich v. Follette*, 20 N.Y. 2d 297 (1967) and New York Criminal Procedure Law Sec. 320.10 (2) (McKinney, 1993).
32. *Rev. Rec. 1938*, III, pp. 2586ff.
33. *Garrity v. New Jersey*, 385 U.S. 493 (1967); *Gardner v. Broderick*, 392 U.S. 273 (1968).
34. *Shales v. Leach*, 119 A.D. 2d 990 (1986).
35. *Rev. Rec.*, III, p. 2571.
36. Ibid., III, p. 2155.
37. 43 N.Y. 2d 1, at 9 (1977).
38. *Matter of Bernstein v. Toia*, 43 N.Y. 2d 437 (1977).
39. *People ex rel. Board of Charities v. New York Society for the Prevention of Cruelty to Children*, 161 N.Y. 233 (1900).
40. *Rev. Rec. 1938*, IV, p. 2954.
41. Warren Moscow, *The New York Times*, July 24, 1938, IV, p. 10; July 19, 1938, p. 6.
42. *Laws of New York*, Chap. 559, p. 1944; Chap. 725, p. 733.
43. Wallace Sayre and Herbert Kaufman, *Governing New York City* (New York: Russell Sage, 1960), pp. 107, 176.
44. *Rev. Rec.*, II, pp. 1400–1401.
45. Hindman, "The Convention of 1938," p. 341, examines the responses.
46. "The Constitution of the State of New York, as Revised with Amendments Passed by the Constitutional Convention . . . ," *Documents of the Constitutional Convention of 1938*, Doc. No. 15, 8. Moscow, *Politics in the Empire State*, p. 170.
47. Report of the Committee on State Finance and Revenues, *Documents of the Constitutional Convention of 1938*, Doc. No. 3, p. 3.
48. Hindman, "The Convention of 1938," pp. 309–315, provides more information on the positions taken by the various bar associations on this question.
49. *Rev. Rec. 1938*, III, p. 1901.
50. Ibid., II, pp. 797–798.
51. 39 N.Y. 2d 136 (1975).
52. *Rev. Rec. 1938*, IV, pp. 2633; Report of the Committee on Social Welfare, *Journal and Documents*, Convention Doc. No. 7.
53. *Rev. Rec. 1938*, III, p. 2492.
54. Ibid., II, p. 1078.
55. Ibid., II, p. 1077.
56. Constitutional Convention, 1938, *Journal and Documents*, Document No. 6, p. 5.
57. Ibid., p. 6.
58. Temporary State Commission on the Constitutional Convention, *Local Finance*, Staff Report No. 3, 1967, p. 99.
59. *Rev. Rec. 1938*, II, p. 1081.
60. Temporary Commission on the Revision and Simplification of the Constitution, *Constitutional Tax Rate Limits*, Staff Report No. 31, 1959, p. 59. The legislature created two tax stabilization reserve funds in 1946; although these funds were helpful in meeting deficits incurred between 1949 and 1951, they have not been built up to the levels anticipated in the State Finance Law.
61. *Rev. Rec. 1938*, II, p. 1079.
62. 268 NY 52 (1935).
63. *Rev. Rec. 1938*, III, pp. 2259, 2268.

64. The following relies on the careful researches of Ann Marie Hauck Walsh, "Public Authorities and the Shape of Decision Making," in Jewell Bellush and Dick Netzer, eds., *Urban Politics NEW YORK STYLE* (Armonk, N.Y.: M. E. Sharpe, 1990), pp. 199-200.

65. Hauck, "Public Authorities," p. 200.

66. Hauck, "Public Authorities," pp. 196-197, 213-217, examines in some detail the various reasons for their growth.

67. 243 N.Y. 231 (1926); *Rev. Rec. 1938*, III, pp. 2262-2263.

68. *New York Real Property Tax Law*, secs. 200-202 (McKinney, 1984).

69. 37 N.Y. 2d 1 (1975).

70. *People ex rel. Town of Pelham v. Village of Pelham*, 215 N.Y. 374 (1915).

71. *Rev. Rec. 1938*, II, pp. 1332-1370; W. Bernard Richland, "Constitutional City Home Rule in New York: II" *Columbia Law Review* 55 (1955), p. 605.

72. *Rev. Rec. 1938*, II, pp. 935-936.

73. *Journal of the Convention* (1938), pp. 481-482. Moscow, *Politics in the Empire State*, pp. 290-210.

74. The search for a "New Republic" compatible with these developments was a prominent part of intellectual and political activity in the first quarter of the twentieth century. See Charles Forcey, *The Crossroads of Liberalism: Croly, Weyl, Lippmann and the Progressive Era, 1900-1925* (New York: Oxford University Press, 1961).

75. Convention President Frederick E. Crane, *Rev. Rec. 1938*, I, pp. 67-68.

76. Hindman, "The Convention of 1938," p. 385. The other major study of the convention, Vernon O'Rourke and Douglas Campbell, *Constitution-Making in a Democracy: Theory and Practice in New York State* (Baltimore: Johns Hopkins Press, 1943), pp. 189-190, draws similar conclusions.

77. Ibid., pp. 189-190.

78. Ibid., p. 211.

79. Donald Roper,"The Governorship in History," in Robert Connery and Gerald Benjamin, eds., *Governing New York State: The Rockefeller Years, Proceedings of the Academy of Political Science* 31 (May, 1974), p. 17.

13

Constitutional Change Between Conventions: 1938–1967

THE 1938 CONVENTION revised and reorganized the constitution, providing for a more rational arrangement of the material. Placed under separate articles were provisions concerning conservation (XIV) and canals (XV). Executive budget amendments were transferred to Article VII (state finance). The twenty articles organized by the convention are currently in operation in the state.

In the thirty years between the 1938 and 1967 conventions, ninety-three amendments were approved. Their distribution among the twenty articles is provided in Table III-A. The most significant changes were effected in articles VI (judiciary), VII, VIII (state and local finance), and IX (local government). The local government article was revised in 1963, a major step toward a unified court system was adopted in 1961, and significant liberalizations in the tax and debt limits in Article VII and VIII were approved between 1949 and 1953. Finally, by the slim margin of 125,599 votes, the electorate in 1957 rejected a constitutionally mandated ballot question on holding a constitutional convention.

THE COMMISSION AND CONSTITUTIONAL REFORM: 1938–1967

In anticipation of the vote on whether or not a convention should be held as required by Article XIX, Governor Averell Harriman signed a bill in 1956 creating a fifteen-member Temporary State Commission on the Constitutional Convention. When a dispute developed between Republican leaders and Harriman over appointment of a chair, Harriman appointed Nelson Rockefeller, on the assumption that Rockefeller had no political ambitions![1] Five members were appointed by the temporary president of the senate, five by the speaker of the assembly, and five by the governor.[2] This commission was given three responsibilities: to study proposals for change and simplification of the constitution, to collect and present information and data useful for the delegates and electorate prior to and during the convention, and to issue reports and recommendations to the governor and the legislature. The *First Interim Report* was filed in February 1957. It was a brief outline of the state's constitutional history and the proposed program of the commission.[3]

The commission held a series of public hearings throughout the state to provide citizens and organizations an opportunity to present suggestions and proposals for constitutional revision and simplification. In September 1957 a *Second Interim Report* was presented[4] which digested (by subject matter) the various proposals for revision gathered by the commission. In the spring of 1957 the commission created an Inter-Law School Committee on the Problem of Simplification of the Constitution. The committee examined fifty-four sections in nine articles, recommending elimination, as superflous and outmoded, twenty-three of them. Other sections were deemed so cumbersome and "harmfully detailed" that they could "be rewritten and substantially shortened."[5]

During the first ten months of 1957, debate took place on the question of whether a constitutional convention was the most appropriate vehicle for achieving constitutional reform. Democratic Governor Harriman supported the call for a convention. Furthermore he called for the adoption of a new procedure in changing the constitution, a constitutional initiative, whereby voters could initiate amendments to the constitution, thereby eliminating dependence on the legislature or a constitutional convention. The latter proposal received little support. New York State has never proved fertile ground for the constitutional initiative. Such proposals, periodically introduced in the legislature and at constitutional conventions have never been successful.[6]

Republicans strongly opposed calling a convention, ostensibly on financial grounds, but more likely because a convention might redress the inequality in legislative reapportionment favoring upstate Republican areas. Republican leaders did not oppose revision altogether; they simply asserted that the legislative course was the better avenue for accomplishing needed revision.

The call for the convention was defeated by a vote of 1,242,538 to 1,368,068. Support was concentrated in New York City, with opposition coming from upstate Republican areas. Democratic leaders generally supported a convention and Republican leaders opposed or remained silent. Republican Nelson Rockefeller, chair of the Temporary Commission, whose purpose was to prepare for a convention, took no active role in support of the convention.

The terms of the statute required the commission's termination on February 1, 1958 if the convention call was defeated. The defeat, however, created considerable discussion over the value of continuing the constitutional studies initiated by the commission. That discussion grew out of earlier debates over the best means for achieving constitutional revision. The legislature adopted a concurrent resolution setting up a Special Legislative Committee on the Revision and Simplification of the Constitution, consisting of fifteen citizens appointed in the same manner as its predecessor. Nelson Rockefeller was again appointed chair and the staff of the first commission was retained by the committee. Its mandate, now changed in light of the defeat of the constitutional convention, was to submit to the legislature proposals for the revision and simplification of the constitution. In December 1958 Rockefeller resigned as chair to assume the governorship, and David Peck, former presiding judge of the Appellate Division, was appointed chair of a reformed Temporary Commission on the Revision and Simplification of the Constitution. That commission ordered the preparation of forty background studies on various aspects of the constitution. Ultimately, thirty-five reports were produced between 1959 and 1961 when the commission's authorization expired. These reports were detailed analyses of nearly every article in the constitution.

All the commissions recommended simplifying the constitution by removing anachronistic and/or excessively detailed parts. The reports also made substantive recommendations in such areas as home rule for local government and the removal of tax and debt limits. A number of the commission's recommendations were adopted by the legislature and approved by the voters, including a new article on local government, a new article on the militia, and removal of obsolete material from Articles I and XIII. These commissions had their roots in the committees and commissions first employed in the late nineteenth century, occasionally independent of any constitutional convention, as was the Constitutional Commission of 1872 and the Judiciary Commission of 1890, and sometimes as preparation to the convening of a constitutional convention, as in 1915 and 1938. The 1957 commission marked the first time a preparatory commission was formed prior to a vote on the holding of a constitutional convention. The goal was to provide sufficient time for a thorough study of areas and issues in need of attention. The success of these commissions provided ample evidence that important if non-controversial constitutional reform could be accomplished in the absence of a convention. The fact that more controversial issues such as reapportionment and state and local tax and debt limits were the subject of careful scrutiny but no action suggests that such issues might require a convention or outside intervention.

Article I

Article I, the Bill of Rights, was amended nine times. Two permitted exceptions to the prohibition on gambling (Sec. 9). The first, in 1939, allowed parimutuel racetrack betting within legislatively prescribed conditions. The stated purpose of this amendment was to produce additional revenues for the state. The amendment was permissive only and did not create a right to parimutuel betting.[7] This was the first step in returning to the pre-1894 state policy of tolerating certain forms of gambling. The second exception, in 1957, authorized municipalities, with voter approval, to allow certain organizations to conduct designated games of chance. The fact that many religious and charitable organizations operated bingo games to raise funds for worthy purposes, and in so doing risked criminal penalties, promoted this amendment. The gambling was confined to nonprofit, charitable, and religious organizations, with all proceeds exclusively devoted to purposes of the organization, and had a limit of $1,000 on the prizes awarded at any given event. Governor Averell Harriman had recommended legislation permitting church bingo; however, the legislature chose the safer route of a constitutional amendment.[8] Legislation pursuant to this amendment created a State Lottery Control Commission to administer the Bingo Licensing Law.

A 1966 amendment to this section allowed the state, for the first time in the twentieth century, to operate a lottery system, with the proceeds designated exclusively for the support of education. The access to a heretofore untapped source of revenue was the main justification for this amendment. The amendment was not self-executing. The legislature had to "authorize and prescribe" the game by a statute known as the New York State Lottery for Education Law (1967). The debate in the senate suggests that there was no intention to do more than carve out a specific exception to the general prohibition against lotteries and gambling.[9] The opening of gambling enterprises on Native American Reservations under a federal law allowing high-stakes gambling on reservations, the decision of Ontario Province to approve casino gambling in the Canadian town of Niagara Falls, and the prospect that states like Massachusetts might approve riverboat gambling, have given impetus to proposals for a constitutional amendment permitting casino gambling in New York.[10]

The 1938 convention inserted a significant qualification to the right against self-incrimination by permitting a prosecutor to compel any public officer to testify before a grand jury about conduct in office or risk loss of employment. In 1944, a city official refused to waive immunity to testify concerning conduct in office and was removed, but assumed a newly created position, thereby circumventing this qualification. Subsequently, the Court of Appeals ruled that no provision existed that disqualified the official from holding any other office.[11] Anticipating a reccurrence, this section was amended in 1949 to prevent an official so removed from holding public office for five years. One additional amendment was added in 1959, again to alter the effects of a court decision. A public official refused to testify under waiver of immunity when called before a grand jury. When an attempt to remove him from office was made, an appellate court ruled that "in the absence of constitutional direction" the state could not remove one from office because of a refusal under waiver to testify as to conduct in a prior office.[12]

Section 1 contains the famous "law of the land" clause, as well as the first substantive right mentioned in the constitution, the right to vote. Both protections originated with the 1777 Constitution. It was amended to authorize the legislature to provide, by general law, that no primaries be held where there are no party contests for nomination to public office or election to party positions. It was primarily a cost-saving measure and was expected to save hundreds of thousands of dollars.[13] Although there appeared to be no constitutional right to a primary system and the current law protected full and fair participation in the nomination and election of candidates, the language of court decisions raised uncertainties regarding the constitutionality of such legislation.[14] In such circumstances an amendment was a more judicious way to proceed. Primaries would still be held when contests developed through the filing of independent petitions. Also, write-ins would still be permitted in general elections. The provision seems more appropriately placed in Article II.

Two amendments in 1963 and 1964 concerned the taking of private property and the power of eminent domain. The 1963 amendment repealed a provision allowing municipalities to take more property than needed for construction of public projects (Section 7e). The repeal was necessitated by the complete revision of the local government article in that year. It was superceded by a new provision of Article IX, Section 1e, providing local governments with eminent domain power, thus enabling them to appropriate private property for public use, including excess land and property sufficient to provide for appropriate disposition.

The 1964 amendment repealed Section 7b. That provision established the forums in which compensation for takings would be provided. It had a tangled history stretching back to the 1846 convention.[15] This section permitted four alternative forums: a jury, the Supreme Court without jury, the Supreme Court with an official referee, and a commissioner system. Since both state and federal constitutions contain judicially enforceable requirements for awarding just compensation in condemnation cases, the Inter-Law School Committee on Simplification of the Constitution concluded that there was "no reason why the legislature should not be left free to fashion procedures for ascertaining what compensation is just without detailed constitutional hints and nudges."[16] In 1962 an amendment to Article I repealed Sections 10, 13, and 15. Section 10 proclaimed all lands of the state to be allodial, that is, owned freely without obligation and not subject to restrictions existing with feudal tenures. The Inter-Law School Committee recommended its elimination, writing: "there are no feudal chiefs to whom New Yorkers must crook their knees now, and there would be none if this constitutional verbiage were to disappear."[17]

ARTICLE II: SUFFRAGE

Article II was amended nine times between 1938 and 1967. All the amendments concerned residency requirements or absentee voting provisions, and all had a liberalizing effect on those requirements. Section 1 had gone practically unchanged since an 1874 amendment prescribing a one-year residence the in state, four months in the county, and thirty days within the election district. Such requirements were instituted to allow voters sufficient time to familiarize themselves with the candidates and issues and to assure that they were bona fide residents of the state and locality in which they voted.[18]

The 1943 amendment altered the requirement from a four-month residence in the county to a four-month residence in the county, city, or village. A 1945 amendment added a clause permitting citizens to vote who satisfied residency requirements and then moved to another election district in the same county less than thirty days before the election. Allowing such individuals to vote would not jeopardize the original purposes of residency requirements (Sec. 1). In 1947 an amendment to Section 2 permitted more extensive use of the absentee ballot. The absentee provision was first adopted in 1919, after studies revealed that over 300,000 voters were disenfranchised by virtue of unavoidable absence.[19] The 1947 modification permitted the legislature to enable those to vote by absentee ballot who, because of duties, occupation, or business (including those of family members) are required to be elsewhere. The amendment was necessitated by the fact that during the war many citizens working outside the state and nation in the war effort were not permitted to cast ballots because they were not members of the armed forces.[20] In 1951 the phrase "in time of war" was deleted, thus allowing members of the armed services to vote by absentee ballot during peacetime. This amendment recognized that significant numbers of military personnel would be stationed abroad for the foreseeable future. It extended the same privilege to family members.[21]

Voters residing in villages and cities of over 5,000 inhabitants were required to register personally. A 1951 amendment dispensed with this requirement for voters in the military service and veteran hospital patients and their families outside New York (Sec. 5). The application for an absentee ballot would constitute personal registration where such was required.[22] Absentee ballot privileges were further extended in 1955 to those unable to appear personally at polling places due to illness or physical infirmity (Sec. 2). It would also permit these voters to register without doing so in person (Sec. 5). The method and proof required for such registration would be determined by the legislature.[23] In 1963 the legislature was authorized to grant absentee voting privileges to persons who, for acceptable reasons, may be absent from their residence, in effect granting to the legislature the power to determine who can exercise the privilege and under what conditions. This amendment eliminated the cumbersome process of having to amend the constitution each time a new class was made eligible. The section, however, does not grant a constitutional right to an absentee ballot, and the courts have been deferential to the legislature regarding its application. The state's refusal to provide an absentee ballot for a citizen vacationing during a special election was sustained.[24] Absentee ballot procedures are governed by the state's election law, and, with regard to presidential and vice-presidential elections, by amendments to the Federal Voting Rights Act of 1970.

In response to the increasingly mobile character of Americans, a 1966 amendment substantially reduced residency requirements. The earlier one-year requirement was estimated to have disenfranchised upwards of 20% of the voters. This amendment reduced the requirement to three months. Various groups supporting these changes argued that three months was sufficient time to get acquainted with the issues.[25] The three-month standard, however, did not meet federal standards, and the Court of Appeals, following the Supreme Court's ruling in *Dunn v. Blumstein*,[26] held this requirement in violation of the equal protection clause of the Fourteenth Amendment.[27] The current standard set by the Supreme Court is thirty days, superceding Section 1 of the New York Constitution. A second amendment that same year extended the provision authorizing absentee registration to those unable to appear personally for registration if their occupation or business required absence from the county of their residence. The previous clause limited the extension to those out of the state.

ARTICLE III: THE LEGISLATURE

Nine amendments were adopted during this period, none involving significant changes. A 1943 amendment specified the residency requirements for election to the senate or assembly following readjustment or alteration of senate or assembly districts.

In 1943 an ordinance divided the town of Hempstead in Nassau County, creating two state assembly districts in the second senate district. In *Tishman v. Sprague*[28] the Court of Appeals invalidated that division on the grounds that it violated Section 5 of Article III, which stated that no town shall be divided in the formation of assembly districts. An amendment approved in 1945 permitted such division.[29]

Until 1947 legislative salaries were fixed by the constitution. Each salary adjustment required a constitutional amendment. In 1947 an amendment to Section 5 transferred that decision to the legislature. An election must intervene between a vote to increase salaries or allowances and receipt of those increases. This change was recommended by the Joint Legislative Committee on Legislative Methods, Practices, Procedures and Expenditures (1946). That committee believed the legislature would be responsible, and in any case public opinion would control urges to abuse that power.

The final change concerning salaries came in 1964 with the deletion of an obsolete clause which had permitted a one-time salary allowance adjustment to the prohibition against salaries or allowances being increased or diminished during the term for which the legislator had been elected.

A second paragraph to Section 22, defining requirements of tax laws, allowed the legislature to adopt the federal definition of income for purposes of the state income tax, thus simplifying the preparation of state income tax returns. By drawing on the large store of federal precedents interpreting the income tax law, the task of administering and clarifying state law would be reduced significantly.[30]

In 1962 Section 3, delineating the boundaries of senate districts in detail, was repealed. Those boundaries became obsolete as a result of legislative adjustments of senate districts after each decennial census. The section contained references to "the Town of Flatbush in the County of Kings" and the "City of Brooklyn," among others. The repeal did not effect the law regarding apportionment; it merely removed obsolete material from the constitution. The amendment also repealed the provision involving the conditions under which the legislature could regulate construction and operation of street railroads. The provision was deemed statutory in character and obsolete, as there were no street railroads in New York! Both repeals were adopted on the recommendations of the Temporary Commission on the Revision and Simplification of the Constitution.[31]

A new section, 25, was adopted in 1963. It was an enabling measure designed to empower the legislature to ensure, as far as possible, the continuity of governmental operations in the event of grave emergency brought on by nuclear attack or natural disaster.[32] Various attempts have been made to use this section to circumvent constitutional restrictions. When the federal courts declared New York's apportionment plans unconstitutional, this provision was invoked as a basis for suspending Section 2 of the article (number and terms of senators and assemblymen). The court, in *Matter of Oran*, rejected these arguments.[33] Similar attempts were made to invoke the provision in connection with the fiscal emergencies that confronted state and local governments in the 1970s. In each case, the court rejected this argument on the grounds that the section was intended to apply to disasters associated with nuclear attacks and natural catastrophes that disrupt state operations.[34] Without such a narrow interpretation of emergency, Section 25 is an open invitation to trump the constitution any time a crisis develops.

Unquestionably the central focus of constitutional developments associated with Article III is the issue of reapportionment. Largely the work of the 1894 convention, as reaffirmed by the 1938 convention, the method of reapportionment was so structured as to favor rural and upstate interests at the expense of the downstate New York City area. That reapportionment plan was declared invalid in *WMCA Inc. v. Lomenzo*.[35] Specifically, it held that insofar as the requirement that no county shall be divided in the formation of senate districts (Sec. 4) interferes with achieving equal population in all senate districts, that provision is invalid. The provision allowing one assembly seat for each county was also voided. The federal rulings which constituted the reapportionment revolution of the 60s were a major precipitating factor in the 1967 constitutional convention in New York. Although the state complied with federal court rulings and substantial equality has been achieved, this compliance has not prevented the legislature from engaging in partisan and bipartisan gerrymandering, as characterized by legislative apportionment plans in the 70s and 80s. The clause requiring districts to be "compact and contiguous" is a potential safeguard against this gerrymandering, but the Court of Appeals has not applied it with much rigor.[36] Though superceded by federal constitutional law, these sections remain in the constitution.

Article IV: The Executive

Three amendments addressed the question of succession. The importance of this question is underscored by the frequency with which governors of New York have resigned. Governor Daniel Tompkins resigned to accept the vice-presidency of the United States; Martin Van Buren left office to become President Andrew Jackson's secretary of state; Grover Cleveland was elected president of the United States and resigned the governorship a few weeks prior to his inauguration; Charles Evans Hughes relinquished office to accept a United States Supreme Court seat; Governor Herbert Lehman resigned in 1942; and Nelson Rockefeller resigned in 1973 to accept appointment as vice-president of the United States.

The 1938 convention continued the succession provisions, with one modification. In the event that the office of governor was vacant and there was no lieutenant-governor, the temporary president of the senate or the speaker of the assembly, if there were no temporary president, would serve until the next general election, occurring not less that three months following the vacancy (Sec. 6). It remained unclear whether the governor and the lieutenant-governor, or only the governor, were to be chosen at that election, but the one elected was only to serve out the balance of the previous office-holder's term.

In July 1943, barely six months after inauguration, Lieutenant-Governor Thomas W. Wallace died. A dispute arose as to whether an election of his successor was required at the next general election. The Court of Appeals affirmed without comment an appellate court decision holding that such an election was required.[37] Reaction was immediate and negative. Governor Thomas Dewey criticized the decision as incompatible with the 1937 amendment which set the term of office for the four statewide elected officials at four years. "With the administration less than one year old, with the nation at war, and there being no other major contested candidacies or state issues, it became necessary for the people of the state to choose a successor to their Lieutenant-Governor."[38]

On recommendation of the governor the legislature passed, and the voters approved, an amendment removing this ambiguity. It prohibited any election for lieutenant-governor being held "in any event except at the time of the electing a governor" (Sec. 6). The temporary president of the senate would perform the duties during such vacancy.

A 1949 amendment anticipated the possibility of the death of a governor-elect. It was apparently prompted by the death of a governor-elect in Georgia.

Until 1953 the governor and lieutenant-governor were not elected jointly; candidates from different parties could be—and were—elected. Having a governor and lieutenant-governor from different political parties, or from ideologically opposed wings of the same party, created serious problems. A responsible, cohesive administration necessitated the election of a governor and lieutenant-governor from the same party.[39] This amendment bracketed the two officers on the voting machine so that a vote for one gubernatorial candidate was automatically a vote for the running mate. New York was the first state to have candidates for the two top offices run as a team in the general election. Twenty-one states have followed that example. However, since the governor does not necessarily select a running mate, this provision guarantees only compatible political parties but not necessarily personal or political compatibility.

The 1953 amendment also increased salaries of the governor from $25,000 to $50,000 and of the lieutenant-governor from $10,000 to $20,000.

A 1963 amendment codified the succession provisions and eliminated constitutionally mandated salary figures for the two offices, leaving the setting of salary to joint resolution of the senate and assembly (Secs. 3, 6).

The 1963 revisions were the last modifications to the succession provision of Article IV. The lieutenant-governor becomes governor in the event of the governor's death or resignation, serving in that office for the remainder of the governor's term. The lieutenant-governor acts as governor in the event that the governor is impeached, absent from the state, or otherwise unable to discharge the powers and duties of the office. The line of succession devolves from the temporary president of the senate to the speaker of the assembly. The legislature was authorized to provide for further devolution by statute (Sec. 6). This latter provision was inserted with the possibility of nuclear disaster in mind.

Although there have been attempts to amend this provision further, particularly in regard to the question of a governor's disability, such attempts have been unsuccessful.[40]

Article V

Nine amendments were added to this article. Three concerned executive department structure, three three others concerned veteran preference in civil service, and the remainder expanded the duties of the comptroller, eliminated obsolete material, and altered a section to conform to changes made in the election of the governor and the lieutenant-governor.

The 1925 reorganization of the executive department as revised by the 1938 convention provided for eighteen civil departments in state government and limited the power of the legislature to create new departments. In 1943 an amendment creating a Department of Commerce was adopted. A Division of Commerce had been established in 1941, but it was believed that a state containing the commercial center of the nation should give the commerce division a status and independence commensurate with its significance. In 1987 the legislature changed the name of this department to the Office of Economic Development.

In 1959 similar considerations led to the creation of the Department of Motor Vehicles. The Bureau of Motor Vehicles existence as part of the Department of Taxation and Finance suggested that motor vehicles were perceived primarily as a revenue source. It was evident that more was involved, including traffic regulation, safety programs, and the coordination of activities of related agencies and associations. To provide it with the "prestige, status and independence" necessary to perform these varied tasks, departmental status was provided.[41]

The most significant change in the executive department occurred with a 1961 amendment providing greater flexibility for the governor and legislature to restructure executive department functions. Between 1925 and 1960 responsibilities and activities of the state increased substantially. The budget mushroomed from $239 million to over $2 billion, and the number of employees increased from 29,000 to over 100,000. The executive branch expanded accordingly, with 136 independent or quasi-independent agencies and approximately 90 advisory boards and councils.[43] A special study group reported that many of these agencies were created to avoid the constitutional limit on the number of departments, and that this practice had impaired the efficient operation of the government. The recommendations of the committee provided the basis for the reorganization accomplished by this amendment.

The amendment retained the limit on the number of departments (twenty), but deleted their names and authorized the legislature to create executive offices of the governor and reduce the number of departments if deemed necessary (Sec. 2, 3, 4). The removal of department names allowed flexibility in assigning new functions to constitutional departments, and the creation of executive offices would allow the governor to retain essential staff units and would eliminate the use of that department as a catch-all for a variety of administrative functions more appropriately placed in line departments.[43]

Three amendments related to veterans preference in civil service. Preference for veterans predated the Civil Service Law of 1883. That law, continuing a preference in appointment and promotion and preference for disabled war veterans, was placed in the constitution in 1894. In 1945 Section 6 was amended to extend the preference to non-disabled veterans, the latter given preference over non-veterans but only after first preference was given to disabled veterans. For the first time, veteran's preference for retention in service was granted. Protracted litigation, administrative difficulties, inequities among veterans, and preference to less qualified candidates led to the revision of this section in 1949. That amendment eliminated the "absolute preference" accorded to war veterans and substituted preference in the form of bonus examination credits.[44] A 1964 amendment deleted the provision relating to the special preference granted certain veterans taking civil service examinations prior to January 1, 1951.

The 1953 change in Article IV, Section 6, preventing the election of a lieutenant-governor except at the time of electing a governor, was paralleled in this article by a similar requirement for the comptroller and attorney general, thus providing a uniform procedure for the four officers chosen in state-wide elections. The legislature was authorized to provide for the filling of vacancies in these two offices. The provision concerning vacancies in the offices of comptroller and attorney general is still an issue. By 1995, proposals had received first passage which would eliminate the power of the state legislature to provide for the filling of vacancies and would delete the prohibition that no election for either office shall be held except at the time of electing a governor. These proposed amendments have as their objective the removal of any legislative and executive influence created by these provisions.[45]

In 1955 the comptroller was given additional authority pertaining to the assessment and taxation of real estate. This could be done only through an amendment, as Section 1 prohibited the legislative assignment of additional duties to the controller beyond those incidental to the ones specified therein. This prohibition, added by a 1925 amendment, was prompted by a dual fear: that the legislature might reduce the authority of the office to the point where there would be no independent audit of state finances, or that the office would be further burdened with administrative functions, making it difficult for the comptroller to perform the crucial functions specified in Section 1.[46] Additionally, it is claimed that some of these functions, e.g., that of custodian and investor of state funds, are incompatible with the role of the comptroller as an auditor. These criticisms have deep roots in the state's constitutional history and have found expression in the prohibition in this section against assigning the comptroller administrative tasks.[47]

The last of the amendments passed in 1962 repealed Section 5. That section, added in 1846, abolished all offices for weighing, measuring, gauging, and inspecting merchandise, produce, and the like. It was added to rid the state of this swarm of public officials, mostly patronage recipients, engaged in the enforcement of the mass of legislation in this area. The amendment was based on recommendations of the Inter-Law School Committee on the problem of simplification of the constitution. The section was a classic example of a constitutional dead letter, a relic of a bygone era. Despite its sweeping proscription, New York State remains actively engaged in large-scale inspection, and employs a legion of inspectors vastly more extensive than anything envisioned by the delegates in 1846. At best the section was irrelevant; at worst it "cast a shadow over a flourishing and widely accepted inspection program."[48]

Article VI: The Judiciary

Between 1846, when the first major reorganization of the judiciary was accomplished, and 1961, when voters approved a complete revision of the court system, the judiciary article was the subject of a Judiciary Commission (1890), a Judiciary Convention (1920), and more amendments than any article in the constitution.

In 1943 an amendment to Section 7 accomplished technical changes in the jurisdiction of the Court of Appeals, extending it in certain areas and restricting it in others. The power of the legislature to abolish the appellate jurisdiction of that court was limited to appeals taken as a matter of right, unless a state or federal constitutional question was involved. If the legislature did abolish this class of appeals, such appeals could still be taken by leave.[49] Section 7 was again amended in 1951 to provide greater opportunity for review of administrative determinations.

In 1947 a third method of removing judges was added to the constitution (Sec. 9-a). Reports of judicial misconduct appeared to be on the increase, and established procedures were perceived as inadequate. Impeachment, the oldest method, was controversial and rarely used. The likelihood of removal by concurrent resolution of both houses by a two-thirds vote was also remote (Sec. 23). There was a need for an independent body to investigate, evaluate, and, where necessary, discipline judges.[50] Believing the legislature overburdened with the constraints of its own business, this amendment embodied a variant of the California plan for judicial discipline.[51] It instituted a Court on the Judiciary, composed of the chief judge and the senior associate judge of the Court of Appeals, with one judge from each appellate division (Sec. 22b). This court would require the concurrence of four of the six members for the removal or retirement of judges. The establishment of a court on the judiciary was the first of three attempts to provide an effective mechanism for disciplining judges.

In 1949 the Court of Claims, a statutory court possessing exclusive jurisdiction to adjudicate private claims against the state and claims against certain agencies of the state, was granted constitutional status. Until 1977 it was the only major court whose members were non-elective. The provision called for appointment by the governor with the consent of the senate (Sec. 23). Various commissions have recommended abolition of the court and merger of its functions with those of the Supreme Court. Nevertheless, when the 1961 unification and reorganization of the court system took place, this court was retained.[52]

Amendments in 1951 and 1953 increased the monetary jurisdiction of the city courts of New York City and county courts beyond the boundaries of cities. As dollar amounts are set by the constitution, depreciation of the dollar necessitates periodic adjustments. The increases, from $3,000 to $6,000, would reduce the number of cases coming to the supreme court.

In 1951 the people also approved an amendment allowing judges on the Court of Appeals to serve in the armed services without relinquishing their position. Prior to passage, judges wishing to serve were compelled by Section 19 to resign from the bench. This exception was extended to justices of other courts in 1955.

A series of amendments addressed the issue of inter-court transfers and temporary assignment of judges. A 1953 amendment allowed the temporary assignment of judges to terms of courts in New York City, which suffered from congested calendars (Secs. 14a, 15a). In 1955 the governor was permitted to appoint, for ninety-day periods, temporary judges or justices in the City of New York. Absences of judges due to illness or disability aggravated delays in justice. The transfer of judges permitted by the 1953 amendment had merely shifted the problem.

In 1961 New York undertook its first court reorganization since 1846. The court reorganization amendment, which took effect in 1962, represented an attempt to transform a largely autonomous collection of courts into a unified state court system. New York's state court system had been labelled "a classic example of an outmoded court system."[53] From 1848 to 1953 twenty-five commissions and committees were created to recommend solutions for New York's tangled court structure.⁵⁴ In 1956 a Temporary Commission on the Courts recommended to the governor and legislature that the state's courts be consolidated to become part of a single, integrated, statewide system, centrally administered.⁵⁵ That plan received a cool reception and the commission was allowed to go out of existence in 1958. Groups such as the League of Women Voters and the Citizen's Committee for Modern Courts kept the idea alive until Chief Judge Charles Desmond of the Court of Appeals, the head of the Judicial Conference, could prepare a substitute plan. That plan became the basis for the 1962 amendment.⁵⁶

The purpose of the revision is clearly stated in the opening sentence: "There shall be a unified court system for the state" (Sec. 1). Although the amendment achieved some consolidation—abolishing eight courts, mainly in New York City—it made provision for eleven different trial courts in the state. The decisions to continue these separate courts were not founded on the recommendations of the Temporary Commission on Courts; rather, these courts remained as a result of the opposition from these courts and their supporters.⁵⁷ The article contained liberal provisions for transferring cases and, as far as possible, use of "full time judges." These judges were prohibited from practicing law or engaging in any other profession or business which would interfere with the performance of their judicial duties. Members of the Court of Appeals, justices of the Supreme Court, surrogate judges, and judges of Family Court could be removed for cause and retired for any mental or physical disability preventing proper performance of their duties, by a Court on the Judiciary upon notice and hearing. Other judges could be removed by the relevant appellate division for cause with notice and public hearing.

Administration of the court system was vested in the appellate division subject to the authority of an Administrative Board of the Judicial Conference. That board would consist of the chief judge of the Court of Appeals as chair and the presiding judges of the four appellate departments (Sec. 28). Centralized authority, however, was not achieved by this structure. As former Chief Judge Lawrence H. Cooke noted: "responsibility was divided often in unclear and inconsistent ways, among the judicial conference, the Administrative Board, the Chief Judge of the Court of Appeals, and the four appellate divisions."⁵⁸ An informal arrangement whereby the presiding judges relinquished day-to-day administrative responsibility to a single administrative judge enabled the system to operate reasonably well.

The article prescribed the number of judges and justices on each of the courts, the method of selection, and their terms in office. The tenure varied from four years for town and village courts to fourteen for Court of Appeals judges and Supreme Court justices. With the exception of judges of the Court of Claims, the judges and justices of these courts were elected.

Provision was made for centralizing budget requests. The proposed annual budget of the courts was to be forwarded to the administrative board of the judicial conference or to the conference as a whole for review and recommendation. It was then forwarded to the appropriate authorities: with respect to expenses borne by the state, to the governor and legislature, and with respect to expenses borne by counties and municipalities, to the appropriate local bodies. The legislature was authorized to delegate in whole or in part to a court or to the judicial conference any power of the legislature to regulate the practice and procedures of the judiciary, or to retain that power (Sec. 30).

The 1961 amendment permitted judges of the Court of Appeals, Supreme Court, or appellate division to serve beyond the retirement age of seventy when certified as to their physical and mental capacity to perform judicial duties, in trial or special term, for two-year periods until the age of seventy-six (Sec. 25b). In 1966 an amendment allowed retired appellate division judges to serve in the appellate division without being limited to trial or special term. It was considered a more effective use of their talents and experience. That same year, voters rejected an amendment which would have allowed retired judges of the Court of Appeals to serve on that court, and they disapproved an amendment allowing all other judges to serve beyond retirement.

Article VII: State Finance

This article was subjected to amendment twelve times between 1938 and 1967. All but one of the amendments were authorizations for the state to incur debt otherwise not permitted by the constitution. They are as follows: diversion of $60 million of grade crossing elimination bonds for construction of state highways (Sec. 14, 1941); authorization of tax revenue stabilization reserves (Sec. 18, 1943); debt for payment of bonuses to war veterans (Sec. 18, 1947, 1949); empowering the legislature to increase pensions of members of the state retirement system (Sec. 8, 1951); authorization of debt for expansion of the state university system (Sec. 19, 1957); extension of the time of payments of notes and obligations for money borrowed in anticipation of bonds issued for housing purposes from two to five years (Sec. 9, 1958); authorization for the state to loan money to non-profit corporations not to exceed $50 million for industrial and manufacturing plants providing additional employment in depressed areas (Sec. 8, 1961); expanding legislative power to authorize loans of state funds to improve employment opportunities in any area of the state (Sec. 8, 1966); empowering the legislature to provide for education and support of the mentally ill or emotionally disturbed (Sec. 8, 1966); permitting the state to increase the amount of pension benefits of widows or widowers of retired members of the state pension system (Sec. 8, 1966). These amendments either allowed exceptions to debt not otherwise permitted and/or are explicit exceptions to the prohibition on the use of state money or credit for private corporations, associations, or individuals (Sec. 8).

One amendment concerned the budgetary process. It changed the date for the budget submission in all but the first year of the governor's administration. In such specific years it required budget submission on or before the first Tuesday following the first meeting of the legislature, giving the legislature, the fiscal community, and the general public an additional three weeks to review the budget (Sec. 2, 1965).

These exemptions reflect the increasing role the state was taking in the management of the economy. The protean character of a dynamic economy, along with the corresponding activism of the state, required periodic adjustments to a constitution whose basic premise is that government should be limited in the extent to which it can incur debt or use its money or credit. Two of these amendments illustrate this tension.

A 1943 amendment established a tax stabilization fund as a buffer against fluctuations in the general business cycle. The measure was constitutionalized, in part—as noted by its chief sponsor, Assemblyman Abbott Low Moffat—because "there is no way under the present constitution that this can be done without the danger that some subsequent legislature will raid the reserve for political purposes."[59] The existence of such a fund in the constitution raises a number of questions. Does it further segment and add complexity to the reporting and interpreting of the state's fiscal activities? Is the creation of such a fund the proper subject for constitutional treatment? The intention of the provision was to limit legislative action concerning use of the funds, but that objective is blunted by its broad and permissive wording.[60]

A second illustration of this tension is the 1956 amendment permitting the use of state funds in support of institutions devoted to aiding the emotionally and mentally handicapped. The exemption was added to a list which already included education and the support of the blind, deaf, and dumb, the physically handicapped, and juvenile delinquents. As the memorandum of the Joint Legislative Committee on Mental Retardation and Physical Handicap noted: "When the constitution was last written there was little of the present awareness of mental retardation, mental illness or emotional disturbance as manifold and serious problems of our society."[61]

Article VIII: Local Finance

Debt Limits

The debt limitations fashioned by the 1938 convention reflected a Depression-era mentality. The difficulties New York and other cities throughout the state experienced in the management of their debt was cause for deep concern. There was sentiment, especially among taxpayer groups, that had the debt limits been tighter and applicable to all local governments, such difficulties might have been avoided.[62] For the next ten years this article remained unchanged. Local government finance improved, as did business conditions, and, most importantly, the war years effectively halted local public works projects and borrowing. Old debts were gradually retired, with little new accumulation. These conditions resulted in an expansion of local government's constitutional debt margins.

The end of the war generated a wave of construction projects and municipal improvements, accompanied by a resumption of borrowing. Concern arose over the possibility of local governments reaching their debt limits. The computation of these limits on the basis of a five-year average valuation meant that any rise in real estate values would come rather slowly. There was also concern about municipalities' ability to finance current operations under the existing tax limits.[63]

In 1947 state comptroller Frank Moore organized a Committee on Constitutional Tax and Debt Limitations and City School Fiscal Relations to report on these developments and make recommendations. The committee issued a series of reports between 1948 and 1950.[64] From these recommendations six constitutional amendments were passed between 1949 and 1953.

The first, in 1949, exempted debts of revenue-producing undertakings proportionately to the extent that their net revenues, after operations and maintenance, covered and were applied to debt service. Under the law in operation at that time, total debt exclusion was permitted where the project was wholly self-liquidating. Supporters saw no reason why proportionate exclusion should not be permitted when the project was partially self-liquidating (Sec. 5). Two other changes in 1949 allowed New York City to issue $150 million in bonds outside the city's debt limit for hospital purposes, and reduced the maximum term for future bonds for rapid transit and dock purposes from fifty to forty years. The first two measures eased debt limitations on municipalities; the third tightened them. Since bonds issued over the longer periods were not necessarily tied to self-liquidating projects, it was believed that they jeopardized the financial status of municipalities and were in need of more control. The ten-year reduction in the life of such debt was seen as "a step in the right direction."[65]

These 1949 measures were deemed insufficient to satisy the swiftly mounting financial requirements of local governments; therefore, the committee submitted a series of recommendations which formed the basis for future amendments approved by the electorate in 1951.

Of major significance was the redefining of the base for determining debt limits from a five-year average of assessed value to a five-year moving average of full value. Full valuation was the assessed value adjusted by state-determined equalization ratios. The committee believed that "Assessing at less than full value . . . has destroyed any relationship between borrowing under the existing debt limit and ability to pay."[66] The committee further believed the shift would restore that relationship and put all municipalities on the same footing. Whatever the intended goal, the actual effect increased substantially the base and thus thus local borrowing power, particularly for the smaller localities. The Staff Report of the 1959 Temporary Commission on Constitutional Debt Limits noted that "there had never been any other relationship between [borrowing power and ability to pay] than the one based on the under-valued assessments." The conversion to full valuation "did not represent a return to an originally intended type of debt limit, but rather constituted a change to a new and never before contemplated type of debt limit."[67] Data not examined by the comptroller's committee demonstrated that under the proposed changes, increases in the borrowing power of most local governments would be so great as to make their debt limits irrelevant.[68] As a way of offsetting these increases, debt limits were lowered for all towns, villages, and counties (except Nassau) from 8% to 7%, and from 9% to 7% for cities with populations under 125,000—not a significant offset, in the opinion of the Staff Report. The establishment of a separate debt limit for city purposes and school districts wholly or partly within cities of less than 125,000 was a significant change and is discussed below.

The 1949 amendment permitted proportionate exclusion from municipality debt limits for capital projects to the extent to which they were self-supporting. This provision, helpful for the outstanding debts of operations or projects already underway, offered no relief to new borrowing for undertakings designed to be revenue-producing. A second amendment in 1951 provided a remedy for that situation. It allowed excluding, prior to the first year's operating expense, of up to 75% of debt for purposes expected to be fully or partially self-supporting (Sec. 5). One important effect of this amendment was to reduce or eliminate the need for counties and municipalities to create local authorities as devices for circumventing restrictions on borrowing.

The third change exempted from the debt limits of localities other than New York City the so-called "phantom debt." Phantom debt has been described as follows:

> ... paper debt resulting from the requirement of the 1938 constitutional provision that whenever all or part of the cost of a capital improvement is required by law to be financed by a direct budgetary appropriation or short-term tax notes the taxes therefor [sic] may be raised outside the tax limit, but that the taxes so excluded from the tax limit must be charged to the debt limit over future years in the same manner as if the cost had been financed by the issuance of bonds maturing in equal annual installments over the full period of probable usefulness of the improvement established by law.[69]

The debt is "phantom" in that the amount so charged to the debt limit has been paid and is not an actual obligation. This amendment would allow cities other than New York, villages, and school districts overlapping cities, unless otherwise provided by the legislature, to levy taxes for direct appropriations for capital purposes outside the tax rate limit without charging the cost of the object thus financed against the debt limit. The exclusion of New York City was not explained by the committee, but suspicions about the city's "lack of fiscal responsibility" may have been behind the limit on how far New York City's property could be taxed. However, New York City was permitted to borrow $500 million outside its debt limits for subway construction (Sec. 7).

The last change, effected in 1951, involved debt restrictions and school districts. The amendments established separate debt limits for school districts completely or partly within the boundaries of cities with less than 125,000 inhabitants (Sec. 4). A reduced debt limit of 7% was established for the cities in this classification, and a separate school district debt limit of 5% was established. School districts could increase this limit with the approval of 60% of those voting on the request and the consent of the Board of Regents and the Comptroller. The latter provision was inserted to allow for flexibility in the face of an anticipated demand for school building construction. Two justifications were offered for the establishment of separate debt limits for these school districts. The present constitution acted as a barrier to school district reorganization in and near cities, because "in some cases reorganization would bring presently excludable school debt within the city's debt limit."[70] The main reason, however, was to give these school districts some control over and responsibility for their fiscal affairs.

The last change approved by the voters allowed the City of New York to exclude from its constitutional debt limit the amount of bonded debt for school purposes that was supported by state school aid, up to $2.5 million. It was a continuous exemption and could be reused as the debt was repaid. Revenue to support the debt service was derived from state aid, not real estate taxes. The provision increased the debt contracting power of New York City by $40 million and was aimed at helping the city finance its schools and other capital improvements.[71]

A final set of amendments, passed in 1953, resulted from the recommendations of the comptroller's third report. One permitted any local government to contract indebtedness for a supply of water in excess of its needs for sale to any other public corporation or improvement district, e.g., water, sewer, or drainage (Sec. 2a). That amendment also permitted the legislature to authorize two or more public corporations and improvement districts to provide a common water supply, and for them to contract joint indebtedness for such purposes. The amendment was aimed at eliminating the financial difficulties interfering with the distribution of water by localities and with their ability to plan effectively and efficiently for anticipated water needs. The ability of municipalities to borrow for their own water supplies for their own use was not in question, but the restrictions on the lending of their credit for another municipality's purpose (Art. VIII, Sec. 1) cast doubt on their ability to sell surplus water to these municipalities. This amendment removed those doubts and, it was believed, would encourage the development of one large supplier of water rather than multiple, smaller suppliers, thus providing more economical and satisfactory service.[72] Once the practice of intergovernmental cooperation was established in the constitution, extension to related areas followed. In 1955 two amendments granted exemptions for debt contracted for sewage disposal and drainage and extended the intergovernmental cooperation provisions to those areas. Section 2a spelled out, at some length, legislative procedure for the apportionment of this joint indebtedness and how it might provide for the periodical exclusion from debt limits of all or part of any such debt contracted for revenue-producing improvements. A 1959 amendment incorporated into Section 1 the substance of Section 2a, extending it to "two or more such units" rather than "counties, cities, towns, villages, school districts." As the amendment did not replace Section 2a, this was another addition to the mass of verbiage accumulating in Article VIII.

In response to the inability of localities to finance needed sewage treatment facilities within their debt limits, an amendment in 1963 exempted all such indebtedness incurred between 1962 and 1972 for such facilities. In 1963 a major revision of the local government article (Art. IX) effected a minor change in Section 12 of Article VIII.

A second amendment excluded budget notes (those issued in anticipation of collection of taxes or other revenues) from constitutional debt limits of counties, cities, towns, villages, and school districts where debt limits apply (Sec. 2). Those notes must be reimbursed from taxes levied within constitutional tax limits, and, except for New York City, are also subject to the constitutional debt limit. A special exemption had allowed New York City to exclude from its debt limit such borrowings up to one-tenth of one percent of its five-year assessed valuation. There was no logical reason to charge budget notes to both tax and debt limits, so they were excluded from the debt but not the tax limits, and the special exemption for New York City, now superfluous, was removed.[73] A final amendment exempted from the debt limit any local government certificates of indebtedness issued for purposes other than capital improvements, not to exceed two years.

Tax Limits

The 1938 convention had extended the tax limits to all cities and villages of the state. Between 1938 and 1945 these limits caused difficulties for localities—not, however, due to increased expenditures, but rather because of the decline in the assessed valuation of property during the period. The decision of the 1938 convention to convert from current assessed valuation to a five-year average assessed valuation failed to appreciably lessen the strain exerted by the tax limits. That situation was to change with the postwar expansion of local government activities and the concomitant rise in expenditures. Real estate taxes used to fund this expansion were proving inadequate. Assessed valuations were rising slowly as a result of the brake on taxing intended by the five-year assessed valuation requirement. That rate was lower than the current assessed valuation throughout the state.[74] Conversely, counties with cities under 100,000, towns, and school districts which were not subject to tax limits were not experiencing the same difficulties. The financial crisis confronting localities in postwar New York was a crisis of cities and villages.

Anticipating such problems, the state created a number of commissions which recommended a variety of measures concerning local finance. Legislation was approved augmenting state aid to schools and granting localities more power to levy a variety of special non-property taxes. However, none of these measures effectively addressed the financial needs of the cities, particularly those with more than 100,000 inhabitants.

Late in 1947 Comptroller Frank Moore organized the Committee on Tax and Debt Limits and City School Fiscal Relations. That committee's recommendations were embodied in amendments passed between 1949 and 1953. Five changes were effected by these amendments. A five-year *full* valuation was substituted for the five-year average *as-*

sessed valuation. The intent was to eliminate artificial variations in taxing power resulting from variations in local assessments. Its effect was a considerable expansion of the tax limits for practically every local government to which such limits applied. In the rationale offered by the committee for the change there is no mention of this effect. The committee focused exclusively on the equalization of the limits and the uniform protection to real estate from excessive taxation.[75] Tax limits were extended to all counties outside New York and fixed at the maximum of 1.5%, with the proviso that the limit could be raised to 2% by the legislature. These measures, according to the 1959 staff report of the Temporary Commission on Constitutional Tax Limits, "put a very wide gap between the existing or any probable future tax rate and the constitutional tax limit based on true value. In effect therefore, for most places, the constitutional tax rate limit might just as well have been repealed."[76]

A third change extended tax limits to school districts partially or wholly in a city with fewer than 125,000 inhabitants. Levies for educational purposes were excluded from the 2% tax limit for all cities with less than 125,000 inhabitants and for villages supporting education in their general budgets.

School district tax limits were set, ranging from 1.25% to 2%. School districts whose limits were less than 2% were permitted to increase their limits in increments of 0.25% to a maximum of 2%. Approval of at least 60% of the qualified voters was required, and only one increase could be approved every five years (Sec. 10e). The 1949 amendments lengthened and complicated Section 10, making subsequent amendments inevitable.[77] The last change effected by the 1949 amendment was aimed at preventing municipalities from circumventing the real estate tax limit by levying taxes outside the tax limit for debt service on improvements while simultaneously using the revenues from the improvements for general municipal operating expenses. This was accomplished by requiring revenues from municipal improvements to be used first for the payment of operating expenses and then for debt service for the improvement.[78]

The 1951 amendments primarily concerned debt limitations. One change, affecting tax limits, allowed municipalities to exclude from their tax limits those taxes levied for financing capital outlays on a pay-as-you go basis.

In 1953 the electorate approved other changes recommended by the Moore Committee. School districts were authorized, with the approval of the voters, to increase their tax limits by 0.25% once a year instead of once every five years. In the face of abnormally large increases anticipated in student population and the effects of inflation, it seemed prudent to allow school districts to approve moderate increases every year rather than every five years.[79] New York City's tax limit was increased from 2% to 2.5% and the tax limits on the counties which make up the city went from a potential 2% to zero, giving the city the opportunity to raise additional revenue from real estate. A clarifying amendment to Section 10a stated that no contractual relationship was established between bondholders and municipalities concerning revenue and revenue-producing improvements. As towns were not subject to tax limitations and were unaffected by the provisions of 10-a, reference to them in the section was deleted.[80]

The impact of these changes was uneven. Uniform tax limits disregarded variations in scope, size, and extent of revenue need of localities. Large cities with extensive revenue needs were left to strain under the limits, while other municipalities had limits far higher than any foreseeable revenue needs. For example, the shift to full-valuation tax base "gave the city only some four percent gain in taxing power under the old equalization rates and only eleven percent gain under the new equalization rates."[81]

Article IX: Local Government

The 1938 convention had incorporated the city and county home rule amendments of 1923 and 1935, respectively, into Article IX. That article contained both an affirmative grant of power "to adopt and amend local law not inconsistent with the constitution and laws of the state relating to the property, affairs or government" (Sec. 12), and restrictions on state legislative interference in matters where municipalities had affirmative power.

The first amendment to Article IX following the 1938 convention occurred in 1945. That amendment allowed the local governing body to overrule, by a two-thirds vote, disapproval of a request for a local or special law by a county executive. Prior to this amendment the constitution, in effect, gave the county executive an absolute veto over such requests.

In 1958 a significant extension of county home rule was granted. Power was conferred on all counties outside the City of New York to prepare and adopt alternative forms of government. Prior to this change, the legislature provided the alternative forms to be adopted. Counties would now be permitted to alter their charters as they deemed necessary without recourse to the state legislature. The amendment did, however, contain certain conditions on the exercise of that power. No alternative form of government could take effect without receiving a majority of votes in the area of the cities considered as separate units and in the area of the county outside the cities. Previously the legislature was able to eliminate this dual requirement if the alternative form did not involve any transfer of function. The explanation given for this change was that "even changes other than transfers of functions may affect the urban and rural parts of a county quite differently."[82] When a change involved a transfer of functions involving villages, this new section required that transfer must have approval by "all the villages so affected as one unit" (Sec. 2c), thus necessitating a triple majority. Concern for loss of popular control and fear of being overwhelmed by other governmental units, particularly cities, prompted these concurrent majority requirements. The 1958 amendment also removed certain ambiguities and clarified provisions relating to procedures for local requests for special legislation.

The 1958 amendment extended county home rule, but did not extend home rule to either towns or villages. The counties were not satisfied with the extent of their home rule powers. The County Officer's Association called for "the broadest home rule powers consistent with our legal concepts."[83] The 1956 Temporary State Commission on the Constitutional Convention, in anticipation of voter approval of the convention of 1957, recommended extending home rule to villages and towns and expanding county home rule. In addition, it recommended eliminating the barriers (concurrent majorities) to consolidation and annexation of local units.[84] When the 1957 call was rejected by the voters, its successor was the Temporary Commission on the Revision and Simplification of the Constitution. That commission went further and recommended a new local government article.[85]

Perhaps in response to past failures to develop a distinction between matters of state concern and matters of local concern and the unsympathetic judicial response to such attempts, the commission suggested an approach that would give local government the freedom to exercise any power or function not denied it by general law.

> Legislative power, except as limited by the general statute of local government, is vested in every county, city, town and village. The legislature shall act in relation to such local governments only by general laws which apply alike to all counties, cities, towns or villages. . . .[86]

This approach amounts to a "grant of power" which the commission characterized as "coming by the Constitution directly from the people to every county, city, town and village. . . ."[87] As a 1967 staff report on local government stated, it was "a directive to the Legislature to share an unspecified portion of its legislative power with local governments."[88] The effectiveness of such an approach depended on the character of the first statute of local government. That statute, as recommended by the commission, would provide for: the organization and, to the extent necessary, classification of the basic units of local government; the exercise of power granted by the new article to local government to legislate on any subject except as limited by general law; and the ability of local governments to enter into agreements of cooperation with other governments in providing services and functions. Recognizing this statute as the core of the matter, the commission recommended that it be drawn up prior to submission of the amendment to the people. As the commission wrote, "the proposed Local Government Article assumes the existence of the General Statute of Local Governments as a necessary condition to its own effectiveness."[89]

In 1961 the task of drafting such a statute was referred to the recently created State Office for Local Government. In the process of operationalizing the commission's plan, the office encountered what it believed to be insurmountable obstacles to drafting such an article and decided to abandon the commission's approach and reconstruct the existing article. This task, once completed, was submitted to and approved by the voters in 1963.

The new Article IX is the cumulation of lengthy constitutional debate and experimentation stretching back to the commission of 1872. The article maintained continuity with the home rule tradition of New York, though it introduced some novel features and substantially simplified previous provisions. It extended home rule for the first time to towns and smaller villages (Sec. 1); enacted, for the first time, a "Bill of Rights for Local Governments" (Sec. 1); provided for a statute of local government introducing a new concept in the exercise of home rule powers (Sec. 2b(1)); broadened existing home rule of counties, cities, and larger villages; and expressly repudiated the "Dillon Rule," a rule of statutory construction applied by courts under which powers granted to local governments were to be strictly construed in favor of the state (Sec. 3).

The opening paragraph of Section 1 declares the philosophy underlying the provisions of the article: effective local government and intergovernmental cooperation are "purposes of the people of the state." That announcement is followed by eight items which comprise what is known as the bill of rights for local government. Subdivisions "a" and "b" grant local government the right to have an elective body with authority to adopt local laws. The right to elect and appoint officers by a local electorate is the keystone of local self-government and is an important bulwark against state interference in the form of selection of local officials or the transfer or consolidation of functions among local units. The provision has served to prevent certain state intrusions, but courts have permitted extensive interventions when important state interests are involved.[90] Subdivision "c" permits local governments as authorized by the legislature to join with other government—federal, state and local—to provide cooperatively or by contract any facility, service, or undertaking which each had the power to undertake separately. Providing a constitutional basis for this cooperation removed legal barriers and encouraged local governments to collaborate in eliminating duplicative or overlapping functions. Contracting for or transferring functions would lower costs and allow for more efficient delivery of services. Subdivision "d" encouraged consolidation by annexation, but placed a barrier to that consolidation by requiring approval of the governing boards of the annexed and annexing units as well as a majority vote of the electorate. The approval of the governing boards was inserted at the request of the Association of Towns, who feared loss of their best tax bases without any voice in the matter. When governing boards disagree, the issue is submitted to the Supreme Court for determination on whether the annexation is in the "over-all public interest." Subsections "e" through "h" grant counties the power to adopt, amend, or repeal alternative forms of government or to do the same with forms of their own. This power includes the authority to transfer functions from one unit to another. The exercise of this latter power, however, required concurrent majorities from the areas of the county outside the cities and a majority of the voters in the cities considered as a separate voting unit. If a transfer of functions involved a village in any way, then a majority approval of the vote in all villages affected, considered as one unit, is also required. These requirements, carried over from earlier provisions, are significant obstacles to accomplishing the cooperation through the transfer of functions or consolidation encouraged earlier in Section 1. They reflect the strong commitment local officials and their respective electorates have to their local governments and the concomitant fear, especially on the part of villages, of being swallowed up by other municipalities.

Section 2 is a revised and consolidated section based on provisions going back to the 1846 Constitution. The section begins with a grant of powers to, and limits on, the state legislature regarding local governments. Subject to Section 1, the legislature is directed to enact and, when desirable, amend a statute of local government granting certain powers to local governments. The statute of local government proposed by the Temporary Commission would have given the power of primary responsibility to local government, thus preventing the legislature from acting in those areas without altering the statute of local government itself. When the Office of Local Government abandoned the task of enumerating those responsibilities because of drafting problems, it did not abandon the concept of a statute of local government. Instead it decided that although it was not feasible to grant the home rule powers contained in the statute constitutional status, the statute provided quasi-constitutional protection for these powers. The legislature could act to restrict the powers enumerated in the statute only on action by two successive legislatures and the concurrence of the governor. The powers so granted by this statute, however, were not significant. The seven powers included the ability to acquire real and personal property, adopt, amend, and repeal ordinances, resolutions, etc., acquire, construct, and operate recreational facilities, and levy, impose, collect, and administer rents, charges and fees. The modest powers specified in the statute, as originally adopted, led the Staff Report on Local Government to conclude that "the statute in is present form its little more than an empty shell."[91] In enacting this statute the legislature also made certain reservations, and if state legislation which impinged on a power granted to local governments by the statute is within the ambit created by those reservations, the change can be achieved by ordinary legislative process.

Section 2c is the center of home rule powers. Every local government is granted the power to adopt or amend local laws relating to its "property affairs or government" not inconsistent with the provisions of the constitution or any general laws relating to its property affairs or government. Additionally, local governments can adopt or amend local laws whether or not they relate to the property affairs or government with respect to ten enumerated subjects (Sec. 2c, 1–10). However, the legislature may restrict the adoption of local laws concerning matters other than property affairs or government of a local government.[92] The ten subjects include, among others, membership and composition of the local legislative body; transaction of business; levying and collecting local taxes; and powers, duties, qualifications, number, mode of selection, and removal of officers or employees.

The state legislature has the power to act in relation to the property affairs or government of any local government only by general laws as defined in Section 3d (1) and by special law as defined in 3d (4) on request of two-thirds of the members of a local legislative body or its chief executive officer with the concurrence of a majority of that body and, with the exception of New York City, in the case of emergencies, certified by the governor with the concurrence by two-thirds of the state legislature (Sec. 2b, 2). This significantly alters the provisions of the 1938 convention which had required two-thirds approval of the state legislature even when the local government requested the special legislation. Since the two-thirds rule was intended to protect local government from unwanted local or special legislation, it was unnecessary and confining when the request was initiated by the local government. This section also revives the deleted 1938 provision allowing passage of special legislation by two-thirds vote of the legislature upon message of the governor.

In addition to the state's power to limit local action by general laws and restrict local initiatives in areas unconcerned with the property affairs and government, this section contains another important limitation on local power. Local governments are forbidden to enact local laws impairing the power of any other local government except in the case of transfer of functions under an alternative form of county government.

Section 3 provides that the article should not be read to impair the legislature's power in relation to public schools, the retirement system, the courts, and matters other than property affairs or government of a local government. Section 3(1)c is an express repudiation of Dillon's rule. The remainder of this section defines the operative terms used in the article: "general" and "special laws," "local government," and "people."

Reactions to this article were widely divergent. Supporters heralded it as a new day for home rule in New York.[93] Others were less optimistic, claiming no significant improvements were produced and the balance of power between state and municipalities remained unchanged, with the one exception of home rule status for towns.[94] Subsequent court decisions and legislative acts have tended to support the latter view. In general, the Court of Appeals has followed decisions made prior to adoption of the article, giving "matters of state concern" an expansive reading.[95]

The article has not been without impact. The Municipal Home Rule Law mandated a liberal interpretation of the home rule powers, and both the legislature and the governor have disapproved requests for state legislation when the same results could have been achieved by local law.[96] The Court of Appeals has, on occasion, acknowledged the presence of the new article. In the landmark case of *Matter of Smithtown v. Howell*,[97] the Court of Appeals upheld a locally enacted charter provision superceding a general state law. That decision has been followed by *Matter of Heimbach v. Mills*,[98] upholding a charter provision that placed power to set real property tax equalization rates in an elected county executive rather than with the Board, as provided in the state's real property law.[99] In *Resnick v. County of Ulster*, *Smithtown* and *Heimback* were extended to apply to non-charter counties with regard to issues covered in Section 1b of the article. Ulster County, a non-charter county, passed a local law providing that a vacancy in the office of a county legislator occurring other than by expiration of its term is to be filled by the remaining membership of the body. State law "vests the power to appoint county officers" in the governor.[100]

The general direction of the court decisions has favored state power over local home rule. The adoption of Article IX has resulted in limited success in reversing an entrenched judicial doctrine stretching from Dillon's Rule to *Adler v. Deegan*, a doctrine that continues to undergird the judiciary's approach to home rule in New York.

Article IX is not the only article affecting the exercise of local power. Article VIII contains constitutional provisions limiting the debt and taxing powers of local governments. Home rule is further restricted by the use of state mandates—legislative requirements mandating local governments to provide specific service, meeting minimum state requirements in so doing. Such mandates encompass a wide variety of areas such as health care, social services, education, and solid waste disposal, etc. New York State imposes more than 3,000 mandates on localities and school districts. In some counties (e.g., Erie County, 1990) these mandates are said to consume more than 70% of the county budget. In *Toia v. Regan*[101] the Court of Appeals sustained a mandate that local governments assume 50% of non-federal costs for welfare programs, even though that mandate would severely limit availability of tax revenues, rendering meaningless a county's right to manage its own affairs. *Toia* illustrates the tension between state mandates and the principle of home rule.

Other articles relating to the operation of local government include Article V, Section 6, which prescribes a civil service merit system; Section 7, which establishes a state retirement system with pensions not to be diminished or impaired; Article VI, which provides a court system; Article X, which prescribes the powers of the legislature in creating public corporations (authorities); Article XI, which provides for the educational system; Article XIII, which contains several provisions relating to local office-holding, including filling of vacancies, compensation for constitutional officers, and election of city officers; Article XVI, which contains general provisions relating to taxing authority; Article XVII, which contains provisions relating to public assistance and the social service system; and Article XVIII, which authorizes state and local governments to provide low-rent housing, nursing home accommodations, and urban renewal.

The constitution encompasses a number of values and contains provisions intended to promote those values, only one of which is home rule. The multiple goals embodied in the document inevitably mean that the promotion of one value occasionally will be at the expense of another. Such has been the fate of home rule in New York. The commitment to minimal statewide standards of welfare, safety, health, and the like has taken precedence over the goal of local autonomy

ARTICLE X: CORPORATIONS

The general title of this article is misleading, as its primary significance currently is connected with those sections (5-8) concerned with public corporations or authorities. Under Section 5 these authorities are authorized by special acts of the legislature to incur indebtedness and collect charges for services and facilities furnished by them. Under Section 3 of Article VIII they are prohibited from levying taxes or benefit assessments on real estate. Additionally, under Section 5 of this article neither the state nor any of its subdivisions are permitted to assume liability for obligations incurred by such authorities unless the state is so authorized by constitutional amendment.

Between conventions, beginning in 1951, the article was amended three times to authorize the state to incur such liability. When the decision was made to resume construction of the New York Thruway after World War II, Governor Thomas Dewey and the legislature were unwilling to burden state finances with the cost of construction and maintainence. Instead they created a public authority, and the New York Thruway Authority was created. It was to be self-liquidating and self-financing, with the power to issue bonds and impose tolls. To insure the project and minimize costs, this amendment guaranteed the full faith and credit of the state for the authority's bonds. It is an explicit exception to Section 5 of this article.[102]

A 1961 amendment involved another public benefit corporation, the New York Port Authority. A 1959 special report to the governor recommended that the New York Port Authority undertake to replace antiquated commuter equipment for the New York Central, New Haven, and Long Island Railroads. For the Port Authority to finance the project through a lease-purchase agreement with railroads in precarious financial condition would have adversely affected the authority's credit.[103] To avert this damage to the authority's financial standing, this amendment—another exception to section 5—allows the state to guarantee the bonds.[104]

The final change in Article X, passed in 1961, also involved an exception to Section 5. It established a Job Development Authority to encourage job opportunities in depressed areas of the state. $50 million of the $100 million expected to be raised by issuance of the bonds was to be backed by the state's credit. The loans, restricted to non-profit, local development corporations, were expected to encourage industrial development. Subsequent amendments, discussed below, increased the amount and expanded the businesses eligible for financial asssistance.

Since the state has resorted to public benefit corporations as mechanisms for borrowing without having to obtain voter approval, this article relates directly to the provisions of Article VII and must be included as part of state finance.

Article XI

The educational article was amended in 1962. That amendment eliminated Section 3, relating to the common school, literature, and United States deposit funds. The amendment follows the recommendation of the Temporary Commission on the Revision and Simplification of the Constitution.[105] The amount of money generated by these funds had become insignificant in comparison to the state's contribution to education, and the security of these funds was provided by statutory law.

Article XII: The Militia

Every constitution from 1777 on has provided for the militia. The detailed provisions of earlier constitutions were eliminated by a 1962 amendment following the recommendations of the Inter Law-School Committee.[106] That committee found that the provisions of the article existed by virtue of federal and state legislation, not "because the State Constitution purports to deal with the matter. . . . [E]very single one of its sections is either superfluous or in conflict with the realities of current existence.[107] No other article in the state constitution has been as affected by the operation of federal law as the militia article. The state militia operates largely under detailed federal supervision.[108] Since every section could be eliminated without any significant change in the status and operation of the militia, the amendment was not controversial. It was nevertheless important: it aligned the provisions of the constitution with current realities, thus ending a situation where constitutional provisions, rather than conditioning and limiting the direction of public policy, were themselves being determined by that policy.

The amendment reduced Article XII to one paragraph. The first sentence recognizes the duty of every person to defend and protect the state. The second is an implementing clause, giving the governor and the legislature, within the confines of federal law, the freedom to structure the state's military department as they see fit.

ARTICLE XIII: PUBLIC OFFICERS

In 1962 significant changes were effected in Sections 2, 3, 4, 5, and 7 of this article. The first four dealt with bribery. A review of these sections by the Inter-Law School Committee's Report on the Problem of Simplification of the Constitution revealed that each had been superceded by statutory law which was more detailed and extensive than the constitutional provisions. The sentence in Section 7 that states that elections for those officers not provided for in the constitution shall be prescribed by law, was "in part, statutory; in part, meaningless in law; and in part, obsolete."[109] These recommendations were accepted and the material was eliminated.

The following year minor changes were made to Section 7, making that section consistent with the salary deletions in Article IV. Section 9 of Article VIII, concerning the power of the legislature to regulate wages and conditions of employment, was transferred to this article and created a new Section 14.[110] The last change in this period occurred in 1965. Section 15, relating to the holding of local elections in odd-numbered years, was transferred to this article as a new Section 8.[111]

ARTICLE XIV: CONSERVATION

The 1938 convention created a separate article for the conservation provisions of the constitution. At that time these provisions were primarily, but not exclusively, concerned with the forest preserves of the state. The central provision placed an absolute prohibition on the use of that preserve in the desire to kept it "forever . . . wild." Inevitably, such emphatic language invited numerous modifications.

The article was subject to amendment eight times during the period in question. Four of these allowed special uses such as construction of ski trails and highways, three involved land exchanges, and one placed an additional restriction on the legislature.

The first amendment passed in 1941 illustrates the competing interests and goals that have been the basis for the various exemptions. It permitted the construction of twenty miles of ski trails on the slopes of Whiteface Mountain. Supporters asserted the developments were necessary for New York to compete with the modern resorts in New England and that such a project would bring economic benefit to the surrounding areas.[112] Similar arguments surrounded the passage of a 1947 amendment which also allowed construction of ski trails. The only new restriction on the legislature occurred in 1953 when the voters adopted an amendment limiting legislative power to pass general laws regulating the flow of streams through the construction of reservoirs in the forest preserve (Sec. 2). A forceful and united group of conservationists opposed the development of preserve land for constructing reservoirs for river regulation beyond that allowed for the public water supply and the state's canals. This amendment removed from the section the clause authorizing the legislature to use state forest preserve lands for reservoirs designed to "regulate the flow of streams" but maintained the right to use such lands to a maximum amount of 3% for "municipal water supply and for the canals of the state" (Sec. 2).[113]

Two amendments were passed in 1957. One allowed the state to relocate, reconstruct, and maintain fifty miles of existing state roads. The justification was public safety, as much of this roadway contained dangerous curves and grades.[114] Another exception involving highways was adopted in 1959. It permitted the "Northway," a major north-south route, to cross 254 acres of state-owned forest land. Circumventing the region would have added years to the completion of the route and made construction considerably more expensive. The highway would relieve congestion on the existing Route 9, which was better suited to local traffic, and would enable millions of recreation seekers to reach the Adirondacks quickly and safely.[115]

The second amendment passed that year was the first of three involving land exchanges. Governor Averell Harriman in his 1956 annual message to the legislature proposed additional funds for acquiring lands inside the Blue Line (lands within the confines of the Adirondack and Catskill parks). With this approval the state could selectively sell small scattered parcels of land outside the Blue Line and use the proceeds to acquire new land within the forest preserve. These scattered parcels were of little use and were expensive to administer. Although outside the Blue Line, the parcels became part of the forest preserve through tax proceedings prior to 1926. The 1957 amendment allowed these exchanges to take place.[116] This amendment was an important step in improving the ownership pattern and facilitating the administration of the state forest preserve.

A second exchange was permitted under a 1963 amendment. The exchange in this instance involved state land within the Blue Line. The amendment allowed the exchange of land between the state and the Village of Saranac Lake. The village wanted ten acres of burned-over swampland for refuse disposal and was willing to exchange thirty acres of forested upland, none of which could be used for that purpose.

The last exchange during the period permitted the Town of Arietta in Hamilton County to exchange thirty acres of its land for twenty-eight acres of forest preserve land. This land was necessary to bring the town's airport up to federal safety requirements of a clear zone for takeoffs and landings.

Article XV: Canals

The article was amended once during this period, suggesting the extent to which the canal system ceased to play a significant role in the state's economy. Indeed, the amendment allowed for the transfer of the canal system to the United States government, making it part of the national system of inland waterways. One purpose of the amendment was to relieve the state of the annual burden of maintenance and operation and the expectation that the national government would modernize the canal. The system's annual costs to the state were between six and seven million dollars.[117] The provision is permissive only. It allows the legislature and the governor to make the transfer if they deem it appropriate. Supporters, mostly from the water transportation sector, admitted they had no assurance that the federal government was interested in assuming jurisdiction over the canal, and Governor Rockefeller, although a supporter of the amendment, did not foresee an immediate possibility for the shift in ownership. The opposition, especially the railroads, wanted the canal to stay in its present condition.[113]

Article XVIII: Housing

The housing article, with its incongruous combination of general policy statement and authorization in the opening section and mass of technical, detailed prescriptions and procedures in the following nine sections, was subject to five successful amendments and nineteen proposals authorizing additional debt or subsidies.

By 1967 the article, although in existence barely thirty years, showed signs of age. The eight amendments were attempts to adapt the article to changing conditions and to broader conceptions of urban renewal and community development. Originally the article had excluded villages and counties from its provisions. A 1949 amendment allowed villages with inhabitants in excess of 5,000, when determining their debt limits, to exclude debt from low-rent housing and slum clearance projects from their general debt limits, and if the projects had a net revenue, to exclude the debt from its housing debt limit as well (Sec. 4).[119]

An intriguing constitutional conundrum occurred in 1955 in connection with a second amendment to the housing article. That amendment proposed an increase from $5 million to $34 million in the limit for authorizations of periodic subsidies for low-rent housing (Sec. 3). The problem arose because the state was also submitting a proposition for additional state indebtedness for the construction of mental health facilities and a proposition for additional indebtedness of $200 million for slum clearance and low-cost housing. Section 11 of Article VII prohibited the submission of any law authorizing debt obligation at any general election if any other law or bill was submitted for approval. The proposition involving money for slum clearance did not create the problem because Article XVIII, Section 3 allowed an exception for proposals incurring debt for housing purposes. This left the proposal creating debt for mental health facilities. The attorney general issued an opinion that the submission probably would violate Article VIII, Section 11.[120] In the realization that this would be a re-occurring problem, a 1955 amendment altered Section 3 to stipulate that any law authorizing contracts in excess of such amounts may be submitted to the people at a general election whether or not any other law or bill shall be submitted for approval at such an election.[121]

Two amendments were proposed in 1957. The first, to Section 3, permitted a level payment plan for the amortization of state debt arising out of loans to limited profit housing companies. Both Article VII and the Housing Article required debts of the state to be paid in equal annual installments during the life of the project. This amendment is an explicit exception to that general requirement. Since level debt amortization plans for retiring debt would result in a reduction of initial carrying charges for limited profit housing projects, thus resulting in significantly lower costs, they would encourage the initiation of limited profit housing projects.[122]

The second 1957 amendment added towns and villages to the provision which previously permitted only cities and city housing authorities to exclude, from the 2% housing debt limitation, liability for the repayment of a state loan, except where there is a default on the part of such municipality or authority in paying off the state loan.[123]

The last amendment to the article, prior to the 1967 convention, passed in 1965 and authorized the state to permit the assistance given to middle-income housing to be given also to nursing homes. The provision targeted housing for the elderly whose needs were unlikely to be met by conventional housing, as they would probably reside in nursing homes.[124]

The Housing Article exemplifies the difficulties in attempting to determine the direction and scope of public policy by constitutional means. The ten sections, comprising six printed pages, are congested with labored, detailed language and studded with negatives. Such language invites—even necessitates—regular adjustments by further amendment. The first thirty years of its existence substantiates that charge. Moreover, the electorate has proven particularly hostile to propositions concerning housing, both prior to, and in the quarter century following, the 1967 convention. The reasons are not entirely clear but are likely connected with the fact that voters were asked to judge propositions so complex and technical as to confound most lawyers. The failed attempt in 1964 to revise the article is exemplary. That revision was recommended in the Staff Report of the Commission on Revision and Simplification of the Constitution and the 1961 Inter-Law School Committee.[125] Voters were asked to pass on material which was incomprehensible to all but a few specialists. This scenario would repeat itself in the major revision proposed in 1971 (Community Development Amendment). Housing and urban development would be a major concern at the 1967 constitutional convention.

Article XIX: Amendments to the Constitution

The 1938 convention added a clause to Section 1 of this article which required that the attorney general's opinion be sought on the effects of any proposed amendment on other parts of the constitution. The purpose was to preserve the integrity of the constitution and guard against inconsistencies resulting from such amendments. There was some dispute over whether or not the failure of the attorney general to render such an opinion, or the failure to do so in a prompt fashion, would render the amendment invalid.[126] An amendment adopted in 1941 resolved that question. The failure to render an opinion, or a delay in doing so, does not affect the validity of any such proposed amendments.[127] Since the legislature can also recall a proposed amendment by concurrent resolution if the attorney general finds it inconsistent with other parts of the constitution, the purpose of the provision would not be frustrated by that action.

The opinions of the attorneys general in New York have played a significant role in the state's constitutional history, more so than those of its federal counterpart. These opinions are the only institutionalized alternative to the constitutional rulings of the courts. Although not binding on courts, they are entitled to due consideration. Moreover, a vast number of disputes are resolved by these opinions without their ever reaching the judiciary. The state attorney general is the major source of advisory opinions on the constitution. In some areas, such as conservation (Art. XIV), these opinions have played as great, if not greater, role than the courts in determining what types of actions are constitutionally permissible. The function of these opinions is to narrow the gap between state practice and constitutional requirements. In the areas of conservation and gambling, for example, the prime source of guidance for the state and its localities has been the opinions of the attorney general. Since these areas are seldom litigated, the attorney general's opinions help to insure that state practice bears a reasonable relationship to the requirements of the constitution.

Notes

1. Robert Connery and Gerald Benjamin, *Rockefeller of New York*, pp. 19–20. That position gave Rockefeller visability and familiarity with New York government and politics, both of which would be important factors in his successful run for the governorship in 1958.
2. *Laws of New York*, 1956, Chap. 814.
3. Temporary State Commission on the Constitutional Convention, *First Interim Report*, February 19, 1957. Leg. Doc. (1957) No. 8.
4. Ibid., No. 57
5. *The Problem of Simplification of the Constitution*, p. xiii.
6. Annual Message to the Legislature, *Legislative Annual*, 1957, p. 408. More recently Governor Mario Cuomo, in his message to the legislature, January 1991, proposed a "limited legislative initiative" which would require legislative action on the petition. This measure would not apply to constitutional amendments, but would require an amendment to Article XIX, Sec. 1. Reflecting the antipathy toward such "populist measures" the Committee on State Constitution of the New York Bar Association opposed the measure. New York State Bar Association, *Legislation Report 1991* No. 124, May 31, 1991.
7. *Application of Stewart* 174 Misc. 902 aff'd 260 A.D. 979 (1940).
8. Annual Message to the Legislature, January 9, 1957, *Legislative Annual, 1957*, pp. 406–407.
9. *Opinions of the Attorney-General*, 1984, No. 84-F1, pp. 14–16.
10. See "Riverboat Gambling on the Hudson," *The New York Times*, May 29, 1994, pp. 13ff. "Comptroller's Report: Questions Benefits From Casino Gambling," *The New York Times*, April 3, 1994, I, p. 24.
11. *People v. Harris*, 294 N.Y. 424 (1945).
12. *People v. Doyle*, 286 A.D. 276, at 278 (1955).
13. *Report of the Joint-Legislative Committee to Make a Study of the Election law and Related Statutes*, Leg. Doc. (1959) No. 57 pp. 22–23.
14. *People ex rel. Hotchkiss v. Smith*, 206 N.Y. 231 (1912).
15. See above, pp. 161–162.

16. Report of the Inter-Law School Committee, *The Problem of Simplification of the Constitution*, Leg. Doc. (1958) No. 57, p. 24.
17. *The Problem of Simplification of the Constitution*, pp. 25–30.
18. Temporary State Commission on the Constitutional Convention, *The Right To Vote*, Staff Report No. 4, 1967, p. 30.
19. "For Absentee Voting," *The New York Times*, October 5, 1919, IV, p. 7.
20. "State Voters Face Six Amendments," *The New York Times*, November 2, 1947, p. 6.
21. Memorandum of the Joint Legislative Committee on Election Law, *Legislative Annual 1949*, p. 147.
22. Report of the Joint Legislative Committee to Revise and Recodify the Election Law, Leg. Doc. (1950) No. 43, pp. 23–24.
23. Report of the Joint Legislative Committee to Make a Study of the Election Law and Related Statutes, Leg. Doc. (1954) No. 43, pp. 18–19.
24. *Eber v. Board of Elections*, 80 Misc. 2d 334 (1974). Accord *Fidell v. Board of Elections of the City of New York*, 409 U.S. 972 (1972).
25. Memorandum of Citizens Union of New York City, "Voting, Residency Requirements," *Legislative Annual*, 1965, pp. 258–259.
26. 405 U.S. 330 (1972).
27. *Atkin v. Onondaga County Board of Elections*, 30 N.Y. 2d 401 (1972).
28. 293 N.Y. 42 (1944).
29. "Republicans Keep Nassau Attorney," *The New York Times*, November 7, 1945, p. 5.
30. James B. Lewis, "1959 Tax Legislation," *Legislative Annual 1959*, pp. 313–314.
31. *First Step Towards A Modern Constitution*, Leg. Doc. 1959, No. 58. pp. 57–58.
32. Memorandum of Joint Legislative Committee on Interstate Cooperation, "Continuity of Government Operations," *Legislative Annual 1963*, p. 221.
33. 15 N.Y. 2d 339 (1965).
34. *Flushing National Bank v. Municipal Assistance Corporation*, 40 N.Y. 2d 731 (1976).
35. 377 U.S. 633 (1964).
36. See *Bay Ridge Community Council, Inc. v. Carey*, 66 N.Y. 2d 657 (1985), and *Prentiss v. Cahill*, 73 Misc 2d 245 (1973).
37. *Ward v. Curran*, 266 A.D. 524; aff'd 291 N.Y. 642 (1943).
38. Annual Message to the Legislature, January 5, 1944, *Public Papers of Thomas Dewey 1944* (Albany: Williams Press, 1946), p. 21.
39. Governor's Message, February 9, 1953, *Legislative Annual*, 1953, pp. 318–319. In 1938 Governor Lehman, architect of the "Little New Deal" in New York, arranged to have the lieutenant-governor nomination given to Charles Poletti rather than the incumbent, William Bray, an anti-New Dealer.
40. See the Memorandum and Recommendations of the Law Revision Commission to the 1984 Legislature Relating to Gubernatorial Inability and Succession. *McKinney's 1984 Session Laws of New York*, pp. 2946–2974, 2975–2976.
41. Memorandum of State Public Service Commission, State Department of Motor Vehicles, *Legislative Annual 1959*, p. 301.
42. Temporary State Commission on the Constitutional Convention, *State Government*, Staff Report No. 14, 1967, p. 123.

43. Administration Memorandum, "State Government Reorganization," *Legislative Annual 1954*, pp. 160–161.

44. Memorandum of National Civil Service League, *Legislative Annual 1949*, p. 116.

45. See S. 4595, S. 4596.

46. Temporary Commission on the Revision and Simplification of the Constitution, *Auditing, Accounting and Management of Funds*, Staff Report No. 13, 1958, p. 11.

47. The history and background of these differing understandings is more fully examined in Special Legislative Committee on Revision and Simplification of the Constitution, *Auditing, Accounting and Management of Funds*, Staff Report No. 13 (New York, July, 1958).

48. *The Problem of Simplification of the Constitution*, p. 70.

49. *Eighth Annual Report of the Judicial Council of the State of New York*, Leg. Doc. (1942), No. 16, pp. 170–172.

50. Memorandum of Citizens Committee on the Courts, Inc., *Legislative Annual 1947*, p. 13.

51. See California Constitution, Article VI, Sections 8, 18, for provisions concerning its Commission on Judicial Performance.

52. Ernest Breuer, *The New York State Court of Claims: Its History, Jurisdiction and Reports* (Albany: New York State Education Department 1959, State Library Bibliography Bulletin No. 83).

53. Arthur Vanderbilt, *Improving the Administration of Justice: Two Decades of Development* (Cincinnati: College of Law, University of Cincinnati, 1957), p. 18.

54. Delmar Karlen and Allen Harris, "Judicial Administration in New York: Developments in the Last Twenty-Five Years," *Buffalo Law Review* 15 (Winter, 1965), pp. 329–330.

55. *1956 Report of the Temporary Commission of the Courts to the Governor and the Legislature of the State of New York*. Leg. Doc (1956) No. 18, p. 40–49.

56. In 1934 the legislature created the New York Judicial Council, whose duties were to collect, analyze, and publish statistics, investigate criticisms, and make recommendations concerning the courts of the state. Under its charter it could not supervise or coordinate the work of those courts. As a result of the recommendations of the Temporary Commission on the Courts in 1955, *A Proposal For Judicial Administration of the Courts of New York State*, the legislature took the first step toward statewide central administrative control of the courts. The legislature replaced the Judicial Council with a Judicial Conference. That Conference was given additional duties but did not have the authority to supervise the judiciary.

57. Karlen and Harris, "Judicial Administration in New York," p. 330.

58. Lawrence H. Cooke,"Structural Reform of the Judicial System," in Peter W. Colby, ed., *New York State Today: Politics, Government, Public Policy* (Albany: SUNY Press, 1985), p. 162.

59. "Legislature Gets Tax Reserve Plan," *The New York Times*, February 27, 1943, p. 7.

60. Special Legislative Committee on Revision and Simplification of the Constitution, *Auditing, Accounting and Management of Funds*, pp. 88–90.

61. *Legislative Annual 1966*, p. 155.

62. Temporary Commission on the Revision and Simplification of the Con-

stitution, *Constitutional Debt Limits For Local Government*, Staff Report No. 32, 1960, p 57.
63. Ibid., p. 68.
64. New York State Comptroller, *Reports*, March, 1948, 1949, 1950.
65. Governor's Memorandum, 1949, *Legislative Annual 1949*, p. 163
66. As quoted in *Constitutional Debt Limits* . . . , pp. 70-71.
67. Ibid., p. 71.
68. Ibid., pp. 71-72.
69. Ibid., p. 72.
70. Comptroller's *Second Report*, March, 1949, as quoted in ibid., p. 74.
71. Memorandum of State Department of Audit and Control, *Legislative Annual 1950*, p. 186.
72. Memorandum of State Comptroller's Committee on Problems Affecting the Distribution of Water, *Legislative Annual 1953*, pp. 291-292.
73. Memorandum of Lieutenant Governor's Committee on Constitutional Tax and Debt Limitations and City-School Fiscal Relations, *Legislative Annual 1953*, p. 311. The Comptroller's Committee was renamed the Lieutenant Governor's Committee when Frank Moore became lieutenant-governor in 1951.
74. Temporary Commission on the Revision and Simplication of the Constitution, *Constitutional Tax Rate Limits*, Staff Report No. 31, 1959, p. 70.
75. Comptroller's Committee . . . , *First Report*, March 3, 1948, pp. 4-5; Second Report, March 30, 1949, p. 12.
76. *Constitutional Tax Rate Limits*, p. 86.
77. A Temporary State Board of Equalization and Assessment was established, now a permanent part of state government, whose purpose is to survey the ratio of assessed to full value and to set the equalization rates. These rates determine the amount a locality can tax and borrow.
78. Memorandum of Committee on Constitutional Tax and Debt Limitations, *Legislative Annual 1952*, p. 163.
79. Ibid., p. 163.
80. Ibid., p. 163.
81. *Constitutional Tax Rate Limits*, p. 91.
82. *McKinney's Session Laws 1957*, "Notes to Section 2(c)," p. LXXVII.
83. Temporary State Commission on the Constitutional Convention, Staff Report No. 13, *Local Government*, 1967, p. 76.
84. *Second Interim Report*, pp. 14-18.
85. *First Steps Toward a Modern Constitution*, pp. 14-29
86. Ibid., pp. 16-17.
87. Ibid., p. 19.
88. Temporary State Commission, Staff report No. 13, *Local Government*, p. 77.
89. *First Steps*, p. 21.
90. James Cole, "Constitutional Home Rule in New York: The Ghost of Home Rule," *St. John's Law Review* 59 (1985), pp. 713ff.
91. Temporary State Commission, Staff Report No. 13, *Local Government*, p. 82.
92. Richard Briffault, "Intergovernmental Relations," in Gerald Benjamin, ed., *The New York Constitution: A Briefing Book*, pp. 119-138, puts the 1963 amendment in the larger context of home rule in New York.
93. New York State, Office for Local Government, *Newsletter*, No. 15,

September 18, 1963, p. 3; "Announcement by the Governor of the Introduction in the Legislature of a Concurrent Resolution Proposing a New Article Nine of the State Constitution Relating to Local Government," February 25, 1962, *Public Papers of Nelson Rockefeller, 1962* (Albany, n.d.), p. 824.

94. Reuben A. Lazarus, "Constitutional Amendment and Home Rule in New York State," *New York Law Journal*, 152 (October 13, 1964), p. 4.; Frank Grad, "The New York Home Rule Amendment: A Bill of Rights for Local Government?" *Local Government Law Service Letter*, 14 (June, 1964), p. 9.

95. Galie, *The New York Constitution*, pp. 219–222; Cole, "The Ghost of Home Rule," passim; New York State Legislative Commission on State-Local Relations, *New York's Local Government Structure: The Division of Responsibility: An Interim Report* (Albany, 1983), pp. 13–38).

96. New York State, *Local Government Handbook*, 4th ed. (Albany, 1987), p. 58.

97. 31 N.Y. 2d 365 (1972).

98. 67 A.D. 2d 731 (1979).

99. McKinney's, County Law, Section 400, (7). Relying on the guiding legal principles found in Article IX, Section 1b and 2c(1), the court sustained the law [at 285].

100. 44 N.Y. 2d 279 (1978).

101. 40 N.Y. 2d 837 (1976).

102. Section 2 of Article XVIII (Housing), authorizes cities, towns, and villages to guarantee the principle and interest on, or only the interest on, the indebtedness contracted by public housing corporations, thus exempting financial measures issued for purposes of this article from the prohibitions of Section 5 of Article X.

103. A lease purchase or lease financing is a scheme whereby a governmental unit leases a facility under a long-term contract, whereupon the developer issues revenue bonds to be paid with the rent. When the lease expires, title reverts to the state. The device evades the referendum requirement of Article VII and the debt limitations in Article VIII at the local level. The Empire State Plaza in Albany was constructed under such an arrangement, with Albany County issuing the long-term bonds for the funding. For a skeptical view of this circumvention of debt limits see William Kennedy's "Everything Everybody Ever Wanted," *Atlantic Monthly* 251 (May, 1983), pp. 77–78.

104. Robert W. Purcell, "Special Report to the Governor on Problems of the Railroads and Bus Lines in New York State," mimeo, March 12, 1959, pp. 28–33.

105. *First Steps Towards a Modern Constitution*, p. 62.

106. *The Problem of Simplification of the Constitution*, pp. 161–162.

107. Ibid., p. 142.

108. A review of this federal legislation and its pervasive impact on state policy is provided in the commission's report, pp. 137–142.

109. *First Steps*, p. 49.

110. This material was originally inserted in 1905 as Section 1 of Article XII.

111. The section was added to the constitution by the 1894 convention as Article XI, Section 3, and transferred to Article IX, Section 15 by the 1938 convention.

112. Conservation Department, *Thirtieth Annual Report 1940*, Leg. Doc (1941), No. 37, p. 52.

113. *Interim Report of the Joint Legislative Committee on River Regulation*, Leg. Doc. (1952), No. 51, pp. 56–58.

114. *Report of the Joint Legislative Committee on Natural Resources*, Leg. Doc. (1956), No. 63, p. 257.

115. See the arguments made by Governor Rockefeller, "Statement by the Governor Recommending a 'Yes' Vote on Amendment Number 2 Relating to the Northway," *Public Papers of Nelson Rockefeller 1959* (Albany, n.d.), pp. 1000–1001.

116. Annual Message to the Legislature, January 4, 1956, *Public Papers of Averell Harriman*, 1956 (Albany, n.d), p. 25.

117. "Legislature's Vote Opens Way to End State Canal Control," *The New York Times*, March 30, 1958, p. 76.

118. "Voters to Decide on Canal Control," *The New York Times*, October 25, 1959, p. 58.

119. *Annual Report of the Commissioner of Housing . . . 1949*, Leg. Doc. (1950) No. 14, pp. 43–44.

120. *Annual Report of Attorney General . . . 1954*, pp. 229–231.

121. Unlike housing loans, which are exempted from the simultaneous submission prohibition, capital and periodic subsidies may be made only from monies appropriated from the general funds. The constitution explicitly exempts the former but not periodic subsidy contracts. That was the basis for the attorney general's opinion.

122. Memorandum of State Division of Housing, *Legislative Annual 1956*, pp. 232–233.

123. Ibid., p. 233.

124. Memorandum of Joint Legislative Committee on Housing and Urban Development, *Legislative Annual 1965*, pp. 323–324.

125. Housing and Urban Renewal Staff Report No. 29, 1959, p. 43, and the 1961 Temporary State Commission on the Constitutional Convention, *Simplifying a Complex Constitution*, p. 220.

126. *Annual Report of the Attorney General . . . 1939*, Leg. Doc. (1940) No. 20, p. 358.

127. *Opinions of the Attorney General . . . 1961*, p. 52.

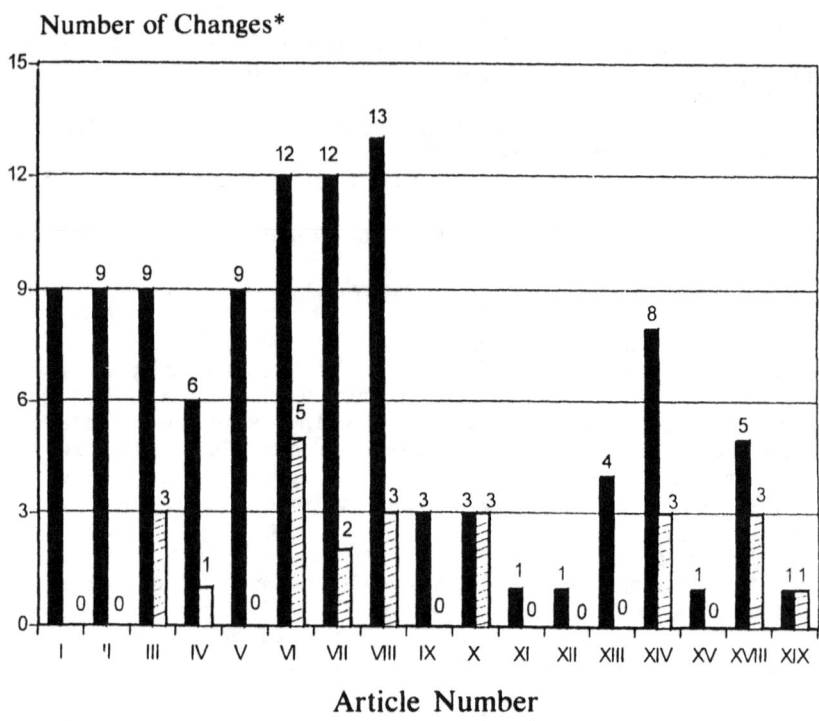

14

Modernizing the Constitution: The Constitutional Convention of 1967

THE YEAR 1957 was selected by the 1938 convention as the target date set for the next referendum, rather than 1956, the actual twentieth year, so that the convention would be in session in 1959, an off year, rather than 1958, when an election for governor would take place. Voters rejected the call.

The next decade brought major changes in New York's political landscape—changes which pushed the state toward a convention. Organized pressure from a variety of civic groups had been growing, and prominent newspapers throughout the state editorialized on the need for a constitutional convention.[1] Howard Samuels, a successful businessman and Democratic candidate for governor in 1962, created a Citizens Committee for a Constitutional Convention, a "non-partisan group organized to obtain an affirmative vote on the referendum question. . . ."[2] The decisive factor on the decision to call a convention, however, came from outside the state—a series of United States Supreme Court decisions declaring many state reapportionment schemes unconstitutional. One such case, *WMCA Inc. v. Lomenzo*,[3] invalidated the apportionment provision of the New York Constitution. Lomenzo acted as a catalyst for the state's civic groups, which coordinated a statewide campaign for a convention. Unable to resolve the reapportionment issue itself, the legislature approved a bill to place the question of a new convention before the voters. The 1964 landslide victory of Democratic President Lyndon B. Johnson helped deliver both houses of the New York state legislature to the Democrats. Believing that they would control any constitutional convention held in the next few years, Democrats were not adverse to holding an early convention. The electorate approved the proposal by a margin of 233,000 votes—1,681,438 (53%) to 1,468,431.

The margin of victory was provided by New York City. No other section of the state supported the call for a convention. The fact that New York State voters had never approved a constitution submitted by a convention called by such a slim margin did not bode well for the success of whatever proposals the convention might produce.

The problem of drawing the district lines to be used in the delegate selection process was compounded when Republicans gained control of the senate in 1966. With the legislature deadlocked, the Court of Appeals approved a plan issued by a judicial commission it had appointed, and delegate selection began. Various groups, including the Committee for a Constitutional Convention, lobbied for non-partisan selection of the at-large delegates.[4] These pleas for non-partisan selection, first voiced during the 1821 convention selection process, suffered the same fate as the earlier appeals. New York's political culture provides barren ground for such non-partisanship. That culture has been described as "highly partisan and party competitive, that is, its politics are set in a context of sharp, relatively evenly balanced, urban/rural rivalry. . . ."[5] Like its predecessors, the convention would be dominated by political professionals and organized along party lines. The impact of this partisanship would be manifest in the way the convention was organized, in the voting patterns, and in the perceptions of delegates and citizens of the convention's decisions. The voters were to elect 171 delegates from senatorial districts and 15 on a statewide basis, for a total of 186. When the elections were completed, Democrats, with the support of the Liberal Party, elected a majority of the delegates (102), Republicans elected 83, and the Conservatives elected one delegate. For the first time in over a century, Democrats would control a New York constitutional convention. Moreover, 90% of the Democratic and Liberal delegates came from the state's five major urban areas, thus insuring that the cities would be the focus of the convention's attention.

Although the delegates did not accurately reflect the state's population, they were nevertheless the most diverse group elected to a constitutional convention in New York's history. Eleven women, eleven African-Americans, seven Hispanics, and a significant number of delegates of Italian, Jewish, and Irish ancestry were present. Two-thirds of the delegates were lawyers, almost one-fourth of them judges. The election of only one farmer as a delegate spoke volumes about the changes in the state between 1846 and 1967. More than eight out of every ten delegates (83%) had previous governmental experiences of one kind or another. The most significant fact about delegate composition would be its partisan complexion.[6] The large number of incumbent and former legislators—thirteen incumbent state legislators and thirty-two former state legislators and congressmen—contributed to the legislative orientation of the delegates. With Assembly Leader Anthony Travia as convention president and Senator Majority Leader Earl Brydges a minority leader, the convention resembled the recently adjourned legislative session. The rules of the assembly were adopted as the convention rules: committees chairs were selected along party lines, and offices and staff personnel of the legislature were used by delegates. The floor leadership system of the legislature was transferred to the convention.

The delegates elected in 1966 began their work in April of 1967 and adjourned six months later on September 26th. They approached the task before them with ample intellectual resources. A series of commissions on constitutional reform had been issuing reports since 1958 on various aspects of constitutional reform.[7] In addition, in 1965, a Temporary State Commission on the Constitutional Convention was appointed and issued fifteen reports for use by the delegates. Modernization, simplification, and reorganization were the dominant themes of these commission reports. That approach would find expression in many of the reforms proposed by the delegates.

THE WORK OF THE CONVENTION

Many issues found a place on the convention's agenda, including legislative reapportionment, metropolitan government, urban revitalization, simplification and modernization of the constitution, reorganization of the judiciary, state and local finance, and repeal of the Blaine Amendment, which prohibited the state legislature from allocating financial aid to parochial schools.

Bill of Rights

The dominance of the convention by the Democratic/Liberal coalition was clearly evident in the revision of Article I, the Bill of Rights. Prompted by the United States Supreme Court's ruling in *Berger v. New York*,[8] which invalidated, on federal constitutional grounds, the state's constitutional and statutory provisions concerning court-ordered wiretaps, the convention tightened requirements for issuing wiretap warrants (Art. I, Sec. 4b) and added an exclusionary rule for violations of this section (Sec. 4c).

A second controversial proposal granted individuals accused of a felony the right to inspect the grand jury minutes when an indictment was obtained without a preliminary hearing (Sec. 5d). The convention also extended the right to jury trial to include defendants charged with misdemeanor crimes punishable by a prison term of six months or more (Sec. 7b).

The delegates also rejected, on federal constitutional grounds, the procedures adopted by the earlier 1938 convention for dismissing public employees who refused to waive immunity before a grand jury. In *Garrity v. New Jersey*[9] and *Spevack v. Klein*[10] the Supreme Court held that dismissal of public officials who refused to waive immunity before a grand jury was in violation of their Fifth Amendment rights prohibiting self-incrimination. The constitutional language adopted by the 1967 convention provided the opportunity for a separate fitness hearing to determine whether the official's failure to cooperate constituted lack of fitness to continue in office. That provision was transferred from Article I and placed more appropriately in the article on Public Officers and Employees (Art. V, Sec. 3).

The delegates amended the clause governing takings of private property to include the phrase "or damaged" along with "taken" (Art. I, Sec. 6), reflecting their belief in the continuing importance of private property rights in the constitutional framework.

One of the most innovative decisions of the convention was a proposal for a consumer's bill of rights (Art. I, Sec. 12). Although it was considered by some observers more appropriate for legislative action, and though it ran counter to the general tendency to remove such statutory material from the constitution, the delegates nevertheless added the provision because the legislature had refused to address the issue. The section provided consumers with protection from unfair, inequitable, or dishonest sales, marketing, and financing practices, and required consumer education as well. The legislature was directed to enact legislation implementing this provision.

The convention explicitly rejected an attempt to permit preventive detention.[11] Instead, it clarified the right of bail in cases where the defendant's appearance is reasonably certain (Art. I, Sec. 8).

The delegates expanded coverage of the state constitution's equal protection clause to include sex, age, and physical handicaps. Had it been adopted, New York would have joined the eighteen states which have adopted "little ERAs" (Art. I, Sec. 3a).

The "Blaine" Amendment

The most controversial issue taken up by the convention was that of state aid to religious schools. The constitutional provision (Art. XI, Sec. 3), popularly referred to as the "Blaine" Amendment, prohibited the state from advancing money or credit, directly or indirectly, to assist educational institutions under the control of religious denominations. Two exceptions were stipulated: examinations and inspections, and transportation for children to and from schools. (The latter exception was added by the 1938 convention.)

As the leading student of the 1967 Constitution commented: "No other issue produced as much mail, no other issue brought as many people to Albany to lobby for their position, no other issue had produced as many advance commitments from delegates prior to the election." Ninety percent of the delegates mentioned the issue during the election process.[12] Particularly effective was the Committee on Educational Freedom (C.E.F.), a group organized to lobby on behalf of repeal, with an aggressive advertising campaign using the Catholic Church as a conduit for its appeal, and claiming the support of more than 120 delegates-elect.[13]

With a majority of the delegates and of the Republican and Democratic leadership committed to repeal, the only remaining obstacles regarded procedure and how to diffuse the inevitable adverse reaction repeal would create. Travia's decision to assign the issue to the Committee on the Bill of Rights and Suffrage rather than the Committee on Education raised speculation that his decision was based on an assumption that the former committee would be more sympathetic to repeal. Both committees, however, were equally supportive of the change. Other factors were involved. Andrew Tyler, chair of the Bill of Rights committee, was an African-American Protestant and would give the appearance of fairness to the committee hearings and deliberations. Additionally, the replacement for Blaine (essentially, the First Amendment establishment clause), would be included in the Bill of Rights along with a standing-to-sue clause, granting any citizen of the state the right to challenge the constitutionality of any state funds expended for sectarian purposes.[14]

Court decisions interpreting the national constitution played a Janus-like role in the debates. On June 1, 1967, while delegates were deliberating, the Court of Appeals upheld the constitutionality, under both the state and national constitutions, of a statute requiring local school districts to purchase textbooks and make them available to public and non-public school children.[15] This decision supported the view that Blaine was no more a barrier to certain forms of aid than was the First Amendment, and that the judiciary as well as the political branches of the government had adopted an accommodationist approach concerning church-state relations, rather than the strict separation view embodied in the Blaine Amendment.[16] Striking support of this view was a statement of the Board of Regents on May 25, 1967, effectively endorsing repeal of the amendment. For some delegates the court's decision in *Allen* provided further reason to retain the clause; for others it gave support for replacing Blaine with the First Amendment establishment clause. The package—repeal of Blaine, its replacement with the First Amendment establishment clause and a standing-to-sue provision—were approved comfortably by a 132 to 49 vote.[17]

When the education article was taken up, the church-state issue again intruded on the debates. An amendment was introduced restricting the use of public funds for construction of facilities for private elementary or secondary education. That amendment was defeated by a closer vote of 74 to 84.[18]

The issue continued to plague the delegates. When the convention addressed the community development article, a proposal considered to be the most important and innovative at the convention, concerns were again raised regarding language that permitted the state to provide financial assistance to aid in the construction of private elementary and secondary schools. The issue was contentious enough to jeopardize its passage. Only a last-minute compromise allayed the concerns of Blaine Amendment supporters and saved the article.[19] The divisive issue raised by Blaine would arise again with the critical decision on separate submission.

No doubt participants believed they were fighting over a matter of surpassing significance. To Dr. Donald Harrington, Liberal Party delegate, repeal of the amendment would alter the character of American life.[20] For supporters of repeal of the amendment it meant the possibility of support for the Catholic school system, which was in serious financial trouble, especially in New York City. Developments in the quarter century following defeat of the constitution suggest that both groups seriously overestimated the impact of the amendment. Support for parochial schools has continued apace, though some legislative policies have run afoul, not of Blaine, but the First Amendment.[21] The debate over repeal of the Blaine Amendment provides a classic example of symbolic politics. The existence of the amendment and what it symbolizes, rather than its impact on the policy process, became the grounds on which the debate took place. Although nothing of substance changed, the retention of the Blaine Amendment provided a reassuring symbol. For opponents of repeal much more was involved than the loss on the specific issue; at stake was the broader symbolic battle being fought over which life style and set of values were to be recognized as normative in the polity.[22]

The Presentation

The Blaine question threatened the convention's working majority again when the issue of presenting its work was addressed. The Committee on Presentation began its deliberations on September 25, 1967. Unlike other convention committees, the Presentation Committee consisted of ten members, with the majority and minority leadership appointing five, respectively. The president of the convention was allowed a casting vote in the event of a tie. President Travia eventually let it be known that he favored single submission. His appointments to the committee were based primarily on loyalty, effectively putting the decision in his hands.

Editorial opinion across the state opposed single submission, and Governor Rockefeller sent a special message to the convention urging separate submission. He proposed that the 1938 precedent be followed, i.e., separate submission of the major substantive amendments, with the remaining items placed in an omnibus amendment.[23] The seven issues he identified were: repeal of the "Blaine" Amendment, a new judiciary article, free public and private higher education, state assumption of local welfare costs, community development, eliminating the referendum for creation of public debt, and legislative reapportionment. Strong arguments were offered for separate submission, including the experience of the 1915 convention. Moreover, one of Travia's major supporters, the Catholic Church, apprehensive of involvement in a partisan conflict, seemed to be retreating from support for single submission. Lieutenant-Governor Malcolm Wilson, a Catholic and a repeal supporter, urged church leaders not to support single submission.[24] Travia broke the tie in committee and a recommendation for single submission went before the convention for deliberation. Realizing that Republican support would not be forthcoming, Travia needed to obtain the votes of 94 of the 102 Democratic delegates. He did so by appealing to party unity and "carrot and stick" pressure. The issue was finally submitted to the convention on September 26, with the 94th vote cast by Travia.[25]

The convention eliminated the clause dealing with libel prosecutions, believing that such language was superceded and unnecessary in view of recent Supreme Court decisions and the convention's decision to adopt an equivalent of the First Amendment.[26] The convention relegated the remainder of the archaic free speech clause to a "Miscellaneous" article (Art. XV, Sec. 8).

Other materials omitted from the Bill of Rights concerned the taking and drainage of swamp lands (Art. I, Sec. 16), the provisions continuing the common law in force (Sec. 14), divorce proceedings (Sec. 9), and the right to recover damages (Sec. 16). These were eliminated because they were judged to be obsolete or statutory in character. Attempts to remove the prohibition against gambling ran into stiff opposition and failed. The convention transferred the ban from the Bill of Rights to the "Miscellaneous" article (XV, Sec. 5).

Suffrage

Article II, Suffrage and Elections, also underwent revision. The delegates drastically reduced its length from nine sections to two, removing provisions thought to be statutory in character such as those establishing details of the voter registration process.[27] Delegates repealed the state's literacy test because they believed problems created by voter illiteracy should not be resolved by a constitutional provision restricting voting but rather by extensive education, a solution more appropriately fashioned by legislative action. The convention also authorized the legislature to lower the state voting age to eighteen (Art. II, Sec. 1).

The Legislature

The convention significantly revised the reapportionment provisions of the legislative article. The convention, as required, adopted the federal standard of "one man, one vote" as the substantive principle for future reapportionment. The contentious question for the convention was: who will redistrict? The legislative stasis preceding the convention regarding reapportionment made it clear that it was too much to expect the legislature to reapportion itself in a manner consistent with court decisions. Therefore, a redistricting commission consisting of five members was established. The temporary president of the senate, the speaker of the assembly, and the minority leaders of the two houses each had one appointment; the chair of the commission was appointed by the Court of Appeals (Art. III, Sec. 2a). The Court of Appeals was explicitly granted jurisdiction to hear challenges to commission plans (Sec. 3). The bipartisan approach avoided the uncertainty connected with a non-partisan commission and was likely to receive media support. It had the additional advantage of excluding the governor from the process. Advancing beyond the federal mandate, the convention also prohibited gerrymandering for any purpose—religious, racial, or political (Art. III, Sec. 2c).

The convention also made several relatively minor adjustments to the structure of the legislature. The delegates added a minimum age requirement of twenty-one for legislators (Art. III, Sec. 8). In an effort to open government to the citizens, a provision was adopted requiring that transcripts of debates be published (Art. III, Sec. 11). More important, the delegates eliminated a series of specific local and private matters previously declared by the constitution to be beyond the legislative purview (Art. III, Sec. 17). The delegates believed it was not possible to list all such matters, and judged the enumeration approach too cumbersome.[28] The legislature was presumed sufficiently responsible to limit its intrusions into private and local matters; and the delegates thought that Article IX on local government provided ample protection for local interests.

Finally, the convention gave the legislature the authority to determine when the governor is disabled (Art. III, Sec. 16f). The decision to include this provision was shaped by the pending Twenty-Fifth Amendment to the national Constitution, which, in the wake of the illness of President Dwight D. Eisenhower and the assassination of President John F. Kennedy, established procedures for determining presidential disability. However, in vesting this power in the legislature, the delegates declined to follow the federal model: the Twenty-Fifth Amendment places principal reliance on the vice-president and the president's cabinet (or such means as Congress may by law provide) in making such judgments, and assigns only the resolution of otherwise intractable disputes to Congress.

Howard Samuels presented what would be the most radical structural proposal submitted to the convention: a 150-member unicameral legislature. It received banner headlines, but—whatever its merits— gained little support among the delegates.[29] The Committee on the Legislature could not muster sufficient votes in support of a four-year term for senators, and sent to the floor without recommendation a proposal containing the previously established two-year term. The four-year senate term had been defeated in 1927 and rejected by the voters in 1938 and again in 1965. With assembly Democrats disinclined to support a measure adding to the prestige or power of the senate, and New York City party leaders unenthusiastic at the prospect of permitting senators the opportunity to seek other office without jeopardizing their current seats, the measure was defeated.

The Executive

The major changes in the executive article were the addition of a section granting the governor the power to execute governmental reorganization plans subject to legislative approval within sixty days, and elimination of the constitutionally established limit of twenty state departments. The convention also eliminated the pocket veto.[30] The new provision required that the governor disapprove a bill within thirty days of the legislature's adjournment; failure to act in the prescribed time frame gave the bill the status of law (Art. III, Sec. 3a).

The only controversial proposal concerning the executive branch was the creation of a state-level department of criminal justice. Bernard Botein, chair of the Committee on the Executive, argued in favor of a single agency to combat a growing crime problem. The fragmented and local character of law enforcement in the state made even their well-intentioned efforts "feeble and sporadic."[31] Acting as the governor's law enforcement arm, the agency would have supervisory as well as coordinating powers over local law enforcement. This proposal raised strong opposition from local law enforcement agencies. The question of whether this power should be placed in the governor's office or under the independently elected attorney-general was a second issue. Chief Judge Charles Desmond of the Court of Appeals moved to delete the word "supervisory" and place the agency under the attorney general. The compromise failed to allay the apprehensions and suspicions of local authorities.[32] With Travia lukewarm on the proposal, the measure failed to obtain the necessary majority required for final passage.

The last alteration involved the Public Service Commission, an agency responsible for regulating the public utilities of the state, including rate-making. The convention reduced office terms from ten to six years and granted the legislature, in joint session, the power to select three of its members. The remaining four members would be selected by the governor (Art. VI, Sec. 8). The new selection plan was expected to yield at least one Democratic appointment.[33]

The Judiciary

As in every other constitutional convention, the reorganization of the judiciary gave delegates as much difficulty as any matter before them. The voters had approved a constitutional amendment in 1961 completely revising the judiciary and calling for a unified court system. Approval of the amendment by over 1.8 million votes was the largest proportion of support for an amendment in New York's history. Despite this successful reform, the judiciary article was still large and cumbersome, its thirty-seven sections constituting 25% of the constitution. The 1961 revision failed to simplify the article, which resembled a detailed statute for the administration of the courts; nor was it successful in relieving the congestion and delays plaguing the judicial system. The disagreements at the convention were so intense, and the delegates so splintered, that the convention only partially achieved the goals of streamlining and abbreviating the article.

Among the major changes adopted were centralizing the administration of the judiciary under the Court of Appeals (Art. V, Sec. 26); statewide financing of the court system (Sec. 11); a provision granting the Court of Appeals original jurisdiction over apportionment cases (Sec. 2c); a provision reducing the number and kinds of automatic appeals heard by the Court of Appeals (Secs. 2c–3); and a provision authorizing the legislature to abolish county courts where appropriate (Sec. 15b).

Environment and Conservation

Continuing a concern with the subject of conservation that originated with the 1894 convention, the 1967 convention adopted a "Conservation Bill of Rights" (Art. VIII, Sec. 3). Declaring conservation and protection of natural resources and of the scenic beauty of the state to be important public objectives, the new provision charged the legislature to reduce air, water, and noise pollution. It also directed the legislature to take measures to protect the state's wetlands and agricultural lands and to regulate the state's water resources. The Conservation Bill of Rights set forth a comprehensive definition of the natural resources of the state.

The convention also mandated the establishment of a State Nature and Historical Preserve, consisting of land, waters, and structures beyond the forest preserve to be acquired by the state because of their "natural beauty, wilderness character, ecological and historical significance" (Sec. 3). The vote of 175 in favor to none against reflected the salience of the environment in the late sixties.[34]

Education

The convention gave the state a broader role in education. The most radical provision adopted by the delegates committed the state to "define a system of higher education . . . encompassing both public and non-public institutions, by programs which may include free tuition, grants, fellowships and scholarships" (Art. IX, Sec. 1b). The state would treat higher education in the same way that it had treated elementary and secondary education since 1894, as a right so fundamental to one's future and well being that access to it should not depend on one's economic status. To emphasize this point the convention added an equality of educational opportunity guarantee (Sec. 2c).

Article VII: State Debt

The convention eliminated the 148-year-old referendum requirement for the assumption of state debt (Sec. 11). This was based on delegate recognization that as important and necessary as projects like urban revitalization were, they were nevertheless unpopular with constitutents. In the six years prior to the convention, three of four amendments to the Housing Article, which would have strengthened the state's ability to support and encourage urban renewal and community development, were voted down. In its place a new requirement was adopted which allowed for debt assumption only if enacted at two separately elected sessions of the legislature, and only if the assumed debt amounted to less than 12% of the state's revenue averaged over the two preceding years (new Art. X, Sec. 11). Another section (11b) allowed for an increase in that limit to 15% with approval of the electorate. Under the new article the state would be permitted to contract with the federal government and with the private sector for the development of its infrastructure.

In an effort to placate those concerned with the possibility of significant increases in state debt, the convention, for the first time, included in the debt limit the liabilities accumulated by authorities (Sec. 19). Despite this last measure, the changes in the new Article X, "State Taxation and Finance," clearly intended to remove restrictions in the area of taxation and debt assumption so that the state might meet "the essential needs of the last third of the twentieth century."[35] Delegates also voiced concern about the increasing role of the federal government, maintaining that where the old constitutional restrictions hobbled state and local governments, the federal government was willing to step in and fill the vacuum.

ARTICLE XI: LOCAL GOVERNMENT

Cities were the focus of attention in the debates over this article. Racial revolts and disorders ignited the nation while the delegates were in session, but these uprisings did not appear to affect the deliberation in any direct way. New York was spared the fate of cities like Newark, Detroit, and Los Angeles. This was due, in no small way, to the leadership and policies of Mayor John Lindsay. Lindsay's support for neighborhood populism worked. His objective was to repair relations with the African-American and lower income communities, to reach out to disgruntled residents and even to gangs of youth.[36] Nonetheless, the "long, hot summer" gave added significance to the debates concerning home rule, local tax and debt limitations, and state aid to the cities. The issue of home rule had been addressed in every convention held in New York since 1867. Supporters of the traditional home rule approach endeavored to prevent the state from intervening in what they considered matters of local concern. At the 1967 convention a group of delegates chose a different approach to the home rule issue. They believed the traditional approach unworkable and outmoded. Major changes had occurred since the home rule issue was first raised. For one, the legislature would soon be reapportioned, removing any unfair advantage rural areas may have possessed. Most significantly, they argued that few, if any, issues were truly local anymore. What was needed were a more clearly delineated pattern of intergovernmental cooperation, a greater role for the state in the form of more assistance to local areas, assumption of certain functions such as welfare costs, and a reorganization of local governmental units, creating more rational, efficient, and responsible local government.

The traditional home rule position was embodied in the 1963 revision of Article IX, and the "neo-reformers" were determined to rewrite that article.[37] The Committee on Local Government debated a replacement for the 1963 article that would incorporate the neo-reformer's ideas. Local units and such multi-county or regional units as the legislature may authorize were vested with all legislative power, except that limited by general law and the constitution. The legislature could act in relation to local government, the chief executive of the locality concurring, and a majority of the governing body or, absent executive concurrence, two-thirds of the governing body. The committee proposal did not make any attempt to separate local from state concerns. Rather, it emphasized cooperation between the state and local governments on the one hand and localities on the other. This approach contrasted sharply with the traditional view, referred to as the "express powers" approach, as it attempts to spell out the powers granted to the local governments and those reserved to the state.[38]

The consistency of the committee's work engendered opposition. Republicans supported the express powers approach; Democrats were divided over which approach to adopt.[39] With the convention deadlocked, a compromise combining the two approaches was proposed.[40] Under this compromise, the article on home rule would contain an express list of powers granted to local governments (Art. IX, Sec. 2c–d), as well as a provision granting all legislative powers to local governments, except those specifically prohibited by the constitution or the general laws (2b). Although this compromise enabled the convention to pass a home rule article, it raised a major problem of constitutional interpretation. If all legislative powers not specifically prohibited were left to local governments, why was a specific list of powers necessary? The attempt to restructure local governments was consistent with neo-reformers' emphasis on cooperation between state and local governmental units. Local government in New York State is composed of 57 counties, 62 cities, 932 towns, and 557 villages, and some 5,000 special-purpose districts and authorities. The fragmented, overlapping character of these units has been the subject of much criticism.[41] Wasteful and inefficient, local governments, particularly in metropolitan areas, made it difficult for voters to hold their officials accountable. In addition, these divisions allowed suburbs to segregate themselves from involvement with the critical problems facing the cities.

Neo-reformers concentrated their efforts on easing local referendum requirements. The revision of the local government article in 1963 made reorganization by annexation or transfer of functions procedurally difficult and politically almost impossible. Annexation required the governing bodies of all units of government affected to agree to the annexation, and the voters to approve by referendum. Transfer of function was no less difficult. Such transfer must be approved by all units of government affected. Thus, if a city and village are affected by the transfer, a triple referendum is required.

The staff of the Committee on Local Government pressed for a proposal that would allow for transfer of functions by a single referendum, considering voters from several local governments involved as one unit. In the presence of strong and widespread opposition from local governments around the state, the committee rejected this idea. On the convention floor an amendment was introduced which would have eliminated the multiple referendum requirement, permitted counties to initiate transfers of functions, and allowed for adoption, repeal, and/or amendment of charter forms of government by a majority of all voters in the county.[42] This amendment aroused powerful opposition from a variety of quarters, including Republicans who did not believe any structural change was necessary, and Republicans from rural areas who reflected the strong opposition from villages concerned about loss of village home rule.[43] Concerned that consolidation would weaken their cities and the Democratic Party politically, upstate mayors from Democratic cities also opposed the measure.[44] Most surprising was the opposition of Democrats from New York City. Having no vested interest in the issue, they opposed the measure for one of two reasons: the measure offered too little, and they wanted to rebuff Convention President Travia, who was involved in an intra-party dispute for leadership with Stanley Steingut.[45] The measure was defeated by a vote of 75 to 95, with 30 Democrats voting against the measure.[46] Delegates did succeed in making sheriff's deputies employees of their respective counties for the first time, thus subjecting them to civil service requirements.

ARTICLE XII (RENUMBERED):
FISCAL HOME RULE AND LOCAL FINANCE

It was clear to neo-reformers that home rule powers without the means of financing their exercises were meaningless.[47] Beneath the issue of political home rule for cities lay the question of the extent to which cities would be permitted to manage their own fiscal affairs. Constitutional tax and debt limits, along with an extensive network of mandates, significantly restrict a municipality's ability to govern itself.

By the mid-sixties in New York the process of metropolitanization had left central cities with populations in need of costly social services—the poor, the uneducated, the elderly, and minorities, particularly African-Americans, and a declining physical plant to maintain. Middle- and upper-middle-income families, as well as industries, were relocating to the suburbs. These migration patterns left cities with shrinking tax bases while they were being asked to provide social services for high-cost, low-income residents and to accommodate a sizeable commuter population. Under these conditions tax and debt limits threatened to undermine the ability of the cities to govern effectively. Traditional home rule advocates proposed granting localities the power to levy non-property taxes, the elimination of tax and debt limits, and the elimination, reduction, or procedural curbing of state mandates. Neo-reformers disagreed. Rather than imposing higher taxes on city residents, they proposed transferring such functions as welfare to the state for financing on a more varied and equitable basis. They also proposed revising state formulas for distributing aid to localities, particularly aid to education, and restructuring local governments through consolidation.[48]

The question of extension of non-property taxing powers to localities found neo-reformers aligned with conservatives, taxpayers, and real estate associations. Though some neo-reformers joined delegates from large cities, most of them opposed this measure, and it was defeated. Aside from what they believed a grievous error in making it easier for cities to tax an already burdened population, reformers thought the measure would simply magnify the worst features of local government: "[Given] the fragmented pattern of [local] government, however, there was considerable opposition to a grant of broad, non-property local taxing powers which would create a tax system as fragmented as the governmental system itself."[49] A compromise measure was offered between giving municipalities unlimited tax power and requiring them to come to Albany for each request, but the measure was defeated by a vote of 68 to 99, with most neo-reformers voting against the measure.[50]

The limitations on municipal revenues forced cities to resort to extensive borrowing and to rely more heavily on state aid. Constitutional debt limits were creating borrowing difficulty, were ineffective, and compelled cities to search for avenues of circumvention. When evasive devices such as the creation of special districts with special borrowing powers were to no avail, they sought legislative assistance for constitutional amendments granting a variety of exemptions from the general prohibition.

By 1967 only a few New York municipalities approached their debt limits. No county in the state had used more than 50% of its capacity, and only six of the sixty-two cities had used more than 50%.[51] Regarding tax limits, a different pattern emerges. While most of the counties and villages had used less than half of their capacity, all six cities with populations exceeding 125,000 had used 90% of their taxing power.

The staff report of the Committee on Local Government contained significant recommendations for change, but the convention was not receptive to extensive changes in the local finance article. The article maintained the basic principles of debt regulation previously embodied in the existing Article VIII: debts should not be contracted for longer than the period of usefulness of that project; full faith and credit of governments and school districts shall be pledged for all borrowing; provision shall be made for appropriation of money for payment of interest on all indebtedness, amortization, and redemption of maturing debt with priority over other obligations. The article contained the provision's exclusions of certain types of debt from the general limitation. In line with the attempt to bring efficiency and effectiveness to local governments, special provisions were established for cooperative financing of local enterprises by local government and other public corporations. These provisions permitted local governments engaged in these cooperative ventures to contract joining debt (Sec. 2(2)). The convention did recommend other changes. For purposes of computing the base for tax and debt limits, communities were permitted to use a three-year rather than a five-year average of the full value of real property. The added flexibility this change would provide was limited by an addition requiring a local referendum to approve any such change (Sec. 14b). Section I of Article VIII was transferred and consolidated into the proposed Article X (taxation and finance). Finally, the 2% debt limit set forth for cities and villages over 5,000 population in Article XVIII (Housing) was transferred to the local finance article and incorporated into the debt limits of those local units (Sec. 4). Debt limits were removed on school districts outside the largest six, and the legislature was to provide tax limits for towns by January 1, 1972 (Sec. 9).

The third fiscal issue concerned mandates. The Committee on Local

Government proposed that future mandates be accompanied by an estimate of the additional annual costs for each local government affected, and successful passage by two successive legislatures. Labor opposition was intense and effective. As in the 1938 convention, civil service unions mobilized successfully to defeat the proposal.[52]

The defeat of local government reorganization, and the failure to obtain significant changes in fiscal home rule powers concerning tax and debt limits, left reformers with three measures they hoped would alleviate, if not resolve, the urban crisis: the transfer of functions to the state, a revised state aid formula, and the replacement of the Housing Article XVIII with a community development article mandating a direct role for the state.

A series of investigations and commission reports concluded that cities were unable to shoulder the burden of welfare costs.[53] The convention accepted this view and mandated that the state assume the costs of welfare. The vote was largely on party lines, with all Democrats voting in favor and all save five Republicans voting against. Supporters argued that the system would be fairer and more efficient and would enable cities to finance other pressing needs.[54] Republicans opposed the proposals on the basis of prohibitive cost and accused the convention of "passing the buck" by requiring the legislature to adopt policies already within its power to implement.[55]

The second measure proposed a change in the state education aid formula. Education was distributed primarily on the basis of real property values per student per school district. This formula did not adequately reflect district needs for state financial aid, and, in fact, discriminated against school districts in the larger cities. Larger cities, already burdened with higher taxes, were also responsible for a higher percentage of disadvantaged students. Rural areas suffered from similar problems. An amendment was proposed to the education article mandating apportionment of state aid in terms of any special educational needs of the districts and the total tax burden of the taxpayers in the district (Art. IX, Sec. 2d).

The third proposal concerned community development. The 1938 convention had previously added a new article (XVIII) on housing, assigning responsibility to the government to address the housing needs of the state. By the 1960s, however, this article was deemed too restrictive as it limited aid to low-income families, excluded counties from its provisions, and required referendum for expenditure of funds. Voters proved to be particularly negative when it came to approving authorizations under this article.

The Committee on Health, Housing and Social Services reported a broad community development proposal intended to replace Article

XVIII. The new article allowed an exception to the prohibition on state or local governments from loaning or giving their money or credit to private entities (Art. X, Sec. 18) and permitted the use of government moneys and credit for "public benefit purposes" to assist programs and facilities related to community development. The article empowered the legislature to create public benefit authorities for community development. With the state-wide referendum requirement for assumption of debt previously removed by the convention, funds for community development could be appropriated without voter approval and could used to aid private enterprises engaged in urban revitalization. Despite a strong endorsement by Governor Rockefeller,[56] major differences existed, particularly over the elimination of the referendum requirement for approving community development projects. Finally, following an intensive and heated debate a compromise was reached which left the basic provisions intact, and the measure passed overwhelmingly, 177 to 2.[57]

The Political Theory of the 1967 Constitution

The values which dominated in the 1967 convention represented a repudiation of much of New York's constitutional history. The delegates made systematic attempts to eliminate obsolete material, as well as subjects which were deemed statutory in character. Examples of the latter include the fraud and bribery provisions of Article II; the divorce clause of Article I, Section 9; and the right to recover for damages in Article I, Section 16. Examples of "obsolete" material removed include the section regarding common law and libel procedure. The convention also streamlined the document by reorganizing the sections, structuring a more logical order, and relegating miscellaneous sections to the final article. The constitution's drafters simplified language throughout. In these respects, the work of the 1967 convention reflected the philosophy of the Model State Constitution drafted by the National Municipal League: modernize, simplify, and shorten. The final product was approximately half the length of the document it was intended to replace.

If there was a central value manifest at the 1967 convention, it was delegate acceptance of an activist state with minimal restrictions on the powers of the legislature to address contemporary social and economic problems. The proposed 1967 constitution, for example, eliminated or eased tax and debt limitations and granted the legislature significant discretion in dealing with community development. Along with the commitment to the idea of an activist state with minimal constitutional restrictions, the 1967 Constitution proposed to transfer to the state government the financing of welfare, the judiciary, higher education, and a major part of community development. In nearly every instance, these new functions and powers were designed to assist the cities.

Not all the actions of the convention, however, were consistent with the Model State Constitution. Controversy surrounding the judiciary doomed attempts to simplify and condense the article, and differences over the nature of home rule left that article muddled by compromise. Nevertheless, the constitution proposed by the 1967 convention shared with the proposed 1915 Constitution a consistency of approach rarely achieved in New York's constitutional history.

THE 1967 CONSTITUTIONAL CONVENTION: AN ASSESSMENT

At the insistence of convention president Anthony Travia, and against the recommendation of Republican Governor Nelson A. Rockefeller and others, the convention decided to submit the constitution as a single package. It was a fatal error, one that repeated the decision of the 1915 constitutional convention.

The constitution encountered opposition from unexpected quarters. The New York Times, the League of Women Voters, the American Civil Liberties Union, the NAACP, and the Citizens Union (excluding its leader, Howard Samuels), most Protestant organizations and denominations, Jewish reform and conservative congregations, and Mayor John Lindsay opposed its adoption.[58] On October 19 the Associated Press published a wire service story concluding that every major New York newspaper was urging rejection of the proposed constitution.[59] The ACLU and the NAACP and various religious organizations apparently based their opposition on the convention's proposed repeal of the "Blaine" Amendment. Republican Party opposition rested primarily on fiscal grounds. Governor Rockefeller's budget director released figures suggesting that the cost of the proposed reforms would exceed three billion dollars after ten years, resulting in an 80% tax boost in that decade.[60] The Liberal Party opposed the 1967 Constitution in part because of the proposed repeal of the "Blaine" Amendment and the failure to achieve court reform. As expected, Republican legislative leaders and county chairs campaigned actively against the charter. More surprising was the Democratic Party's campaign, which was described as "no campaign" at all.[61]

The legislative wing of the Democratic party dominated the convention. Delegates divided into two highly partisan cluster blocs comprised of all but five delegates: Democratic partisans and Republican partisans. "Partisanship in New York was so powerful that it washed out virtually every other possible competitor as a basis for systematic delegate voting behavior in the roll calls studied."[62] The manifestly partisan character of the convention and its decisions, however meritorious, contributed not only to Republican opposition but also to a negative public image that such partisanship inevitably engenders. Travia's executive assistant at the convention, Robert S. Herman, suggested that Travia possessed enormous power "but wasn't really able to exert much leadership over the convention. He began by alienating Earl Brydges, the minority leader, [and created] a very partisan convention where there were only three fairly minor partisan issues . . . I think that showed a lack of leadership" because it mistook "power for leadership."[63] Travia and the Democratic delegates expended a great deal of energy to secure adoption of the document yet seemed incapable of developing a strategy to counter combined media, religious, and partisan opposition.

The partisanship exhibited at the 1967 convention was not inevitable, as a comparison with other states whose political culture and constitutional traditions sustain a more nonpartisan approach reveals. Elmer Cornwell, Jay Goodman, and Wayne Swanson analyzed six constitutional conventions, interviewing convention delegates before and after deliberations on the question of the role of parties. The table below (p. 331) suggests the extent of partisanship in New York and its relative absence in other states. The tension between the idea that delegates should approach the task of reforming the fundamental charter of the state with a larger ken than party affiliation, and the need for parties to organize and take responsibility for the product of constitutional reform, is a concept New Yorkers have not successfully wrestled with. Professor Cornwell and his associates have pointed the way to a healthy balance between the antinomies involved:

> Parties must be involved in successful constitutional revision by convention but not so as to impart too political an image. It is probably also important that party involvement be frank and accepted, and thus a stabilized and stabilizing influence in the deliberations. The delegates will have to play their part in maintaining this balance by being conscious of the need to moderate party spirit.[64]

The proposed constitution had its supporters. Governor Rockefeller indicated his personal decision to vote in the affirmative; Catholic Church leaders remained steadfast; the AFL-CIO endorsed the document, as did orthodox Jewish groups and the New York City Budget Commission. But Rockefeller could not secure Republican leaders or

Republican voters, anymore than the AFL-CIO could drum up enthusiasm among the rank and file. The anticipated Catholic vote failed to materialize and the other groups were too small to affect the outcome.[65]

Attention has been focused on the importance of repeal of the "Blaine" Amendment as a major factor in the defeat of the document. Certainly repeal played a crucial role in the decision of various religious and non-religious organizations to oppose the constitution, but in light of the lack of unanimity among Catholic voters and the size of the defeat, it appears that concerns over cost and partisanship were the crucial factors.[66]

When the votes were tallied, the defeat was a stunning rebuff to Travia and the work of the convention. The voters rejected the constitution by a three-to-one margin. This rejection fostered concern over whether major constitutional reform could be achieved via a constitutional convention. It did not, however, dampen the desire for constitutional reform; some of the proposals set forth in the rejected 1967 Constitution have found their way into the state's public law.

For example, discrimination on the basis of sex, age, or handicap has been made illegal. Open records legislation has been adopted, and a stronger consumer protection agency was a major priority of the administration of Democratic Governor Hugh L. Carey.[67] In 1969 the voters also approved a constitutional amendment establishing a conservation bill of rights; in 1971 the Twenty-Sixth Amendment to the United States Constitution reduced the minimum voting age to eighteen for all elections; and in 1977 the voters approved a constitutional amendment providing for the appointment of members of the Court of Appeals and specifying methods and procedures for disciplining judges. The state now finances the entire court system.

Apart from the matters noted above, the changes proposed by the rejected 1967 Constitution languish neglected. Little change has occurred in the crucial areas of state and local finance, despite the existence in the 1967 document of detailed proposed solutions to recurring problems. This is in sharp contrast to the aftermath of the rejected 1915 Constitution. In that case strong leadership on the part of Governor Alfred Smith, Belle Moskowitz, and Robert Moses resulted in the successful adoption of the major structural proposals made at the 1915 convention. No such leadership was forthcoming in the post-1967 period. No constitutional convention in New York's history was more responsive to the needs of the cities, but its bold initiatives in the areas of welfare, education, and community development, among others, proved too much for the voters of New York.

NOTES

1. For a discussion of the activities of the civic groups, see Donna Shalala, *The City and the Constitution: The 1967 New York Convention's Response to the Urban Crisis* (New York: National Municipal League, 1972), pp. 10–12. Examples of newspaper endorsements include *The New York Times*, editorial, April 9, 1962, p. 28; *Buffalo Courier Express*, May 19, 1965; "Yes on Convention," *Buffalo Evening News*, April 27, 1965, pp. 22.

2. Press release, August 24, 1965, as quoted by Henrik Norman Dullea, "Charter Revision in the Empire State: The Politics of New York's 1967 Constitutional Convention," (Ph.D. diss., Syracuse University, 1982) p. 80.

3. 377 U.S. 633 (1964).

4. See the remarks of political columnist Victor Ostrowjoski, *Albany Times Union*, November 1, 1966, p. 2.

5. Leon S. Cohen, Elmer E. Cornwell, Jr., Jay S. Goodman, and Wayne R. Swanson, *The Politics of State Constitutional Reform: The New York Constitutional Convention 1967–1968* (unpublished manuscript, 1969), p. 1.

6. Less kindly, the press referred to them as "party hacks," *The New York Times*, November 3, 1966, p. 1.

7. There were two of these commissions: an Inter-Law School Committee created by the Temporary Commission in the spring of 1957, and a Special Legislative Committee on the Revision and Simplification of the Constitution, established in 1958. Two reports were issued by the first commission, established in 1956. These were entitled *Interim Report*, 1st–2nd (Albany, 1957). The commission in existence between 1958 and 1960 issued a series of thirty-five staff reports which provided detailed and skillful analysis of the constitution.

8. 388 U.S. 41 (1967).

9. 385 U.S. 493 (1967).

10. 385 U.S. 511 (1967).

11. State of New York, Constitutional Convention, 1967, *Documents*, Doc. No. 18.

12. Dullea, "Charter Revision," pp. 338, 148.

13. The pre-convention efforts of the C.E.F. are carefully examined in Irving H. Freedman, "The Issue of Public Support for Church-Related Education in the 1967 New York State Consitutional Convention: A Study in the Decision-Making Process" (Ed.D diss., State University of New York at Albany, 1969), pp. 72–88.

14. Dullea, "Charter Revision," p. 343.

15. *Board of Education v. Allen* 20 N.Y. 2d 109 (1967); aff'd 392 U.S. 236 (1968).

16. Leonard Levy has concluded that "In a real sense all members of the Court, including even the separationists, have favored accommodation of religion. . . ." *The Establishment Clause: Religion and the First Amendment*, 2nd rev. ed. (Chapel Hill: University of North Carolina Press, 1994), p. 159.

17. *Procceedings of the Constitutional Convention of the State of New York, 1967, Journal*, V, p. 317.

18. Ibid., V, p. 474.

19. *Record*, Pt. 3, IV, p. 722; Article X, Sections 12b, 18a.

20. *Record*, Pt. 1, II, p. 769.

21. E.g., *Lemon v. Kurtzman* 403 U.S. 602 (1971).

22. See Joseph Gusfield, *Symbolic Crusade: Status Politics and the Ameri-*

can *Temperance Movement* (Urbana: University of Illinois Press, 1963); Murray Edelman, *The Symbolic Use of Politics* (Urbana: University of Illinois Press, 1964).

23. *Journal*, V, pp. 477–478.

24. The decision to submit a single package resulted in Wilson's open opposition to the constitution even while Governor Rockefeller indicated that he would "personally" vote for the constitution. Thomas P. Ronan, "Lieut. Gov. Wilson Opposes Charter 'Scoring Package'," *The New York Times*, October 28, 1967, p. 1.

25. *Record*, Pt. 3, IV, p. 821; *Journal*, V, p. 592.

26. *New York Times v. Sullivan*, 376 U.S. 254 (1964).

27. *Documents*, Doc. No. 3.

28. *Documents*, Doc. No. 7.

29. The proposal for a unicameral legislature continues to attract supporters who offer cogent arguments for its consideration. See Gerald Benjamin, "Change the Rules, Change the Games," *Empire State Report* (October, 1991), pp. 37–38.

30. *Documents*, Doc. No. 6..

31. *Record*, Pt. 1, II, p. 679.

32. *Record*, Pt. 1, II, p. 685.

33. Dullea, "Charter Revision," p. 320.

34. *Journal*, V, p. 324.

35. *Documents*, Doc. No. 54, p. 2.

36. Fuller discussion of Lindsay's role and policies is found in Jewel Bellush, "Clusters of Power: Interest Groups," in Jewel Bellush and Dick Netzer, eds., *Urban Politics New York Style* (Armonk, N.Y.: M. E. Sharpe Inc., 1990), pp. 301–305.

37. The terms "traditional Home Rule advocates" and "neo-reformers" are used by Shalala in her careful study of the 1967 convention, cited above in Note 1. That study was based on her dissertation, more provocatively titled "While the Cities Burned: The 1967 New York State Constitutional Convention and the Urban Crisis (Ph.D. diss., Syracuse University, 1970).

38. *Record*, Pt. 2, III, pp. 572–574 (hereafter cited as *Proceedings*, 1967).

39. Henrik Norman Dullea, "Charter Revision," p. 418. Dullea's dissertation is by far the most comprehensive analysis of the 1967 convention and I have profited from it in writing this chapter.

40. Henrik Dullea, "Charter Revision," pp. 418–419. Dullea interviewed key participants involved in the fashioning of the compromise.

41. E.g., Advisory Commission on Intergovernmental Relations, Metropolitan America: Challenge to Federalism (Washington, D.C.: Advisory Commission, 1966); Robert Wood, *1400 Governments: The Political Economy of the New York Metropolitan Region* (Cambridge: Harvard University Press, 1961).

42. *Record*, Pt. 2, III, pp. 591–594.

43. *Record*, Pt. 2, III, p. 595.

44. *Record*, Pt. 2, III, p. 596.

45. As to the first, see Manhattan Delegate Hortense Gabel's remarks, *Record*, Pt. 2, 1967, III, p. 163. As to the second, see Shalala, *The City and the Constitution*, pp. 80–81.

46. *Journal*, pp. 385–386.

47. Jefferson B. Fordham, "Home Rule-AMA Model," *National Municipal Review* 44 (March, 1955), p. 142.

48. Shalala, *The City and the Constitution*, p. 54.
49. Ibid., p. 54.
50. *Journal*, p. 348; (vote) *Record*, Pt. 2, pp. 130–133.
51. Shalala, *The City and the Constitution*, p. 65.
52. *Record*, Pt. 2, 1967, III, pp. 553–556; the vote was 48 to 125, *Journal*, pp. 379–380.
53. See Shalala, *The City and the Constitution*, pp. 85–90, for a summary of these reports.
54. *Record*, Pt. 2, 1967, III, pp. 793–797.
55. *Record*, Pt. 2, 1967, III, pp. 805–806.
56. *Journal*, pp. 172–174.
57. *Record*, Pt. 3, 1967, IV, pp. 626–672; *Journal*, p. 569.
58. Dullea, "Charter Revision," p. 499. In Chapter VII, Dullea gives a full discussion of the line-up of supporters and opponents of the proposed constitution. See also the analysis of the League of Women Voters of New York State, *Seeds of Failure: A Political Review of New York State's 1967 Constitutional Convention* (New York: Shiver Mountain Press, 1973).
59. *The New York Times*, October 19, 1967, p. 66.
60. UPI, "New Charter Requires 80% State Tax Boost in Decade, Hurd Says," *Buffalo Evening News*, October 4, 1967, pp. 1, 6–7.
61. Dullea, "Charter Revision," p. 500.
62. Elmer E. Cornwell, Jr., Jay S. Goodman, and Wayne Swanson, *Constitutional Conventions: The Politics of Revision* (New York: National Municipal League, 1974), p. 60
63. "Interview with Robert S. Herman" in Gerald Benjamin and Robert Nakamura, *The Modern New York State Legislature: Redressing the Balance* (Albany: Nelson A. Rockefeller Institute, 1991), p. 233.
64. Cornwell, et al., *Constitutional Conventions*, p. 60.
65. James R. Dunne, "A Longitudinal Study of the Role Concepts of Delegates to the 1967 New York State Constitutional Convention" (Ph.D. diss., SUNY, Albany, 1972) pp. 257–258.
66. Dullea, "Charter Revision," concludes that "rock-bottom party loyalty from the voters [ironically, the basis for the major decisions at the convention] was all that his [Travia's] proposed constitution received on the most important vote of all" (p. 509). See also William S. Stevens, "Cost Not Politics, Seen Key to Defeat of New Constitution," *Schenectady Union Star*, November 9, 1967, p. 27.
67. Henrik N. Dullea, *The 1967 Constitutional Convention: Outcome and Impact* (Albany: Rockefeller Institute Special Report, Series No. 3, State University of New York, 1984), p. 15. In this report (p. 14), Dullea examines the subsequent fate of various proposals made at the convention, claiming that the incorporation of ideas in the 1967 draft has been "substantial."

PARTISAN AMONG CONVENTION DELEGATES
(in percentages)

	N.Y.	Ill.	Haw.	Ark.	N.Mex.	Md.
Parties will play strong/moderate role	83	84	32	33	24	31
Parties did play a strong/moderate role	90	82	26	22	11	16
Percentage point change	+7	−2	−6	−11	−13	−15

Taken from Elmer Cornwell, Jr., Jay S. Goodman, and Wayne R. Swanson, *Constitutional Conventions: The Politics of Revision* (New York: National Municipal League, 1974), p. 58.

15

Contemporary Constitutional Developments: 1968–1995

IN THE QUARTER CENTURY following the 1967 convention, 4,437 constitutional amendments were proposed, of which sixty-five amendments were passed by the legislature.[1] Forty-three (66%) were successful (see Table IV-A). Over half (24) derived from four articles: VI (judiciary), VII (state finance), VIII (local finance), and XIV (conservation). The most significant changes occurred in the judicial article. Eight amendments modified the selection process for judges on the Court of Appeals, established a centralized system of court administration, streamlined procedures for disciplining judges, and instituted a single state-wide court budget.

The overwhelming number of amendments to the state and local finance articles continued the process of liberalizing tax and debt limits and expanded the bonding power of public benefit corporations such as the Job Development Authority. Two amendments afforded nonprofit and religious organizations more latitude in operating games of chance. However, an equal rights amendment was defeated in 1975 by nearly half a million votes. Four of the six amendments to the conservation article involved land exchanges and authorization to construct a ski trail. Of greater import was a 1969 amendment making it the public policy of the state to conserve, improve, and protect natural resources and the quality of the environment.

ARTICLE I

Two of the three amendments to the Bill of Rights concerned gambling. A 1975 amendment broadened the range of games of chance that religious, charitible, and certain nonprofit organizations were permitted to operate, to include raffles, roulette, etc.[2] Provisions intended to prevent infiltration of organized crime remained unchanged (Sec. 9).

The second amendment gave the legislature authority to periodically adjust (upwards) the maximum prize allowance in church bingo and other games operated by these institutions. The amendment afforded them an opportunity to increase revenue, helped them meet the increasing competition from gambling dollars from Canada, Atlantic City, and Native American reservations, and obviated the need to amend the constitution each time inflation or other factors necessitated increases.[3] The contitutional ceiling had been set at $250 per prize, with a total limit of $1,000 per occasion. Inserting such limits into an article concerned with fundamental rights reflects the haphazard way in which the Bill of Rights was created in New York, as well as a lingering mistrust of the legislature, particularly on the issue of gambling. As a *New York Times* editorial noted: "Good housekeeping and a sense of what properly belongs in a constitution argue for this change."[4] The third change in Article I took place in 1973. Defendants charged with indictable offenses not punishable by death or life imprisonment were afforded the opportunity to waive indictment by a grand jury (Sec. 6). Prior to this amendment the prosecutor was required to seek a grand jury indictment in all felony prosecutions. The professed objective was to "speed disposition of serious cases and help to clear court calendars. . . ."[5] The change also made it possible for a substantial portion of defendants pleading guilty to expedite the process by waiving grand jury indictment.[6] This amendment is an explicit recognition of the extent to which the criminal justice system depends on plea bargaining rather than formal trial.

Article II

In 1995 voters approved a proposition which amended Sections 1, 5, 6, and 8 of Article II. These changes, essentially housekeeping in nature, will bring the state constitution in line with federal voting requirements. The amendment changes the voting age from twenty-one to eighteen, as required by the Twenty-Sixth Amendment; eliminates the literacy test for voting; and reduces the residency requirement to thirty days. In addition, it eliminates the personal registration requirement and the requirement for re-registration of voters who move within a county or within the City of New York.

Article III

Two amendments were adopted to the legislative article. A 1969 provosion altered the requirement in Section 5a with respect to the use of "citizens" as the population base when reapportioning legislative districts. At the turn of the century, when aliens were concentrated in New York City, using "citizens" as opposed to "persons" made a difference in the apportionment of senate and assembly seats. By 1969 the number of aliens in the state was so small relative to the total population that that differentiation was unnecessary. New York State relies on the federal dicennial census, which does not make a distinction between aliens and citizens for purposes of congressional apportionment. As a result, to comply with the citizen-base mandate of this section, New York was compelled to undergo a four-year delay until special census figures concerning aliens were available. In replacing "citizens" with "persons," this amendment reduced that time by half, and saved the state money as well.

In a rare example of a change in the power of the legislative body, a 1975 amendment to Section 18 allowed the legislature to call itself into special session by a two-thirds vote of members of both houses. Historically, special sessions, governed by Section 3 of Article IV, were convened solely by the governor; the legislature was limited to considering only those subjects recommended by the governor. This change gave the legislature more control over its own affairs and reduced what was perceived as undue control over the legislative branch by the executive. Its chief sponsor, Republican Perry Duryea, then speaker of the assembly, expected it to give the legislature recourse when the governor vetoed a bill following adjournment.[7] Furthermore, it would enable the legislature to take up issues it proposed in the petition, not just those specified by the governor. In practice, no extraordinary session has been called by the legislature. It has preferred to recess and reconvene, avoiding the necessity of a two-thirds vote and the restriction of acting only on the items listed in the petition.

Article IV

There was only one amendment to the executive article. It was necessitated by the change in Article III, Section 18, which granted the legislature power to initiate special sessions. The amendment simply made the language of Section 3 consistent with the change in the legislative article.

In the mid-eighties attempts were made to provide a constitutional procedure by which disability of a governor could to be determined. The terminal illness of Governor Ella Grasso of Connecticut and the illness of her successor, Governor O'Neill, precipitated this action. The national government had adopted a procedure in the Twenty-Fifth

Amendment (1967). A 1986 concurrent resolution, sponsored by Senator John R. Dunne and Assemblyman Saul Weprin, would have allowed the governor to declare incapacity or, in the absence of such a self-declaration, permit the lieutenant-governor and legislative leaders to make that determination. If the governor insisted that no disability existed, the issue would go to the Court of Appeals.[8] The resolution failed second passage and was never submitted to the voters. New York currently has no constitutional procedure in cases of executive disability.

The Law Revision Commission also recommended deletion of the phrase "absent from the state" in Section 5. The meaning of the phrase has never been determined. A few courts in other states have interpreted it to mean the physical non-presence of the governor within the state boundaries; others construed it to mean presence outside the state to an extent which affects the ability to govern. Twenty-seven states have a similar interim executive clause, and in some of those states the clause has created problems. In the 1970s California experienced running battles between Democratic Governor Jerry Brown and Lieutenant-Governor Mike Curb. Whenever Governor Brown left the state, Curb vetoed bills and filled vacancies. The same problem plagued Kentucky in the late 1970s. Although New York has yet to experience similar conflicts, the operative word is "yet."[9] Whatever the interpretation, the existence of instant communication and rapid transportation has rendered the original reason for the clause obsolete.[10] No action was taken on this recommendation and the phrase remains in the constitution.

Article V

An amendment to the Officers and Civil Departments article effected a changed in Section 6 concerning veterans preference on civil service examinations. Under that provision, a veteran who was a non-resident at the time of entry into the armed services was not eligible for the veteran's preference. The 1987 amendment entitled such persons to the preference. Sponsors argued that a citizen who had served in the armed services, even if not a resident at the time of entrance into the service, deserves the same benefits and privileges as residents.[11]

Article VI

The judiciary article was subject to extensive change during this period, despite the fact that it underwent complete revision in 1961. Although that revision declared the state's courts a "unified court system," they were anything but. The reorganization established a broad array of discrete courts, distributed administrative authority among the four regional appellate courts, and provided for separate personnel and budget systems, but failed to provide centralized rule-making authority for court procedures. Indeed, the history of court reform in New York since 1961 can be viewed "as an effort to correct the constitutional fiction that the state has a unified court system."[12] The rejection of the 1967 convention's recommendations spurred new efforts at court reform. Governor Rockefeller supported a proposal from The League of Women Voters for a fresh review of court reform. He established a temporary study commission chaired by Republican Senator D. Clinton Dominick, thus known as the Dominick Commission. The commission issued a three-volume report in 1973 containing 180 recommendations, including: central court administration, state financing of all but city and town courts, court merger, discipline of judges by a state commission on judicial conduct and a permanent Court on the Judiciary, and establishment of a district court system in larger counties to replace village, city, and town courts. Governor Rockefeller not only supported the recommendations but also called for gubernatorial selection of judges of the Court of Appeals and Supreme Court, and for screening panels and senate confirmation. The legislature, immersed in a major revision of the state's drug laws, took no action on these proposals, setting up instead another joint legislative committee to study the issues. One minor amendment to the judiciary article in 1973 granted Family Court jurisdiction over the custody of minors in habeas corpus proceedings (Sec. 13). Such jurisdiction would bring an additional resource to Family Court in settling family matters.[13]

While the legislature was deliberating, two events occurred which were to alter the course of court reform in New York. The first involved a change in New York's election law, allowing primary election challenges in judicial elections. For over a century, judges of the Court of Appeals had been selected in state-wide elections. When vacancies occurred they were filled by Republican and Democratic leaders on a bipartisan basis.[14] The change in the election law allowed a high-court candidate to secure party nomination outside the convention process. The result was a series of "election spectaculars for seats on the Court of Appeals."[15]

With the retirement of Chief Judge Stanley Fuld in 1973, Republican Charles Brietel, a former procecutor and respected legal scholar with twelve years as an associate judge, would be, by tradition, the nominee of both parties. However, he obtained only the Republican endorsement. Jacob Fuchsberg, a successful Manhattan trial attorney, won the Democratic primary. Brietel won the bitterly contested election, straining relations with Fuchsberg, who took his seat as an associate judge. In 1974 the Court's sole African-American judge, Democrat Harold Stevens, formerly presiding judge of the Appellate Division of Manhattan, was defeated by his primary opponent. The defeat of Judge Stevens—apparently for no reason but money and partisan politics—convinced Brietel that he should use his position as chief judge to eliminate partisan electioneering for high-court positions.[16]

A Joint Legislative Committee on Court Reorganization was established as a successor to the Dominick Commission. That committee made four major recommendations: appointment of high-court judges by the governor with senate confirmation, restructuring of judicial discipline machinery, state financing of courts, and centralized court management by a chief administrator of the courts appointed by the chief judge, subject to senate approval.

Not content to wait for action from the other branches, Judge Brietel instituted procedures to centralize management of the judiciary. He appointed a state administration, and persuaded the four appellate divisions to delegate management authority over the trial courts to that administration. These two actions centralized the management of the state's court system and effectively created an administrative merger of the New York City trial courts. He followed this bold administrative action with an unprecedented address to the legislature in which he called for reforms similar to those made by the Legislative Committee, adding one proposal conspicuously absent from the list of recommendations: merit selection of judges. In 1974 Brietel's crusade to reconstruct the judiciary of New York received support from gubernatorial candidate Hugh Carey, who assigned court reform a high priority. His election in 1975, along with the Joint Legislative Committee's support for court reform, resulted in the submission of two constitutional amendments that same year. One of these, proposing central court administration and first instance state financing of courts, was defeated by the slim margin of 18,448 votes. Voter concern regarding the costs of such changes most likely played a decisive role in its defeat. The second, proposing a restructuring of the procedure for judicial discipline, was approved. It reconstituted the Court on the Judiciary (Sec. 22) and added a new section (Sec. 36c).

Prior to amendments adopted in 1975 and 1977, judges in New York could be removed from office by one or more of five different procedures. Three primarily involved the legislature, i.e., impeachment (Sec. 24), concurrent resolution of both houses (Sec. 23a), and vote of the senate upon the recommendation of the governor (Sec. 23b). The impeachment provision, unlike the other two, applied to all public officials. Additionally, there were two methods of removal by judicial proceeding: judges of the Court of Appeals, Supreme Court, and Family Court could be removed by the Court on the Judiciary for cause, or they could be retired for any "mental or physical disability" preventing performance of duties. The Court on the Judiciary was established by constitutional amendment in 1948 (Sec. 22). It was composed of the chief judge and senior associate judge of the Court of Appeals and one judge from each of the four appellate courts. The court could be convened only by the chief judge on his own motion or at the request of the governor, the presiding judge of an appellate division, or the executive committee of the state bar association. Upon convening the court, the chief judge was required to notify the governor and the legislature. The legislature could then initiate its own removal proceedings. Between 1948 and 1973 this court was convened only five times.[17] The history of the use—or, more precisely, non-use—of these measures suggests that they were a "shadowy threat" rather than an effective sanction for disciplining judges.[18] The report concluded that incidents of judicial misconduct appeared to be increasing; more importantly, reports of serious misconduct created the perception that such conduct was not properly sanctioned. To remove this perception the committee recommended "substantial revision of existing measures of dealing with complaints of judicial misbehavior. . . ."[19]

The growing dissatisfaction with the disparate system of judicial discipline in general and with the Court on the Judiciary in particular led to the adoption of a 1975 amendment. Various criticisms were directed at the Court on the Judiciary: convening it was cumbersome; when it did convene it addressed major cases but lesser grievances went unnoticed; and it served as investigator, prosecutor, judge, and jury, thus violating traditional notions of fairness.[20] Responding to this dissatisfaction the legislature in 1974 created a Temporary State Commission on Judicial Conduct, which began operations in January 1975.[21] The 1975 amendment created a Commission on Judicial Conduct, consisting of nine members. Three were appointed by the governor, only one of whom could be a lawyer and none of whom could be a judge. The four leaders of the assembly and senate each made one appointment; none of these appointees could be a judge or retired judge. Two appointments, made by the Chief Judge, were to be judges, one from the appellate division of the Supreme Court and the other from a court of record other than the court of appeals. The composition was designed to ensure competence, as well as independence from the three branches of the government. This commission was to receive and investigate complaints from any source concerning qualifications, conduct, or fitness of any judge or justice within the unified court system and was authorized to make an intitial determination whether action of some type be taken against a judge. That determination would be transmitted to the chief judge of the state, who would then notify the judge under investigation; the latter may request a convening of the Court on the Judiciary to consider the charges. That court's proceeding would be conducted by the counsel and staff of the Commission on Judicial Conduct. The governor and legislature at that time would be notified, and they would have the option of undertaking their own removal proceedings in lieu of action by the Court on the Judiciary. The commission was to be a catalyst for convening the Court on the Judiciary. The amendment eliminated the authority of the New York State Bar Association to recommend convening the court. Since that association was not a governmentally created organization with delegated public authority, it seemed inappropriate for it to exercise such power.[22] The amendment also prohibited a judge charged with a felony from exercising the power of office.

Governor Carey, dissatisfied with the 1975 changes and determined to place the issue of court reform before the voters, called the legislature into extraordinary session, limiting that session to consideration of proposals addressing judicial reform. Specifically, the governor proposed adoption of a merit system for selecting members of the court of appeals, establishment of a Commission on Judicial Conduct, and creation of a constitutional office of chief administrator of the courts. The other major aspect of court reform—unification of the court system's budget—would be achieved by statute. The extraordinary session produced three constitutional amendments. These amendments received second passage in 1977 and were approved with comfortable margins by the voters in 1977.[23]

In the first of these amendments, judges of the Court of Appeals were designated appointive positions for the first time in the court's history. The unseemly spectacle of expensive, bitterly contested, partisan elections for seats on the highest court in the state had become a part of the state's history. The judges are currently appointed by the governor from candidates recommended by a Commission on Judicial Nomination, with nominations approved by the senate (Sec. 2d). The commission consists of twelve members serving four-year, staggered terms. Four members are appointed by the governor, four by the chief judge of the Court of Appeals, and one each by the two majority and two minority leaders of the legislature. No more than six may be of the same party, a minimum of four must be non-lawyers, and none can be an active judge. With this amendment the state adopted a version of the "Missouri Plan," so named because its basic principle, merit selection, was first adopted in that state. The elaborate selection process was crafted to ensure the judiciary's independence from any single branch of government, prevent partisanship, and inspire public confidence in its independence and impartiality. The second 1977 amendment created a new centralized system of court administration. The lack of effective court management had been the complaint of a variety of state commissions on court reform. The Temporary Commission on the New York State Court System had concluded:

> If New York is to achieve its long-sought goal of a truly unified court system, that system must be so structured as to allow for far more top-level administrative leadership than has been provided to date. . . . [no] one organization or group . . . [is] ultimately accountable for the functioning of the system as a whole.[24]

A chief administrator of the Courts (or chief adminstrative judge, if the appointee is a judge) would be appointed by the Chief Judge of the Court of Appeals with the advice and consent of an Administrative Board of the Courts (Sec. 28a).

The administrative Board of the Courts consists of the Chief Judge as chair, and the four presiding justices of the appellate division. Centralized administration of the courts would be achieved under the direction of the Chief Judge and the Chief Administrator. Statewide standards and policies governing operation of the courts, promulgated by the Chief Judge in consultation with the administrative board, were subject to approval by the Court of Appeals. Among the Chief administrator's numerous duties are the preparation of the judiciary budget, establishment of terms and parts of court, and the assignment of judges to them. The chief administrator has established the Office of Court Administration (OCA) to assist in the performance of these duties. The amendment achieved its intended results—so much so that some members of the bar, formerly supportive of centralized administration, have criticized the system on the grounds that it has destroyed the judiciary's independence. This criticism seems to confuse administrative functions with judicial functions. The amendment certainly reduced the former but there is little or no evidence that it has reduced the latter.[25]

The final amendment in 1977 streamlined the procedures adopted in 1975 for disciplining judges, and eliminated the Court on the Judiciary. The relationship between it and the Commission on Judicial Conduct proved awkward and the process ineffective. The Commission on Judicial Conduct, established in 1975, was replaced with a new commission possessing the power to monitor and discipline all judges. It consists of eleven members, four appointed by the governor, three by the Chief Judge of the Court of Appeals, and one each by the majority and minority leaders of the legislature. At least two must be non-lawyers, and three—the Chief Judge's appointees—must be judges. They are appointed to four-year, staggered terms. After investigation and a hearing the commission may admonish, censure, remove, or retire a judge. The Court of Appeals may review all decisions of the commission (Sec. 22). This procedure, whereby the same commission investigates, prosecutes, and judges, is open to criticism as contrary to our notion of due process. However, the legislature has fashioned implementing procedures which attempt to guard against this danger.[26] As a result of the 1977 amendment the commission's scope of authority was broadened and the procedures for disciplining judges within the unified court system were streamlined. All formal disciplinary hearings would now be conducted by the commission. The final change, accomplished by the Unified Budget Act of 1976, established state funding of all state, county, and city courts, beginning in 1977.[27] By 1980 the state had assumed the entire capital costs of the operation of all but town and village justice courts.

Taken together, the amendments centralizing court financing, court administration, and disciplinary proceedings did more to achieve a unified court system than the revisions of 1961.

In 1983 the voters approved an amendment to subdivision (f) of Section 26, authorizing the temporary assignment of Family Court judges to the Supreme Court. Under the unamended section, Family Court judges could be assigned to another family court, a county court, or, in New York City, to the criminal or civil courts, but not to the Supreme Court. Family court was once conceived as a specialized forum to give undivided attention to the problems of children and families in crisis; nevertheless, Family Court judges were called to serve temporarily on other courts. Since these judges met the same requirements as for appointment to the Supreme Court, there was no reason to exclude them from temporary service on the Supreme Court. It would add flexibility and fairness to the judicial assignment process, and enable the Supreme Court to take advantage of the valuable expertise judges on family court can provide.[28] In 1985 Sections 11, 15, and 16 were amended to increase the maximum monetary jurisdiction of the county court and the court of city-wide civil jurisdiction for the City of New York from $10,000 to $25,000 and the district court from $6,000 to $15,000. As 1962 was the last time the amount had been adjusted, inflationary pressures caused the amount to be unrealistically low. As a result, litigation had to be commenced in Supreme Court, increasing that court's caseload as well as expenses for the parties. Raising the monetary jurisdiction helped ensure a more efficient distribution of court caseloads and a speedier and less costly disposition of cases.²⁹ For the same reasons, these sections were amended again in 1995, increasing the monetary jurisdiction of both courts to $50,000.

The last amendment to the judiciary article, adopted in 1985, expanded the jurisdiction of the Court of Appeals. A procedure was adopted enabling that court to answer questions on New York Law certified to it by the United States Supreme Court, Federal Courts of Appeals, and appellate courts of last resort in other states (Sec. 3). Federal and state appellate courts are frequently called upon to determine and apply New York Law. When the issue before them has not been settled by New York Courts they had to guess as to the meaning of that law. This certification procedure would enable litigants to obtain a definitive answer before proceeding further, and would facilitate federal-state and state-state cooperation. This procedure had already been adopted by half the states.³⁰

Article VII

Three of the six amendments to this article involved the Job Development Authority, also discusssed in Article X. The remaining three made a minor adjustment to the budget process, expanded pension eligibility, and eased restrictions on the terms of state borrowing.

The Job Development Authority was established in 1961 by constitutional amendment as a bank with three objectives: to stimulate the expansion of businesses already in the state, to encourage companies to locate new plants within the state, and to encourage companies to maintain existing plants, rather than moving outside the state. The Authority was permitted to loan up to 30% of project expenses in connection with the construction, acquisition, or improvement of industrial or business facilities. In 1973 this provision was amended to increase this percentage to 40% (Sec. 8(3)). The change would lower financing costs to businesses assisted by the JDA, thus increasing the likelihood of their success. In 1977 an amendment to Article 7 permitted the enlargement of the class of business eligible to receive financial assistance and allowed loans for renovation as well as new structures. This amendment to Section 8 was necessitated by the prohibition on the loan of state money or credit to corporations, individuals, or associations. A 1985 amendment increased from 40% to 60% the amount per project which the JDA could finance. This change would lower financing costs to businesses assisted by the JDA and would reduce the amount of long-term loans required from banks and other conventional lenders.³¹ The final amendment to this article eased restrictions on the terms of state borrowing by providing flexibility in the scheduling of debt repayment. The state would be permitted to issue bonds that do not require annual interest payments to investors. The amendment authorizes, as an alternative, principle payment or contributions to a sinking fund in installments that result in substantially level or declining debt-service payments. The amendment also expanded the existing provisions regarding the refunding of state debt by specifying when refunding bonds may be issued by the state and what restrictions must be observed.[32] The amendment will permit borrowing for several projects with one bond issue rather than requiring separate issues. The state could then refinance earlier debt without getting new voter approval as long as savings would be obtained by the action.

Article VIII

The local finance article was subject to six amendments between 1967 and 1994. Three were extensions of the ten-year period for exclusion from the debt limits of indebtedness contracted for sewer purposes; two eased tax and debt restrictions for school districts, and one gave local governments more flexibility in choosing debt repayment schemes. In every case the amendments added to the exceptions to the tax and debt restrictions in the article or eased the limitations found therein.

A 1963 change, commencing retroactively on January 1, 1962, permitted municipalities to exclude indebtedness from constitutional debt limits for debt contracted for sewer construction or reconstruction for an eleven-year period (Sec. 5). In 1973 another amendment extended that exclusion another ten years.[33] In 1983 and again in 1993 similar extensions were approved. The state began a major effort to prevent pollution of its water resources with passage of the Water Pollution Control Act of 1949.[34] Among the factors discovered by a Special Committee on Pollution Abatement preventing effective local response to this problem was the inability of some municipalities to "finance construction of needed facilities within the debt margin available to them under present constitutional limits."[35] This amendment eliminated one dimension of the problem. However, faced with other pressing needs such as schools, municipalities were not anxious to make large capital expenditures for treatment facilities, particularly when they could literally dump the problem downstream.[36] Approval of the Pure Waters Bonds by the voters in 1965 provided the necessary funds to encourage local governments to undertake new treatment projects. The current extension will expire in 2004.[37] This third renewal illustrates the ad hoc character of much local debt policy and the accumulations of exemptions which threaten to engulf the general prohibition. The constant need to resort to exemptions also suggests that debt limitations on local governments are too severe and stand in need of more systematic revision.

Two amendments in 1985 addressed school district financing. The first enabled municipalities and school districts to issue sinking fund bonds to be repaid from sinking funds financed by the issuer for any purpose for which serial bonds could be currently sold. The authorization gave municipalities more flexibility in bond markets. New York City was the chief beneficiary of this amendment because an inability to satisfy investor demand for non-serial bonds meant payment of higher interest rates to increase the marketability of serial bonds with less desirable maturities.[38] The second amendment repealed Subdivision (e) of Section 10. The deletion eliminated the constitutional tax limitation on the amount to be raised by real property taxes for school districts located in cities with a population of less than 125,000. School districts in those areas had limits ranging from 1.25% to 2%. The proximate cause of this amendment, *Hurd v. City of Buffalo*,[39] invalidated the practice of many city school districts of treating pensions and social security costs as capital expenses instead of operating expenses, thus avoiding the existing constitutional tax limitations. Constitutional tax limits do not apply to tax levies for debt service or, in localities other than New York City, to expenditures for capital outlays. However, in both cases the legislature must establish a "period of probable usefulness" of the particular object or purpose. Several taxpayer suits challenged this establishment of a period of probable usefulness for what appeared to be current expense items. The statute in *Hurd* established a three-year period of probable usefulness for the cost of pensions and retirement liabilities in the cities of Buffalo, Rochester, and Yonkers. Similar provisions had been applied to the sixty-five small city school districts. The state adopted provisional measures to forestall the immediate impact.

A Temporary State Commission on Constitutional Tax Limitations was formed in 1974. It recommended passage of a constitutional amendment authorizing exclusion of retirement and social security contributions in the computation of constitutional tax limits.[40] This amendment was defeated by over 600,000 votes in 1975. The following year the legislature passed an Emergency City and School District Relief Act, continuing temporary relief to cities and school districts by permitting them to exclude from constitutional tax limitations certain pensions and social security contributions until 1980.[41] In 1978 the court struck down this Emergency Relief Act.[42] A Special Task Force on the Financing of School Districts was created and the legislature adopted its recommendations. Special equalization ratios were instituted for districts and cities hardest hit, and state aid was advanced to finance the "short fall" on a revolving basis. The special equalization did reduce the gap initially from $112 million to $20 million.[43] However, the usefulness of these ratios diminished as the growth of cities' real property wealth slowed. The task force also recommended constitutional amendments. By removing the existing constitutional restriction on the ability of fiscally independent city school districts to raise property taxes, the 1985 amendment would reduce city school district reliance on the emergency state aid.[44]

The last two amendments, approved in 1993, eased restrictions on local borrowing. Section 2 of this article was amended to provide municipalities with greater flexibility in how they pay off debt. This flexibility would enable them to work out the most favorable borrowing terms in a diverse and constantly changing market. The existing requirements operated to produce higher payments by the governments in the early years of a bond's life. This amendment would allow local governments the option of scheduling level annual payments of combined principal and interest. These level payments would assist local budget-makers in their yearly efforts to match spending with revenues. Furthermore, the amendment permits local governments to avoid requirements of annual interest payments if such avoidance would enable them to make a better deal in the money market. Zero-coupon bonds would be possible under this amendment.[45] Municipalities were required to set aside, annually, funds to meet the eventual payments. The provision is an attempt to prevent local governments from postponing payments for future budgets. The amendment did not authorize additional borrowing; it simply allowed greater flexibility in the exercise of currently authorized borrowing power.

Article X

Five of the six amendments to the Corporations article concerned the Job Development Authority. The sixth altered the ownership structure of savings and loan associations.

The Job Development Authority was created by constitutional amendment in 1961 to stimulate business expansion, thus securing and creating new jobs and fostering a favorable climate in the state for business and industry. It was originally permitted to issue $50 million in state-guaranteed bonds to finance the loan program. Following voter rejection of two attempts in 1966 and 1967 to increase that amount, an increase to $150 million was approved in 1969 (Sec. 7, renum. Sec. 8).

Supporters claimed the authority had been effective but had reached its limit of $50 million, and the market was unfavorable to non-guaranteed bonds.[46] For similar reasons a 1981 amendment increased the amount to $300 million, and in 1985 the amount was doubled again to $600 million. In addition, a companion amendment to Article 7, Section 8 increased from 40% to 60% the limitation on the amount of project cost per project which the JDA could finance. No direct expenses to the state were incurred, as the JDA had been self-supporting since 1967, but the state's obligations increased by virtue of the guarantee of the Authority's bonds. In 1991 the maximum amount the legislature may make the state the guarantor of bond issues by the authority was increased to $900 million.

The only amendment not pertaining to the JDA was passed in 1983. A 1874 amendment had prohibited savings and loan associations from possessing capital stock, and trustees were forbidden from sharing in any profits. These associations were looked upon as benevolent institutions, serving the less well-off of the community, and thus any profit-taking was viewed as unseemly. By the 1980s, however, these associations were in financial trouble, having suffered heavy losses which drained their capital (net worth). Private capital necessary to replenish these losses was unavailable because of these prohibitions. To insure viability of the state's thrift industry, this amendment removed the restraint.[47]

Article XIII

Four amendments to the Public Officers article were approved during this period. Three involved alterations to Section 13. The first adjusted the terms of office for district attorneys. The district attorney is a constitutional office: Section 13 specifies it as an elective position with a term of three years. A 1972 amendment provided the option of a three- or four-year term "as the legislature shall direct." The intention was to increase stability in the office and reduce the time and money spent in campaigning. A comparable amendment in 1984 provided the same option for the office of sheriff, for similar reasons. Electing sheriffs every four years would permit voting for these offices to coincide with other local and state elections, when they were likely to receive more attention. An amendment in 1989 removed a clause prohibiting counties from ever assuming responsibility for the actions of the sheriff. This amendment rendered obsolete the provision requiring sheriffs to insure themselves, as counties now have assumed liability for their official actions. Sheriffs were the only public officials personally liable for damages when someone felt aggrieved by their official actions and those of their subordinates. The liability dates back to a period when sheriffs were not paid officials and were, in effect, private entrepreneurs compensated from the fees they collected. That situation ceased in 1934 when sheriffs became salaried employees. This amendment eliminated an obsolete vestige of the earlier system.

An amendment to Section 3, adopted in 1977, was prompted by *Roher v. Dinkins*.[48] Roher held that a part of the education law that allows school board vacancies to be filled for the unexpired terms violated the clause mandating that appointees may hold office for no longer than the commencement of the political year following the first annual election held after the occurrence of a vacancy. In response to this decision, this section was amended in 1977. Its sponsor gave as justification that "political year" as it appears in this section was never intended to apply to the state school system.[49]

Article XIV

Seven amendments were adopted to the conservation article. Four involved land exchanges; two concerned land use outside the Forest Preserve and construction of ski trails, and one considerably expanded the scope and character of the state's conservation policy.

The 1969 amendment renumbered Section 4 as Section 5 and created a new Section 4. That section declares it the public policy of the state to conserve, improve, and protect its natural resources and the quality of the environment. The amendment is identical to the one proposed at the abortive 1967 convention.[50] As that proposal had received unanimous praise at the convention, its immediate adoption is not suprising. It is referred to as the "Conservation Bill of Rights." Sponsors had the ambitious goal of making scenic beauty, unlittered land, clean waters, and unpolluted air as the inalienable rights of each New Yorker.[51] The amendment creates a state nature and historical preserve to protect the heritage of the state beyond the forest preserve. By choosing the adjective "scenic" rather than "natural," the amendment likely includes buildings within its scope. Its range is not limited to large wilderness areas: it includes natural areas or historical sites near metropolitan areas where the need may be greatest. The criteria for preservation are scenic beauty, wilderness character, and geological, ecological, or historic significance. Protection of the kind envisaged by this section was previsously provided, at least in part, by statute. The broad policy goals of the section were implemented by statutes in the 1970s.[52] This amendment constitutionalized these policy goals and provided an all-inclusive preservation policy, including, as it does, wetlands and agricultural lands.

In 1973 voters approved an increase in the size of parcels of land beyond the Adirondack and Catskill Parks (Sec. 3). The term "dedicated parcels" is used to describe those scattered, isolated tracts of forest preserve located in forest preserve counties but lie outside the boundaries of the Adirondack and Catskill Parks. These patches of land are of little value to the state and are a burden financially and administratively. Some are completely inaccessible. A 1957 amendment permitted the state to rededicate or dispose of all such detached parcels under ten acres in size. Although this amendment effectively disposed of 266 parcels, 152 parcels exceeding the ten-acre limit remained.

Three of the amendments involved land exchanges. The first, adopted in 1979, allowed the state to relinquish 8,500 acres beyond the forest preserve to the International Paper Company in exchange for land within the preserve, to simplify land management problems. However, the Sierra Club opposed the exchange, arguing that the state should purchase the land from the company outright. The club feared the exchange would undermine the constitutional guarantee of the preserve's wildness.[54] A 1983 amendment approved an exchange of ten acres of land adjacent to the Sagamore Institute, including buildings within the Sagamore camp complex, for nearly 200 acres of wilderness land of at least equal value within the Adirondack Preserve. If the state took possession of the land it would be required to allow the land to revert to its natural condition. To prevent this, the state sold the land to a private organization now known as the Sagamore Institute. In effecting the exchange the boundaries were drawn so as to preserve ten acres under state control. This amendment permitted the rejoining of the camp complex and allowed maintainence of the buildings on the site.[55] An exchange in 1991 authorized the state to transfer fifty acres of forest preserve land to the Town of Arietta, Hamilton County, in exchange for fifty-three acres of preserve land owned by the town. The Piseco Airport, owned by the town of Arietta, needed land adjacent to the airport to satisfy safety requirements mandated by the Federal Aviation Administration. The land was not expected to be used for commercial purposes. The amendment is permissive only; it does not mandate the exchange, but permits it upon approval of all parties. The last exchange authorized the state to transfer twelve acres of the town of Keene for public use as a cemetery in exchange for 144 acres of land, and an easement over town land in order to restrict further development.[56] An amendment, approved in 1987, permitted three state-owned and operated ski centers to ensure safer skiing and modernization of the trails. The amendment permitted increasing the length and width of ski trails. A constitutional provision specifying the number of miles and width of these trails, previously adopted in 1947, was obsolete in terms of safety, enjoyment, and maintenance.[57]

Article XV: Canals

The sole amendment to the canal article was approved in 1991 and completed the transformation of the canal system from a major economic development of the state to a tourist attraction and recreational facility. Section 1 allowed canal acreage to be used under thirty-day revocable permits. Such limited time periods would not allow for the establishment of commercial enterprises consistent with tourism and recreation. By resorting to long-term leases, the state would maintain control over the rate and nature of development along the canal while promoting tourism. The provision in Section 2 requiring canal revenues to be paid into the general fund was deleted. The section was revised and transfered to Section 3. It created a special fund into which canal revenues shall be deposited. That fund would be used for the maintenance, construction, development, or promotion of the canal and canal lands. The prohibition on toll charges for canal users, approved in 1882, was eliminated so that user fees could be charged for the canal locks. This amendment signalled the state's intention to embark on a multi-million dollar rehabilitation of the canal system for tourism and cultural activities.[58] The 1991 amendment represents a change in policy and attitude from that expresssed in the 1959 amendment which viewed the canal as a financial burden better off as part of the national system of inland waterways. As the 1959 authorization remains in the article, transfer of the canal to the federal government is a possibility, but it is likely that the state will enter the twenty-first century with the canal system in tow.

Article XVI

The taxation article was amended only once since adoption at the 1938 convention. That amendment, adopted in 1983 and known as the Local Development Amendment, was designed to convert economically unproductive, blighted, or deteriorated areas into prosperous, revenue-generating parts of the community. Its provisions permit counties, cities, towns, and villages to employ a technique known as tax increment financing to finance revitalization. A local redevelopment agency is formed to issue bonds to finance projects such as slum clearance, with the bonds repaid from the tax revenues generated from the increased value of the improved area. The amendment was necessary as municipalities were not permitted to contract indebtedness without the pledge of their full faith and credit (Art. VIII, Sec. 2), to incur debt without restriction as to amounts or repayment installments (Art. 4), or to exclude the debt incurred from the municipality's constitutional debt limit.[59]

Article XVII: Social Welfare

The Social Welfare Article was the subject of two amendments since its incorporation in 1938. The first deleted the provision that the head of the Department of Corrections (currently named the Department of Correctional Services) shall be the chairman of the State Commission of Corrections. The chair of the commission, constitutionally authorized to oversee the operation of state prisons and detention centers, was also responsible for the operation of that system. This amendment thus removed an obvious conflict of interest. The separation of personnel, along with the decision to transfer the commission to the executive branch, provided an independence commensurate with its constitutional functions.

The other amendment was in response to acute shortages in hospital and health care facilities during the 1960s. These institutions were facing a major crisis due to the deterioration and obsolescence of their physical plants. Since many of the hospitals were voluntary not-for-profit or limited-profit private enterprises, state financial assistance would contravene Article VII, Section 8, prohibiting the state from giving or loaning its money or credit to any private association, corporation, or undertaking. This amendment removed any uncertainities created by Section 8, thus enabling hospitals and health care facilities to qualify for low-interest loans.[60]

The Call for Reform

In 1991 Governor Mario Cuomo called for a constitutional convention prior to 1997, when the convening of a convention would be required by the every-twenty-years clause of Article XIX. In a Special Message to the Legislature in 1993 he reiterated that call, asserting that a constitutional convention was the only way to overcome the legislative deadlock over issues such as state voter registration laws, campaign finance reform, and the judicial selection process. Other issues mentioned included the death penalty, casino gambling, and term limits. On previous occasions the governor noted the problems of "backdoor financing" and the need to reassess the debt limits on state and local governments. The governor appointed a Temporary State Commission on Constitutional Revision with Peter Goldmark, president of the Rockefeller Foundation, as its chair. This commission was assigned the task of helping New Yorkers use the time leading up to 1997 to inform themselves, define the basic issues, and frame the debate over whether the state is in need of constitutional change.[61] There is no dearth of issues. In addition to those mentioned, the following have been advocated by various groups or political leaders: court consolidation, a unicameral legislature, initiative and referendum, term limits, placing legislative apportionment under control of a nonpartisan body, super majorities for approval of tax increases, recall of elected officials, consolidation of counties and other local governments, a constitutional right to education, constitutional spending caps, requiring a balanced budget, constitutionalizing use of Generally Accepted Accounting Practices (GAAP), requiring reimbursement from the state to localities for expenses mandated by the legislature, and requiring voter approval for moral obligation debt.[62] There are also issues concerning the convention process itself. Should delegates be elected on a nonpartisan basis? Is the current selection method using senate districts as multimember districts combined with at-large elections a violation of the Voting Rights act of 1965? Should there be limited or weighted voting to ensure the process results in a more diverse convention? Should public officials be barred from serving as delegates?[63] Should amending the constitution by legislative initiative be simplified?[64]

The volatile nature of many of these issues, as well as a perception that voters are angry enough to support "radical" proposals, has caused apprehension among a large part of the liberal community over the prospect of holding a convention. Abortion, the death penalty, populist measures such as recall, referendum, initiative, and term limitations, are likely to be raised at any convention held in the next decade. The state's fiscal practices have generated significant support for more stringent budget requirements and caps on expenditures. Liberal Democrats worry about the impact of such restrictions on social welfare programs. Conservatives and various taxpayer groups, however, generally support the call for a convention, believing that fiscal reform is imperative and that the electorate is likely to support such reform. The reversal of positions between 1967 and 1997 over the desirability of holding a convention speaks volumes about both the transformation of New York politics in the past thirty years and the anxious mood of the electorate.[65]

There is general agreement that some reform is needed, though there is dispute as to the direction of that reform and whether a convention is the best way to achieve it. Arguments in favor of a convention include the following: a convention would be able to clear the document of obsolete clauses, simplify its language, and, where applicable, align the document with the mandates of the Supreme Court. A convention would allow a more rational and systematic integration of the 136 amendments adopted since 1938. It would provide the people the opportunity to decide the direction they wish to move concerning the major issues facing the state as it enters the new century. It would give citizens the opportunity to debate and decide issues such as reapportionment, campaign financing, and voter registration reform—issues that the legislature has failed to address.

Arguments against holding a convention include the possibility of controversial and potentially dangerous proposals being placed before an electorate in the mood to entertain such measures.[66] With important and controversial issues to be decided, the convention could propose a constitution whose provisions address those issues, only to have the electorate reject its work, as it did in 1967. The expense of a convention, running into the millions of dollars, is too high, especially in light of that possibility. Submitting the most controversial proposals as separate amendments, as did the 1938 convention, and initiating a well organized active campaign behind the convention's work would lessen the likelihood of a repeat of the 1967 experience. But a constitutional conventional is a risky and unpredictable venture under any conditions. Moreover, alternatives exist for achieving needed reform.

If the experience of the past half century in New York is any guide, then the future of state constitutional conventions is problematic. Voters appear unwilling to approve convening them and/or are unwilling to ratify their efforts. It is likely that the process of piecemeal amendment which has characterized the state's constitutional activity over the past fifty-five years will continue. As an alternative between the incremental change associated with legislatively generated amendments and a convention, the state could employ the constitutional commission to provide intelligent guidance and information on the issues as well as the arguments over whether a convention should be convened. The materials gathered by commissions before the 1915 and 1938 conventions and the work of a series of commissions between 1956 and 1965 had a direct and palpable effect on constitutional change in the state.

In 1993 Governor Mario Cuomo appointed a Temporary New York State Commission on Constitutional Revision without the approval or financial support of the legislature. Cuomo hoped, in vain, for an early legislative call for a convention prior to the every-twenty-year requirement date of 1997. This commission has been charged with examining the process of constitutional change as well as the substantive issues to be considered at a possible convention in 1999. By early 1995 the Temporary Commission held hearings throughout the state, issuing a briefing book, an interim report, and a periodic newsletter (*Constitutional Matters*). It is the most extensive attempt thus far in the state's history to provide for and stimulate public debate on the question of constitutional reform. Unlike previous commissions which focused primarily on providing information for delegates at the convention, the Cuomo Commission directed its efforts as much at educating the public as at providing background for delegates at any future conventions. What impact this approach will have remains to be seen, but if voters in 1997 reject the call for a convention, they will do so on a more informed and rational basis than they did in 1977.

A second option is to appoint a constitutional commission similar to the ones appointed in 1890 and 1920. Its creation would require legislative action and approval of all recommendations, but a prestigious commission, reporting well thought-out proposals for which a consensus has been achieved, would make it difficult for the legislature to ignore its recommendations, and would improve measurably the chances of success with the electorate.[67]

NOTES

1. For a statistical analysis of amendment activity between 1967 and 1993 see Gerald Benjamin and Melissa Cusa, "Amending the New York State Constitution Through the Legislature," in Gerald Benjamin, ed., *The New York State Constitution: A Briefing Book* (Albany: Nelson A. Rockefeller Institute of Government, 1994).
2. Unpublished memorandum of Senator Rolison, S. 2509, as reprinted in Robert Allen Carter, *The New York Constitution: Sources of Legislative Intent* (Littleton, Co.: Fred B. Rothman & Co., 1988), p. 10.
3. Unpublished memorandum of Senator Saul Weprin, S. 21002, as reprinted in Carter, *New York Constitution*, p. 10.
4. "Editorial," *The New York Times*, November 2, 1984, p. A26.
5. *Public Papers of Nelson Rockefeller, 1971* (Albany, n.d.), p. 1152.
6. Governor's Memorandum, "Grand Jury Indictment, Waiver," *Legislative Annual*, 1973, p. 6.
7. See his remarks in "Duryea Bids Legislature Have Power to Call Special Session," *The New York Times*, March 17, 1974, p. 5; and the remarks of Democratic Assemblyman Alan Hevesi,"Legislature Aims For Wider power," *The New York Times*, April 25, 1974, p. 45.
8. *Memorandum in Support, 1986*, No. 3619, microfiche, New York State

Library; and *Memorandum of Law Revision Commission Relating to Gubernatorial Inability and Succession, Absence from the State and Filling Vacancies in the Office of Lieutenant Governor*, No. 8365, microfiche, New York State Library.

9. G. Scott Thomas, "Vacancy in Office No. 2," *Empire State Report* (April, 1986), p. 34.

10. *Memorandum of Law Revision Commission*, No. 8365.

11. *Memorandum in Support*, Assembly No. 3621, microfiche, New York State Library.

12. Frederick Miller, "New York State's Judiciary Article: A Work in Progress," in *Effective Government, New For the New Century: A Report to the People, the Governor and the Legislators of New York* (Albany: The Final Report of the Temporary New York State Commission on Constitutional Revision, February, 1995), p. 84.

13. *The 1958 Report of the Temporary Commission on the Courts*, Recommendations for the Reorganization of the Structure of the Courts of the State of New York and Their Administration. Leg. Doc. (1958) No. 36, pp. 12–13.

14. This bipartisanship was made possible because cross endorsements were permitted and party leaders controlled the conventions at which nominations were made.

15. Miller, "New York State's Judiciary Article," p. 90.

16. Ibid., p. 91.

17. . . . *And Justice for All*, Report to the Temporary Commission on the New York State Court System, Part I (Albany, January, 1973), p. 57.

18. *Report of the Joint Legislative Committee on Court Reorganization*, Leg. Doc. (1973) No. 24, pp. 14–15.

19. Ibid., p. 17.

20. Ibid., pp. 17–18.

21. *McKinney Session Laws*, 1974, chaps. 739–740.

22. *Report . . . on Court Reorganization*, p. 19.

23. A challenge to these amendments based on the method by which they were submitted to the voters was rejected by the Court of Appeals in *Frank v. New York*, 44 N.Y. 2d 687 (1978).

24. . . . *And Justice for All*, Pt. I, pp. 7–9.

25. On this point, see the remarks of Lawrence Cooke, former Chief Judge of the State of New York, "Structural Reforms of the Judicial System," in Colby, ed., *New York Today* (Albany: SUNY Press, 1985), pp. 167–168.

26. *McKinney's 1978 Session Laws of New York*, Chap. 156. The legislation requires that a judge being investigated has a right to counsel at all stages of the investigation, and that the commission must make available to the judge copies of all documents intended for presentation at such hearings and any written statements by witnesses who will be called to give testimony. The judge shall have the right to call and cross-examine witnesses and present evidentiary material. Records of the commission are confidential and are not made available to the public.

27. *Laws of New York*, 1949, Chap. 666.

28. *Memorandum in Support, 1983*, S. 990, microfiche, New York State Library.

29. Robert Connery and Gerald Benjamin, *Rockefeller of New York* (Ithaca: Cornell University Press), p. 334.

30. Memorandum of the Law Revision Commission to the 1984 Legislature,

"Relating to Certification of Questions of Law to the Court of Appeals," *McKinney's 1984 Session Laws of New York*, pp. 2976, 2982.

31. *Governor's Program Bill 1984 Memorandum*, No. 8808, microfiche, New York State Library.

32. Official Summary of the Amendment as provided by the State Board of Elections, July 30, 1993.

33. An amendment which would have accomplished the same thing with less explicit wording was narrowly defeated by the voters in 1971.

34. *Laws of New York*, 1949, Chap. 666.

35. Joint Legislative Committee on Interstate Cooperation, *Progress Report of the Special Committee on Pollution Abatement*, Leg. Doc. No. 59, 1948, p. 31.

36. Connery and Benjamin, *Rockefeller of New York*, p. 334.

37. The original ten-year exclusion was intended to enable local government to participate in the state's assistance program without the fear that by incurring indebtedness for sewer purposes their debt-incurring power would lessen for other important public improvements.

38. *Memorandum of Claudia Wagner, New York City Representative 1985*, No. 6219, microfiche, New York State Library.

39. 41 A.D. 2d 402 (1973), aff'd 34 N.Y. 2d 628 (1974).

40. *Final Report*, Albany, New York, February 15, 1975, p. 1.

41. *McKinney's 1976 Session Laws of New York*, Chap. 349.

42. *Bethlehem Steel Corporation v. Board of Education of City School District of Lackawanna*, 44 N.Y. 831 (1978), aff'd, 61 A.D. 2d 147 (1978).

43. *Local Government Handbook*, 4th ed. (Albany: Department of State, 1987), p. 188.

44. *Memorandum in Support 1983*, No. 1638, microfiche, New York State Library.

45. Zero-coupon bonds are bonds that do not pay interest. Their yield depends on reinvestment of coupons. To succeed, they must be heavily discounted.

46. Governor's Memorandum, "Job Development Authority Bonds," *Legislative Annual 1969*, p. 237.

47. *Memorandum in Support 1983*.

48. 40 A.D. 2d, 956, 1976; aff'd 32 N.Y. 2d, 180 (1973).

49. Memorandum of Assemblyman Robert Stavisky, as quoted by Carter, *New York State Constitution*, p. 163.

50. Proposed 1967 Constitution, Article VIII, Sec. 3.

51. *Proceedings . . . 1967 Constitutional Convention*, II, Record, Pt. 1, p. 939.

52. E.g., "Environmental Conservation Law," *Laws of New York*, Chap. 140 (1970); and the State Environmental Quality Review Act of 1975, which requires an environmental impact statement for any project having a "significant effect on the environment." *Environmental Conservation Law*, Sec. 8010912 (2) (McKinney, 1984).

53. *The Future of the Adirondack Park* (Albany: Temporary Study Commission on the Future of the Adirondacks, 1970), p. 49; Memorandum of Assemblyman Glenn H. Harris, "Disposition of Forest Preserve Lands," *Legislative Annual 1973*, p. 15.

54. Editorial, *The New York Times*, November 2, 1979, p. A30.

55. *Memorandum in Support, 1983*, A. 2903, microfiche, New York State Library.

56. *Memorandum in Support, 1990*, S. 8926, microfiche, New York State Library.

57. *Memorandum, Concurrent Resolution of the Senate and Assembly,* 1987, No. 8377, microfiche, New York State Library.

58. *Memorandum in Support, 1989*, S. 5706, microfiche, New York State Library.

59. *Memorandum in Support, 1983*, S. 1154, microfiche, New York State Library. Senator Joseph R. Pisani, the chief sponsor of the amendment, produced two documents in support of change: *Tax Increment Financing: A Public/Private Partnership in Community Development* (Albany: State Senate, 1982); and *The Local Development: It Isn't New, It's Just New in New York* (Albany: The Legislative Commission on Public/Private Cooperation, Senator Joseph R. Pisani, Chairman, 1983).

60. Fuller description of the state of the hospitals and health care facilities, and the rationale for the amendment, is found in Governor Rockefeller's "Message Relative to Hospitals, Nursing Homes and Health Care Facilities," *Public Papers of Nelson Rockefeller 1968,* pp. 177–183.

61. Temporary New York State Commission on Constitutional Revision, *Mission Statement* (Albany, 1993).

62. For fuller discussion of these proposals see *Getting New York's Fiscal House in Order: The Need For Long Term Budget Reforms* (Albany: Staff Report to Senator Joseph Bruno, Chairman, Legislative Committee on Public Private Cooperation, May, 1989); *Report of the American Society of Public Administration, Constitutional Revision Committee, Subcommittee on State and Local Finance, November, 1991* (Albany, mimeo, 1991); Richard Dollinger [Democratic State Senator, 54th District], "A Constitutional Convention Needed to Put the State Back Together," *Buffalo News*, October 23, 1993.

63. These questions, among others, are explored, and tentative recommendations made, in *The Delegate Selection Process*, The Interim Report of the Temporary New York Commission on Constitutional Revision, March, 1994 (Albany: The Rockefeller Institute of Government, 1984).

64. For exploration of this question see Gerald Benjamin and Melissa Cusa, "Amending the New York Constitution Through the Legislature," pp. 65–71.

65. See Peter J. Galie, "A Pandora's Box? Holding a Constitutional Convention in New York," *Effective Government Now for the New Century: A Report to the People, the Governor, and the Lesiglators of New York* (The Final Report of the Temporary New York State Commission on Constitutional Revision, February, 1995), pp. 69–81.

66. See the supplemental statements of commission members Peggy Cooper Davis and Margaret Fung to the Final Report of the Temporary New York State Commission on Constitutional Revision, February, 1995, *Effective Government Now for the New Century,* pp. 30–31.

67. See Robert Williams, "The Role of the Constitutional Commission in State Constitutional Change," in *The New York Constitution: a Briefing Book,* pp. 73–79.

Constitutional Changes
1968–1995

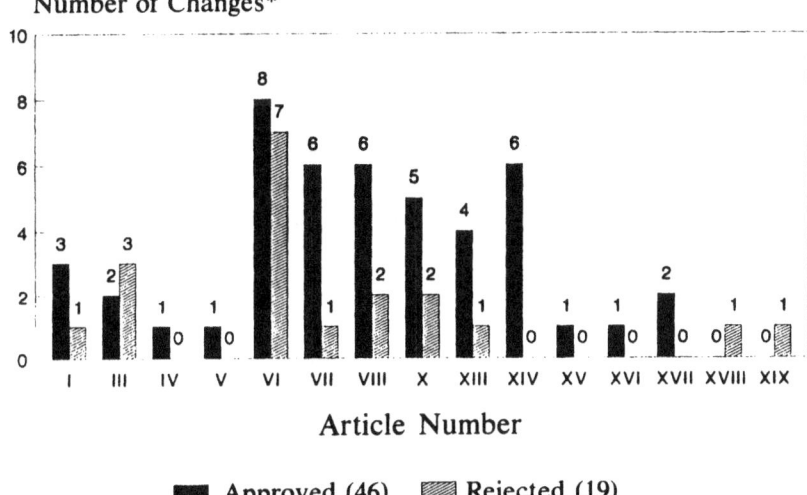

Article Number

■ Approved (46)   ▨ Rejected (19)

*Some proposed amendments affected more than one article.

16

Toward the Year 2000: Reflections on New York's Constitutional Tradition

THE CURRENT NEW YORK CONSTITUTION comprises twenty articles containing over 50,000 words. Six provide the framework for government: the Legislature (Art. III), the Executive (Art. IV), the Judiciary (Art. VI), State Offices (Art. V), Public Officers (Art. XIII), and Local Government (Art. IX). Two establish the rights of citizens: The Bill of Rights (Art. I) and Suffrage (Art. II). Ten—half the constitution—concern substantive or policy issues: State Finance (VII), Local Finance (VIII), Corporations (X), Education (XI), Defense (XII), Conservation (XIV), Canals (XV), Taxation (XVI), Social Welfare (XVII), and Housing (XVIII). Finally, Article XIX allows for amending the constitution, and Article XX concerns the time of taking effect.

The fundamentals of the state constitution were shaped in the nineteenth century. Three defining factors stand out: an aversion to special legislation, democratization of the polity, and constitutionalizing of public policy.

That tradition understood the government's role as limited not so much by an ideology of laissez-faire as by an ideology which saw government as a neutral actor in judging competing claims of those who would have it act for their benefit. Government would intervene when a clear public purpose justified action, but would not intervene when such action advanced the interest of one group or individual at the expense of another. The real bête noire for nineteenth-century constitution-makers was special privilege in the form of special charters, and special legislation. Much of their effort was concentrated on preventing passage of such special legislation. In pursuit of this goal numerous restrictions were placed on the legislature concerning both the substance of, and procedures for, passing legislation, and limitations on the amount of debt the state could incur without referendum approval by the electorate. It was an approach consistent with the vision of a republican government independent of faction and acting only for a clear public purpose. The result of such attempts were numerous restrictions on the power of the legislature. The history of constitutionalism in nineteenth-century New York indicates the difficulty of maintaining that vision.

Democratization of the constitution complemented and reinforced this development. Between 1821 and 1894 the electorate was expanded and large numbers of public offices, including judicial offices, were made elective. Such democratization diffused power and responsibility, making it difficult for the governor to administer effectively or control the executive branch and for the electorate to hold anyone responsible for government action or inaction.

A third significant development shaping the constitution in the nineteenth century was the constitutionalizing of public policy. The 1777 Constitution contained an article on the militia, along with a clause protecting Native Americans from land fraud. However, the process of constitutionalizing public policy began with the decision of the 1821 convention to place the state's canal policy into the constitution. Subsequent conventions and amendments added corporations, education, finance, taxes, conservation, housing, social welfare, and labor. The pattern in almost every case was the same. Constitution-makers took already existing legislative policy and incorporated it into the constitution. In some cases this incorporation was done in response to interest groups or reform movements wishing to ensconce their policy goals in the constitution, making those policies more resistant to alteration; in others, policies were incorporated for symbolic reasons—providing legitimacy and status to the values and policies in question.

These policy provisions took two forms: proscriptive and prescriptive. The clearest examples of proscriptive policies are those preventing state intervention with the forest preserves, the prohibition, until 1959, against selling or leasing the canal system, provisions preventing state assumption of debt without referendum, and the clauses preventing municipalities from exceeding certain tax and debt limits. Other policy provisions are prescriptive in nature: they authorize and encourage, but do not require, the state to take any specific action. The section of Article XIV declaring "the policy of the state to conserve and protect its natural resources and scenic beauty and encourage the development and improvement of its agricultural lands" is a prime example. It is not self-executing, nor is there a specific mandate: the language is precatory, allowing the legislature leeway as to how much is to be done and at what pace. The housing article is similar:

"The legislature *may* [my emphasis, here and following] provide in such manner, and by such means and upon such terms and conditions as it *may* prescribe for low rent housing. . . ." Two policies, social welfare and education, seem to fall somewhere between the two forms. The education article directs that the "legislature *shall* provide for the maintenance and support of a system of free common schools. . . ." The social welfare article declares that "the aid care and support of the needy are public concerns, and *shall* be provided by the state . . . in such manner and by such means, as the legislature *may* from time to time determine." In both cases there appears to be a constitutional minimum: that free common schools shall be maintained and some aid to the needy must be provided. It is likely that the state's judiciary would require at least that. The language has not required much more, and the courts largely have left the matter to legislative descretion. There is scant evidence that these prescriptive policy provisions have had any significant impact on the policy choices of the legislature. Indeed, most were the public policy of the state in statutory form before constitutional incorporation. The extensive support for housing, social welfare, and education policies is likely a function of social conditions and political demands and not based primarily on constitutional language or court decisions. This is not to say that there is no impact. The language provides a standard to which those advocating additional educational programs, welfare, and housing can repair. These articles provide constitutional grounds for a judiciary so inclined to demand more of the state, and they remind citizens of the goals and values they have determined to be fundamental.[1]

The situation is more complex with the proscriptive policies. Some have been remarkably successful. The "forever wild" clause has played a major role in preserving the forest preserve. Undoubtedly the strong consensus regarding the value of such a preserve, partly created and reinforced by the clause as well as by attorney generals' opinions strictly interpreting the clause, have contributed to the success of this constitutional provision. Nevertheless, it is an example of successful policy-making by constitutional provision.

The case of the strict limitations on the incurring of state debt, and the comparable restrictions on municipalities, is more problematic. The requirement that state debt be limited without the referendum approval of the electorate has been ineffective in limiting state debt or protecting the state's credit status. By 1990 New York ranked ninth among states in per capita debt and sixteenth in debt as a ratio of personal income. In 1990 both Standard and Poor's and Moody's Investment Services gave New York the lowest long-term credit rating in the state's history.[2] The explanations for such failure are multiple and complex. The overriding reason appears to be the conflict between the debt provisions and the rise of an activist state facing problems of a intractable and recurring, if not permanent, nature. The positive state, created in response to citizen demand for action and for control of elected officials, has reinforced and enhanced those expectations. State spending continues to grow faster than the economy of the state, partially due to new programs—including the war on drugs, which dramatically increased correction expenses—and partially due to continued escalation of Medicaid costs. Periods of slowed economic growth cause "the state's recurring revenues to fall substantially below its ongoing expenditures, exacerbating the problem."[3] In a sluggish economy with spending outdistancing revenues, politically difficult choices had to be made. Too often taxes were deferred by employing the expedient of delaying payment for future generations.

These pressures for increased spending are likely to continue in the near future. The issue of the continued viability of constitutional tax and debt limits must be considered in this context. Two methods were used to meet the increasing demands being made on the state. The first was the method of constitutional amendment. The state requested voter approval of amendments permitting exceptions to the referendum requirement. Twelve of the exceptions have been adopted in this century. Of equal or greater significance has been the resort to what critics have labelled "Backdoor Financing."[4] A major device for circumventing the constitutional prohibition against borrowing without referenda has been the public benefit corporation or public authority. Its most important characteristic is the power to issue bonds to finance operations, usually the construction of capital projects. Since the constitution prohibits assumption of debt without voter approval, the bonds of these authorities cannot be supported by the full faith and credit of the state. The authorities are able to sell bonds on the strength of their revenue-producing capacity, e.g., The New York Thruway Authority, or, if that is insufficient, because they are backed by a "moral obligation" on the part of the state. The state's practice of assuming a "moral obligation" to compensate for any deficits incurred by these authorities has blunted the impact of the restriction on state debt. By the early 1980s there were forty-three public authorities with statewide or regional responsibilities. The Court of Appeals, in a series of decisions, has upheld the practice of allowing the state to caution investors purchasing bonds from these authorities that the state is not legally obligated to guarantee such bonds, while simultaneously declaring that the state had a "moral obligation" to do so.[5] By the mid-seventies the state had eighteen moral-obligation bonding authorities with a total debt of $8.2 billion, almost tripling the size of the state's "full faith and credit" debt.[6] By 1995 the state's long-term debt stood at $28 billion, with only $5 billion (19%) of that figure approved by voters. That debt costs the taxpayers $2.6 billion in interest annually. This is in striking contrast to 1960, when all state debt was approved by the voters.[7] By the 1980s the state's complex public authority system was the largest in the nation. A series of commissions were established before and after New York City's financial problems in the mid-seventies, including the Temporary Commission on the Powers of Local Government and the Moreland Commission.[8] The Moreland Commission was established to study the authority system in general; it made sweeping recommendations emphasizing the need for more accountability and access.[9] The 1990 Report of the Commission on Government Integrity urged the creation of another Moreland Commission.[10]

The state does exercise some control over these entities, requiring that all authorities with outstanding loans, appropriations, or other special state funds must submit budget reports to the finance committees of the legislature and the budget director. Selective audits of their finances and performance review of borrowing proposals by the state comptroller, a Public Authorities Control Board for some state authorities, and program-related approval by the legislature are also required.[11] These controls are thought inadequate by many legislators, watchdog groups, and students of authorities.[12]

Another budget contrivance is the resort to "one shot" revenue sources to balance the budget. A prime example of this is the 1991 Attica Prison sale to the Urban Development Corporation (UDC) for $200 million. This sale helped balance the budget, but will eventually cost the state over half a billion dollars in principal and interest on bonds the UDC will sell to produce the $200 million. The use of these one-time revenue sources postpones confronting the basic imbalance problems.

The lease purchase device is the second method employed to avoid the state debt referendum requirement. The state contracts with another level of government or an authority for a long-term lease of a capital project such as a hospital or office building. The entity building the project issues bonds which are paid off with the rent from the government unit using the building. When the bonds are paid, the lease expires and the government agency using the facility assumes ownership. In that fashion the state built the Albany Mall. Then-Comptroller Arthur Levitt argued that financing the mall "circumvents the constitutional procedure which requires public approval of state debt by a voter referendum."[13] Though advocating an end to this "back-door financing," Governor Cuomo sold Attica Prison to the Urban

Development Corporation, which issued bonds to pay for it and then leased it to the state.[14]

In May 1993 the Court of Appeals issued a potentially far-reaching ruling in the *Matter of Schulz v. State of New York*.[15] The court dismissed the challenge to the leaseback of Attica Prison on grounds of untimeliness, but overruled or modified earlier rulings, and allowed taxpayers to challenge the state's borrowing practices.[16] *Schulz* appeared to signal a new attitude on the part of a court traditionally unwilling to involve itself in financial questions during economic crises and whose decision to apply the minimal scrutiny standard in the area of debt limitation has contributed to making these provisions largely irrelevant in controlling state debt. However, in *Schulz v. State of New York* (1994)[17] the court reaffirmed its traditional position, rejecting a challenge to legislation authorizing bond issues by the Metropolitan Transit Authority (MTA) and the Thruway Authority. The challenge was based on Article VII, Section 11, which mandates that state contracts for debt must be submitted to public referendum. Since the legislation authorizes authorities to issue bonds while explicitly disavowing any obligation on the part of the state, moral or otherwise, for such debt, the state claimed that it had not, in fact, contracted any debt. The court, taking the disclaimers in the legislation at face value and reading Section 11 narrowly, agreed with the state. Dismissing the political reality that such debt would almost certainly be assumed by the state, the court concluded: "our constitutional limitations . . . have consistently been construed as addressing legally binding debt."[18] In addition to reaffirming its policy of minimal scrutiny, the court hinted its unwillingness to shoulder the burden of upsetting precedents upon which "reliance has been placed in the financial marketplace. . . ."[19] The court's concluding remarks indicated that the solution to the "stretchings" and "gimmickry" inflicted on the debt clause "is appropriately directed to the public arena where it is indeed under serious consideration."[20]

A third device used by the state to avoid constitutional limits is the practice of "spring borrowing." The constitution authorizes the state to borrow funds to meet "casual deficits or failures in revenues, or for expenses not provided for. . . ." Relying on this clause for approximately thirty years, the state has been using tax revenue anticipation notes (TRANS) to fund school aid and cope with revenue shortfalls during the fiscal crisis of the 1970s. As Robert Kerker, former deputy chief budget examiner, has observed:

> The state's ability to authorize and pay school aid in one fiscal year without paying for it until the next (taking advantage of the "magic window" afforded by differences in the state and school district fiscal years)

enables the state to roll over its debt each spring, contravening the spirit, if not the letter, of Section 9.[21]

The willingness of the legislature and governor to resort to numerous strategies to circumvent the debt requirement with the connivance of the judiciary has severely limited the effectiveness of the constitutional debt policy. Governor Cuomo and a significant portion of the legislature have recognized these failures and committed themselves to reform.

The state has taken a series of measures to address the fiscal condition of the state. Among these are GAAP (Generally Accepted Accounting Principles) budgeting, i.e., budgeting on an accrual rather than a cash basis, and "capping legislation" that restricts the amount of moral obligation bonds a public benefit corporation may issue. The Budget Accountability Reform Act of 1981 required the state to present a budget and audit in accordance with GAAP, but the legislation did not require a balanced budget on a GAAP basis.[22] In 1984 the Citizens Budget Commission, a private organization dedicated to providing research and making recommendations on fiscal reform, called on the state to adopt a GAAP balanced budget. The state did enact the New York Local Government Assistance Corporation Act of 1990, which requires the state to abandon the practice of borrowing billions of dollars each spring to pay for routine expenses such as aid to school districts.[23] It created the New York Local Government Assistance Corporation, a public benefit corporation, authorized to issue long-term obligations to fund payments to local governments traditionally funded through the state's annual seasonal borrowing. The LGAC has a limited bonding authorization of $4.7 billion, minus the proceeds of the bonds issued by the corporation. The new procedure will reduce the delays local governments suffer in receiving state aid for their own budgets, and eliminate borrowing at costly short-term interest rates. The interest on that borrowing was running between 143 and 214 million dollars per year by the mid-eighties.[24]

The Citizens Budget Commission has recommended changing the fiscal year to July 1–June 30, to complete the reforms begun by the 1990 legislation and embodied in the constitutional proposals. In 1943 the fiscal year was altered from July through June to April through March for the purpose of improving the budget and cash-flow patterns. Since that time the patterns of revenue collections and disbursements have changed radically, creating what is referred to as the "magic window," the gap between state and local fiscal years, which enables the state to pay school aid in one state fiscal year without actually paying for it until the following year. In conjunction with the Local Assistance Corporation Act of 1990, a change in the budget year would end the necessity for annual spring borrowing and enable the executive to incorporate January tax collection data in the revenue estimates for the new fiscal year.[25]

The governor has called for a constitutional convention to revise, inter alia, the finance articles of the constitution. By 1994 the legislature approved to constitutional debt reform proposals which would significantly alter the character of the debt practice of the state.[26] The proposed amendment would:

1. Ban use of authorities to finance capital projects for the state, back-door financing, lease purchase arrangements, and selling prisons or highways to balance the budget. The Urban Development Corporation (UDC), e.g., would no longer build state prisons.
2. Require a multi-year state capital financing plan with a mandate that state debt be used to support only capital projects.
3. Compose a cap on all state debt, the ceiling allowing outstanding revenue bonds equal to no more than 4.4% of New Yorkers' personal income. This would be the first time since 1846 that the state would be permitted to incur general long-term debt without voter approval. General obligation bonds approved by the voters would be in addition to, or outside of, the personal income cap. The limit or cap in that case would be at the discretion of the voters.
4. Authorize the state to borrow above the specified limit without voter approval to meet economic emergencies and court decisions. Inclusion of court decisions was prompted by the financial crises created by decisions like *Hurd v. City of Buffalo* (see p. 341) and potentially disruptive consequences of *In the Matter of Schultz v. State of New York*, which allowed taxpayer suits challenging state spending schemes.
5. The state would be authorized to issue special revenue bonds secured by dedicated revenue sources such as the sales tax. The higher rating received by bonds from Wall Street would mean lower interest rates.
6. The state would be authorized to propose more than one bond issue on the ballot in any given year, encouraging the state to pursue smaller, narrowly focused bonding programs and expanding the role of voters in decisions on state debt.[27]

The package of reforms would be the first major change in the way New York incurs debt since 1846. These proposals were soundly rejected by the voters in 1995, with nearly 60% voting against the proposition. A number of forces combined to defeat the proposition: voters were clearly suspicious about the impact of the changes and the willingness of the legislature to propose effective debt reform; the state Conservative Party, supporters of Ross Perot, upstate Democrats like State Senator Richard Dollinger and Robert Shultz, a critic of state fiscal practices, all opposed the measure vigorously. Supporters, like State Comptroller H. Carl McCall, admitted that the legislature should have imposed stricter guidelines and tighter caps on borrowing.[28] The legislature has before it other bills which would impose stricter debt controls, and voters will have an opportunity to revisit the question in 1997 when they will be asked whether they wish to hold a convention to revise the state's constitution.

The tax and debt limit policies for local governments have suffered a similar fate. Municipalities, chafing under the weight of these limits, have resorted to constitutional and extra-constitutional avenues to avoid the restraints. Article VIII is crammed with so many exceptions to the debt and tax limits that the force of the original prohibitions has been diluted, and the provisions have become nearly unreadable. Like the state, municipalities have employed a series of devices to circumvent the limitations, including the creation of local authorities, lease purchase agreements, and using TANS (tax anticipation notes) to roll over debt.

The fiscal crisis of New York City in the mid-seventies illustrates the failure of the constitutional restraints, and some reasons for that failure. The largest of American cities failed to meet its financial obligations. It had been resorting to a variety of questionable practices, such as issuing short-term revenue and tax anticipations notes (TRANS) to balance the budget, and relying on authorities. The city, with the authorization of the state, continually pursued a policy of deficit financing.

The constitutional limits failed to prevent this crisis for a number of reasons. The constitution does not limit the amount of short-term debt that the legislature can authorize the city to issue, and the city relied heavily on that short-term borrowing as well as on capital expenditures to finance operating expenses. The limits failed because city officials, assuming the basic strength of the city's economy, continued to increase spending to satisfy requests for social services and union demands. The limits failed because both Democratic and Republican politicians, under pressure to satisfy the myriad demands and reflecting in their ideologies their respective constituents, paid lipservice to the limits while undermining them.[29] The limits failed because there was no effective watchdog to insure compliance with the spirit, as well as the letter, of the constitution. The judiciary abdicated any meaningful role in enforcing the document's provisions. Even the bond markets did not signal an alarm until the bubble had burst. Moody's Investors Service maintained the city's "A" rating until threatened defaults were imminent in late 1975.[30] Finally, it has been suggested that the article's complexity provoked "compliance with its letter rather than its spirit."[31] It should be noted that New York's failure to provide full and accurate information concerning its actual financial situation contributed to the crisis; constitutional debt limits, as such, cannot be expected to prevent constitutional legerdemain.[32] Although New York City is an extreme case, other municipalities, e.g., Yonkers, have resorted to similar practices.

Although intense support exists in some quarters for continuing these limits, scholarly studies and a variety of commissions over the past forty years have concluded that these limits have failed and should be eliminated or replaced.[33]

A similar pattern is found with tax limits. Municipalities have demonstrated their ingenuity in avoiding these limits.[34] The existence of strict prohibitions clashed with what decision-makers thought necessary to address citizen demands and financial difficulties, and therefore the restrictions failed to obtain the political consensus which might have sustained them. Instead, they were viewed as unnecessary obstacles rather than legitimate and important safeguards. In such an environment few constitutional provisions can survive, let alone be effective.

In the Housing Article nine of its ten sections were so detailed as to invite obsolescence. Five of the eight amendments proposed between the 1938 convention and the 1967 convention were approved. A complete revision, effected at the 1967 convention, was rejected by the voters along with the proposed constitution. In 1971 a major revision establishing a community development article, including counties heretofore excluded, was defeated by over one million votes. Since then the state has not placed any amendments to this article on the ballot. A combination of legislative enactments and liberal court decisions has rescued the article from complete obsolescence but has not entirely eliminated the difficulties created by outmoded conceptions of housing and the cumbersome technical procedures and limitations.[35]

A very different strategy was adopted with regard to the articles dealing with defense (militia), canals, and taxation. The defense article was reduced to two sentences. That decision reflected the fact that for some time federal law had determined the contours of militia policy, and the remaining details could be more appropriately handled by statute. The canal article was stripped of all but two major provisions. Section 1 contains the famous prohibition on the sale or lease of the canal, which is currently contradicted by Section 4, which allows the state to transfer the canal to the national government. The article on taxation consists of six sections; all but the last, the local development amendment of 1983, are brief. It grants all taxing authority to the legislature, places few limitations on the power to tax, largely declares statutory law, and serves as a guarantee against any radical legislative change in the tax system. This strategy has effectively deconstitutionalized policy in all three areas.

It would appear that constitutionalizing public policy is more likely to have an impact when couched in the language of "thou shalt not" rather than when phrased in prescriptive or precatory language and when there are individuals or organizations willing to undertake litigation. Having an impact is not the same as achieving the intended results. Prohibitory language has been successfully employed in the "forever wild" provision but less successfully in other areas such as debt and tax limitations. Placing public policy in the constitution is an attempt to micro-manage the government by constitutional amendment and has had limited success in New York. The record suggests that without a strong and sustained political consensus, policy provisions are susceptable to erosion by periodic constitutional amendment, evasion by ingenious devices, hostility or indifference from the judiciary, or pre-emption by federal law or Supreme Court decision.

The document created by these developments was intended to prevent abuse and limit government. That inevitably meant making it difficult to take bold, swift, coordinated action. The executive branch was decentralized; with most top offices elective, collective leadership was difficult if not impossible. The judiciary was an uncoordinated agglomeration of courts. Much twentieth-century constitutional change in New York has been directed at overcoming the effects of this tradition.[36] The process began with the short ballot, the executive budget, and the general strengthening of the governor's office; the process continued, especially after World War II, with the liberalization of the debt and tax limitations on state and local governments, and reached the judiciary with amendments in 1961 and 1977 that centralized the administration of the courts.

Other changes were precipitated by forces external to the state—in particular, the decisions of the Congress and Supreme Court. The most spectacular examples were the Supreme Court's reapportionment decisions, which invalidated much of the apportionment section of Article III. In addition, the federal judiciary has voided the literacy and residency requirements of Article II, the mandatory retirement policy for judges, and the wiretapping provisions in Article 1, Section 12. The Twenty-Sixth Amendment, which sets the voting age at 18, pre-empted the state's twenty-one-year requirement. Congress has pre-empted most of the militia policy and the labor provisions of Article 1. As the federal government moved into policy areas traditionally thought to be the domain of the states, constitutional policy provisions were preempted or subordinated to the national effort.

THE INSTITUTIONS

The Executive

The governor of New York is one of the most powerful in the nation. That position, in large measure, rests on the powers provided in the constitution. In part, this position also derives from his role as party leader, and the prominence the governor gains by virtue of being the chief executive of one of the largest and most important states in the Union. Most of New York's twentieth-century governors have been national figures. How much the constitution is responsible for this is debatable, but the fact that the constitution provides the framework and opportunity for this leadership, and sufficient power to attract individuals of ambition and vision, is significant. Nelson Rockefeller, echoing Alexander Hamilton in the *Federalist Papers*, put it succinctly: "Great men are not drawn to small office."[37]

The Legislature

In the nineteenth century the legislature dominated state government. That dominance has been eclipsed by the governor; its policy options have been restricted by a variety of state constitutional provisions and pre-empted by Supreme Court decisions and federal law. Nevertheless, the legislature has managed to preserve for itself an effective and important role. It has taken the lead in the twentieth century in providing an optimistic, active approach in meeting the needs of the public in such areas as health, welfare, discrimination, and education, and has been a national leader in innovative policy-making to which the federal government as well as other states have looked for models and inspiration. In the past twenty years it has attempted to modernize and professionalize its operation and has taken steps to exercise greater control over its own environment.[38] A 1971 report of a Citizens Committee on State Legislatures rated the New York Legislature the second most effective in the nation.[39]

The Judiciary

The New York judiciary is the largest, busiest, most complex, and most expensive in the Western world. It employs over 3,000 judges and magistrates and over 11,000 non-judicial personnel handling millions of actions, proceedings, and indictments every year. Its budget in the mid 1990s, including town and village courts, approached one billion dollars.[40] Historically, the state's judiciary has suffered from decentralization, congestion, and a lack of co-ordination. The constitutional amendments in 1962 and 1977 went a long way in achieving a unified court system, though increasing litigation in both the criminal and civil areas has frustrated attempts to eliminate the congestion.

Despite these problems, the New York judiciary, as many have noted, has always been in the vanguard in providing a forum for solving new legal problems. It has produced some of the giants of American law, including Chancellor James Kent and Benjamin Cardozo. The court continues to play an active role in interpreting the state constitution, especially with the provisions contained in the Bill of Rights. In numerous areas, particularly regarding criminal procedure rights, the Court of Appeals has provided more protection for rights than has the U.S. Supreme Court in interpreting comparable national provisions.[41]

Dissatisfaction with the judiciary, however, continues. The League of Women Voters has pointed out that, notwithstanding the unification in 1962, eleven different courts of original jurisdiction continue in existence. The League recommended completion of the consolidation that began in 1962 and has also called for the creation of statewide district courts to replace all city, town, and village courts outside of New York City, and the merit selection of judges.[42] A growing number of organizations, including the New York Bar Association and the New York State Commission on Government Integrity, have called for a nonpartisan appointive system for judicial selection.[43] The Bar Association endorsed a system of selection in which judges would be nominated by screening committees and then appointed by the governor or local elected leaders. This recommendation was prompted by the Bar's concern that election of judges appeared to exclude women and minorities; as of 1993, approximately 13% of judges were women and 8% were Hispanics or African-Americans.[44] The Commission on Government Integrity made a similar recommendation, based on its view that party control in the case of judicial elections undermines the moral foundations of the judiciary by threatening its independence. The Bar Association Report was spurred by the possibility that New York's selection system may violate the Federal Voting Rights Act of 1965, which has been applied to the selection of judges. One year after the report, the Justice Department announced that the control exercised by Democratic Party leaders over the selection process in the Bronx, Brooklyn, and Manhattan violates the Voting Rights Act.[45]

The New York Constitution has provided successful governmental institutions. Examined separately, these institutions work reasonably well. How well has the constitution as a whole served the state? How is the impact of the constitution on the state's successes and failures assessed? What connection, if any, exists between the state's development and its constitutional structure? It is not enough to point to the state's prosperity or its role as financial and communications capital of the nation. Earlier commentators simply connected the state's successes with the constitution. That connection, however, should be demonstrated, not assumed. This is especially true in light of contemporary scholarship questioning the extent to which constitutional forms are key variables in effecting political, social, and economic change.[46] Conversely, a variety of scholars have taken the opposite view, viz., that constitutional forms are crucial, and the particular forms adopted have had the effect of making workable government difficult, if not impossible. The doctrine of the separation of powers has been the focus of these criticisms. This separation has resulted, so the argument goes, in divided and deadlocked government. The doctrine may have been appropriate for the eighteenth and nineteenth centuries, but a complex, rapidly moving social order requires coordinated, responsible government.[47] A case in point is the relationship between the development in the economic and constitutional systems in nineteeth-century New York.[48]

New York actively supported business enterprises through subsidies and other forms of aid throughout the nineteenth century. This active support helped make New York the leading industrial state by 1850. As the corporation was becoming the dominant business form, a centralized and integrated economy was being created. Simultaneously, constitutional reforms were expanding the electorate and increasing the decentralization and fragmentation of the political system. The result was a fragmented and politically undeveloped constitutional system facing an increasingly efficient and integrated economic system. The limitations placed on the government, and the diffusion of power caused by expanding the electorate and designating numerous offices elective, prevented the political system from effectively directing the course and character of economic modernization as well as moderating the deleterious effects of that modernization. The decisions at the 1846 constitutional convention to democratize and diffuse power was consistent with a traditional distrust of political power and in line with developing notions of democracy which had taken hold in most parts of the state. They were also decisions that made an activist, coordinated government all but impossible. However one judges the pluses and minuses, clearly these constitutional choices had a profound impact on the transformation of New York in the nineteenth century.

Similarly, in the twentieth century the debt and tax limitations have had important consequences on the fiscal practices of state and local governments. These restrictions have made it difficult to develop rational financing policies while simultaneously failing in their primary goal, the prevention of significant debt accumulations.

The third aspect of our constitutional system that has had important consequences for the state's social and economic practices is home rule. The home rule provisions largely protect traditional community patterns and make it difficult to achieve annexation or consolidation of functions or establish rational and comprehensive policies to deal with urbanization and metropolitanization. The limits on local debt and taxes are, of course, related to the issue of home rule. The state has yet to confront directly the relationship between the current debt and tax restrictions in the constitution and the contemporary financial needs of local governments.

Contrarily, the New York Constitution is a document which has effectively accommodated new social forces, expanded the electorate, and developed a system of civil liberties which, in a number of areas, is more protective of liberty than is the national Constitution. It is a constitution which has committed the state symbolically, and to some extent instrumentally, to the protection of social and economic as well as political rights.

The New York Constitution is an imperfect document, much in need of reform. On April 20, 1987, the 210th anniversary of the New York Constitution, the country was simultaneously celebrating the 200th birthday of the United States Constitution. *The New York Times* observed: ". . . the New York Constitution, which is older and longer— at times unfathomably longer—doesn't even warrant a public seminar on its 210th birthday, which happens to be today. Yet it too is a document that is worth pondering."[49] New Yorkers have demonstrated a willingness to ponder and revise, and there is no reason to believe they have abandoned that tradition. In 1997 they will be asked, in accordance with the every-twenty-year clause, whether they wish to approve a call for a convention to revise and amend the constitution, or whether they will be content to end the century with the constitution they adopted just prior to its beginning.

Notes

1. See Peter Galie, "The Other Supreme Courts: Judicial Activism Among State Supreme Courts," *Syracuse Law Review*, 33 (1982). Stanley Mosk, "The Emerging Agenda in State Constitutional Rights Law," in John Kincaid, ed.,

"State Constitutions in a Federal System," 496 *Annals of the American Academy of Political and Social Science* (March, 1988), pp. 54-64.

2. The rankings are found in *Debt Capacity and Control Analysis: An Update From the Office of the State Comptroller Edward V. Regan* (Albany, September, 1989), Appendix A; "Moody's Find Risk in Albany Budget," *The New York Times*, June 7, 1990, p. B1.

3. Cynthia Green, "Defeating the Deficit," *Empire State Report* (March, 1989), p. 29. Green's article is an adaption of a Citizens Budget Commission Report issued in January 1989. Ms. Green is senior research associate.

4. Humphrey S. Tyler, "The Steady Growth of Backdoor Financing," *Empire State Report* I (June, 1975), p. 211.

5. The line of cases stretches from *Comereski v. City of Elmira* 308 N.Y. 248 (1955) to *Wein v. State* 39 N.Y. 2d 136 (1976) and *New York Coalition v. Coughlin*, 103 A.D. 2d 40, aff'd 45 N.Y. 2d 248 (1984).

6. Tyler, "The Steady Growth . . . ," p. 222.

7. Figures used by Comptroller McCall, "Change Would LImit State Debt," p. B-3. It has been suggested by Raymond Keating, chief economist for the Small Business Survival Committee in Washington, that if all state-related debt is accounted for, as done by the Commerce Department, the state's total outstanding debt is around $50 billion.

8. *Strengthening Local Government in New York*, Part 2, 1973, pp. 83-88.

9. *Restoring Credit and Confidence: A Reform Proposal for New York State and Its Public Authorities* (Albany, March 31, 1976).

10. Bruce A. Green, ed., *Government Ethics Reform for the 1990s* (New York: Fordham University Press, 1991), pp. 340-378.

11. *Laws of New York*, 1975, Chap. 479; 1971, Chap. 440; 1976, Chap. 621; 1976, Chap. 38; 1983, Chap. 838; 1975, Chaps. 868, 869, 870. Annmarie Hauck Walsh, *The Public's Business: The Politics and Practices of Government Corporations* (Cambridge: MIT Press, 1978), p. 281.

12. See the remarks in Keith Henderson, "Other Governments: The Public Authorities," in Jeffey M. Stonecash, John White, and Peter Colby, eds., *Governing New York*, 3rd ed. (Albany: SUNY Press, 1994), pp. 220-222.

13. *Memorandum of Arthur Levitt on the South Mall Contract*, May 11, 1965.

14. Sarah Lyall, "Cuomo Proposes To End 'Back Door' Financing," *The New York Times*, January 9, 1993, p. 28.

15. 81 N.Y. 2d 336 (1993).

16. *Wein v. Comptroller of the State*, 46 N.Y. 2d 394 (1979) and *New York State Coalition for Criminal Justice v. Coughlin*, 64 N.Y. 2d 660 (1984).

17. 84 N.Y. 2d 231 (1994).

18. at 250. Contrast the court's stance with Governor Hugh Carey's response to the failure of the Urban Development Corporation to meet its financial obligations: "These likely results are unthinkable and unacceptable." Governor's Messages to the Legislature, "Message of Necessity," Feb. 26, 1975, *New York State Legislative Annual, 1975*, p. 407.

19. at 250.

20. at 251.

21. Robert Kerker, "State Government Finance," in Benjamin, *The New York State Constitution: A Briefing Book*, p. 164.

22. *Laws of New York*, Chap. 405.

23. Ibid., Chap. 220.

24. Arthur J. Kermer, "Changing State's Fiscal Year Can Help Eliminate Budge Impasses," *Empire State Report* (December, 1986), p. 48.

25. See Citizen's Budget Reports, *Reforming New York State Finance*, Vol. 52, No. 1, January, 1985; *Reducing New York STate's Deficit*, Vol. 53 No. 1, January, 1986. Alex Storozdynski, "The State's Fiscal Abyss," *Empire State Report* (January, 1992), p. 29. The extent of dissatisfaction with the state's way of handling the budget had brought together an "unprecedented coalition of business, human services and good government groups to form the Alliance for State Budget Reform" (Storozdynski, "The State's Fiscal Abyss," p. 29).

26. S. 4358, S. 4359.

27. See Patrick Bulgaro, "Debt Reform Comes to New York State," *Empire State Report* (May, 1993), pp. 19–20.

28. James Dao, "In 128 Words, a Question on State Borrowing," *New York Times*, November 6, 1995, p. B6; Richard Dollinger, "Don't Let State Borrow More," *Buffalo News*, November 1, 1995, B-3; H. Carl McCall, "Change Would Limit State's Debt," *Buffalo News*, November 1, 1995, p. B-3. Shultz and others filed suit to have the proposition split into five separate questions because it calls for an amendment to five sections of the constitution. A favorable decision in state Supreme Court was overturned by the appellate division just prior to the election.

29. Examples of current political conflicts which have interfered with achieving fiscal reform are recounted in Alex Storozynski, "The State's Fiscal Abyss," pp. 27–30.

30. Hauck, *The Public's Business*, pp. 78, 134–35. Under Rockefeller "the brokers had proved a good deal more generous than the voters," p. 276.

31. Association of the Bar of the City of New York, Local Finance Project, 1979, p. 8.

32. Martin Shefter, *Political Crisis/Fiscal Crisis: The Collapse and Revival of New York City* (New York: Basic Books, 1985), pp. 106–107.

33. Association of the Bar of the City of New York, *Local Finance Project*, pp. 10–17; New York State Constitutional Revision Commission, *Constitutional Debt Limits on Local Government*, Staff Report No. 32, 1960, pp. 92ff. New York State Assembly, *Report of Speaker's Task Force on Constitutional Revision* (Albany, 1976), pp. 10–18; Cf. *Constitutional Revision in New York* (Albany: New York Public Interest Research Group Inc., 1977). The Citizens Budget Commission has not recommended elimination of the debt limitation. Along with its call for a balanced budget on the basis of GAAP, it has recommended reduction of unnecessary and inappropriate state spending (New York exceeds the national spending average by 38%), and increases in sales and income taxes where necessary (Cynthia Green, "Defeating the Deficits," p. 24).

34. Temporary State Commission on Constitutional Tax Limits, *Report*, February 15, 1975 (Albany, New York), pp. 16–18, discusses five methods of avoidance.

35. Eugene J. Morris,"Housing and Urban Development: Problems Facing the Constitutional Convention," *The Record of the Association of the Bar of the City of New York* 21 (1966), p. 145. John P. Dellera, "County Powers in Assisted Housing Programs: The Constitutional Limits in New York," 20, *Fordham Urban Law Journal* 109 (1993).

36. For a succinct overview of this development in the context of general trends in New York's constitutional history see Gerald Benjamin, "Constitutional Revision in New York: Retrospect and Prospect," in *Essays on the*

Genesis of the Empire State (Albany: New York State Bicentennial Commission, 1979).

37. As quoted in Gerald Benjamin, "The Governorship in an Era of Limits and Changes," in *New York State Today*, 2d ed., Peter Colby and John K. White, eds. (Albany: SUNY Press, 1989), p. 144.

38. For summary of these trends see Gerald Benjamin and Robert T. Nakamura, "the Modern New York Legislature," *Rockefeller Institute Bulletin*, 1991 (Albany: Nelson A. Rockefeller Institute of Government, SUNY), pp. 11–14.

39. *State Legislatures: An Evaluation of Their Effectiveness* (New York: Praeger Publishers, 1971), p. 88.

40. *14th Annual Report of the Chief Administrator of the Courts for Calendar Year 1991* (New York City, 1992), p. 4.

41. Joseph Bellacosa, "The New York Constitution: A Touch of Class," *New York State Bar Association* 59 (April, 1987), and the studies cited above, p. 7n5.

42. *The Judicial System in New York State* (New York: League of Women Voters of New York State, 1978), pp. 31–36, and *Order in the Courts: Weighing the Impact of Court Merger, Appellate Reform and Judicial Selection Proposals in New York State* (Albany: New York State Senate Judiciary Committee, January 1986). The latter report supported merger, but recommended retaining the election of judges.

43. Green (ed.), *Government Ethics*, pp. 270–301; Matthew Hickerson, "Electing Judges: The Blind Vote," *Empire State Report* (February, 1992).

44. Sarah Lyall, "Bar Association Urges System of Panels to Nominate Judges," *The New York Times*, May 27, 1993, p. B7.

45. Kevin Sack, "New York Faces Changes in Selection of Judges," *The New York Times*, December 7, 1994, p. 1.

46. See, e.g., Robert Dahl, *A Preface to Democratic Theory* (Chicago: University of Chicago Press, 1956).

47. James MacGregor Burns, *The Deadlock of Democracy* (Englewood Cliffs: Prentice Hall, 1963); James L. Sundquist, *Constitutional Reform and Effective Government* (Washington, D.C.: Brookings Institute, 1986).

48. The following relies on the work of L. Ray Gunn, *The Decline of Authority: Public Economic Policy and Political Development in New York State, 1800–1860* (Ithaca: Cornell University Press, 1988).

49. The Editorial Notebook: "New York's Old and Fat Constitution," *The New York Times*, April 20, 1987, I, p. 18. Similar sentiments are expressed in "Why the Town of Keene needs your OK for Its Cemetery: Odd Votes Are Decreed by Outdated Constitution," editorial, *Buffalo News*, November 5, 1995, p. F–8.

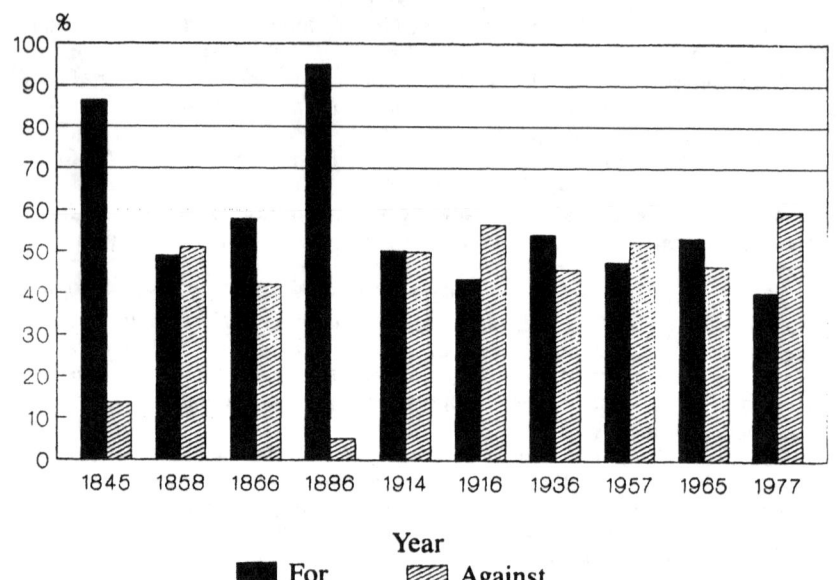

New York Constitutional History: A Guide to Sources and Commentary

THE CONSTITUTION

The New York Constitutions of 1777, 1821, 1846, and 1894, including amendments, can be found in volume five of Francis Thorpe, ed., *The Federal and State Constitutions, Colonial Charters and other Organic Laws* (Washington, D.C.: Government Printing Office, 1909), 7 vols.; William Swindler, ed., *Sources and Documents of the United States Constitutions* (Dobbs Ferry, N.Y.: Oceana Publications, 1978), 10 vols. Volume 7 contains the 1777, 1821, and 1846 Constitutions, as above, as well as the 1897 Constitution and the proposed constitution drafted by the 1967 convention. The text of the current constitution can be found in *The Constitution of the State of New York Amended to 1992*. This publication is updated periodically by the New York Secretary of State and is available from that office. The current constitution, annotated clause by clause, can be found in *McKinney's Consolidated Laws of New York*, Book 2 as supplemented, and *New York Consolidated Law Service* [CLS], Volume 42–42A. All proposed amendments to the constitutions are printed in the *Session Laws of New York*, published annually. *The New York Times* reports on and summarizes proposed amendments before the November general elections at which such amendments are voted upon. Robert Allan Carter's *New York State Constitution: Sources of Legislative Intent* (Littleton, Colo.: Fred B. Rothman & Co., 1988) provides a list of sources by section for the constitution. It is an excellent research tool for locating convention debates, legislative documents, commission reports, and governor's papers pertaining to the various sections of the document. Peter J. Galie's *The New York State Constitution: A Reference Guide* (Westport, Conn.: Greenwood Press, 1991) provides explanatory material and historical background for each article of the current constitution.

There are a number of sources for the meaning and intent of the constitutional provisions. In addition to the constitutional convention debates noted below and the debates on amendments proposed by the state legislature, there are three other authoritative sources. The most important of these are the decisions of the state judiciary, especially the decisions of the Court of Appeals. The decisions of the latter are reported in the *New York Reports* and in the *North East Reporter*. The *Formal Opinions of the Attorney General* are a second authoritative source of constitutional interpretation. The attorney general is frequently called upon to render opinions on the meaning of various constitutional clauses. These opinions are published annually in the *Report of the Attorney General*. Finally, the public papers of the governors contain information on constitutional intent, as governors usually offer justifications for the amendments they propose and/or support.

The Background

Alexander Flick, ed., *The History of the State of New York* (New York: Columbia University Press, 1933–35), 10 vols., provides extensive treatment on a variety of topics by the best historians of the day. A good, comprehensive, one-volume history of the State of New York, though in need of updating, is David Ellis, et al., *A History of New York State*, rev. ed. (Ithaca: Cornell University Press, 1967). Journals containing relevant articles are *New York History, New York Historical Society Quarterly* (ceased publication 1988), and the *New York Bar Journal. Empire State Report* contains articles on current aspects of New York State goverment and politics. Journals not specifically connected with New York but which contain pertinent materials are *State Government* and *The National Civic Review*. The latter contains articles and items related to all aspects of state constitutional development, including a yearly summary of amendments passed or rejected in the states. Relevant articles will also be found in the law reviews published by each of New York's law schools.

Documents pertinent to constitutional developments during the colonial period are collected in E. B. O'Callaghan, John R. Brodhead, and Berthold Fernow, eds., *Documents Relative to the Colonial History of the State of New York* (Albany: Weed, Parsons & Co., 1853–1857), 15 vols. For the laws of the colonial period: *Laws and Ordinances of New Netherland, 1638-1674*, compl. & trans. E. B. Callaghan (Albany: Weed, Parsons, 1868). Works which provide specific background on political and legal developments before the adoption of the first constitutions are: Robert C. Ritchie, *The Duke's Province: A Study of New York Politics and Society 1664–1691* (Chapel Hill: University of North Carolina Press, 1977); Patricia U. Bonomi, *A Factious People: Politics and Society in Colonial New York* (New York: Columbia University Press, 1971), who picks up the story at the opening of the eighteenth century and takes it up to the 1770s; and Mary Low Lustie, *Privilege and Perspective: New York's Provincial Elite, 1710–1776* (Cranbury, N.J.: Associated University Presses, 1995).

General Works on New York's Constitutional History

There is no general work which covers the constitutional history of New York into the twentieth century. Charles Z. Lincoln, *The Constitutional History of New York From the Beginning of the Colonial Period to the Year 1905* (Buffalo: William S. Hein, 1994 [Rochester: Lawyers Cooperative, 1906]), 5 vols., is the most comprehensive and reliable history. University Microfilms, Ann Arbor, Michigan, reproduced the volumes on microfiche in 1971. It includes, in addition to pertinent colonial documents, texts of the first four state constitutions and their amendments. It is a remarkable effort by a delegate to the 1894 convention and legal advisor to Governors Morton, Black, and Roosevelt. In spite of its legalistic approach every student must depend on this work. J. Hampden Dougherty, *Constitutional History of the State of New York*, 2nd ed. (New York: Neale Publishing Co., 1915) is a generally reliable one-volume treatment of roughly the same period. Robert Ludlow provides a workmanlike overview of constitutional developments in "Constitutional and Related Aspects From 1801 to the Constitutional Convention of 1894," and John Baker adds a short chapter on the 1894 convention in David McAdam et al., eds., *History of the Bench and Bar of New York* (New York: History Co., 1897), 2 vols. A few articles provide broad overviews. Benjamin F. Butler, "Outline of the Constitutional History of New York," *Collections of the New York Historical Society*, 2nd Series (New York: Bartlett & Welford, 1848), II, pp. 9–75. Butler's long essay is one of the earliest attempts to survey New York's constitutional history. Henry Wayland Hill, "An Analysis of Constitutional Change in New York State," *Publications of the Buffalo Historical Society* (Buffalo: Peter Paul Book Co., 1896); Ruth Kessler, "An Analysis of Constitutional Change in New York State," *New York University Law Quarterly* 16 (November, 1938), p. 101; Frances D. Lyon, "The New York Constitutional Conventions," *Proceedings of the New York State Historical Association* 37 (1939), p. 51; Frank Moore, "Constitutional Conventions in New York State," *New York History* 38 (1957), p. 3; Franklin Feldman, "A Constitutional Convention in New York: Fundamental Law and Basic Politics," *Cornell Law Quarterly* 42 (1957), p. 329; Richard I. Nunez, "New York State Constitutional Reform—Past Political Battles in Constitutional Language," *William and Mary Law Quarterly* 10 (1968), p. 366. Gerald Benjamin, "Constitutional Revision in New York: Retrospect and Prospect," *Essays on the Genesis of the Empire State* (Albany: New York State Bicentennial Commission, 1979) provides a succinct and perceptive summary of the major constitutional values which have guided constitution-making in New York.

Bibliographies

The single best bibliography on the constitutional history is Ernest Breuer, *Constitutional Developments in New York 1777–1958: A Bibliography on Conventions and Constitutions with Selected References for Constitutional Research* (Albany: New York State Library Bibliography Bulletin, No. 82, 1958). Mr. Breuer issued two updates to this work: *Constitutional Developments in New York 1958–1967, A Temporary Supplement* (Albany: mimeograph, 1967); and *New York State Constitutional Convention of 1967, A Second Supplement* (Albany: mimeograph, 1970). Dorothy Butch's *New York State Documents: An Introductory Manual* (Albany: New York State Library Bibliography Bulletin No. 89, 1987) provides general information about official publications of New York State. It covers all publications connected with the New York State Constitutions, statutes, and administrative laws as well as the legislative, executive, and judicial branches. It is an excellent starting place for the student of the New York Constitution. The entries are annotated with helpful information about the location and character of the documents in question. Ellen Gibson, *New York Legal Research Guide* (Buffalo: Wiliams S. Hein, 1988) also contains an excellent section on the documentary sources of the New York Constitution. Cynthia E. Browne, comp., and Richard H. Leach, intro., *State Constitutional Conventions: From Independence to the Completion of the Present Union 1776–1959* (Westport, Conn.: Greenwood Press, 1973), lists the publications of state constitutional conventions, commissions, and legislative and executive committees for all states. *State Constitutional Conventions, Commissions and Amendments, 1959–1978: An Annotated Bibliography*, Nicholas Olcott, bibliography editor (Washington, D.C.: Congressional Information Service, 1981) continues the coverage of the Browne volume. Both these volumes are valuable for their extensive coverage as well as their citations to a recent microfiche collection. The Congressional Information Service has been reproducing these documents in its multistate microfiche series *State Constitutional Conventions, Commissions and Amendments*. The bibliographies by Brown and Olcott include the microfiche numbers for each bibliographic entry. The Library of Congress has a microfilm series entitled *Records of the States of the United States of America*, Walter Jenkins, ed. (Washington D.C. and University of

North Carolina, 1949). Section C includes early constitutional records of New York covering the years 1776–1846. Ellen Gibson's entries are keyed to this series, and I have noted the New York documents contained in the series by section and reel number. Balfour J. Halevy (with supplement by Myron Fink, comp.), *A Selective Bibliography of State Constitutional Revision*, 2nd ed. (New York: National Municipal League, 1967) is arranged by topics and, within topics, by state.

THE CONSTITUTION OF 1777

The Sources

The proceedings of the first convention are found in the *Journal of the Provincial Congress, Provincial Convention, Committee of Safety and Council of Safety for the State of New York From 1775–1777*, I (Albany: T. Weed, 1941) [Congressional Information Service, microfiche number 1, hereinafter CIS-NY]. The 1777 Constitution is reprinted in Lincoln, I; Thorpe, V; and Swindler, VII. Lincoln also reprints copies of destroyed drafts of the Constitution of 1777.

Commentaries

Three works treat New York's first constitution in comparative perspective. Allan Nevins, *The American State During and After the Revolution* (New York: Macmillan, 1927) is pioneering but essentially descriptive. Two more analytical works are Willi Paul Adams, *The First American Constitutions: Republican Ideology and the Making of State Constitutions in the Revolutionary Era* (Chapel Hill: University of North Carolina Press, 1980); and Donald Lutz, *Popular Consent and Popular Control: Whig Political Theory and the Early State Constitutions* (Baton Rouge: Louisiana State University Press, 1980).

Earlier treatments can be found in Lincoln, I, pp. 471–595, and Dougherty, Chapter II. A shorter account, which puts the adoption of the constitution in a larger political context, is Carl Becker's *History of Political Parties in the Province of New York, 1760–1776* (Madison: University of Wisconsin Press, 1909). Becker's work is much broader than the title suggests and is a pioneering analysis of the social and economic interests which led to independence. His final chapter examines the new state government. Elisha Douglass, *Rebels and Democrats* (Chapel Hill: University of North Carolina Press, 1955) follows Becker's class conflict approach to constitutional change. The most sophisticated recent examination of the origins of political parties in New York is Alfred Young, *The Democratic Republicans of New York:*

The Origins 1763–1797 (Chapel Hill: University of North Carolina Press, 1967). Young provides useful information on the 1777 Constitution and the extent of suffrage before and after its adoption. E. Wilder Spaulding's "The State Government Under the First Constitution," in *The New State*, Volume IV of Flick, ed., *History of the State of New York*, sees the document as a triumph of the minority party of privilege. Among more recent studies, Bernard Mason's *The Road to Independence: The Revolutionary Movement in New York 1773–1777* (Lexington: University of Kentucky Press, 1966) stands out, along with his essay "New York State's First Constitution," in *Essays on the Genesis of the Empire State* (Albany: New York State Bicentennial Commission, 1979). Mason's work is a careful analysis of the drafts of the 1777 document as well as the divisions among the delegates. He argues convincingly that John Jay's role in drafting the document has been exaggerated. William Polf's *1777: The Political Revolution and New York's First Constitution* (Albany: New York Bicentennial Commission, 1977) is a pamphlet-size essay which analyzes the structure and powers of each branch of the new government and how the constitution handled the questions of rights and suffrage. It also reprints the 1777 Constitution.

Richard B. Morris, "John Jay and the New York Constitution After Two Hundred Years," in *Essays on the Genesis of the Empire State*, reasserts the older view that John Jay was the major force in shaping the content of the constitution. Patricia U. Bonomi's "Constitution-Making in Time of Trouble," in the same volume, focuses on the impact of the war on drafting the document. Edward Countryman, *A People's Revolution: The American Revolution and Political Society in New York 1760–1790* (Baltimore: Johns Hopkins Press, 1981) has some evaluative comments on the character of the 1777 Constitution which should be compared to those of Young, Douglass, and Mason. His dissertation, "Legislative Government in Revolutionary New York" (Ph.D. Diss., Cornell University, 1971), contains biographical information on members of the Provincial Congresses as well as an analysis of the 1777 Constitution. Building on the work of Mason, Countryman views the constitution not as the work of a few key influentials but rather the product of the whole convention.

THE CONVENTION OF 1801

Records

There are two available sources of the convention's work. *The Journal of the Convention of the State of New York, 1801* (Albany: John Barber,

Printer to the Convention, 1801) [CIS-NY 5], and the *Journal* as published by Catine and Leake, Printers to the State, in 1821. The amendments adopted at the convention are reprinted in Lincoln, I, pp. 189–191.

Secondary Sources

Commentary is provided by Lincoln, I, pp. 596–612, and Dougherty, Chap. IV. The latter treats both political and constitutional aspects of the convention. Jabez Hammond, *The History of Political Parties in the State of New York*, 4th ed., 3 volumes (Syracuse: Hall Mills & Co., 1851), is still the best general treatment of this topic. Hammond was a contemporary public figure who knew many of those he wrote about. He describes the political conflicts and events surrounding the convention. H. L. McBain, *DeWitt Clinton and the Origins of the Spoils System in New York* (New York: Columbia Studies in Economics and Public Law, Vol. 28, No. 1, 1907), undertakes a partial defense of Clinton's patronage practices.

THE CONVENTION OF 1821

Records

Report of the Proceedings and Debates of the Convention of 1821, N. Carter and W. L. Stone, Reporters, M. T. C. Gould, Stenographer (Albany: E. & E. Hosford, 1821) [CIS-NY 8] (L.C.C.: Reel 1). DaCapo Press reprinted this edition in 1970. A report based on the Carter and Gould edition was published by J. Seymour Printer in 1821. *Journal of the Convention of the State of New York, 1821* [CIS-NY 7] (L.C.C.: Reel 1) (Albany: Catine & Leake, Printers to the State, 1821). The constitution is reprinted in Thorpe, V, Lincoln, I, and Swindler, VII. The *Journal of the Convention* is the daily record of the actions taken by the delegates. The Reports, though not transcripts, constitute the official record of the convention.

Commentaries

Lincoln, I, pp. 613–756, and Dougherty, Chaps. V—VIII, provide accounts of the convention. Merrill Peterson, ed., *Democracy, Liberty and Property: The State Constitutional Conventions of the 1820's* (Indianapolis: Bobbs Merrill, 1966) has an excellent essay on the 1821 convention, putting its work in the context of what other states were doing during the 1820s. It includes excerpts from the debates of the convention. Older studies of the political and economic forces underlying the convention's work are Dixon Ryan Fox's "New York Becomes a Democracy," in Flick, ed., *History of the State of New York*, VI, *The Age of Reform*. This essay is based on his fuller treatment of the period, entitled *The Decline of Aristocracy in the Politics of New York, 1801–1840* (New York: Columbia University Press, 1919). Also valuable is Jabez Hammond, I. Donald B. Cole, *Martin Van Buren and the American Political System* (Princeton: Princeton University Press, 1984) emphasizes the role of Van Buren in leading the Bucktail majority at the convention. The two institutions abolished in 1821—the Council of Appointment and the Council of Revision—have been well studied. Alfred B. Street, *The Council of Revision of New York* (Albany: William Gold Publisher, 1859), Frank Prescott and Joseph Zimmerman, *The Council of Revision* (Albany: Graduate School of Public Affairs, State University of New York at Albany, 1973); J. M. Gitterman, "The Council of Appointment in New York," *Political Science Quarterly* 7 (1892), p. 80; and Hugh M. Flick, "The Council of Appointment in New York State: The First Attempt to Regulate Political Patronage, 1777–1822," *New York History* XV (1934), p. 353. The question of African-American suffrage at the convention is thoroughly examined by Phyllis F. Field, *The Politics of Race in New York: The Struggle for Black Suffrage in the Civil War Era* (Ithaca: Cornell University Press, 1982). Marvin Meyers, *The Jacksonian Persuasion* (New York: Vintage Books ed., 1960) places the convention in the context of the origin and development of party alignments as well as in the broader movement he labelled "Jacksonian Persuasion." Two dissertations have focused on the convention. Helen Young, "A Study of the Constitutional Convention in 1821" (Ph.D. Diss., Yale University, 1910) examines the convention's work in light of the changes that had taken place since 1777. John Casais, "The New York Constitutional Convention of 1821 and Its Aftermath" (Ph.D. Diss., Columbia University, 1967) concentrates on the factional alignments and voting patterns at the convention. George P. Parkinson, "Antebellum State Constitution-Making: Retention, Circumvention, Revision" (Ph.D. Diss., University of Wisconsin, 1972) place the New York convention in a comparative context.

The Convention of 1846

Sources

Reports of the Debates and Proceedings of the Convention for the Revision of the Constitution of the State of New York, 1846, reported by W. G. Bishop and W. H. Attree (Albany: Evening Atlas, 1846). An alternative source is reported by S. Croswell and R. Sutton (Albany: Argus Printers, 1846). Neither of these are verbatim records. *The Journal of the Convention of 1846* (New York: Carroll and Cook, 1846) [CIS-NY 13] (L.C.C.: Reel 2). The constitution as revised is reprinted in Lincoln, I, Thorpe, V, and Swindler, VII. For amendments to this constitution from 1847–1867, see Lincoln, II, pp. 218–240.

Commentaries

There is no monograph on the 1846 convention. Lincoln, II, pp. 9–217 gives extensive treatment. Less extensive treatment is given by Dougherty, Chaps. VIII–IX. E. P. Cheney, "The Anti-Rent Movement and the Constitution of 1846" in Flick, ed., *History of the State of New York*, VI, *The Age of Reform*, as the title indicates, focuses on the connection between the anti-rent movement and the convention. Edna Jacobsen, "New York's Constitution: A Hundred Years Ago," *New York History* 45 (1947), p. 191, is a short summary of the major changes made at the convention and contains some interesting social background on the delegates. Hiram P. Hastings, lawyer and Democratic supporter of Van Buren, published *An Essay on Constitutional Reform* (New York: Globe Job Office, 1846) just prior to the convention. It is a jeremiad calling on all friends of reform to "Awake! Arouse!" (p. 4). Another contemporary account by a prominent lawyer-politician is Benjamin Butler's "Outline of the Constitutional History of New York, An Anniversary Discourse," op. cit. L. Ray Gunn, *The Decline of Authority: Public Economic Policy and Political Development in New York State 1800–1860* (Ithaca: Cornell University Press, 1988) contains the most sophisticated analysis of the convention's work (Chap. 6), and is one of the few works to attempt to demonstrate a relationship between constitutional change and economic development. Marvin Meyers, *The Jacksonian Persuasion*, examines the convention's work with special attention to its treatment of the business corporation. Hendrick Hartog, "Because All the World Was Not New York City: Governance, Property Rights and the State in the Changing Definition of a Corporation, 1730–1960," *Buffalo Law Review* 28 (1979), p. 91, documents the complex process by which governmental corporations like New York City were losing their autonomous legal identity and becoming an adjunct of the state administrative system while the private corporation was emerging from its "publicness." Treatment of the African-American suffrage issue is found in Phyllis Field, *The Politics of Race*. Francis Bergan, *The History of the New York Court of Appeals, 1847–1932* (New York: Columbia University Press, 1985) provides information on the origin of the Court of Appeals in the 1846 convention. Patricia McGee, "Issues and Factions: New York State Politics from the Panic of 1837 to the Election of 1848" (Ph.D. Diss., St. John's University, 1970), places the convention in the context of the factionalizing and realignment of politics in New York during the 1840s. Parkinson, "Antebellum State Constitution-Making," looks at the changes effected by "radicals" in a comparative context.

From 1847 to 1894

Sources

Records of the convention of 1867: *Journal of the Convention of the State of New York* (Albany: Weed, Parsons & Co., 1867) [CIS-NY 19]. *Proceedings and Debates of the Constitutional Convention of the State of New York* as reported by Edward F. Underhill (Albany: Weed, Parsons & Co., 1868), 5 volumes [CIS-NY 20]. The proposed constitution is available as the *Amended Constitution of the State of New York Adopted by the Convention of 1867* (Albany: Luther Caldwell, 1868). The Constitutional Commission of 1872: The record of the commission was never published, so the *Journal of the Constitutional Commission . . . 1822–1873* (Albany: Weed, Parsons & Co., 1873) [CIS-NY 25] is the only source of the commission's activities. The results of its work is found in *Amendments Proposed to the Constitution of the State of New York . . .* (Albany: Argus Printer, 1873). The records of the Judiciary Commission of 1890 were never published, so the *Journal of the Constitutional Commission, 1890–1891* (Albany, 1891) [CIS-NY 28] is the only record of their deliberations. The commission issued reports which are listed in Breuer and Gibson.

Commentaries

Francis Lieber, a professor of constitutional Law at Columbia law School and a conservative political theorist, published an address he gave before the New York Union League Club, *Reflections on the Changes Which May Seem Necessary in the Present Constitution of the State* (New York: Union League Club, 1867). The essay was meant to influence the work of the 1867 convention. David Dudley Field, the great advocate of codification of the laws and author of the Field Code of Civil Procedure, published *Suggestions Respecting Revision of the Constitution of New York* (New York: Wm. Read Steam Job Printer, 1867). His suggestions were in the form of a proposed constitution meant to provide a model for the 1867 convention. Lincoln, II, pp. 18–

125, and Dougherty, Chaps. X–XIV, cover the period in question thoroughly. Lincoln also reprints the proposed constitution. More recent treatment is found in Finla Crawford, "Constitutional Developments, 1867–1915" in Flick, *History of the State of New York*, VII, *Modern Party Battles*. Homer A. Stebbins, *A Political History of the State of New York 1865–1869* (New York: Columbia University Press, 1913), IX, is a summary of the convention's work and a commentary on the politics therein. James C. Mohr, *The Radical Republicans and Reform in New York During Reconstruction* (Ithaca: Cornell University Press, 1973) is a more recent treatment which is kinder to the Radical Republicans, but focuses primarily on the convention's handling of the question of African-American suffrage.

THE CONVENTION OF 1894

Documents

A large number of publications accompanied the calling of the 1984 convention. Thirteen volumes of preparatory materials were published for the use of the delegates. The volumes are listed by title in Breuer, *Constitutional Developments*, and Butch, *New York State Documents*. The convention itself produced eleven volumes of documents, records, proeedings, and a journal. The *Record of the Proceedings* (Albany: 1894) was published in six volumes and was revised and indexed in five volumes by William H. Steele (Albany, Argus Company, 1900) [CIS-NY-31]. *The Journal of the Constitutional Convention* consists of two volumes published in Albany, 1894 [CIS-NY 30]. It was also revised and indexed in one volume (Albany: Argus Company, 1895) [CIS-NY 30]. The 1894 Constitution is reprinted in Thorpe, V; Lincoln, IV; Swindler, VII. Lincoln annotates the constitution.

Commentary

Lincoln devoted an entire volume to the work of the 1894 convention. Dougherty gives much less—and less well organized—coverage in Chaps. XIV–XVIII. Good brief summaries of the convention's accomplishments are found in Finla Crawford, "Constitutional Developments," and Frank T. Hamlin, "The New York Constitutional Convention," *Yale Law Journal* IV (June, 1895), p. 213. Three recent works, all of which put the convention in the larger context of New York politics and which focus on the role of the Republican party at the convention, the impact of interest groups, and regional considerations, are Samuel T. McSeveney, *The Politics of Depression: Political*

Behavior in the Northeast, 1893–1896 (New York: Oxford University Press, 1972); Richard L. McCormick, *From Realignment to Reform: Political Change in New York State 1893–1910* (Ithaca: Cornell University Press, 1981); and Robert Crosby Eager, "Governing New York State: Republicans and Reform, 1894–1900" (Ph.D. Diss., Stanford University, 1977).

The Convention 1915

Sources

The Journal of the Constitutional Convention, 1915 (Albany: J. B. Lyons, 1915) [CIS-NY 36]. The debates are in two forms: *The Record of the Constitutional Convention, 1915* (Albany: J. B. Lyons, 1915), 4 vols., and the *Revised Record of the Constitutional Convention* (Albany: J. B. Lyons, 1916), 4 vols. [CIS-NY 37]. There were a large number of preliminary publications in connection with the convention. These are listed in Breuer and Butch.

A copy of the full text of the revised constitution was reprinted in *The New York Times*, September 12, 1915, pp. 18–21.

Commentaries

Best of the early works are Finla Crawford, "Constitutional Developments 1867–1915" and Alden Chester's *Courts and Lawyers of New York: A History 1609–1925* (New York: The American Historical Society, 1925), 4 vols., Volume II, entitled *A History of State Government and Constitutional History*, which contains a chapter on the Constitution of 1915. The only monograph on the convention is by Thomas Schick, *The New York State Constitutional Convention of 1915 and the Modern State Governor*, published by the National Municipal League (Sowers Printing Co., 1978). This work focuses on the convention's attempts at governmental reorganization, but slights the impact of political parties and political factors in general. A good corrective, emphasizing the latter, is Gerald McKnight, "The Perils of Reform Politics: The Abortive New York State Constitutional Reform Movement in 1915," *New York Historical Society Quarterly* LXIII (July, 1979), p. 203. Schick provides a full bibliography of materials relating to the 1915 convention.

1916–1938

Sources

The Judiciary Convention of 1921: Breuer, Butch, and Gibson have complete listings of proceedings, documents, and the manual. The convention's recommendations are found in *Report to the Legislature* . . . Leg. Doc. (1922) No. 37, (Albany: J. B. Lyons, 1922).

Commentaries

The convention is discussed in Bergan, *History of the New York Court of Appeals.* Alden, op. cit., treats the Judiciary Convention of 1921 in the context of his analysis of the Judiciary Act of 1925. The way in which executive reorganization and the constitutional reforms advocated by the 1915 convention were achieved is described in Finla Crawford, "Recent Political development, 1915–1935," in Flick, *History of the State of New York*, VII, *Modern Party Battles*. Robert A. Caro, *The Power Broker Robert Moses and the Fall of New York* (New York: Random House Vintage Books, 1975) provides a more recent discussion of Governor Smith and Executive Reorganization.

THE CONVENTION OF 1938

Sources

As with the 1915 convention, preparatory work was undertaken. The materials assembled under the direction of Charles Poletti, and known as the *Poletti Report*, are an invaluable source of legal and historical information concerning New York State's constitutional development. The report consists of twelve volumes. These as well as other materials connected with the convention are listed in Breuer, Butch, and Gibson. The activities of the convention are found in *The Journal of the Constitutional Convention . . . 1938* (Albany: J. B. Lyons, 1838) [CIS-NY 47]. *The Record of the Constitutional Convention, 1938* (Albany: J. B. Lyons, 1938) 3 vols. A *Revised Record* was issued in 4 volumes by the same publisher in 1938 [CIS-NY 48].

Commentaries

The only published monograph on the convention, Vernon O'Rourke and Douglas Campbell's *Constitution-Making in a Democracy: Theory and Practice in New York State* (Baltimore: Johns Hopkins Press, 1943) is the first study of New York conventions to focus on interest-group activity and partisanship. A similar approach, but with more attention to the specific issues, is Wilbert L. Hindman, "The New York Constitutional Convention of 1938: The Constituent Process and Interest Activity" (Ph.D. Diss., University of Michigan, 1940). Freida A. Gillette, "The New York State Constitutional Convention of 1938" (Ph.D. Diss., Cornell University, 1944) describes the major issues and how they were handled, and concludes with an analysis of partisan divisions on each of these issues. An early attempt to relate the convention decisions to public opinion is Madge Mckinney, "Constitutional Amendment in New York State," *Public Opinion Quarterly* 3 (Oct. 1939), p. 635. Also useful is Arthur E. Sutherland, "Law Making by Popular Vote: Some Reflections on the New York Constitution," *Cornell Law Quarterly* 24 (1938), p. 1. Articles by delegates to the convention are noted in Hindman, p. 422.

BETWEEN CONVENTIONS, 1939–1966

Sources

A list of amendments to the 1894 Constitution between 1939 and 1967 can be found in *The Legislative Manual 1988–89*, published by the Secretary of State of New York. The three Temporary Commissions on Constitutional Revision (1957–1961) held hearings and issued interim and topical reports on all aspects of the constitution. These, as well as the unpublished materials of the commissions, are listed and discussed in Breuer, Butch, and Gibson. These reports provide an excellent picture of the idea of constitutional reform in the late fifties and early sixties, as well as useful background information.

Commentaries

Guthrie Birkhead, Jr., *A Right to Choose: The Prospective Constitutional Convention in New York State*, prepared for the Citizenship Clearing House (Syracuse: Syracuse University Press, 1957), summaries the pros and cons of a convention as well as the major issues that would have faced the convention. Birkhead also provides a list of organizations active in constitutional reform or who had taken a position on the question of reform. Franklin Feldman, "A Constitutional Convention in New York: Fundamental Law and Basic Politics," *Cornell Law Quarterly* 42 (1957), p. 329, put the upcoming vote on the 1957 convention in the context of the political limits to constitutional reform. Volume 31 of the *St. John's Law Review* (1957) is devoted to the question of whether there ought to be a constitutional convention in 1959.

THE CONVENTION OF 1967 AND BEYOND

Sources

The Temporary Commission on the Constitutional Convention issues a series of fifteen reports on a variety of topics. These have been bound in two volumes (Albany, 1966). The New York State Department of Audit and Control issued a five volume series entitled *Comptroller's Studies for the 1967 Constitutional Convention* (Albany, 1967). The *Hearings of the Temporary Commission*, held throughout the state, were bound in five volumes of mimeographed transcripts (New York: Ralph Fink, 1966). *Proceedings of the New York State Constitutional Convention* (Albany, 1968), 12 vols., contains the journal, the debates, proposed amendments, and documents of the convention [CIS-NY 75A-75F]. The proposed constitution can be found in *Text, Abstract and Highlights of the Proposed Constitution of the State of New York* . . . (Albany: Legislative Index Co., 1967).

Commentaries

Ernest R. Breuer, *New York State Constitutional Convention of 1967: A Second Supplement* (Albany: mimeograph, 1970), updates his earlier bibliography and contains a list of archival material held by the New York State Library in Albany. The League of Women Voters of New York published a pamphlet entitled *The 1967 New York State Constitutional Convention* (New York: Foundation for Citizen Education, 1966). It provides useful background information as well as the League's position on constitutional reform. The Citizens Union of New York City's position is presented in *New York State Constitutional Convention 1967: Citizens Union Position Papers 1-19* (New York: mimeograph, 1967). Two other sources of information and reform proposals are Sigmund Diamond and Nancy Lee, eds., "Modernizing State government: The New York Constitutional Convention of 1967," *Proceedings of the Academy of Political Science* 28 (January, 1967) and Columbia School of Law, *Essays on the New York Constitution* (bound mimeograph, 1966). The articles in the former are general discussion with comments by noted scholars and/or political figures; the latter is a more technical examination of constitutional problems with specific proposal for reform. Elmer E. Cornwell, Jr., Jay S. Goodman, and Wayne R. Swanson put the 1967 constitutional convention in the context of six other state constitutional conventions held between 1964–1970 in *Constitutional Conventions: The Politics of Revision* (New York: National Municipal League, 1975). Donna E. Shalala, *The City and the Constitution: The 1967 New York Convention's Response to the Urban Crisis* (New York: National Municipal League, 1972), provides an excellent view of the convention's work in relation to its treatment of urban problems, as well as an analysis of the divisions among reformers. Though written from its own perspective, the League of Women Voters of New York, *Seeds of Failure: A Political Review of New York State's 1967 Constitutional Convention* (New York: Mt. Shiver Press, 1973) is an informative overview of the convention as well as the reasons for its failure. Richard I. Nunez, "New York State Constitutional Reform—Past political Battles in Constitutional Language," *William and Mary Law Quarterly* 10 (1968), p. 366, puts the failure in the context of earlier conventions. Lewis B. Kaden, "The People: No! Some Observations of the 1967 New York Constitutional Convention," *Harvard Journal of Legislation* 5 (Summer, 1968), p. 343, and William Vanden Heuval's "Reflections on Constitutional Change," *New York State Bar Journal* 40 (June, 1968), p. 261, while recognizing the inevitability of partisanship at conventions, make recommendations as to how it can be reduced or limited. *The New York Times* is an excellent source of information and opinion on the convention and it product.

The 1967 convention has been well covered in the dissertation literature. The fullest coverage is given by Henrik N. Dullea, "Charter Revision in the Empire State: The Politics of New York's 1967 Constitutional Convention," (Ph.D. Diss., Syracuse University, 1982). This work examines the forces leading to the convention, plots regional, partisan, and ideological divisions using roll call votes and interviews with participants, and explores the reason for its failure. The Nelson A. Rockefeller Institute of Government published a much shortened version of this dissertation as one of its Rockefeller Institute Special Reports under the title *The 1967 Constitutional Convention: Outcome and Impact* (Albany: State University of New York, 1984). More specific in their focus are James A. Dunne, "A Longitudinal Study of the Role Concepts of a Select Group of Delegates to the 1967 State Constitutional Convention" (Ph.D. Diss., State University of New York at Albany, 1972); Carol S. Greenwald, "Lobbyist Perceptions of the 1967 New York State Constitutional Convention" (Ph.D. Diss., City of University of New York, 1972); and Irving H. Freedman, "The Issue of Public Support for Church Related Education in the 1967 Constitutional Convention: A Study in the Decision-Making Process" (Albany: State University of New York at Albany, 1969).

Little has been published on the need for constitutional reform since 1977. The New York State Assembly appointed a Speaker's Task Force on Constitutional Revision in 1975. That task force issued a brief report entitled *Constitutional Revision in New York State* (Albany, 1976). Intended to be preparatory for the 1977 referendum, it reiterated arguments of earlier commissions about the need for major constitutional reform and called for the appointment of a new temporary commission to educate the voters on the connection between the state government's inability to meet their needs and the defects of the constitution. No commission was created. A similar brief report was issued by the Assembly's Committee on the Judiciary, *"Shall There Be A Convention to Revise the Constitution and Amend Same?" A Report of the New York State Assembly Standing Committee on the Judiciary* (Albany, 1977), which concluded that a convention was the only appropriate forum for effective reform.

There is no constitutional history which treats the period from World War II to the present. The temporary State Commission on Constitutional Revision appointd by Governor Cuomo in 1993 published *The New York Constitution: A Briefing Book* (Albany: Nelson A. Rockefeller Institute of Government, 1994), which contains up-to-date articles on various aspects of the contemporary New York Constitution. Robert Connery and Gerald Benjamin, *Rockefeller of New York* (Ithaca: Cornell University Press, 1979) is an informative survey of public policy of the state between 1960 and 1980, as well as an examination of Rockefeller's performance as governor. Joseph Zimmerman, *The Government and Politics of New York* (New York: New York University Press, 1981); Jeffrey Stoncash, John White, and Peter Colby, eds., *Governing New York State*, 3rd ed. (Albany: State University of New York at Albany, 1994); and *A Guide to New York State Government* by the League of Women Voters (Croton-on-Hudson: Policy Studies Associates, 1989) are useful, balanced descriptions and analyses of New York government and politics.

Table of Cases

Adler v. Deegan 251 N.Y. 467 (1929), 221, 227 n.61, 291.
Application of Stewart 174 Misc. 902; aff'd 260 A.D. 979 (1940), 299 n7.
Atkin v. Onondaga County Board of Elections 30 N.Y. 2d 401 (1972), 300 n 24.
Atkins v. Kansas 191 U.S. 207 (1903), 173.
Bay Ridge Community Council, Inc. v. Carey 66 N.Y. 2d 657 (1985), 300 n36.
Bennett v. Boyle 40 Barb. 551 (1864), 224 n2.
Berger v. New York 388 U.S. 41 (1967), 235–236, 308.
Bethlehem Steel Corporation v. Board of Education of City School District of Lackawanna 44 N.Y. 2d 831 (1978), 353 n42.
Board of Education v. Allen 20 N.Y. 2d 109 (1967); aff'd 392 U.S. 236 (1968), 310–311.
Boykin v. Alabama 395 U.S. 238 (1969), 259 n30.
Browne v. City of New York 241 N.Y. 96 (1925), 227 n65.
Cancemi v. People 18 N.Y. 128 (1858), 224 n5.
City of Clinton v. Cedar Rapids and Missouri River R.R. Co. 24 Iowa 455 (1868), 185 n58.
City of New York v. DeLury 23 N.Y. 2d 175 (1968), 258 n13.
Comereski v. City of Elmira 308 N.Y. 243 (1955), 371 n5.
Cosby v. Van Dam (N.Y., 1733), unreported opinion, 25.
Dash v. Van Kleeck 7 Johns. 477 (1811), 79.
Dawson v. Horan 51 Barb. 459 (1868), 135 n16.
Donohue v. Copiague Union Free School District 47 N.Y. 2d 440 (1979), 170.
Dorsey v. Stuyvesant Town Corporation 299 N.Y. 512 (1949), 234.
Dunn v. Blumstein, 405 U.S. 330 (1972), 267.
Eber v. Board of Elections 80 Misc. 2d 334 (1974), 300 n24.
EEOC v. Wyoming 460 U.S. 266 (1983), 258 n14.
Esler v. Walters 56 N.Y. 2d 306 (1982) 139, 233 n15.
Fidell v. Board of Elections of the City of New York 409 U.S. 972 (1972), 300 n24.
Flushing National Bank v. Municipal Assistance Corporation 40 N.Y. 2d 731 (1976), 300 n34.
Forsey v. Cunningham (N.Y., 1764), unreported opinion, 25–26.
Frank v. New York 44 N.Y. 2d 687 (1978), 352 n23.
Garcia v. San Antonio Metro Transit Authority 469 U.S. 528 (1935), 258 n14.
Gardner v. Broderick 392 U.S. 273 (1968), 237, 309.
Gardner v. Newburgh 2 Johns. 162 (1816), 79.
Garrity v. New Jersey 385 U.S. 493 (1967), 237, 309.
Greaton v. Griffin 4 Abb. Pr. (New Ser.) (N.Y. 310) (1968), 125.
Green v. Shumay 39 N.Y. 418 (1868), 135 n7.
Hellerstein v. Assessor of the Town of Islip 37 N.Y. 2d 1 (1975), 251.
Hurd v. City of Buffalo 41 A.D. 2d 402 (1973) aff'd 34 N.Y. 2d 628 (1974) 342, 364.
In Re Guden 171 N.Y. 529 (1902), 141.

TABLE OF CASES

In Re Jacobs 98 N.Y. 98 (1885), 80–81.
Ives v. South Buffalo Railroad 201 N.Y. 271 (1911), 205.
Katzenback v. Morgan 384 U.S. 641 (1966), 225 n16.
Knight v. Campbell 62 Barb. 16 (1872), 135 n16.
Kundolf v. Thalheimer 12 N.Y. 533 (1855), 125.
LaGuardia v. Smith 228 N.Y. 1 (1942), 185 n58.
Lemon v. Kurtzman 403 U.S. 602 (1971), 327 n21.
Levittown Union Free School District v. Nyquist 57 N.Y. 2d 27 (1982), 170.
Mapp v. Ohio 367 U.S. 643 (1961), 235.
Matter of Bernstein v. Toia 43 N.Y. 2d 437 (1977), 259 n38.
Matter of Grilli 110 Misc. 45 (1920), 206.
Matter of Heimback v. Mills 67 A.D. 2d 731 (1979), 290.
Matter of Jensen v. Southern Pacific Railroad Co. 215 N.Y. 514 (1915), 205 n10.
Matter of Orans 15 N.Y. 2d (1964), 269.
Matter of Ryers 72 N.Y. 1 (1878), 161, 184 n11.
Matter of Schulz v. New York 81 N.Y. 2d 336 (1993), 362, 364.
Matter of Smithtown v. Howell 31 N.Y. 2d 365 (1972), 290.
New York State Coalition for Criminal Justice v. Coughlin 103 A.D. 2d; aff'd 45 N.Y. 2d 248 (1984), 371 n5, 372 n16.
Newell v. People 7 N.Y. 9 (1852), 118.
Oneida County v. Berle 49 N.Y. 2d 515 (1980), 212.
Pelham v. Village of Pelham 215 N.Y. 374 (1915), 250, 259 n70.
People ex rel. Board of Charities v. New York Society for the Prevention of Cruelty to Children 161 N.Y. 233 (1900), 259 n39.
People ex rel. Bush v. Thorton 25 Hun 456 (1881), 140.
People ex rel. Carter v. Rice 135 N.Y. 473 (1892), 167.
People ex rel. Collins v. Mclaughlin 128 A.D. 599 (1908), 162.
People ex rel. Einsfeld v. Murray 149 N.Y. 267 (1896), 226 n60.
People ex rel. Everson v. Lorillard 135 N.Y. 285 (1892), 143.
People ex rel. Fernando Wood v. Simeon Draper et al. 15 N.Y. 532 (1857), 127–128.
People ex rel. Hotchkiss v. Smith 206 N.Y. 231 (1912), 299 n14.
People ex rel. Pulman v. Henion 64 Hun. 471 (1894).
People ex rel. Robin v. Hayes 163 A.D. 725 (1914), 189.
People ex rel. Rohrlich v. Follette 20 N.Y. 2d 297 (1967), 259 n31.
People ex rel. Sturgis v. Fallon 152 N.Y. 1 (1897), 161–162.
People ex rel. Town of Pelham v. Village of Pelham 215 N.Y. 374 (1915), 251.
People v. Bowen, 21 N.Y. 517 (1860), 123, 156 n15.
People v. Coler 166 N.Y. 1 (1900), 205, 232.
People v. Cosmo 205 N.Y. 91 (1912), 224 n5, 258 n29.
People v. Croswell 3 Johns. 337 (1804), 86.
People v. Defore 242 N.Y. 13 (1926), 259 n24.
People v. Doyle 286 A.D. 276 (1955), 299 n12.
People v. Foot 19 Johns. 58 (1821), 75.
People v. Harris 294 N.Y. 424 (1945), 299 n11.
People v. Laude 81 Misc. 256 (1913), 161, 184 n17.

People v. Molyneux 40 N.Y. 113 (1869), 177.
People v. Phillips unreported case (1813), 49.
People v. Richter's Jeweler's Inc. 291 N.Y. 161 (1943), 235.
People v. Tremaine [I] 52 N.Y. 27 (1929), 211.
People v. Tremaine [II] 281 N.Y. 1 (1939), 225 n33.
People v. West Chester County National Bank 231 N.Y. 465 (1921), 216.
Prentice v. Cahill 73 Misc. 2d 245 (1973), 300 n36.
Re Members of the Court of Errors 6 Wendell 158 (1830), 105–106.
Resnick v. County of Ulster, 44 N.Y. 2d 279 (1978), 290.
Robinson v. Cahill 303 A. 2d 273 (N.J. 1973), 185 n50.
Robinson v. Zimmerman 268 N.Y. 52 (1935), 222, 248.
Roher v. Dinkins 40 A.D. 2d 956; aff'd 32 N.Y. 2d 180 (1973), 344–345.
Rutgers v. Waddington (N.Y., 1784), in Robert Morris ed., *Select Cases of the Mayor's Court of New York City 1674–1784* (1935), 58–59, 79.
Schulz v. State of New York 84 N.Y. 2d 231 (1994), 362.
Shales v. Leach 119 A.D. 2d 990 (1986), 259 n34.
Tishman v. Sprague 293 N.Y. 42 (1944), 268.
Toia v. Regan 40 N.Y. 2d 837 (1976), 281.
Tucker v. Toia 43 N.Y. 2d 1 (1977), 238.
Ward v. Curran 266 A.D. 524; aff'd 291 N.Y. 642 (1943), 300 n37.
Wein v. Carey 41 N.Y. 2d 498 (1977), 212.
Wein v. State 39 N.Y. 2d 136 (1975), 243, 371 n5, 372 n16.
Welsh v. United States 398 U.S. 333 (1970), 186 n72.
White v. New York Central Railroad Co. 216 N.Y. 653 (1917), 224 n10.
Williamsburgh Savings Bank v. State 243 N.Y. 231 (1926), 250.
Wiltwych School for Boys Inc. v. HIll 11 N.Y. 2d 182 (1962), 170.
WMCA v. Lomenzo 377 U.S. 633 (1964), 67, 269, 306.
Wynehamer v. New York 13 N.Y. 378 (1856), 80, 93 n38, 121.

INDEX

Absentee ballot, 196, 207, 267–68
Adams, John, 39
Adams, Willi Paul, 27
Administrative Board of the Judicial Conference, 276
Administrative Board of the Courts, 340
Albany Mall, 362
Albany Regency, 97
Amending process: absent in Constitution of 1777, 48; and distinction between fundamental and statutory law, 61; and the 1801 Convention, 66; and convention of 1821, 72–73; of 1846, 109–110; of 1938, 256–57; legislative method provided, 30; and coincident submissions, 179–80; ease of, 4–5; role of attorney-general in, 298
American Civil Liberties Union, 324
American Labor Party, 230
Andros, Governor Edmund, 19
Appellate Division of Supreme Court: created, 155; restructured, 170; jurisdiction of, 195; size of, 214; granted constitutional status, 215; removal process, 337–38
Apportionment: and Constitution of 1777, 41; and convention of 1801, 67–68; of 1821, 83; 121–22; of 1894, 166–69, 183; of 1938, 242–44, 257; declared unconstitutional, 270–72; and convention of 1967, 308, 315; and amendment of 1969, 334–35
Articles of Confederation, 61
Assembly: size of, 41, 67, 123, 169; term of office, 122, 163 208; and power to originate money bills, 41, 83. *See also* Legislature; Apportionment
Assembly Judiciary Committee, 189
Association of Towns, 289
Attica Prison: 362-363

Attorney general: in the colony, 26; and convention of 1821, 78; made elective office, 105, 112; and election of, 123; elected with governor, 274; and role in constitutional interpretation, 255, 299–300, 360
Authorities. *See* Public benefit corporations

Banks: chartering of, 83; protests against, 97–98; and convention of 1846, 103–104; and Commission of 1872, 147. *See also* Corporations
Barnes, William, 191
Baxter, George, 16
Beard, Charles A., 193, 200
Becker, Carl, 39
Bicameralism: in Constitution of 1777, 41; theory behind, 44–45
Bill of Rights, state: and Committee on Government of Provincial Congress, 37; absence of in 1777 Constitution, 48–49; adoption of statutory, 50–51, 60–61; adopted at 1821 convention, 47–48; and convention of 1867, 121; and Constitution of 1938, 7–15; moved to Article I, 161; and convention of 1967, 309–311; and social rights, 3–4. *See under separate rights*
Bill of Rights, U.S.: 2, 85
"Bill of Rights for Local Government": 288–289
Bingo Licensing Law: 265
Bipartisan Election Boards: adopted at 1894 convention, 164
"Blaine" Amendment: in convention of 1894, 172–73, 183–184; in convention of 1967, 310–313; role in defeat of 1967 Constitution, 327. *See also* Education; Board of Regents; Religious liberty

INDEX 399

Board of Equalization and Assessment, 251
Board of Regents: creation of 21, 171; as head of Department of Education, 194; function of, 4, 172; and constitutional amendment of 1925, 171–77. *See also* Education; "Blaine" Amendment
Board of Social Welfare, 239
Botein, Bernard, 316
Brown, Jerry: 335
Bribery. *See* Corruption
Brietel, Charles, 336–337
Brydges, Earl, 309, 326
Bucktails: and convention of 1821, 72, 76, 83
Budget Accountability Reform Act of 1981, 364
Burr, Aaron, 67, 104
Butler, Benjamin, 37

Cambreling, Churchill, 95, 99
Canals: and convention of 1821, 83, 86–88, 91; of 1846, 96–97, 104; of 1867, 117–18, 123, 125–26; and amendment of 1874, 148; and convention of 1894, 173; of 1915, 197–98; and amendments of 1918, 1921 and 1933, 220; and convention of 1938, 253; and amendment of 1959, 296; of 1991, 349. *See also* Debt, state; Legislature
Cardozo, Benjamin, 223, 370
Carey, Governor Hugh: and judicial reform, 326, 337; 339
Catholics: in colony, 10; restrictions on, 23, 29, 49–50; and opposition to "Blaine" Amendment, 172–73; and repeal of "Blaine" Amendment, 312, 314; support of 1967 convention, 327–28
Chancellor: and Constitution of 1777, 43, 46, 51; of 1801, 65; of 1821, 82–83; of 1846, 98, 106; office abolished, 106. *See also* Kent, James
Chancery Court: in colony, 25; and Constitution of 1777, 43; of 1821, 82; abolished, 106
Charles II, 22, 29
Charter of Liberties and Privileges: of 1683, 21–22, 238; of 1791, 23–24

Charters: in colonial period, 1, 5–6, 11–12, 23–25. *See also* Charter of Liberties and Privileges
Choate, Joseph, 160–61, 182
Citizen's Budget Commission, 364
Citizen's Committee for a Constitutional Convention, 306
Citizen's Committee for Modern Courts, 277
Citizen's Union of New York, 231, 326
City courts, 276, 341
Civil Service Law of 1883, 274
Clayton Anti-Trust Act (1914), 234
Cleveland, Governor Grover, 271
Clinton, Governor DeWitt, 66, 67; 71
Clinton, Governor George, 27, 29, 37, 57, 64–65
Colden, Lieutenant-Governor Cadwallader, 24–26
Commission of Appeals, 124; 150. *See also* Court of Appeals
Commission on Government Integrity, 363, 370
Commission on Judicial Conduct, 338–339
Commission on Judicial Nomination, 339
Commission on the Powers of Local Government, 363
Commission to Devise a Plan for the Government of Cities in the State of New York (1875), 149, 155
Commissioner of Education, 171–72. *See also* Education
Committee on Constitutional Tax and Debt Limitations (1947), 280ff, 284ff
Committee on Educational Freedom, 312
Committee on Government of the Fourth Provincial Congress, 7–10
Committee on Health, Housing, Social Services, 323–324
Committee on Local Government, 320–321
Common law: in colonial period, 9, 16, 24, 25, 27, 30; and Constitution of 1777, 45, 50, 58; and convention of 1967, 314
Commonalty, 7, 9–10
Comptroller: and convention of

123; of 1915, 194; and Commission for Reconstruction of State Government, 210; and payment of state debt, 217; and budget preparation, 212; and convention of 1938, 243, 247; and amendment of 1955, 274; and amendment of 1951, 282; and public benefit corporations, 363. *See also* Moore, Frank; Levitt, Arthur; McCall, H. Carl

Conservation: in convention of 1894, 173; of 1938, 220; of 1967, 318, 327; and amendments, 220, 295–97, 327, 347–49; influence of attorney generals' opinions, 66; and "Conservation Bill of Rights," 327. *See also* "Forever Wild" provision

"Consumer Bill of Rights," 311, 318, 328

Constitutional Commission, 154–55, 263–64, 352–53. *See individual commissions*

Constitutional Commission of 1872, 1–2, 139ff, 155, 168

Constitutional Convention: method for calling, 99, 111; required every twenty years, 111, 159, 179, 308, 352; rules concerning, 179–80; and convention of 1867, 130–31. *See also Delegates*

Constitutional Convention Commission (1915), 193

Constitutional Convention Committee (1938), 231–32

Cooke, Lawrence H., 276

Corporate charters: special, 4–6, 15, 17–18, 32, 146; general, 102–103, 106–107, 112–113; municipal, 106. *See also Corporations*

Corporations: and convention of 1846, 102–103; amendments concerning attacks upon, 232–233. *See also* Public Benefit Corporations

Corruption: and convention of 1846, 100–101, 103; and canal construction, 118, 122, 125–26; and New York City, 126–29; and bribery of public officials, 130;

and the electoral process, 137–140; and legislative process, 143; and Tweed Ring, 145; and debt levels, 147; and municipal government reform movement, 148–150, 177; and convention of 1894, 163–65; and Governor Sulzer, 189–90; and prosecution of public officials, 238–39, 266–267, 311; and judiciary, 337–41

Council of Appointment: and Constitution of 1777, 42–43, 46; precipitates convention of 1801, 64–65; in convention of 1801, 67; and "spoils system," 74–75; criticisms of, 72, 74–75; and power to nominate, 59, 74; abolition at the convention of 1821, 77–78, 82, 90

Council of Revision: and Constitution of 1777, 41, 42, 43, 46–47; and veto of wartime legislation, 57, 59–62, 72–75; and convention of 1821, 78–79, 88–90. *See also* Judicial Review

Council of Safety, 57ff

Countryman, Edward, 44

County court, 106, 124–25, 214, 276, 214, 317

Court of Appeals: creation of, 106; and convention of 1846, 106, 110–12; of 1867, 124; and Judiciary Commission of 1890, 153–54; and convention of 1894, 169; of 1915, 195; and Judicial Convention of 1921, 214; and convention of 1938, 242–43; of 1967, 318; amendments concerning, 275–77, 335–342; and second division, 150; membership and size of, 214–15; and protection of rights, 80–81. *See also* Judicial review; Judiciary; Commission of Appeals

Court of Assizes, 19

Court for Trial of Impeachment and Correction of Errors: and Constitution of 1777, 41, 43–44, 46–47, 51; of 1821, 82, 89; and judicial review, 111–12; abolished, 105–106

Court of Claims, 125, 134; 215, 276
Court of Oyer and Terminer, 25
Court on the Judiciary, 276, 338–40
Courts of Admiralty, 43
Crane, Frederick E., 221, 232
Cuomo, Mario, 348, 350, 361, 363

Daly, Charles, 131
Debt, local: in Constitution of 1846, 102, 106; of 1894, 176–77; of 1938, 225ff; of 1967, 322–23; and public benefit corporations (authorities), 247; and Constitutional Commission of 1872, 144–46; and Tilden Commission recommendations, 148–50; and amendment of 1884, 151–52; liberalizations of and exemptions from debt limits, 218–20, 280ff, 343ff; criticisms of, 366–67. See also Local government; Home rule; Taxation; Public benefit corporations; Local government; New York City
Debt, state: and convention of 1821, 83; of 1846, 96–97, 100–101; of 1915, 197–98; of 1938, 240, 244–245; of 1967, 318–19; and amendment of 1854, 117; and the Constitutional Commission of 1872, 146; exemptions from debt limits, 216–18; amount of, 19; method of payment of, 342; and Backdoor financing, 352, 362–63; and Job Development Authority, 342; criticism of debt limits, 360ff, 372; and public benefit corporations (authorities), 362–63; and court challenges, 117–118, 292; reforms of, 365ff; and spring borrowing, 264–65; and lease purchases, 363–64. See also Canals
Delegates: background of in convention of 1801, 66–67; of 1821, 75–76; of 1846, 99–100; of 1867, 119; of 1894, 160; of 1915, 189–90; of 1938, 233–34; of 1967, 118–119; selection process, 119, 159–60, 179, 232–33; credentials of, 179

Democratic Party. *See chapters on individual conventions*
Democratic-Republicans: in convention of 1801, 64, 66–67; and convention of 1821, 71, passim
Department of Commerce, 273
Department of Corrections, 350
Department of Criminal Justice, 316
Department of Education: 171–72, 194
Department of Efficiency and Economy: and role in 1915 convention, 193
Department of Environmental Protection, 249
Department of Motor Vehicles, 273
Department of Public Instruction, 171. *See also* Education
Department of Taxation and Finance, 273
Desmond, Charles, 277, 317
Dewey, Governor Thomas, 213, 236–37; and election of lieutenant-governor, 271; views on balanced budget, 213
DeWitt, Charles, 40
Dillon's Rule, 186 n58, 288, 291
District attorney, 131, 346
Dix, Governor John, 147
Domestic Relations Court (Family Court): authorized, 214; jurisdiction expanded, 336; judges to serve on Supreme Court, 341; removal of, 277, 338
Dominick Commission: 336
Dongan, Governor Thomas: 20, 23
Donnelly Act (1935), 235
Double jeopardy, 85
Duane, James, 59
Due process of law: in colony, 21–22, 30; and 1777 Constitution, 48–49; and convention of 1821, 80–81; and impeachment procedures, 189–91. *See also* Law of the land; Substantive due process
Duer, John, 88
Duke's Laws, 18, 29
Dunne, John R., 335
Dunnigan, John, 236–37

Duryea, Perry, 334
Dutch (in colonial period), Chapter I, passim
Dyer, William, 19–20

Education: and Constitution of 1777, 55 n56; initial provision for, 88; funds from the sale of state lands, 88; in convention of 1846, 104, 109; of 1867, 130, 134; of 1894, 171; of 1915, 194; of 1938, 253; and amendment of 1962, 294; of 1966, 266; of 1967, 318. *See also* Board of Regents; "Blaine" Amendment
Eisenhower, Dwight D., 316
Emergency City and School District Relief Act (1976): 344
Eminent domain: and Constitution of 1846, 109; of 1894, 162; and amendments of 1919, 204; of 1963 and 1964, 267. *See also* Just Compensation
Equal Protection Clause: in convention of 1915, 197, of 1938, 235–36, 269–70; of 1967, 311
Equal Rights Amendment, 311, 332
Erie Canal, 87, 96, 100. *See also* Canals
Executive branch: reorganization of, 194–95, 200–201, 208ff, 224–25. *See also* Governor; *individual departments and offices*
Executive budget: and 1915 convention, 194–95; adoption of, 217ff; amendment concerning, 278; reforms of, 351, 363, 365–67

Factionalism, in colony, 10–28; and 1777 Constitution, 48; and convention of 1821, 74
Federal Omnibus Crime Control and Safe Streets Acts (1988), 238
Federal Voting Rights Act (1965), 269
Federalist Papers, 132, 140
Federalist political theory: and 1777 Constitution, 47–58; and convention of 1821, 88–89, 90–91; of 1846, 105–111; of 1867, 131–32; and Constitutional Commission of 1872, 140; and legislative branch, 140
Federalists, 64–65, 71, 75–76. *See also* Federalist political theory
Fenton, Governor Reuben, 118, 127
Fifteenth Amendment, 133, 138
Fifth Amendment, 237, 308
First Amendment, 85–86, 311
Flowers, Governor Roswell, 180–81
"Forever Wild" provision, 2, 173, 295, 361. *See also* Conservation
Fourteenth Amendment, 197, 235–36, 269
Fourth Amendment, 236–37
Fourth Provincial Congress of New York (1776), 36, 38
Fox, Dixon Ryan, 75
Free Banking Act of 1838, 97
Freedom of speech: in colony, 11, 29–30; protected in convention of 1821, 85–86; and convention of 1967, 313. *See also* Libel
Freedom of the press. *See* Freedom of speech
Freehold. *See* Suffrage
Fuchsberg, Jacob, 337
Fuld, Stanley, 336
Fuller, Charles, 164

Gambling: statutes concerning, 162–63; exemption for pari-mutuel racetrack betting, 266; exemptions for games of chance, 266; 332–33; and courts, 163; and casino gambling, 351; and convention of 1967, 314–15. *See also* Lotteries
General Assembly of Province of New York, 21
General incorporation. *See* Charters
General legislation, 121, 143–44, 161–62; defined, 221–22, 290–91
Generally Accepted Accounting Principles (GAAP), 351, 365
Glorious Revolution, 23–24, 29
Glynn, Governor Martin, 188, 190–91
Goldmark, Peter, 351
Governor: and Constitution of 1777, 42, 45–46, 47, 50–51; and convention of 1846, 105; of 1967, 316–17; term of office of, 46,

INDEX 403

81–82, 141, 170; veto power of, 46, 81, 89; 123; power of appointment, 123; and removal of district attorney, 139; power to convene legislature, 46, 141; salary of, 81, 141, 272; elected with lieutenant-governor, 272; succession of, 170, 242–45, 271–72; disability of, 334–35; importance of, 369. *See also individual governors;* Council of Appointment; Council of Revision; Executive branch; Executive budget
Grand jury: right to indictment by in colony, 22, 30; right to inspect minutes of, 310; waiver of by public employees, 196, 238–39, 266–67, 311, 333. *See also* Self-incrimination
Grasso, Ella, 334
Greeley, Horace, 99, 119
Gunn, L. Ray, 112

Habeus Corpus, 60, 85
Hammond, Jabez, 97
Hamilton, Alexander, 49, 58–59
Hamilton, Andrew, 86
Harriman, Governor Averell, 263–64, 266, 296
Harrington, Dr. Donald, 311
Harris, Ira, 129
Hempstead Convention, 19–20
Herman, Robert S., 327
Hill, Governor David, 148, 159–60
Hoffman, Governor John, 137, 143, 155
Home rule: definition of, 156 n34; in convention of 1846, 104, 106–107, 113; of 1867, 126ff; of 1894, 174–76, 184; of 1915, 196, 262; of 1938, 252–53; of 1967, 319ff; and Tilden Commission, 148ff; dissatisfaction with, 220–221; amendment of 1923, 221; of 1963, 286ff; and court challenges, 222–23; and public benefit corporations (authorities), 223; and county government, 208, 223–24, 286–87; and towns and villages, 287; limitations on,

291–92. *See also* Local government; Local debt; New York City
Horsemanden, Daniel, 26
Housing: and convention of 1938, 239–240, 256, 258; of 1967, 324–25; amendment of 1949, 297; of 1955, 297–99; of 1957, 298; of 1965, 298; and community development, 299, 319, 323–24; as constitutional obligation, 239, 360
Hughes, Governor Charles Evans, 192, 211, 271
Hunt, Governor Washington, 118
Hurst, James Willard, 181

Impeachment: origin and purpose, 43, 44, 189; definition of impeachable offense, 189; in 1777 Constitution, 43–44; and Constitution of 1821, 83; of Governor Sulzer, 189–191; criticism of procedure, 190–91; and court interpretations, 190. *See also* Court for Trials of Impeachment and Correction of Errors
Indians: 12, 23, 333, 360
Initiative: constitutional, 264; local, 292
Inter-Law School Committee: creation of, 264; recommendations of, 268, 275, 295, 299, 329 n7
Isaacs, Stanley, 191
Ives Pool Hall Law (1887), 162

James, Duke of York, 16–20; as King James I, 22–24
Jay, John, 1, 37–39, 42–43, 48, 50, 56, 64–66
Jay, Pierre, 50
Jefferson, Thomas, 44, 109
Jews: in colony, 10, 18, 23, 28; and convention of 1867, 60; of 1967, 308, 326
Job Development Authority, 332, 342, 345
Johnson, Lyndon B., 307
Joint Legislative Committee on Court Reorganization: 336–37
Joint Legislative Committee on

Legislative Methods, Practices, Procedures and Expenditures, 270
Judges. *See individual courts*
Judicial Conference, 277
Judicial review: 3; origin and development in New York, 58–59, 78–81, and exercise by Court of Appeals, 81, 111–112, 162, 205–206, 217, 221–23, 236, 237, 268–269, 362, 364; and certiorari power, 195; and 1938 convention, 243–44. *See also* Council of Revision
Judiciary: in colonial period, 18; and Constitution of 1777, 43, 46; of 1821, 75, 82–83; of 1846, 98–99, 105–106; of 1867, 124–125; and the Judicial Commission of 1894, 153–55; and Constitution of 1894, 170–71; of 1915, 195; and Judiciary Convention of 1921, 214–16; and convention of 1938, 243–44; and amendments, 275–78; budgets for, 278; 1961 reorganization of, 275–78; and convention of 1967, 317–18; and restructuring by amendments, 335–2; current condition of, 329, 369–70
Judiciary Commission of 1890, 152–54; and cnvention of 1894, 170, 274
Judiciary Convention of 1921, 171, 214–16, 275
Jury: size of, 18, 121; right to trial by in colony, 18, 22, 26, 30; and Confiscation Act of 1779, 59; and denial of, 206; and Constitution of 1777, 49; in libel prosecutions, 85; and taking of private property, 109, 205, 266–67; in misdemeanor cases, 311; waiver of, 196, 205, 238; and non-unanimous verdicts, 205
Just compensation: required by 1846 constitution, 109; and amendment of 1913, 205; and amendments of 1963 and 1964, 266–67. *See also* Eminent domain
Juvenile Court, 196, 214

Kammen, Michael, 24
Kempe, John Tabor, 26
Kennedy, John F., 315
Kent, James, 72, 73, 370
Kerker, Robert, 364–65
Kieft, William, 12–13
Kincaid, John, 3
King, Governor John, 127–28
Kingston, N.Y., 37–38
Klein, Milton, 41

Labor Bill of Rights, 5, 235
LaGuardia, Mayor Fiorello H., 230–32
Lauterbach, Edward, 162
Law of the land: first appearance in colony, 20, 26, 30; and Charter of Liberties and Privileges (1683), 22; and 1777 Constitution, 45, 267. *See also* Due process of law
Law Revision Commission, 335
Lawyers: role in colony, 24–25; at convention of 1846, 99; of 1867, 119; of 1894, 160; of 1938, 233; of 1967, 309
League of Women Voters: 277, 325, 336, 370
Lease Purchase Device. *See* Debt, state
Legislature: during colonial period, 26–27; and Constitution of 1777, 40; and republican ideology, 44–45, 73–74, 105, 140–41; size of, 65, 67; procedures of, 103–104, 142–43, 169–70, 122; powers of, 41; qualifications, 315; authorized to call special session, 334; role in impeachment, 83, 189–91; and disability of governor, 316, 334–335; salary of, 83, 122, 195, 207–208; limitations on, 83–84, 103–105, 121, 142–43, 180, 183; and problem of special legislation, 103–104, 143–44, 208, 196, 316; and holding of civil office, 195; authorizes convention of 1801, 99; authorizes convention of 1821, 73–74; authorizes convention of 1846, 99; and deadlock over calling of 1894 convention, 159–60; evaluation of, 371; role in

constitutional commissions, 137–38, 192–93, 214, 233–34, 263ff; role in constitutional revision, 109; granted emergency powers, 270. *See also* Representation; Apportionment; Assembly; Senate; Bicameralism; Suffrage
Lehman, Governor Herbert, 230–36, 270
Leisler, Jacob, 23
Levitt, Arthur, 363
Libel: in colony, 29–30; and state constitution, 85–86, 314
Liberal Party: and convention of 1967, 309–310, 313, 326–27
Lieber, Francis, 129
Lieutenant-governor: created in 1777 Constitution, 42; made president of the senate, 42; qualifications of, 142; salary of, 142, 195, 271–72; and succession to governor, 242–43, 271–72; when acting governor, 195, 334; term of office, 170; method of election, 271–72; election to fill vacancy, 271–72; member of Court of Impeachment and Correction of Errors, 82; and 1915 convention, 195; of 1938, 242–43; and amendment of 1945, 271; of 1949, 272
Lincoln, Charles, ix, 52 n14, 78, 80, 92 n17, 119, 137 n2, 163, 172
Lindsay, Mayor John, 318, 326
Literacy test. *See* Suffrage
Livingston, Robert, 37–39, 56
Local Development Amendment, 349–50
Local laws, 221–22. *See* Special legislation
Long Island: 15–18, 20
Lotteries: in colonial period, 88, 162; banned at 1821 convention, 88; in convention of 1894, 161–62; in Bill of Rights, 333; state lottery for education authorized, 266. *See also* Gambling
Lovelace, Governor Francis, 19
Low, Seth, 191, 193
Lutherans, 10, 18, 28
Lutz, Donald, 1, 47

Machold, H. Edmund, 211
Madison, James, 47–48, 71, 132
Magna Carta, 9, 20, 25, 27, 45, 60
Major's Court: in New York City, 58
Marcy, William, 99
Marshall, Louis, 191
Mason, Bernard, 38
McBain, Howard, 18, 221
McCall, H. Carl, 373 n7
Merit selection. *See* Public officers
Metropolitan Police Force: 127–28
Metropolitan Transit Authority: 364
Militia: in the Constitution of 1777, 84; in convention of 1821, 84–85; of 1867, 178–79; of 1894, 177–78; and amendment of 1962, 294–95; and national Constitution, 294–95, 369; and religious exemption from service, 86
Miller, Governor Nathan, 210–11
Model State Constitution, 6, 325–26
Moffat, Abbot Low, 249, 279
Moore, Frank, 280
Moral obligation debt, 361–65
Morris, Gouverneur, 38, 46–48
Morris, Lewis, 25
Morris, Robert, 103
Moscow, Warren, 140
Moskowitz, Belle, 201, 209–210, 328
Moses, Robert, 201, 209–210, 234
Municipal Home Rule Law: 291
Murrin, John, 22
Murphy, Charles, 209
Murphy, Henry C., 106
Murray, William S., 241
Murry, John, 58

NAACP, 326
Nature and Historical Preserve, 317
Nelson, Samuel, 99
New Netherlands, 12, 16–17
New York Bar Association, 153, 161, 339, 370
New York Bureau of Municipal Research, 193
New York City: growth of, 126, 167–68; and votes for constitutional conventions, 264, 309; courts of, 276–77, 341; registration requirements, 268–69; representation, 36–37, 108, 169,

241–42, 271; corruption in, 127ff, 145, 177; and home rule, 174ff, 221–24, 252–53, 286, 290, 319, 321; debt of, 219–21, 244–46, 322–24, 366–67; impact on 1894 convention, 165, 176, 184; problems, 318
New York City Transit Authority, 248
New York City Water Board, 249–50
New York Local Government Assistance Corporation Act, 365
New York Port Authority, 293
New York State Constitutional Convention Commission (1915), 193
New York State Lottery for Education Law (1967), 266. *See also* Education
New York State Thruway Authority, 248, 293, 362, 364
New York Times: 133, 232, 333, 372
Nichols, William, 163
Nicolls, Richard, 17–20, 29

O'Brien, John Lord, 191
O'Brien, Morgan, 191
Office of Court Administration, 340
Office of Local Government, 288, 289–90

Paine, Thomas, 39
"People's Constitution," 110
Percy-Gray Law, 162–63
Poletti, Charles, 233, 235
Poletti Report. *See* Constitutional Convention Committee of 1938
Preamble: of the 1777 Constitution, 40–41; and the 1821 convention, 75
Private laws. *See* Special legislation
Private property: importance of, 21, 27–28, 198; right to, 109; and taking clause, 121, 161–62, 204–205, 266–67, 310, 313. *See also* Eminent domain; Substantive due process; Just compensation
Privy Council, 17, 26, 46, 61
Progressive Movement: and convention of 1894, 184; of 1915, 192, 200; program of, 225

Proportional Representation, 242, 257
Provincial Assembly, 16
Public Authorities Control Board, 362–63
Public benefit corporations (authorities): nature and rise of, 248–49; in convention of 1938, 248–49; court interpretations concerning, 248ff, 364; and debt limits on, 319; criticisms and reform of, 362–63, 364. *See also* New York Thruway Authority; Job Development Authority; New York Port Authority; Urban Development Corporation; Water Finance Authority
Public officers: bribery of, 138–39, 165, 295; and merit selection of, 165–66, 272–74; and regulation of wages and hours, 206; and taxation of compensation, 252; and waiver of immunity, 238–39, 311; and veteran's preference, 156, 274, 335; pensions of, 254, 278. *See also individual offices*
Public purpose doctrine: and the convention of 1821, 79; and issuance of debt, 146; 1919 amendment, 205; and amendment of 1963, 266
Public Service Commission, 317

Quakers, 10, 18, 23, 28, 84

Race. *See* Suffrage
Radical Republicans: and convention of 1821, 82, 84, 88, 89; of 1867, 118–119, passim
Railroads: protests against, 97; proposal to vest power of government in New York Central Railroad, 118; and convention of 1867, 122; of 1894, 163, 165; amendments concerning grade crossings, 219, 254–55
Referendum: and debt approval, 101, 325; evasion of, 217, 218; proposed amendment on, 365; and annexation procedure, 321; in general, 138

Registration. *See* Suffrage
Religion, 18. *See* individual religious groups
Religious liberty: in colony, 16–18, 22–23, 27–29; and constitution of 1777, 49–50; and convention of 1821, 86; of 1846, 109; and establishment of religion, 22, 29, 49, 86. *See also* "Blaine" Amendment; Catholics; Quakers
Representation: *See* Apportionment; Legislature
Representative government: and growth of assemblies, 9, 11–13, 14ff, 16; and Hemstead Convention, 17–18; and English rule, 18ff; and dangers of assembly government, 40. *See also* Republican government; Legislature
Republican Party. *See chapters on individual conventions, passim*
Republicanism: in colonial period, 22–23, and constitution of 1777, 44; judiciary review, 61–62; Chancellor Kent's view of, 72–73; and legislative supremacy, 73–74; and convention of 1821, 77; of 1894, 182
Riegelman, Harold, 245
Right to bail, 22–23
Right to confront witnesses, 121
Right to counsel: in colony, 18, 30; in Constitution of 1777, 49; current status, 2–3
Right to fish, 121
Right to peaceably assemble and petition, 121, 161
Right to picket, 235
Right to recovery in wrongful death, 163
Riots: during colonial period, 11; and seizure of Fort George, 31; anti-rent movement, 98; and New York Police, 128
Robinson, Governor Lucius, 148–49, 151
Rockefeller, Governor Nelson: role in constitutional reform, 264–65, 297; and convention of 1967, 313–14, 325–26; and role of governor, 369; and reform of the judiciary, 336; resigns office, 271
Roosevelt, Governor Franklin, 231–32
Root, Elihu, 160, 163, 172, 188, 191, 193, 201
Root, Erastus, 76
Ruggles, Charles, 110

Sage-Maier Bill, 211
Samuels, Howard, 308, 315, 325
Schurman, Jacob, 191
Schuyler, Philip, 64
Scots, 10
Scott, John Morris, 40
Seabury investigation, 237
Search and seizure: protection against in 1867 convention, 121; and expansive reading of state clause, 237; provision added by 1938 convention, 236; exclusionary rule, 236–37. *See* Wiretapping
Secret ballot, 39, 45, 57, 165
Secretary of State, 105
Self-incrimination: in colony, 30, 85; and public officials, 196, 238–39, 266–67, 392. *See* Grand jury
Senate: size of, 41, 67, 140, 167–69; term of office, 121–22, 140, 242; selection of presiding officer, 108. *See also* Legislature; Apportionment
Separation of powers: and Constitution of 1777, 44, 45, 47; of 1821, 75, 88–89; of 1846, 105–106, 110–111; of 1915, 199–200; criticism of, 371
Seward, Governor William, 96, 99
Sheriff, 42, 78, 91, 346
Sierra Club, 348
Simpson, Kenneth F., 232, 241
Slavery, 2, 48, 60–61
Sloughter, Henry, 23
Smith, Governor Alfred: and convention of 1915, 191, 201; of 1938, 232–34, 242, 249; role in government reorganization, 209–211, 328
Smith, William, Jr., 9
Social welfare: and convention of

1915, 198-99; of 1938, 239-40, 258; role of government in, 239, 256-58; burden on cities, 324; and convention of 1967, 324, 328; transfer of financing to state, 326; and amendments of 1973, 350; affirmative rights to, 238-40
Special Committee on Pollution Abatement, 343
Special legislation: and Constitution of 1846, 103-104; of 1867, 122; and Constitutional Commission of 1872, 142-44; and convention of 1894, 174; and Home Rule movement, 221-22, 290
Special Legislative Committee on the Revision and Simplification of the Constitution, 265
State Commissioner of Corrections, 350
State Comptroller's Committee on Constitutional Tax and Debt Limitations and City School Fiscal Relations, 280ff.
Statute on Local Government, 288
Steingut, Stanley, 320
Stevens, Harold, 337
Stimson, Henry L., 191
Stuyvesant, Peter, 13-16, 28
Substantive due process, 80-81, 181, 205-206. *See also* Due process of law
Suffrage: and freehold requirement, 22, 39-40, 45, 47, 56, 76-77; and African-Americans, 48, 60, 76-77, 90, 107-108, 110-12, 119-20, 131, 133, 138; and aliens, 108, 333-34; and women, 107, 112, 120, 138, 160, 161-64, 196, 198, 201, 206-207; and literacy, 120, 207, 315, 368; and age, 120, 315, 333; residency requirements, 120, 268-270, 333; and registration, 163, 165, 241, 268-70, 333; and oath of alligiance, 27. *See also* Absentee ballot; Secret ballot; Bribery
Sulzer, William, 189-192, 209
Superintendent of Common Schools, 171. *See also* Education
Supreme Court: in colonial period,
24ff, 43; reorganization of, 82-83, 106, 214; justices to sit on Court of Appeals, 151; creation of appellate division, 154, 170; jurisdiction of, 14; number of justices, 82, 124; term of judges, 124, 277-78; removal of, 98, 275-76, 368; made elective, 105; numbers increased, 154, 170, 214. *See also* Judiciary; Appellate Division
Surrogate Court: given constitutional status, 106; term, 215; removal of, 217
Swedes, 10

Taft, William Howard, 193
Tammany Hall, 72, 165, 174, 176, 199, 209, 231-32
Taxation: during Dutch rule, 12ff.; and representation, 10, 19-21, 27; on war profiteers, 60; direct, 96; on real and personal property, 322-23; prohibition on granting exemptions from, 143; recommendations of Commission of 1877, 149-50; limits on city powers, 152; and convention of 1915, 197; method of assessment, 204, 218-19; authorities, 247; local powers concerning, 247-48, 284-86, 290; and the convention of 1938, 250ff.; and role of comptroller, 274; and amendment of 1985, 344; evasions of constitutional limitations, 344-45, 368; and Local Development Amendment, 349-50; and use of federal definition for income tax, 270; and tax stabilization fund, 279
Temporary Commission on the Courts (1956), 277
Temporary Commission on the Future of the Adirondacks, 348
Temporary Commission on the New York State Court System, 340
Temporary Commission on the Powers of Local Government, 363
Temporary State Commission on Constitutional Revision (1993), 351
Temporary State Commission on

Constitutional Tax Limitations (1974), 344
Temporary State Commission on Judicial Conduct, 338
Temporary State Commission on the Constitutional Convention (1956), 263–64
Temporary State Commission on the Constitutional Convention (1965), 207, 310
Temporary State Commission on the Revision and Simplification of the Constitution (1959), 264, 271, 287, 294
Tenant farms, 9–10, 60, 98, 107
Third Provincial Congress of New York (1776), 36–37
Tilden, Governor Samuel, 99, 119, 149
Tilden Commission. *See* Commission to Devise a Plan for Government of Cities
Tompkins, Governor Daniel, 68
Townsend, Miles, 129
Travia, Anthony, 309, 311, 313, 316, 320, 325–27
Treasurer, 105
Tyler, Andrew, 312
Tyron, Governor William, 58

Unicameralism, 39, 316, 351
Unified Budget Act of 1976, 341
United Nations Declaration of Human Rights, 258
United States Constitution: and preemption of state constitutional provisions, 50, 207, 235, 294; provisions on militia, 84–85; impact on state constitution, 85, 89, 121, 316, 334–35; and suffrage restrictions in New York, 138; and state equal protection clause, 235–36; and state search and seizure clause, 235–36; and state right to counsel, 238; and state waiver of immunity provision, 238–39, 310–11; and state welfare provisions, 258; and state residency requirements, 269–70; and state reapportionment provisions, 271–72, 308; and state separation of church and state clause, 311–13; compared to state constitution, 1ff., 47, 372
Urban Development Corporation (UDC), 362–65

Van Buren, Governor Martin, 76, 89–90, 271
Van Dam, Rip, 25
Vested rights, doctrine of, 79
Veteran's preference. *See* Public officers
Veto: in Constitution of 1777, 44, 46, 47; and convention of 1821, 78; in U.S. Constitution, 89; and convention of 1867, 123, 132; and Constitutional Commission of 1872, 141; use by Governor Hoffmann, 143; and convention of 1967, 316
Viva Voce Voting, 39, 57
Voting Rights Act of 1965, 351, 370
Voting Rights Act of 1970, 269, 370

Wagner, Robert F., 191, 233
Wallace, Lieutenant-Governor Thomas W., 271–72
Water Authority, 250
Weed, Thurlow, 97, 99
Weinfeld, Edward, 235
Weprin, Saul, 335
Westervelt, Jacob, 127
Wheeler, William, 117, 119–20
Whig Party, 99–100, 127
Whig political theory, 40, 47–48, 111
White, Andrew Dickinson, 119
Whitman, Governor Charles, 191, 211–13
Wickersham, George, 191
William III, 23–24
Wilson, James, 49
Wilson, Lieutenant Governor Malcolm, 313
Wisner, Henry, 37
Wood, Mayor Fernando, 128
Worker Compensation Law, 205–206

Yates, Abraham, 39–40
Yates, Robert, 37, 40, 46, 49

Zenger, John Peter, 11, 29–30, 86

www.ingramcontent.com/pod-product-compliance
Lightning Source LLC
Chambersburg PA
CBHW071952290426
44109CB00018B/1995